Winner of the PEN/Jacqueline Bograd Weld
Award for Biography

A Best Book of
Vulture • NPR • Rollin
The Globe and Mail (Toron

"Whenever I've been asked why Dilla was special, I didn't feel like I had the right vocabulary to explain his importance—specifically the way he made work that was so perfectly imperfect that it redefined the way I thought about art. Dan Charnas to the rescue. He scaled the mountain of Dilla's complex career and sent back instructions so that others could make the climb. This book is a must for everyone interested in illuminating the idea of unexplainable genius."

—Questlove

"Charnas's main reasons for writing [*Dilla Time*] are not only to make Dilla's contributions to music known but to also explain that the devotion from fans is justified."

—Eric Ducker, *The New York Times*

"[*Dilla Time* does] what good music books should: send you back to the source material . . . *Dilla Time* is an important piece of music writing, affording its African-American subject the respect that the rock establishment has long accorded its white heroes."

—*The Economist*

NEW YORK TIMES BESTSELLER

"The greatest hip-hop producer of all time is getting the love and care his legacy deserves. *Dilla Time* is a master class."

—dream hampton

"With this assiduously researched, stirringly told, and expansively elucidated accounting of J Dilla's life as muse, mythos, and generationally transformative composer of hip-hop beats, Dan Charnas has provided readers with an alchemist's cookbook of its titular, wizardly subject."

—Greg Tate, author of *Flyboy in the Buttermilk*

"*Dilla Time* is a portrait of a complex genius taken too young, as well as a glorious study of the music and culture he created."

—Liza Lentini, *Spin*

"The book's heart is its rich, evocative musicological analysis, complete with rhythm diagrams, of Dilla's beats ... Charnas's engrossing work is one of the few hip-hop sagas to take the music as seriously as its maker."

—*Publishers Weekly* (starred review)

"I look at J Dilla as a man who redefined the word 'innovative.' This book makes you feel like you traveled his journey every single step."

—DJ Premier

For the official *Dilla Time* listening guide, please visit www.DillaTimeBook.com.

Praise for *Dilla Time*

"[This is] no ordinary book . . . It's equal parts biography, musical analysis and cultural history delving deep not only into Dilla's history and music but also into the histories of rhythm and his hometown of Detroit."
—Jem Aswad, *Variety*

"An ambitious, dynamic biography of J Dilla, who may be the most influential hip-hop artist known by the least number of people . . . A wide-ranging biography that fully captures the subject's ingenuity, originality, and musical genius."
—*Kirkus Reviews* (starred review)

"J Dilla turned what one generation deemed musical error into what the next knew to be musical innovation. In this splendid book, Dan Charnas offers an uncanny mix of research and vision, documentation and interpretation, plenitude and momentum. *Dilla Time* is definitive. And exhilarating."

—Margo Jefferson, author of
Constructing a Nervous System and *Negroland*

"In the way that J Dilla's music was a portal for us to hear our world and feel the pulse of life anew, Charnas has made a portal through which to understand our time—historical time, musical time, and James Yancey's own time—in a new way. *Dilla Time* is a book that will be read and re-read with as much pleasure as we have listened and relistened to Dilla's music. A masterpiece."

—Jeff Chang, author of *Can't Stop Won't Stop*

"How can one be both universally revered and massively underappreciated? Filled with impeccable reportage, elegant prose, and incandescent anecdotes, *Dilla Time* is more than an urgently needed biography of hip-hop's most revolutionary producer. It is a testament to the never-ending struggle between creativity and mortality."

—Rob Kenner, author of *The Marathon Don't Stop:*
The Life and Times of Nipsey Hussle

Noah Stephens

DAN CHARNAS
DILLA TIME

Dan Charnas is the author of the definitive history of the hip-hop business, *The Big Payback*. He is also the author of *Work Clean*, a book that applies chefs' techniques to almost any life situation. The cocreator and executive producer of the VH1 movie and TV series *The Breaks*, he lives in Manhattan and is an associate professor at the Clive Davis Institute of Recorded Music at the NYU Tisch School of the Arts.

Also by Dan Charnas

The Big Payback: The History of the Business of Hip-Hop

Work Clean: The Life-Changing Power of Mise-en-Place to Organize Your Life, Work, and Mind

DILLA
TIME

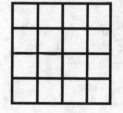 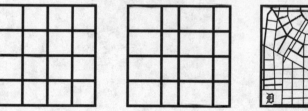 

DILLA TIME

The Life and Afterlife of J Dilla, the Hip-Hop Producer Who Reinvented Rhythm

DAN CHARNAS

With musical analysis by JEFF PERETZ

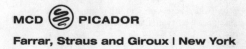

MCD ⊜ PICADOR

Farrar, Straus and Giroux | New York

For my one and his two

MCD
Picador
120 Broadway, New York 10271

Copyright © 2022 by Dan Charnas
All rights reserved
Printed in the United States of America
Originally published in 2022 by MCD / Farrar, Straus and Giroux
First paperback edition, 2023

Illustration credits can be found on pages 459–460.

The Library of Congress has cataloged the MCD hardcover edition as follows:
Names: Charnas, Dan, author.
Title: Dilla time : the life and afterlife of J Dilla, the hip-hop producer who reinvented rhythm /
    Dan Charnas ; with musical analysis by Jeff Peretz.
Description: First edition. | New York : MCD / Farrar, Straus and Giroux, 2022. | Includes
    bibliographical references and index.
Identifiers: LCCN 2021042472 | ISBN 9780374139940 (hardcover)
Subjects: LCSH: J Dilla, 1974–2006. | J Dilla, 1974–2006—Criticism and interpretation. | Sound
    recording executives and producers—United States—Biography. | Rap (Music)—Production
    and direction—History. | Rap (Music)—History and criticism. | Musical meter and rhythm.
Classification: LCC ML420.J113 C53 2022 | DDC 782.421649092 [B]—dc23
LC record available at https://lccn.loc.gov/2021042472

Paperback ISBN: 978-1-250-86297-6

Designed by Gretchen Achilles

Our books may be purchased in bulk for promotional, educational, or business use. Please
contact your local bookseller or the Macmillan Corporate and Premium Sales Department at
1-800-221-7945, extension 5442, or by email at MacmillanSpecialMarkets@macmillan.com.

Picador® is a U.S. registered trademark and is used by Macmillan Publishing Group, LLC, under
license from Pan Books Limited.

For book club information, please visit facebook.com/picadorbookclub or email
marketing@picadorusa.com.

mcdbooks.com • Follow us on Twitter, Facebook, and Instagram at @mcdbooks
picadorusa.com • Instagram: @picador • Twitter and Facebook: @picadorusa

10   9   8   7   6   5   4

Man that is born of woman is of few days and full of trouble. He cometh forth like a flower, and is cut down; he fleeth also as a shadow, and continueth not.

—JOB 14: 1–2

time is imperfect measure
knowing
this is nothing
short of knowing god

—TINA ZAFREEN ALAM

He'll change the expression on your face
When you just see that boy fly . . .

—PYE HASTINGS,
from Caravan's "A Very Smelly, Grubby Little Oik,"
as sampled by J Dilla

CONTENTS

Contents

Go

A NOTE FROM THE AUTHOR

This is a book about a hip-hop producer who changed the path of popular music.

The career of James Dewitt Yancey was short, lasting around a dozen years—from his first release in 1993 on a small record label in his hometown of Detroit until his death in Los Angeles in 2006 at the age of thirty-two from a rare blood disease. In that time, no record he produced rose higher than #27 on the *Billboard* Hot 100 chart.

That fact is remarkable because Yancey—first known as Jay Dee and then as J Dilla—collaborated with some of the most popular artists of his time, like A Tribe Called Quest, Busta Rhymes, the Roots, D'Angelo, Common, and Erykah Badu, and influenced the music of superstars like Michael and Janet Jackson. What's more, J Dilla continues to inspire and provoke new artists who rose to fame after he died, from the rap icon Kendrick Lamar to the jazz pianist Robert Glasper to dozens of pop acts.

When you ask J Dilla's more successful hip-hop contemporaries like Dr. Dre and Pharrell to name peers they admire, Dilla is always near or at the top of their lists. Despite his short life span and low profile, J Dilla was, and remains, the producer's producer, the inspiration for inspirers, or, as the Roots' drummer Ahmir "Questlove" Thompson says, "the musician's musician's musician."

After his death, J Dilla achieved a popularity he never experienced in life. "Dilla Days" are now celebrated annually around the world from New York to Miami to London, attracting fans and followers by the thousands. News outlets like NPR and *The Guardian* document his influence in the pop and jazz worlds. Tributes flourish on record and onstage: New York's Lincoln Center and the Detroit Institute of Arts have hosted homages to the late producer. His work and his influence are studied by musicologists, by recipients of MacArthur "genius" grants and Guggenheim fellows. Colleges and universities have created courses dedicated to studying and interpreting Dilla's work. Foundations fund educational programs in his name. He's had scores of records dedicated to his memory and symphonies arranged around his music. He even had a street named after him in Montpellier, France.

All these accolades leave us with a question: *Why does this hitless hip-hop producer have such a persistent presence in the music world?*

In *Dilla Time*, I offer a simple answer: Because J Dilla transformed the sound of popular music in a way that his more famous peers have not. He is the only producer-composer to emerge from hip-hop and, indeed, all electronic music to fundamentally change the way so-called traditional musicians play. And the core of Dilla's contribution is a radical shift in how musicians perceive time.

Before J Dilla, our popular music essentially had two common "time-feels"—straight time and swing time—meaning that musicians felt and expressed time as either even or uneven pulses. What Dilla created was a third path of rhythm, juxtaposing those two time-feels, even and uneven simultaneously, creating a new, pleasurable, disorienting rhythmic friction and a new time-feel: Dilla Time. What follows is the story of how that happened and what it means.

This book emerged from a class I teach on J Dilla at New York University's Clive Davis Institute. Its roots go back to my time in the music business as a talent scout, record executive, and beatmaker, and to a trip I made to Detroit in the summer of 1999 with my friend and colleague Chino XL to work with the producer then known as Jay Dee. But *Dilla Time* is journalism, not memoir. I do not consider myself an expert on J Dilla, but a student who has spoken to the real experts, the people who lived and worked and studied with him, whom you will meet in this book. My aim was to be faithful to them, and to tell their stories from each of their perspectives. The narrative is based on more than 190 interviews conducted over the course of four years, and the text and dialogue herein are the result of reporting and research. Where my sources' perspectives and stories conflict, I have noted that in the footnotes. James lived with that conflict, and we must too. (You may read more about my process in the Reporter's Notes and Sources section in the rear of the book.)

James Dewitt Yancey created a succession of aliases—Silk, Jon Doe, Jay Dee, J Dilla—and in *Dilla Time* I use them interchangeably, depending on who is speaking or thinking about him and what appellation they preferred. Mostly here, he is as his closest friends and family called him, James.

Dilla Time is not a simple biography of J Dilla, but is about what he means in history. No one innovates and influences in a vacuum. Thus *Dilla Time* follows the stories of other people: his parents and siblings, mentors and protégés, colleagues and followers, friends and lovers. Influence takes time, so this book begins before J Dilla's birth and ends well after his death. Innovation happens with new tools, so this is a book about music-making machines. Everything happens somewhere, and thus this book is also about Detroit, its citizens, and their encounter with the machine.

Thus the chapters of *Dilla Time* compose a grid of two separate but complementary tracks—the *biography* of J Dilla and the people around him, and the larger context of music and *musical time*.

I was accompanied in this latter endeavor by a vital expert, my colleague at NYU, the musicologist Jeff Peretz. When I began teaching a musical concept called "Dilla Time" to my students in 2014, it was Jeff who validated my argument and helped me deconstruct it. Jeff and I began formulating the musical pedagogy in this book during my Dilla course, and we developed it over time in conversations with each other, with our students and colleagues, and with other musicians. Jeff reviewed every word in the music chapters, created many of the original charts and analyses, and developed the visual language that this book uses to illustrate rhythmic concepts.

For those who don't know much about hip-hop or J Dilla, I offer what I hope will be both a compelling biography and a book about music that builds those concepts step-by-step. For those who already count themselves as informed Dilla fans, I hope *Dilla Time* confirms your admiration and deepens your understanding.

I also reframe the discussion of J Dilla and challenge some clichés about the man, his music, and his legacy that have ossified over the years.

My students were barely in grade school when J Dilla died. When I ask them why they've elected to take a course on him, the word that comes up most often is *love*. J Dilla's music evokes feelings, and the language of feeling suffuses much of the writing about him: how Dilla felt music and how we feel in return. There is something transcendent and evocative about his work that seemingly goes beyond analysis.

What this approach possesses in spirit it lacks in specificity. In promoting J Dilla merely as a musical mystic, even the greatest Dillaphiles miss something crucial: what J Dilla actually *did*, *how* he did it, and why it is *important*. J Dilla's music was an act of calculation as well as feeling; two legitimate but different kinds of intelligence. Some of his closest collaborators agree. As DJ Jazzy Jeff told me: "You can follow the method and you won't have the feeling. You can have the feeling but no success because you have no method." D'Angelo agrees that time itself can be both felt *and* measured: "You can do both," he says. "Beat machines taught us that."

Thus what J Dilla did, the instinctive *and* the methodical, deserves analysis: to be quantified—or *quantized*, if you prefer.

James himself did not analyze or theorize much about his approach. "I just want to make some shit" is a typical way he expressed himself when asked. He didn't have a grand formula. But J Dilla did develop key techniques. And he *knew* he had a sound. He was acutely aware of its influence and often unhappy about hearing people emulate his style. I doubt he would have made an argument for his own significance. But that's my job, not his. So I am going to quantize J Dilla a little bit, break him down. And that's needed: contrary to the trope that he was simply a great drummer who happened to play the drum machine, he was actually a *programmer* who used and mastered the features of the equipment on which he worked.

This polarity—the facts of Dilla versus the emotion of Dilla—often approaches the tension between sacrilege and gospel. In the decade after his death, Dilla's musical concepts circumnavigated the globe, but that feat has often been overshadowed by the intense feelings inspired by J Dilla's music and story. A culture emerged around his memory, one with its own pantheon and lore: His mother and brother took prominent roles in promoting his work after his death, becoming public figures themselves. His mother in particular became engaged in a public struggle with her son's estate, followed by open conflict among Dilla's family and friends over the stewardship of his legacy and the propriety of projects made and events held in his name. To this day, J Dilla fans are confused about who is actually in charge, and conflicted about who should be. I hope to impart some clarity about the battle for his remains.

All the mysticism and myth about J Dilla engendered a kind of deification that has become profoundly creepy to some family, friends, and fans. The adulation has created skepticism among people who otherwise admire his work.

There is, on my shelf as I write this, a figurine of J Dilla that was commissioned by his estate and sold to fans around the world. It's adorable: His trademark Detroit Tigers cap atop his head, a silver donut hanging from a chain around his neck, and a tiny MPC drum machine under his arm. His nose is a button, his eyes tiny dots, his limbs exaggerated. It reminds me of another widely circulated piece of fan art, distributed online in 2010 by the graphic artist DeadlyMike, an illustration of J Dilla as the *Peanuts* character Schroeder, hunched over an MPC instead of a piano. The figurine, like the portrait, is comforting to people, especially considering how horribly he died: *Dilla as eternal child*. But that doll is also there to remind me: *That is not James.*

Dilla Time is not the Book of St. James, scripture from the Church of Dilla. In these pages you will not meet a god, though some have called him that. Instead, you will get to know a beautiful, complicated man with both virtues and flaws. James Yancey possessed an evolved musical sensibility; he was generous, smart, and deeply funny. In other areas—relationships with friends, with women, and with his daughters;

his ability to care for others and ultimately for himself—he was not quite as consistently refined. And James, like everyone in this book, gets to be human.

The best answers to cliché, myth, and skepticism are the facts and good context. I wrote *Dilla Time* to honor James's life and make plain his achievements. I argue that his work is every bit as transformative and revolutionary as acclaimed geniuses like Louis Armstrong, Billie Holiday, Thelonious Monk, John Coltrane, and James Brown. And if you don't know these folks, or why they're significant, I'll explain that too.

Let's go.

DILLA
TIME

1.
Wrong

Twenty years before the Roots became the house band for NBC's *The Tonight Show* in 2014—placing them at the epicenter of the American cultural mainstream—they were an obscure hip-hop act promoting their first album on the road, opening for only slightly less obscure hip-hop acts.

The Roots' twenty-three-year-old drummer, Ahmir Thompson, was their de facto leader, with his trademark afro their de facto logo. The world would later come to know him as Questlove. But on this evening in 1994, outside a small North Carolina venue, he was an unknown.

After the Roots' performance, Questlove settled into a car, en route to an interview at a nearby college radio station, while the headliners, the Pharcyde, took the stage for their set. As the beats from the club drifted out into the parking lot, Questlove asked the driver to wait. He rolled down the window to listen. Something in the drums sounded . . . wrong.

What was Questlove expecting to hear? What all who listen to popular music expect: a steady beat.

One sound—whether the bang of a drum or a note struck on a piano or a bird's chirp—doesn't become music until a second sound occurs; either at the same time, called *harmony*; or at another moment in time, called *melody*; the ordered spacing of those sounds in time called *rhythm*.

Thus all music begins with the second event. The indivisible number of rhythm is two, for it is the space between the first and second beat that sets our musical expectations and tells us when to expect the third, and so on.

The common rhythm of our popular music is counted in multiples of either two or three. Most often, we count in "measures" or "bars" of fours: *one-two-three-four, one-two-three-four*. But in that rhythm, the back-and-forth of the *one* and *two* stays well defined. In modern popular music, we tend to stomp our feet on beats one and three (the downbeat), and clap our hands on beats two and four (the backbeat). So it sounds something like this: STOMP-clap!-STOMP-clap!

TRY IT YOURSELF: A STEADY BEAT

Stomp your feet and clap your hands alternately as you count to four:

1	2	3	4
STOMP	CLAP	STOMP	CLAP

Outside that North Carolina nightclub, what Questlove heard was different. The claps, which should have carried that steady backbeat, slid into place just slightly after he expected to hear them. Each clap sounded like a book falling down onto its side just after being set upright on a shelf. The weirdest part was the kick: the drum sound played with the foot to carry that "stomping" downbeat. The kick drum was chaotic. It would appear on the "one" and then not show up when he expected it to hit on the "three." Instead, it would pop into view in irregular places, not places that felt familiar or safe to a drummer, the musician most responsible for delivering a stable, dependable pulse. He'd never heard a drumbeat so inconsistent in a rap song, a genre of music made on machines, all with dependable digital clocks. It sounded, as Questlove would later describe in colorful language, like what would happen if you gave a baby two tequila shots, placed her in front of a drum machine, and had her try to program a beat. Nothing was exactly where he expected it to be. And that's what made it exhilarating.

Questlove ran to the stage door. After convincing the security guards that he was, in fact, one of the musicians, he stood backstage and listened to the song. The next day he asked his tourmates: *What was that first song y'all did where the kick drum was all over the place?*

That was "Bullshit," they answered, one of the songs from their new album. *Produced by that kid we told you about, Jay Dee.*

Questlove flashed back to his conversation a couple of weeks prior with the four members of the Pharcyde backstage at Irving Plaza in New York, when he told them how excited he was that Q-Tip from A Tribe Called Quest—one of the most popular and creative groups in hip-hop and Questlove's musical "North Star"—was going to be producing tracks for their upcoming album. *Not Q-Tip,* they replied. *Tip's boy from Detroit.* They pointed to a rather unremarkable-looking young man sitting on a couch nearby. And Questlove recalled being disappointed, and rather disinterested in meeting whoever it was.

Now he was interested.

The next year, the recording engineer Bob Power sat behind a mixing board in New York's Battery Studios during a recording session for the fourth album from A Tribe Called Quest. Power was middle-aged, Jewish, a trained musician who had forged an unlikely creative partnership with the three Black kids from Queens since the beginning of their careers. They gave him a crucial education in the methodology of hiphop beatmaking. And the members of Tribe, in turn, found in Power a trusted ear, a sound man who helped them combine disparate sampled sounds from dozens of different records into seamless songs, and could navigate the tangled terrain of electronic music production, coaxing different machines with different clocks to synchronize with each other.

Power had developed a rhythm with the group's two producers, the lead vocalist, Jonathan Davis, who performed under the name Q-Tip, and the DJ, Ali Shaheed Muhammad. Power knew what to expect from them and they shared a language to communicate musical ideas. But that dynamic changed on this album with the addition of another, outside producer. Some new kid Q-Tip found in Detroit named Jay Dee.

Power listened to one of Jay Dee's tracks for a song called "Word Play" as he recorded those sounds from a digital drum machine onto a huge, two-inch-wide reel of magnetic tape able to hold twenty-four separate tracks of audio at once.

Power squinted. Something sounded wrong.

The drums were . . . weird. The snare drum on the backbeat landed a little off, but the kick drum just bounced all over the place. The whole thing sounded sloppy, like the kid didn't even care where the drums fell. Like he didn't really have much musical or technical knowledge.

Power wanted to say something, but he knew he couldn't. Q-Tip and the guys in the crew seemed to be keen on Jay Dee, and Power was always wary of overstepping his bounds. So he held his tongue.

But Power thought: *Man, this shit is fucked up.*

Later it occurred to Bob Power that maybe that was the whole point.

I n 1997, at another recording studio in New York City, the singer D'Angelo assembled a band to record his second album. In addition to Ahmir "Questlove" Thompson on drums, there were James Poyser on keyboards and Roy Hargrove on horns. The odd man out in this crew of young Americans was the London-based bassist Pino Palladino.

Palladino had started his career in the 1970s and worked as an in-demand studio and stage player for most of the eighties and nineties with artists like Eric Clapton, Elton John, Melissa Etheridge, and Phil Collins. But in all his years as a professional sideman, Palladino had never quite played the way D'Angelo was now asking him to do. "D" wanted Palladino to place his notes far behind the beat, meaning that Palladino's bass notes would drop just after the listener expected to hear them. Palladino understood this as a technique from jazz, backphrasing. But what was different here was how severe it was and how it deliberately clashed with Questlove's metronomic drums.

Palladino came to understand that the time-feel D'Angelo was pursuing owed a great deal to another, transient figure in Electric Lady Studios—someone whom all the accomplished musicians in the sessions, especially D'Angelo, regarded with a kind of reverence; not a musician, actually, but an electronic beatmaker. Questlove in particular had come to worship Jay Dee as a guru who liberated him from the idea of keeping perfect time, and instead imparted a permission to be loose, to be human, to be wrong.

Over the course of the next several years, Jay Dee would become the rhythmic patron saint of that studio band—a collective that would collaborate on myriad projects. Palladino left in 2002 to join the legendary rock band the Who, a gig that lasted for the next fifteen years. But the sessions with D'Angelo, Questlove, Poyser, and Jay Dee—who had taken to calling themselves the Soulquarians—were among the most transformative and liberating Palladino had ever experienced, and these tracks would end up being a career-defining body of work for him, influential to countless musicians thereafter for the rhythms that Palladino himself described as "wobbly" and "messed up."

When Palladino played the songs for musician friends of his, they invariably remarked:

The timing is kinda weird.

S*loppy. Drunken. Limping. Lazy. Dragging. Off.*

Questlove had heard all these terms used to describe the music of Jay Dee, who in midcareer switched his sobriquet to J Dilla.

But it wasn't until he came to Detroit to visit Jay in his home studio that he understood that the producer wasn't sloppy at all.

In the basement of a small ranch house on the corner of Nevada and McDougall in a neighborhood called Conant Gardens, Questlove witnessed J Dilla the craftsman, with an almost spiritual devotion to repetition, process, and order. Every day, no matter how late Jay stayed up, he rose at 7:00 a.m. From 7:00 to 9:00 a.m. he swept, wiped, and dusted every inch of his studio while listening to music, usually records that he had recently purchased, listening for sections to sample and manipulate on his Akai MPC3000 drum machine. He didn't just skip through the records, "needle-dropping" for interesting parts. He listened to entire songs, listened and listened. His vigilance was almost always rewarded by an element deep within a track. From 9:00 a.m. until noon, he made "beats," or individual rhythm tracks for rappers to rhyme on or singers to sing over. He created them quickly, one after the other, finished them, and then moved on. At lunchtime, he took a three-hour break. Sometimes he'd use that time to pick up visiting musicians and artists at the airport and take them back to his home studio. Then he'd work again from 3:00 p.m. until 8:00 or 9:00 p.m., and use the rest of the evening to hang out—go eat, go to the strip club—often returning to make more beats. That routine yielded both innovation and a prodigious body of work. J Dilla was prolific, producing hundreds upon hundreds of individual beats.

The young Detroit producer had other behaviors that seemed eccentric to his collaborators, friends, and family. When they ambled around his home, they found what many of them describe as the cleanest house they ever saw. If they walked to his bedroom, they'd find his clothes ordered and displayed in an almost boutique-like fashion. If they opened his refrigerator, they'd see everything in it organized just so, the soda cans lined up in straight rows, the labels all turned to face the same way. He kept notebooks filled with drafts and revisions of lyrics; with lists of tasks and sample ideas and detailed song arrangements. Anyone who ever got close to J Dilla discovered the truth about the man and, by extension, his music. Not a single thing was out of place. Everything was exactly where he wanted it to be.

J Dilla's rhythms were not accidents, they were intentions. Yet even the biggest fans of his style initially heard them as erratic. Why? Their reactions had everything to do with those rhythms *defying their expectations*. To understand the music of J Dilla, we must examine that process of subversion.

How our rhythmic expectations came to be is as much a tale of geography as it is musicology. Our musical expectations are governed by our *location*: where we're from, and where we've been. So, before we meet James, we need to first take an important journey—from Europe to Africa to America—and on that trip we are going to need maps. In positioning J Dilla, a map of one place in particular tells us much of what we need to know.

2.
Straight Time/Swing Time

La ville du détroit is what the French called the place: "the village on the strait," a fur-trading post beside a narrow, straight passage between two great lakes, founded in 1701 by a naval officer named Cadillac. One hundred and four years later, after the English took *le Détroit* from the French and the American colonists took Detroit from the English, President Thomas Jefferson sent an emissary there to serve as the Michigan Territory's chief justice. By the time Augustus Woodward arrived, the entire town had burned to the ground after a barn fire, its six hundred inhabitants huddled beneath makeshift shelters.

Woodward—who fetishized all things Roman and Greek, and who'd written a book called *A System of Universal Science* to organize all the knowledge of the human race—did not see the burning of Detroit as a human crisis, but as an opportunity to impose his ideals of perfection and order upon a tabula rasa. Woodward stood on a high boulder with his surveyor and envisioned a new city rising from the ashes.

He drafted a plan of interlocking equilateral triangles, each side exactly four thousand feet long. He began with the first triangle, the base of which ran parallel to the river. At this triangle's center was the survey origin point near his rock, which he saw as a military parade ground he dubbed in Latin "Campus Martius." Six avenues extended from the central square. The three points of the triangle would be rounded out for other, circular plazas and parks, each themselves the end points for other, inverted triangles.

Woodward's design for Detroit was among the first radial city

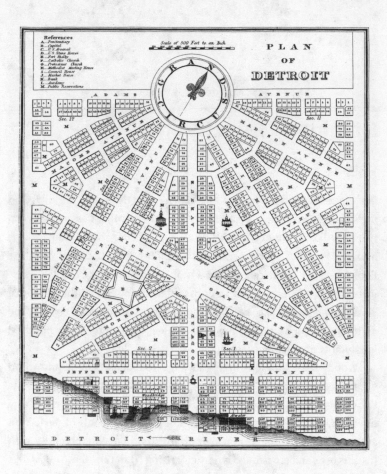

plans in history. It was practical, allowing the city's expansion simply by adding more triangles. And it was beautiful: elaborated on paper in 1807, the City of Detroit unfurled as a resplendent mosaic of alternating triangles arranging themselves into tiled hexagons; their interior avenues, circles, and rectangular campuses forming flowers of latticework. It was a design of rigid mathematics, in multiples of three, imposing its order on the American landscape and upon everybody within it.

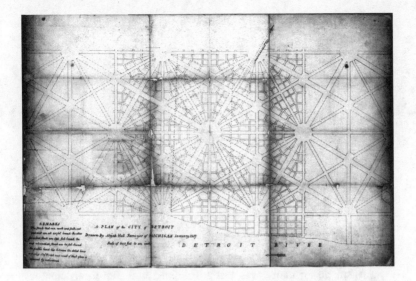

mposing order, *their* order, was an obsession for the Europeans before and during the colonial enterprise. European cultures had developed precise rules for everything: in architecture, and in music. Some musical rules were governed by physics—for example: a vibrating length of string, cut in half, will produce a vibration twice as fast, resulting in a tone that seems to the human ear the *same* as the first, but *higher* in pitch.

But almost every other European "rule" about music was really a choice. The reason that the above phenomenon is known as the "octave" is that Europeans decided to devise a system making that higher tone the eighth step on a scale of seven degrees or notes. Europeans created a second tonal system, dividing this same distance into twelve smaller, equidistant steps. Again, a choice. Those choices—the seven- or twelve-note scale over even rhythms counted in multiples of either two or three—evolved over hundreds of years into a common practice that determined what Europeans would hear as musical and what they wouldn't.

But there were other ways to conceive of music. The Greeks, much earlier, had devised a ten-tone triangular system of harmony called the

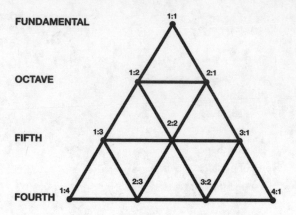

tetraktys. Asian cultures divided the distance of an octave into scales with five, seven, twelve, twenty-two, and fifty-five steps.

African performance was less formalized and more participatory than the European system. The African concept of pitch was much more granular, what we now call *microtonal.* And Africans evolved a more complex rhythmic sense, wherein two different pulses were often laid on top of each other, played simultaneously, called polyrhythm; for example, a chunk of time counted in twos and threes *at the same time.* Polyrhythm was the sound of two or more strands of rhythm happening at once, at seeming cross-purposes to each other, but part of a whole.

Our musical expectations are governed by where we're from. Pitting twos against threes in this manner was foreign to the European practice. What the Africans heard as music, Europeans heard as wrong, alien, uncivilized. When the Europeans came to impose their will upon the Africans, these cultural biases played no small part in their justification for what would become the most atrocious imposition in human history, the transatlantic slave trade.

The calculus of colonizers met new realities on the ground, and their schemes often yielded unintended consequences. The citizens of Detroit hated Woodward and his perfect plan, as did Michigan's new governor, Lewis Cass. So they sabotaged it. Cass sold off new lots north

TRY IT YOURSELF: MONORHYTHM/POLYRHYTHM

STEP ONE: Tap your LEFT hand on your knee to a 2 count

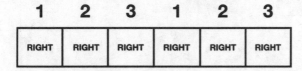

1	2	1	2
LEFT	LEFT	LEFT	LEFT

STEP TWO: Tap your RIGHT hand on your knee to a 3 count

1	2	3	1	2	3
RIGHT	RIGHT	RIGHT	RIGHT	RIGHT	RIGHT

STEP THREE: Now do both at the same time

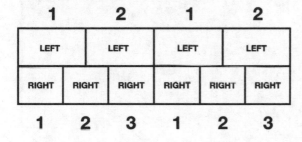

1		2		1		2	
LEFT		LEFT		LEFT		LEFT	
RIGHT	RIGHT	RIGHT	RIGHT	RIGHT	RIGHT
1	2	3	1	2	3

Not so easy, is it?

of Woodward's first triangle, blocking the plan's inland expansion and decapitating the top half of what Woodward envisioned as "Grand Circus Park," henceforth only a semi-circus. French farmers on either side of town sold their lands piecemeal, blocking the paths of many crosstown roads, their borders becoming long streets that preserved the farmers' names— Beaubien, Campau, Moran, Chene. City merchants and politicians decided to ignore Woodward's plan for the bottom of his triangle and developed it on a simple gridiron of streets at right angles to each other, the linear twos of the merchant class wedging a ragged interruption into the graceful rhythm of Woodward's baroque threes, two things happening at once, at cross-purposes to each other. A polyrhythm of conflicting intentions.

Thomas Jefferson's Land Ordinance Act required another grid, aligned with true north, an act of violence upon the land presaging another on Indigenous people. In Michigan the borders of these grid squares, measured in miles, came to be defined by roads running in long straight lines with no regard for topography. As Detroit grew, these became the "Mile

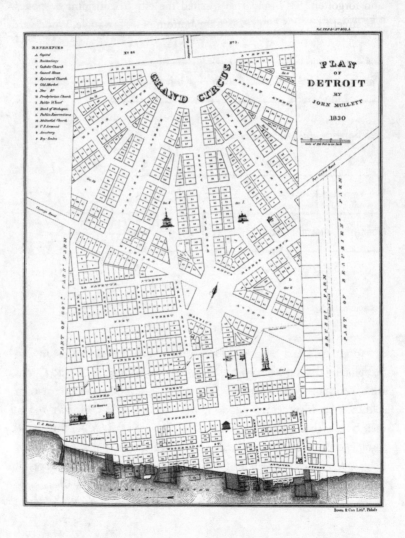

Roads" that ran east to west across the city, conflicting with the cross-town roads that ran parallel to the river. Now Detroit had two, misaligned grids. Wherever Detroit didn't name the mile roads, it numbered them by their distance from Campus Martius. When Detroit eventually finished expanding northward, it set its border at a road called "8 Mile."

Little remained of Woodward's vision in downtown Detroit: fragments of three triangles, like shards of an artisan's elegant tile, shattered and forgotten. Six broad roads exited the city like disjointed spokes. The street that would have been the bottom of that triangle, Woodward named for his benefactor, Jefferson; and the street that bisected the triangle, he named for himself, though he later claimed that he called it "Woodward Avenue" only because it ran *toward the woods*. That road became the central axis of a city where the streets on the west side didn't match up with the streets on the east. Some zagged in odd places and others dead-ended. Others were built in broken sections. In the city on the strait, nothing would be exactly straight.

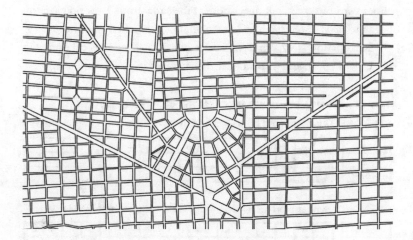

Woodward and Jefferson were hypocrites: fans of grand plans with fatal flaws; peddlers of platonic ideals they didn't practice; prophets of freedom who owned slaves. They wouldn't live to see the disorder their order created.

—————

After Europeans abducted Africans and took them across the Atlantic, African men and women had to disguise their religious and musical practices in order to preserve them. In South America and the Caribbean, African gods were rebranded under a Catholic veneer, so African polyrhythm persisted within it.[*]

But in the Protestant English colonies that became the United States, religious practices from Africa were forbidden, and polyrhythm vanished. Musical expression outside Christian hymns was suppressed; drumming, especially, was seen as clandestine communication and tantamount to insurrection. Wherever the African retentions and inheritances surfaced, they did so most often in a European frame: the seven-note scale, but breaking the rules just a bit; the performance word-for-word and note-for-note, but deviating just a bit. In North America, the greatest African inheritance—that polyrhythmic sense— was restrained by the European practice of one even pulse counted in either twos or threes, but never both at the same time. How polyrhythm began to peek out, just a bit, is in a phenomenon called *syncopation*.

Syncopation is what happens when we don't hear musical events in places we expect, and instead hear those events in places we don't.

TRY IT YOURSELF: UNSYNCOPATED vs. SYNCOPATED

STEP ONE: Unsyncopated beat—count out loud while stomping/clapping

Count	1	n	2	n	3	n	4	n	1	n	2	n	3	n	4	n
CLAP																
STOMP																

STEP TWO: Syncopated beat—count out loud while stomping/clapping

Count	1	n	2	n	3	n	4	n	1	n	2	n	3	n	4	n
CLAP																
STOMP																

[*] For example, the Afro-diasporic religions condomblé and santeria would spawn the musical lineage that led to polyrhythmic genres such as samba and bossa nova in Brazil and rumba and son cubano in Cuba, respectively.

Syncopation imported the surprise of polyrhythm into the mono-rhythms of North American music without the polyrhythm itself. The pulse was counted in twos, but the events often happened in the places where a superimposed pulse of threes might put them. Syncopation was the ghost of polyrhythm, the spirit of Africa still following its progeny through time and space, through slavery to emancipation and beyond.

African Americans at the turn of the twentieth century didn't call it syncopation, they called it *ragging*. To "rag" a tune was to mess around with where you put notes while holding the pulse. As pianos became a feature of middle-class American culture, African American pianists applied their rhythmic sensibilities to the instrument. With Scott Joplin's performance at the Chicago World's Columbian Exposition in 1893 and the publication of his "Maple Leaf Rag" in 1899, the genre of *ragtime* was born. This ragged, rolling, disorienting music where notes came in odd places was an expression of cultural freedom, and thus of defiance. Ragtime roiled white America: young people generally greeted the defiance of rhythmic expectation with surprise and delight; older whites recoiled from the disorder. For the next three decades, ragtime became America's chief popular music, boosting the growth of the fledgling sheet music and record business.

In the bars and bordellos of early-twentieth-century New Orleans, ragtime became the foundation for another genre of music. *Jazz*, in one sense, was what happened when multiple musicians ragged a tune, separately but simultaneously, a pleasant confluence of cross-purposes. Jazz was also fed by another emerging genre of African American music from the countryside. The *blues*, by the 1900s, had evolved into a distinct form: a particular harmonic movement and structure, a microtonality that could be achieved only on instruments like the guitar by "bending" strings to try to get to the notes *between* the notes on the European scale. And though the blues was counted just as European music was—in twos or threes—it, too, showed a ghost of African polyrhythm. The rhythm of the blues had acquired a particular uneven gait. And thus the emergence of jazz and blues did something else: they created an entirely new way—an *African American* way—of relating to musical time.

――――――

n European music, time was expressed, with rare exceptions, as a straight, even pulse.*

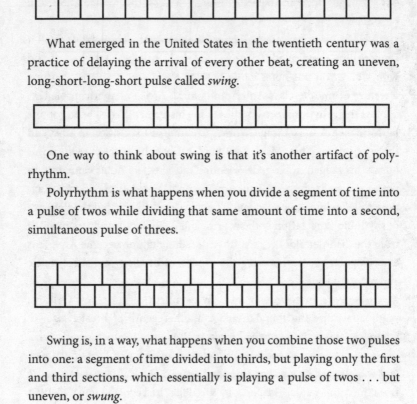

What emerged in the United States in the twentieth century was a practice of delaying the arrival of every other beat, creating an uneven, long-short-long-short pulse called *swing*.

One way to think about swing is that it's another artifact of poly-rhythm.

Polyrhythm is what happens when you divide a segment of time into a pulse of twos while dividing that same amount of time into a second, simultaneous pulse of threes.

Swing is, in a way, what happens when you combine those two pulses into one: a segment of time divided into thirds, but playing only the first and third sections, which essentially is playing a pulse of twos . . . but uneven, or *swung*.

---

* A phenomenon called notes inégales in classical music and the dragged second beat of the Viennese waltz are two of those exceptions.

In practice, however, swing is more complex than this simple math. Some musicians swing a rhythm only slightly, and some more severely. The expressions of long-short vary from performer to performer, an expression of individual, human time; and a reflection of the movement of the human body and a musical tradition wedded to dance.

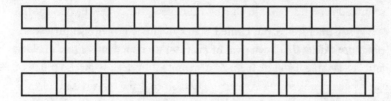

Swing as a time-feel would permeate blues, jazz, and nearly every American musical genre to follow: from rhythm and blues to country and western, from rock to soul, from funk to disco, from punk and new wave to hip-hop and electronic dance music. Swing time is now an integral part of the American musical expectation, and thus our global musical expectation.

Listening To:
The Difference Between Straight and Swung

One of the greatest examples of the difference between straight and swing time occurs in one of the world's best-loved and widely known classic rock songs: "Bohemian Rhapsody" by Queen.

Begin listening at the 3:40 mark. Freddie Mercury wrote this section as a mock opera, performed as European classical music is, in straight time. We are still in straight time at 3:57 when the chorus sings the words: *Beelzebub has a devil put aside for me.*

They will repeat the words "for me" two times. By the end of the second repetition, at 4:05, we are in swing time. Do you hear the difference?

In making a sudden switch from opera to rock 'n' roll, the song not only shifts from straight to swung, it symbolically crosses the Atlantic, making the journey from Europe to America in eight seconds.

Swing signifies the difference between European and African American rhythmic feels. It's performance based, not scripted or notated. It adopts the unique qualities of the player.

One musician in particular would help to encode swing into jazz, and thus put the time-feel in the center of all American popular music thereafter: Louis Armstrong, who began in New Orleans, then built his reputation and influence in Chicago and New York, where he became the one musician whom everyone tried to emulate. His methods presaged a subgenre of jazz that became America's youth dance music in the 1930s and '40s, taking its name from Armstrong's time-feel: *swing*. So much of what pop music became, Armstrong established: the improvised solo; the bluesy, bent way of singing and playing; even the archetype of the Black performer "crossing over" to white audiences. But Armstrong's delaying of time had the greatest influence. Almost every performer in jazz and pop, whether peer or protégé, took something from him: Billie Holiday and Duke Ellington, Bing Crosby and Frank Sinatra. In the Armstrong style, which became the popular style, he sang or played in a devil-may-care fashion, as if he was in no hurry to get where he was going. *I'll get there when I get there. I'll see you when I see you. It'll be worth the wait.* In jazz, "cool" was manifested by delay and defiance of expectation.

Louis Armstrong's musical journey north was part of a larger, dire exodus from the American South, as whites enacted laws that segregated Black Americans and stripped them of their franchise, using terror and violence to enforce them. In the Great Migration, from 1915 until the passage of the Civil Rights Act in 1965, around six million Black men, women, and children fled the former Confederate states. The closest and safest northern destination for many Black southerners were the cities of the Midwest, one of which offered a particular promise of prosperity.

Edward "Red" Cornish—born January 2, 1903, the son of an Irish American landowner and one of his Black sharecroppers—left Maryland in 1916, alone on a train at the age of thirteen. He arrived in Detroit and found work at the Ford Motor Company.

Two years earlier, Henry Ford had put the word out that he was doubling the company's minimum wage to five dollars a day. For working
men, this was an unbelievable sum. But Ford's factories, machines that
made machines, had an appetite for men. Ford did something else that
many of his peers didn't do: he hired Black workers. His reasons for doing
so are as complex and suspect as the man himself: Ford desired a control-
lable, loyal workforce that would reject unionism and communism.

Fleeing Jim Crow and attracted by the prospect of paying work, Black
Americans flooded Detroit, by the hundreds, then by the thousands. In
1920, the Black population was 40,000. By 1930 it was 120,000. In the
years after World War II it would more than double again, to 300,000.

The place on the disorderly map where Black Detroiters were compelled to live was a dilapidated neighborhood called Black Bottom—so
named for the color of the riverside soil—pushing northward along
Hastings Street into a Jewish neighborhood called Paradise Valley. It
swelled with tens of thousands of new arrivals crushed into abysmal
housing so scarce that it actually cost more to rent there than it did in
the white neighborhoods that surrounded it—neighborhoods that had
plenty of space to let but none for Black people. The racial animus in Detroit was so vicious that the white citizens created one of the most active
KKK chapters in the North, prompting many in Black Bottom to portray
Detroit as living "up South."

Only a few other tiny pockets of Detroit welcomed Black renters
and homeowners. One was located on the East Side near 7 Mile Road,
on lands once owned by Detroit's foremost white abolitionist. That man,
Shubael Conant, sold his property with the caveat that there could never
be any restrictive covenants barring their sale to Black or Jewish people,
as was common practice. The neighborhood that grew on those lands
became the city's first Black middle-class district, Conant Gardens.*

---

* Conant Gardens was not insulated from its white neighbors' brutality. The federal government planned a
new housing project there for working-class Black families during a World War II housing shortage. The project was initially opposed by Conant Gardens' Black middle-class community organization, but facing white
opponents' unequivocal bigotry ("We want our girls to walk on the street not raped," read one leaflet), Black
residents united against an armed white mob in early 1942. The Sojourner Truth Homes began taking
Black tenants a few months later under the protection of the National Guard. The conflict presaged the anti-
Black race riots that racked Detroit the following year.

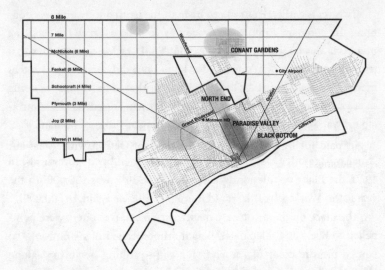

"Ford's," as Detroiters called the Ford Motor Company, was the single largest employer of Black Americans in the city; Detroit's Black churches functioned as hiring halls and its ministers were empowered as recruiters. It was the lowest, the dirtiest, and the most dangerous work—most Black men were hired as janitors or in the foundries; and it wasn't always the five-dollar day promised. But it was enough to support a family.

"Red" Cornish married a pretty girl from Georgia and had children. His daughter Maybeline started a family with a young man, Thomas "Suge" Hayes, who had himself fled Alabama for Detroit the day after his high school graduation in 1948. Suge worked at Ford's, too, until he found some more nefarious hustles to support five children, including Maybeline's daughter, Maureen.

And the man who married Maureen Hayes, Dewitt Yancey, worked for Ford almost his entire adult life, even while he struggled to make a career for himself in music—which had become the second industry in Detroit's burgeoning Black community.

T he restaurants, lounges, and hotels of Paradise Valley became vital venues for the development of syncopated and swung music in the city on the strait: jazz and blues; then the blues' brazen, uptempo child, rhythm and blues. An archipelago of Black churches spawned generations of musicians and singers. The Detroit Public Schools, segregated as they were, provided comprehensive music education. And Detroit, imperfect as it was, fostered Black prosperity, which enabled not only the purchase of musical instruments, but also a worldview that allowed for the pursuit of fulfillment after generations of struggle for survival— a gift paid for by the mothers and fathers of Detroit with sweat and sleeplessness.

Berry Gordy II and his wife, Bertha, followers of Booker T. Washington's philosophy of self-reliance, opened a grocery store in Black Bottom that bore Washington's name, and other businesses, too, instilling in their eight children a similar entrepreneurial spirit. "Ber-Berry" was the name of the family fund into which all the Gordys—adults and children—were required to deposit regularly, a modest reserve of capital out of which the children could draw a loan for any venture approved by the family members. In 1959, the Gordys' son Berry III applied for a loan to start a record company, and after much debate, he was given $800.

During his teenage years on Hastings Street, the junior Gordy caught the fever for jazz and blues, and began writing songs. A job on the Ford line became an opportunity to write them to the rhythms of the machines. Gordy's songs for Jackie Wilson—"Reet Petite," "Lonely Teardrops," and "To Be Loved"—made him a hitmaker. His new record company was a chance to retain his equity and control, its name turning the Detroit penchant for ethnic diminutives—Corktown for the Irish, Poletown for the Polish, Jewtown for the Jews—back around on the motor city itself: Motown.

Operating from a modest two-story house on West Grand Boulevard, Motown became one of the most successful independent record labels in the country and, eventually, the largest Black-owned business in America. Gordy got there by taking a cue from Ford's moving assembly line. Motown would be a machine, a full-service music manufacturer that plucked artists from Detroit's Black neighborhoods, matched them with material written by teams of songwriters, produced those records with a crew of peerless musicians, and debated their quality before releasing them. The artists were drilled in manners, dress, dance; their careers managed and tours booked by Motown. Thus Gordy created the modern concept of artist development, and over the years launched the careers of artists like Smokey Robinson, Diana Ross and the Supremes, Mary Wells, Kim Weston, Marvin Gaye, Stevie Wonder, the Temptations, Martha Reeves, and the Jackson 5, as well as songwriting-production teams like Holland-Dozier-Holland. Tens of millions of Motown records sold across the globe, and on each of them, a map—all roads leading to Detroit.

Motown forged a brand of rhythm and blues that combined its musicians' swinging sophistication with its singers' church musicality, and executed this blend, called "soul," with pop form and commercial intent. Gordy's mottoes for Motown, "Hitsville, U.S.A." and "The Sound of Young America," became self-fulfilling prophecies. Motown's records were hits on the R&B and pop charts in equal measure—so equal that *Billboard* magazine eliminated its segregated charts for several years due to Motown's musical subversion, until a British band, the Beatles, invaded the charts with their own riff on Detroit's musical ideas.

Berry Gordy in some measure became the foremost practitioner of Booker T. Washington's theories of apolitical Black capitalism as power. Others in Detroit saw the need for a power more explicit. Elijah Poole, renaming himself Elijah Muhammad, founded in Detroit a Black-centric Muslim creed, the Nation of Islam. The churches of Detroit marshaled an army of volunteers and a wave of capital for the Civil Rights movement to overthrow Jim Crow in the South. The dry run for the March on Washington was Detroit's Walk to Freedom, down Woodward Avenue on a June day in 1963, after which Martin Luther King Jr. auditioned an early version of his "I Have a Dream" speech in front of a crowd of Detroiters. With them came white progressives, politicians, and trade unionists, who had for one reason or another, at this moment, found common cause with Black Americans. As Black Detroit marched America into its future, there was, for a brief moment, a sense that the road ahead was clearing.

———

A few months after the March on Washington, engineers from Motown dragged recording equipment around the corner from the studios on West Grand Boulevard to the King Solomon Baptist Church, where they taped a speech by the chief spokesperson for Elijah Muhammad's Nation of Islam. The Michigan-bred Malcolm X lampooned the March on Washington as a sellout by "Negro" leaders to white interests seeking to blunt Black grassroots political power.

"You was talking this march talk on Hastings Street!" he boomed—adding, as an aside, "Is Hastings Street still here?"

It wasn't.

The main artery of Black Detroit had been flattened to build one of several new freeways allowing unimpeded travel from Detroit to the expanding suburbs, which were chewing up land and filling Thomas Jefferson's square-mile grid boxes with tract housing. In other cities, "urban

renewal" projects ended up being little more than "Black removal" programs; but in Detroit's new order, those plans were executed with explicit racism. Black Bottom and Paradise Valley had produced a community, their streets a matrix for a singular culture. Now Detroit's chief Black neighborhoods were systematically erased from the map. The organs of Black nightlife were removed to create a new medical center. Streets that traversed Black Bottom and Paradise Valley were spliced, fractured, ruptured, disconnected. Old addresses disappeared under a huge freeway cloverleaf. Years later, the Detroit historian Herb Boyd would write, almost with a shrug: "The altering of neighborhood grids was something most Black Detroiters had grown accustomed to."

With Black Bottom disappearing, Edward "Red" Cornish had earned enough at Ford's to move out of the neighborhood and help his daughter Maybeline buy a house on the Far East Side, on Garland Street, into which she, her daughter Maureen, and her other children moved after Suge was sent to prison.

The smashing of Black Detroit, combined with policing by a particularly brutal force, boiled over in 1967 after police raided a West Side after-hours club. In the five-day rebellion that followed, forty-three people died, the National Guard was called up, and over four hundred buildings were destroyed by fire and looting. It marked the beginnings of a power shift. Whites had already been moving north of 8 Mile Road, and now they did so in greater numbers, taking their tax dollars with them. Jobs evaporated with automation and plant closings. Detroit real estate values plummeted, city services dwindled, and crime spread. The neighborhood around Maybeline and Maureen Hayes's house on Garland emptied: the grocery store, Sylvetti's Italian Market, the butcher shop, all gone.

The coup de grâce came from Berry Gordy himself when he moved his entire company to Los Angeles in 1972. Motown had become a synonym for Detroit, and it was Detroiters' pride and joy; but it was a business, not a birthright, owned by a capitalist, albeit a Black one.

The Motown Sound was already on its way out because both music and Detroit had been seized by a new rhythmic development, another African American invention, the first real jump since swing.

Funk, most simply, was a change in rhythm's center of gravity. The transformation in popular music was drastic, occurring over the course of just a few years.

In the early 1960s, musical time—whether in twos or threes, whether straight or swung—had an overall even keel expressed as a back-and-forth ticktock between the one and the two, the downbeat and the backbeat. Motown music exemplified this evenness. Listen to "My Guy" by Mary Wells from 1964: notice the even back-and-forth between the kick drum on the downbeat and the snare and claps on the backbeat.

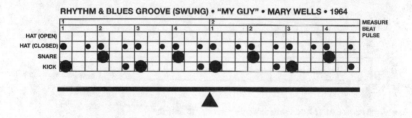

Now listen to "Cold Sweat" by James Brown—a song released only three years later, in 1967—which tilted the emphasis toward the first downbeat, or as Brown called it, the "One."

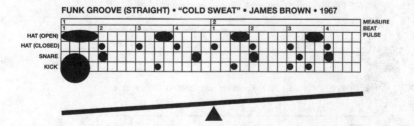

"Cold Sweat" shifted the balance to the One so heavily that the measures after it felt like a suspension, a held breath, building the tension for two whole measures before the next occurrence of the One.

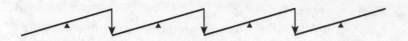

TRY IT YOURSELF: SHIFTING TO FUNK

STEP ONE: Start a four-count ("one-two-three-four" and repeat).

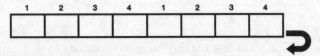

STEP TWO: Clap your hands on every "2" and "4."

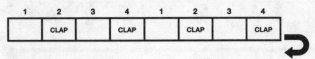

STEP THREE: Add foot stomps on every "1" and "3."

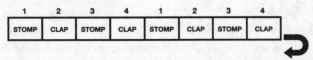

Listen to the evenness of this rhythm. This is a *standard rhythm & blues groove*

STEP FOUR: Stop stomping. Keep clapping your hands.

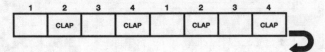

STEP FIVE: Add a big foot stomp on just the first ONE, and repeat.

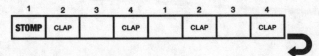

Notice the difference. This is a *funk groove.*

Funk was a rhythmic system of tension and release *over time*, but also *simultaneous* tension between some players exercising maximum restraint and others exhibiting maximum expressiveness. Most of all, funk was a science of subverted expectations, syncopation taken to its ultimate destination. With funk, things weren't always where you thought they'd be. In "Cold Sweat," the first couple of beats created *stability*, but the next few kicks and snares came *later than expected*, increasing *instability*, a pleasant disorientation and reorientation—with sudden silences *creating suspense* before the return of the One.

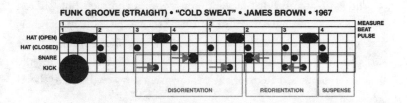

FUNK GROOVE (STRAIGHT) • "COLD SWEAT" • JAMES BROWN • 1967

The drums weren't the only instrument to play with rhythmic expectation, because in funk, every instrument was used as a drum, especially the bass guitar, which also began to take on the melodic work. Funk made the bass line prime.

In the late 1960s into the 1970s, James Brown solidified and codified funk through a series of songs that built out this aesthetic like "Sex Machine" and "Give It Up or Turnit a Loose." By the end of the 1960s, even Motown's grooves had changed. Stevie Wonder, for example, had gone from the even-keeled "Uptight (Everything's Alright)" to one-centric rhythms like "For Once in My Life" and "Signed, Sealed, Delivered I'm Yours." But funk was a set of ideas that could be heard across all genres. The hard rock band Led Zeppelin's lead-footed John Bonham was highly influenced by James Brown and his drummers, like Clyde Stubblefield. Almost no corner of global pop went untouched by this particularly American rhythmic idea: reggae, Afrobeat, even country music. And though disco would even out the tilted nature of funk in the 1970s, much of what passed for disco was simply funk by another name. By the end of the decade, funk informed a new genre, hip-hop.

Aside from James Brown, no person was more influential in the growth of funk than George Clinton.

C linton first hit Detroit in 1962, he and four friends in rumpled suits tumbling out of a souped-up Pontiac Bonneville for an audition with Motown. Clinton and his group, the Parliaments, were literally a barbershop quintet. They cut heads for a living in New Jersey; they drove six hundred miles overnight because they dreamed of cutting records in Detroit.

The Parliaments didn't leave Motown with a contract. But Clinton found work as a songwriter, and by 1967 he gave the Parliaments their first hit, "(I Wanna) Testify," on the small Detroit label Revilot. But the Parliaments couldn't find another hit, and they weren't made for the slick, choreographed R&B of the Motown era anyway. Instead, they'd create a new one.

The transformation happened in May 1968, during a ten-day residency at the Phelps Lounge at 9006 Oakland Avenue in the decaying north end of Paradise Valley. The Parliaments were third on the bill with several other R&B and soul artists like Jimmy Ruffin, Bettye LaVette, and Carl Carlton. The Parliaments began as one of those class acts in their suits and slicked-back hair. But as the days went by, George Clinton and the band became more uninhibited. Clinton stuck his head under a faucet and his process regained its curl. The next evening he came onstage in just a diaper. Some of the band followed, in ever-more-ridiculous costume, from sunglasses and bell-bottoms to duck feet and rooster heads. By the end of those ten days at the Phelps, the Parliaments were gone. Funkadelic had been born.

It would take longer for the sound of the new group to coalesce. The center of gravity came in the form of William "Bootsy" Collins, a veteran of James Brown's band. Brown had beaten the One into Bootsy's brain, and the bassist imposed Brown's ruthless rhythmic rigor on Clinton's crew of freethinkers, a new order within the disorder. Throughout 1973, their work at United Sound Systems Recording Studios, just seven blocks from Motown's now-deserted offices, made them Detroit's innovators. Clin-

ton released the music under two entities: Funkadelic and Parliament—
and the bands soon melded in fans' language into one collective: P-Funk.

I n 1975, Parliament released a song called "Chocolate City," which celebrated a demographic shift taking place in cities all over the United
States, Detroit included.

That shift—which saw Black people numbering around half of Detroit's population of 1.5 million—had already swept a Black man from
Black Bottom into the mayor's office. In late 1973, Coleman Young, a
union organizer turned state senator, defeated the ex–police chief who
created a program, under the apt acronym STRESS, that had killed nearly
two dozen Black men in the previous couple of years.

After Coleman Young won the election, Black Detroit rejoiced as he
threw a hex on the city's criminals, both without and within the police
department: "It's time to leave Detroit. Hit 8 Mile Road!" *Our way, or the
highway.*

Old Detroit was dead. Its creators left behind a broken, disordered
maze. New Detroit would be a Black city, a metropolis of the future.

Nothing symbolized the spirit of Detroit's moment—the embrace
of both possibility and impossibility, the sublime and the absurd, both
the love and the satirization of Black life—quite like George Clinton's
magnum opus, *Mothership Connection*, an album that coalesced all the
elements of future funk: the creation of outlandish characters like Star
Child and the marshaling of synthesizers and electronics, all contained
in the Mothership, a warp-drive Cadillac, its occupant a space-age, flam-
boyant, slang-talking hustler, a mirror of Detroit's street culture.

The Mothership became a totem of a larger Black American worldview: a cultivated, exuberant dream-sense of the future, spirits both
ancient and new, bound with the sciences—math, physics, machines,
technology—offering the possibility of flight. In later years, Black scholars would give this aesthetic a name: Afrofuturism. They'd point to the
Mothership, and the Phelps, and United Sound Systems, and to Detroit,
a place where the past, present, and future all happened simultaneously,
as Afrofuturism's vital incubator. As such, Detroit's map—a ruptured,

offset, conflicted ghost of polyrhythm—could be more than a record of what had been. It might also be a prediction of things that had not yet come to pass.

Star children, aliens on Earth, being born in the shattered grid.

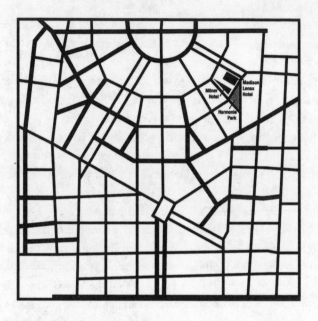

3.
Play Jay

One evening in the fall of 1974, the nineteen-year-old grandson of Red Cornish, Herman Hayes, drove downtown to see his infant nephew, James.

Herm parked his car near Grand Circus Park and walked to the nearby Madison-Lenox Hotel, where his big sister Maureen now lived with her new husband—Beverly Yancey, a musician whom everyone called by his middle name, Dewitt. When Maureen let him into their apartment, Herm hollered. There was little James, a fat baby perched upright on the knee of his father. Dewitt was holding the wobbly infant vertical with his left hand curled gently around the back of James's neck. With his right, Dewitt's fingers thumped a rhythm on James's belly, just as Dewitt would pluck his upright bass, singing along . . .

Booom-badu-bup-boooom. Badooom-bup-boooom.

"Dewitt," Herman said. "You're playing your *son*?!"

"It's the only way I can get him to shut up and stop crying," Dewitt replied. Maureen shook her head. That wasn't even the half of it. James wouldn't sleep at night without some kind of music, either on the stereo, or Dewitt playing his bass, or—as it was tonight—Dewitt playing James.

As Dewitt tapped his foot, James bounced, his round eyes and tiny ears wide open. Herm sat down and watched the father put the bass lines into him.

B orn February 7, 1974, James Dewitt Yancey represented a second chance at building a family for both of his parents.

Maureen Hayes came from Black Bottom. Her family lived in the upstairs flat of an old house on Antietam Street, oil-burning stove in the middle of the dining room. With four younger siblings—Terone, Reta, Clarice, and Herman—Maureen was saddled with their care while her mother, Maybeline, worked a succession of jobs: switchboard operator, bookbinder; and her father, Thomas "Suge" Hayes, made deliveries of bootlegged corn liquor. Sometimes he'd pile the children into his black 1949 Mercury to fetch his ingredients, sending each of them into different markets to buy five-pound bags of Domino sugar, and he always left a pad and pen near the house phone so they could take orders whenever someone called for "the milkman." Maureen felt as much apart from this world as she was a part of it: she had fallen in love with opera after studying classical voice at Miller Junior High. Her aunt, a music teacher, occasionally gave her tickets to the Detroit Symphony Orchestra; Maureen and her friend from glee club donned their freshly pressed school uniforms, taking the bus to join the white-gloved ladies and besuited gentlemen at the Ford Auditorium. Back in Black Bottom, no one shared her passion. Girls at school teased her about her singing. Her mother, Maybeline, listened to country music. Maureen brought her sister Reta to a concert, thinking it might give her some culture. Reta fell asleep. Her brothers got their hands on her two favorite records—a 45-rpm single of Nina Simone's "I Loves You, Porgy," and an album by her idol Leontyne Price, the first Black prima donna at the Metropolitan Opera— and threw them around until they cracked. Her alienation began to make more sense to her when she turned fifteen and needed her birth certificate to apply for a summer job. According to the City of Detroit's records, there *was* no Maureen Hayes. Her legal name was Maureen Renee Shearod, the daughter of Maybeline Cornish and George Robert Shearod, to whom her mother was still technically married. A number of disconnected memories came rushing back to Maureen in a thunderclap, moments that now made sense when joined together—being left behind when her younger siblings went off to spend their summers in Alabama with Suge's family; the Christmas card from Suge's sister that she found open on her mother's bed: *I'm putting $400 in this envelope and I want you to spend $100 on each one of my babies.* Maureen, who'd never received any money, did the math and told her mother: *Aunt Mag can't count. There's five of us.* Maybeline told Maureen not to read her letters and to mind her business. Suge and his children never wavered in their embrace of Maureen; she felt some distance nonetheless.

By the time Maureen came of age, the neighborhood had been upended, and so had her family. Suge had grown his hustle into a large drug operation, shacking up with a girlfriend while running cocaine out of the City Airport Inn on Gratiot; Maybeline, with help from her father, Red Cornish, bought a new home on Garland, pregnant with Suge's fifth child, Albert, while Maureen was expecting her first, Kenya, fathered by a young man from the neighborhood. The next few years were a traumatic blur. She moved in with a new boyfriend, a drug dealer and user who grew increasingly abusive. While Maureen was pregnant with his son, Kenya died under his care—*a bad fall*, he claimed. Maureen fled to her family's home and had her second child, Andre, while mourning her first. She cared for Andre for the first few years of his life, but eventually gave him to his paternal grandmother as a way to keep Andre and herself safe, and perhaps a way to survive that chapter of her life by shutting it out.

Maureen started over. She promised God she'd go to church. She created a workaday life for herself with a clerical job at the IRS. Her dreams of a performing career had long since faded when she was introduced to Dewitt Yancey, who had never stopped chasing his.

The Yancey family's music history ran decades deep. Dewitt's parents, William and Beverly, had both migrated from the South and played piano accompaniment for silent films in movie halls. They had twelve children: James, Blanche, Webster, McCoy, Clemmer Geno, Robert Lee, Alberta, Annabelle, Thelma, Martha, Cecelia, and, born in 1932, Beverly Dewitt, a boy named for his mother. Dewitt saw combat in the army during the Korean War, and carried with him thereafter what later generations would call posttraumatic stress. When he was discharged, he came home and went to work on the Ford line, but music was his preoccupation even when it wasn't his occupation. In the late 1950s, his brother Geno worked with a singing group, the Ambassadors, for whom Dewitt wrote and produced records. Later, Dewitt and his songwriting partner Johnny Thornton coaxed a young gospel singer to record a couple of their songs. Kim Weston was uncomfortable with secular music at first, and it took a few years until Thornton and his cousin Eddie Holland convinced her to sign with the record company Holland worked for, Motown. Weston went on to record a handful of hits for the label, including "Take Me in Your Arms (Rock Me a Little While)" and "It Takes Two" with Marvin Gaye.

But Dewitt had moved on by the time Kim Weston's career took off. He joined another singing group, the Ivies, who recorded songs for Roulette and Brunswick Records, and whose leader, Aaron McCray, turned down an offer from Motown because the money wasn't right. Sometimes billed as the "Sensation Ivies," they also recorded sides for singer-entrepreneur Johnnie Mae Matthews, one of the first Black women to found and operate her own independent label, Northern Records, and sang backup on her 1961 single "My Little Angel." In the years to come, Matthews became a friend and mentor to Dewitt Yancey, who wrote, recorded vocals, and arranged for Matthews's groups like the Eldees.

Dewitt would tell his family and friends that, in the late sixties, he had another brush with Motown, ghostwriting a song called "It's a Shame" and selling it to the label—which, according to Dewitt, gave him a Ford Cortina; gave the song to the Detroit Spinners; and gave the writing credit to Stevie Wonder, Syreeta Wright, and Lee Garrett. "It's a Shame" became the Spinners' first hit in 1970.[*] But Dewitt Yancey had little to show for all his work, neither in credits nor cash. He'd married a

---

[*] Dewitt's ex-wife Alice Scarbough Yancey says that she witnessed Dewitt writing this song; and members of the Yancey and Hayes families have long taken Dewitt's authorship as a given. I was unable to find corroboration for this story from anyone on the Motown side. None of the people I interviewed who were involved in the recording of "It's a Shame"—including Dennis Coffey, Paul Riser, and G.C. Cameron, the lead singer of the Spinners—have a memory of Dewitt Yancey or his involvement. Cameron's narrative of the song's creation is quite specific: "When I came home from Vietnam in '67, Stevie Wonder became my best friend . . . One night . . . we were at a club somewhere hanging out in Detroit . . . and he said, 'Look, man, I got this tune for you.' And we came back to his mother's house. He lived in the basement, because houses in Detroit had beautiful, big basements. That's where he kept his clavinet. And he sat down on the stool of the clavinet, and he went [sings the melody that would become Dennis Coffey's guitar intro]. And I say, 'I like it.' They called us the next day and said, 'Stevie needs you guys in the studio to record tomorrow.' And on the third day I recorded 'It's a Shame.' That was 1970." Though it was not unheard of for Motown songwriters to buy others' work and present it as their own, the only way for Dewitt Yancey's story to be true is if Stevie Wonder, one of the most prolific and original songwriters of the twentieth century, also engaged in this practice. Did Stevie Wonder get this song from Dewitt Yancey? A representative of Wonder, his brother Calvin Hardaway, relayed this answer to me through Paul Riser: "No."

woman named Alice Scarbough and they'd had three children—two girls, Beverly and Tracey, and a boy, Mark, whom everyone called Dewayne. Dewitt's work at the plant was the thing that kept the family afloat. By 1973, Dewitt's first marriage was over and he was living in a room at the Madison-Lenox Hotel.

Maureen met Dewitt when a mutual friend heard her sing and convinced Dewitt to invite her to one of his rehearsals. Dewitt liked Maureen's voice enough to bring her to an audition at a nightclub, the Hideaway, where the owner offered her a regular gig on the spot. It was all too much for Maureen, who worked full-time and took accounting classes at night. But Dewitt kept inviting her to rehearsals and Maureen, for some reason, kept finding the time. She liked this generous, gregarious man who seemed to think nothing of giving his time and effort to all these musicians and singers. She was twenty-two, he was thirty-eight. They had both just been through separate, significant splits. But she knew Dewitt was a good provider, working every shift he could at Ford, doing his music thing when he couldn't; and a good father, taking his kids every weekend. She made a silent vow: *I'm gon' get him.*

M oving into Dewitt's home, Maureen tried to be respectful of his children, who reacted to their father's new wife in different ways: The eldest daughter, Beverly, fourteen, was polite. The boy, Dewayne, thirteen, brooded. Tracey, eight, was resentful and possessive of her father. At first, the weekends were not comfortable.

James changed things. Since Maureen had brought her son home from Zieger Hospital, Dewitt's girls doted on him. James had a healthy appetite, and Maureen was tiny, so she carried the heavy boy in a sling around her belly. Maureen and the girls laughed at James's little feet rotating like propellers whenever he would eat his favorite food—Gerber Hawaiian Delight. By the time James was six months old, the doctors told Maureen that she needed to restrict his diet. But it soon became clear to them that James took the world in through his ears more than his mouth.

When he wasn't using his son as a musical instrument, Dewitt played his upright bass; James startled both his parents by singing along and matching Dewitt's pitch. When Dewitt put James Brown on the stereo system, little James Yancey would pull himself up by the netting of his playpen and dance. When James got big enough to move around on his own, records became his thing: crawl to the turntable and watch the label spin. When James was old enough to walk, Dewitt took him record shopping as a treat, and James soon got his own portable, battery-powered record player. Dewitt would return from his shift at the plant to bring James to nearby Harmonie Park for some fresh air, and James would insist on bringing that record player with him. He'd load a stack of 45-rpm singles onto his chubby arms, pushing his hands through the spindle holes and letting them dangle; then James would sit and play records for his fellow Detroiters. Passersby were amused at the sight of this toddler playing grown-up music. They'd make requests—*You got any James Brown?*—and little James knew exactly what records they meant. He couldn't yet read, but he could find the right records using the color of the labels as a guide.

At that very moment, six hundred miles to the east, a new scene of park-and-street DJs was emerging in New York City; a culture that didn't yet have a name. James, at the age of two, was with them in spirit, spinning 45s in the streets of the city on the strait.

Through Dewitt's drive, Maureen found her singing voice again, but she discovered that their home had room only for Dewitt's dreams. When James was a baby, she'd enrolled in a correspondence course to finish her accounting degree; Dewitt didn't like her studying and taking time away from the family, and Maureen never finished the course. On their first Christmas together, Dewitt began making a gift list for their children, and on it, four names. *Dewitt can't count*, Maureen thought. *There are five children: Beverly, Tracey, Dewayne, James . . . and Andre.* Maureen had already noticed Dewitt's lack of interest when Andre came for the rare visit. She had hoped Dewitt's heart might warm to him as hers had for his children. But in that moment, she decided to stop trying.

Maureen buried her wants because she wanted, most of all, to be married. So she sang when Dewitt wanted to sing, rehearsing until she lost her voice. She bowled when Dewitt wanted to go bowling, his favorite family pastime. And when the owner of a nearby hotel restaurant, the Milner Grill, wanted to turn his business over to Dewitt, Maureen found herself running it: cooking, waiting on the counter, operating the register, serving cube steaks and salads, up before dawn and closing after dark, while James kept himself occupied with a crayon and paper, sitting at a table in the back. Things got harder: Maureen gave birth to a girl, Martha, born in late spring 1977. When an ectopic pregnancy sent Maureen to the hospital, her recovery spelled the end of the Yanceys' adventure in food service. By then, Maureen had taken responsibility for another child who wasn't hers, Earl Hurst. A year younger than James, Earl was the son of an unmarried couple who lived in the Milner Hotel, where the Yanceys had moved to run the restaurant—the father, Earl Sr., worked long hours; the mother was a white woman who seemed disinterested in parenting altogether. Maureen grew fond of the boy and, with financial support from Earl Sr., she and Dewitt took him in. After a couple of moves, Maureen found a bigger place for their expanding family, a three-bedroom wood-frame house in Conant Gardens, on Wexford Street, where her sister Clarice already lived.

A tiny pocket of blocks on the East Side between 6 and 7 Mile Roads, Conant Gardens was the kind of place where Maureen knew the children could have more space and enjoy, for the first time, a backyard. But her apartment-dwelling downtown kids were terrified of bugs, flying insects, and dirt. They preferred to stay inside: Earl drawing, Martha writing, James playing records. Still, their house was a short walk to good schools and a great African Methodist Episcopal church, Vernon Chapel. Dewitt and Maureen joined the choir, but the music was—even for Maureen's refined tastes—a tad *too* proper. So the Yanceys also hosted Positive Force, an after-service Sunday singing group for more raucous praise sessions. Dewitt often grilled in the backyard; for a goof, Dewitt had Maureen modify an apron so that when he raised it to wipe his face, out popped a long, brown tube shaped like a penis, complete with black wool around the base to simulate pubic hair. The apron was such a popular gag that he and Maureen started selling them to church friends, the fabric customized for skin tone. It was one of several family side hustles: lawn care, a reupholstery business. With half of Dewitt's check going to support his older children, Maureen had to keep her hands moving.

The Hayes siblings were frequent visitors. Herman had become a professional chef and now had a job making donuts, and would often stop by after work at Dewitt's behest to bring a dozen. Herm's own kids were sick of them, and of the smell of fryer oil on their father's work clothes. One day, Dewitt discovered that Herm's regular box had gone missing from the kitchen. He found it empty, under James's bed. After the bust, James began needling Herm regularly. Herm shook his head—the kid barely said two words to anyone but had plenty to give his uncle the third degree about some damn donuts.

As the kids grew, Dewitt wrestled with the machines at Ford's Rouge and Saline plants, then at Livonia Transmission; driving by way of surface streets because he was rattled by the freeways, and because his car would occasionally break down. He'd relax at home by recording himself singing, assembling three-part harmony on a chunky tape deck. And he continued to moonlight for Johnnie Mae Matthews's Northern Records, running rehearsals out of her West Side basement and recording at United Sound. Maureen endured these interminable sessions even though she had grown to hate them. Because these engagements often ran late into the night, the children had to attend them as well: James, Earl, and Martha in their street clothes or in their pajamas, roaming the same studio halls that George Clinton walked, or curled up with a blanket in a corner, trying to get some sleep before school. James stayed up and watched the action, class in session.

James was quiet, in part, because he stuttered. His father was a stutterer, too; when Dewitt was a child, sometimes he would have to lie down and cross his arms against his chest, holding opposite shoulders, just to get the words out.

But mostly James didn't talk because he was listening. Where oth-

ers' energies went into their output, James used his own to process input. When the Yanceys arrived at Grandmother Maybeline's house on
Garland for family functions, they entered to the cheers and hollers of
the Hayes clan. But while the adults carried on and the rest of the kids
ran around outside, James drifted over toward the dining room and the
wooden cabinet containing Maybeline's stereo. He'd slide down on his
knees on the plush red carpet and examine each record, one by one.
Then he'd walk to the staircase that led down to the basement, where
Herman had tacked up two dozen record album covers at Maybeline's
request—Nancy Wilson, Sam Cooke, Aretha Franklin, Dinah Washington, Smokey Robinson, Marvin Gaye, Mary Wells. James—carefully,
carefully—removed the four pins from the corners of one of them. He
flipped the cover to the back and read all the text he could; and, if there
was an inner sleeve that had liner notes on it, he read that, too. For Maybeline, her wall of album covers was decoration. James saw them as code,
and looked behind the mosaic to see the information that most intrigued
him: the names of the musicians who played on each of the songs and of
the people who wrote them; the places where those songs were recorded
and the producers who brought those sessions into being. After studying
these details, saving them, he would flip the album back, hold it against
the wall, and—carefully, carefully—place the tacks back in the tiny pin-
holes so no one would be the wiser. Then James would move on to the
next record and repeat the process.

At first, James's relationship to music was about absorbing rather
than creating. It was Maureen—remembering how hostile her childhood environment was to her own musical aspirations—who took the
initiative to enroll five-year-old James in Saturday morning piano lessons at the Krainz Woods Music School. The classical rigor of the place
delighted Maureen, but she soon noticed how James would drag behind
her as they walked to his lessons. The musical director at Vernon Chapel
AME proposed a solution: Kenneth Minor ran his own music school,
much less formal, more inclusive of popular styles. James liked these lessons a bit more. After a time, James declared that he wanted to play the
drums. Maureen told him that she couldn't afford a whole set for him,
but she had saved enough by the Christmas of James's eighth year to

buy him a good snare from the JC Penney catalog and some brushes. Within a few weeks, she remarked that James was making that single snare drum sound like a full kit. Dewitt and Maureen soon drafted him to be the regular drummer for their jazz-and-gospel singing group, the Larks, who emulated the tight harmonies and vocalese techniques of the Manhattan Transfer.

At Farwell Junior High School, the music teacher Peggy McConnell paired James with the cello; and though the instrument was taller than he was, James was equal to its challenges, putting some of Dewitt's low-end legacy to work. James applied himself with similar dedication to the baritone sax. McConnell began to rely on James—always game, always prepared—as a model for her other students. He played in the Detroit Public Schools "Area E" orchestra at events around the city; in the audience at Kettering High School, Maureen cried. Dewitt enrolled James and Earl in a program run by the woman whose career he helped launch: Kim Weston—at the behest of Mayor Coleman Young—had created an expansive summer cultural curriculum for the city's school-age children. Launched in 1977, the annual Kim Weston Festival of the Performing Arts offered training in a variety of disciplines from music and dance to culinary and clerical work. Dewitt put James in instrumental instruction and Earl in visual arts.

And then there were Friday nights in the Yanceys' living room, where Maureen and Dewitt led their children, family, and friends in a weekly variety show in which everyone was required to perform. Dewitt trotted the children out to sing "Mr. Sandman" by the Chordettes; the arrangement of which, naturally, he'd taught them. For a time James, Earl, and Martha billed themselves as their own singing group, "The Yancey Kids." They wrote songs, one of them called "Like a Zombie," with Earl singing lead and James on drums, convinced that they had a huge hit on their hands. They put on home concerts and made tickets by cutting up sheets of paper. On Sundays there was choir and band at Vernon Chapel, where James, Earl, and Martha sang and James played drums.

On other days at the church there were Boy Scouts for James and Earl, and Girl Scouts for Martha; and during summers, a junior police cadet program where James, among other activities, volunteered to visit the homes of senior citizens. Maureen thought James's choice was a bit unusual for a child his age, but James told her that he liked hearing their stories.

And they liked him, too. Who wouldn't? The kid was all ears.

The Hayes clan called the Yancey family "a band of Gypsies," always moving as a pack, whether walking to the convenience store or de-camping from one house to another. They relocated across the street to a new home on Wexford, and then southwest a few blocks to a house on the corner of McDougall and Berry. Everywhere they went, their routines remained.

On one hand, that rigidity made sense in a city that was increasingly depopulated and dangerous. On James's eleventh Halloween in 1984, 810 buildings across Detroit were set afire during "Devil's Night," an annual American adolescent tradition twisted into a grim ritual, equal parts nihilism, protest, and landlord arson. While suburban cynics deni-grated Detroit from afar and voyeurs came to gawk, Detroit's community institutions, including Vernon Chapel, started offering "Angel's Night" events as a way to keep kids off the streets. Conant Gardens was spared the worst, much safer and more stable than many neighborhoods closer to the city's center, but on the quality-of-life spectrum, the community that began in the 1940s as a Black middle-class village now leaned closer to slum than suburb.

On the other hand, Dewitt never wanted anyone out of his sight, and that restricted Maureen's movements as well. Dewitt could get jealous and downright paranoid when it came to his young wife. Maureen and her siblings chalked up Dewitt's conservative thinking about women and marriage to him being so much older than her. It was all relative: Dewitt was a far cry from his brother Geno, who lived with a virtual stable of cowed women and whom the Hayes family suspected of being a pimp. Dewitt had a sense of humor that could lift everyone's spirits; but he could, at any moment, turn dour and deeply insecure. Maureen never knew when those bursts of anger would come.

Perhaps it was because Dewitt disapproved of her taking an office job, or because of the remoteness she felt from her first son, Andre, or the loss of her first daughter, Kenya, but as the years progressed Maureen created a career caring for children. Maureen began watching a neighbor's boy who had scoliosis; then started looking after a couple of latchkey kids. After taking some referrals from Vernon Chapel, Ruby Williams, one of the church administrators, asked Maureen if she'd join their day care operation and take some early childhood classes to get certified.

"Mr. Yancey would never allow it," Maureen replied. She called him "Mr. Yancey" now, a measure of the distance between them.

Williams approached Dewitt on her own, telling him how the church might lose the day care if he couldn't convince his wife to take these courses. Maureen stifled a giggle when Dewitt mentioned that her taking college classes might be a good idea. It had only taken a dozen years for him to come around. Then Maureen discovered that she was pregnant again. It was her birth control that failed, but she didn't speak to Dewitt for weeks. She had been looking forward to some freedom now that her kids were old enough to look after themselves. Now she'd have to wait. John Yancey was born on October 13, 1986. He looked uncannily like James.

Shortly after John's birth, Maureen enrolled in classes at the Dearborn campus of the University of Michigan, to which Dewitt drove her, complaining for miles and miles about the weather, and about her attending a white college in the suburbs instead of a school in the city. Maureen took the reins of Vernon Chapel's day care, but her marriage remained a disappointment.

James, the listener, took it all in: the tension between a father whose dreams had been truncated by the music business and a mother whose dreams had been truncated by his father.

One day Reta Hayes regaled Dewitt with the story of a younger Maureen's romantic aspirations, imitating her sister in a lilting, saditty voice: "Maureen used to say, 'I want a haazzzzband! I want a haazzzzband!'"

"And that's just what she got," Dewitt replied. "A has-been."

Dewitt and Maureen had programmed James with the music of their lives—jazz, soul, gospel, classical. His ten-year-old body contained at least fifty years' worth of code: bass lines and drum riffs, melodies and cadences. But as he got older, James began to program himself. Detroit had a Black-owned TV station, WGPR, and on it, a uniquely Detroit music and dance show: *The Scene*, hosted by Nat Morris, featuring futuristic music and otherworldly dance moves that made *Soul Train* look tepid by comparison. On the radio, two DJs brought distinct approaches to their shows. The Electrifying Mojo, on WJLB-FM, created an eclectic, ecumenical mix of electronic-driven funk and soul, one of the first DJs in the nation to throw his support behind a little-known Midwestern artist, Prince. Meanwhile, Jeff Mills on WDRQ-FM balanced New York rap records with a growing crop of local Detroit tracks, some made by Mills's friends who were creating their own distinct genre of electronic music.

These sounds were different from the music of James's parents. That difference came into stark relief for James in 1984 with two rap songs out of New York: "Sucker M.C.'s" by Run-DMC and "Big Mouth" by Whodini. These were not normal instruments he was hearing. The drums on these records didn't sound anything like the drum set he played in church. They were so loud that they seemed to fill every available sonic space: unwavering, relentless, perfect in their uniformity and repetition. The kick drum vibrated so low that it shook the floor. The vocals on "Big Mouth" stuttered, like he did; but on purpose, like they were being cut up somehow, starting and stopping short, starting and stopping again.

James didn't yet know that these sounds were made on machines.

But in that moment he decided—however this music got made—that's the way he wanted to make music, too.

4.
Machine Time

The first music-making machines were built not for making music, but to keep time.

The clock has been twinned with sound and song since its beginnings in ancient China—a water-powered mechanism that struck a bell—through its evolution into the ubiquitous towers in Europe that chimed on the hour. Thus it was the watchmakers of eighteenth-century Switzerland who created the innards for the earliest music boxes, in which a coiled spring rotated a cylinder with bumps on its surface, bumps that struck metal tines that produced musical tones spaced in time. Another machine, powered by spring and pendulum, was soon created to help musicians themselves measure time more precisely: the metronome.

The dawn of the Machine Age brought with it this new conception of time, one disconnected from biological rhythms and instead externalized to devices against which the individual, human sense of time could be measured and regimented. And with machines came new inventions to automate music-making. As the piano industry boomed in the late 1800s so too did the sales of new "pianolas"—pianos that played themselves, powered by pneumatics, and programmed with long paper rolls, long grids of holes that triggered the keys, working on the same principles as the first music boxes: a wind-up mechanism that was able to trigger sounds in sequence.

These developments ultimately led to the first electronic music machines that used circuitry to generate and trigger sounds. In 1920, the Russian inventor Leon Theremin created a device that produced a wavering tone that could be raised or lowered in pitch by moving his hands

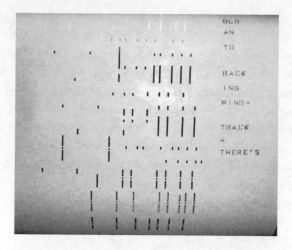

within the machine's electromagnetic field. *Sound synthesis* was born. But Theremin also worked on ways to *remove* his hands from the process, creating an early version of a drum machine with his Rhythmicon, a machine that played itself, the first electronic *sound sequencing*.

In 1952, at his New York laboratory, Manhattan Research, Inc., Raymond Scott took those concepts further. Scott created a keyboard version of the Theremin called the Clavivox, an endeavor in which he was assisted by a young technician, Bob Moog. The sounds the Clavivox generated were uncanny, and marketed that way. An early advertisement proclaimed: "Raymond Scott Clavivox can sound 'something' like a vocalist, not a voice; a clarinetist, not a clarinet; a violinist, not a violin." Like Theremin, Scott sought to make playing automatic, creating a device he called the "Wall of Sound": a machine six feet tall and thirty feet wide composed of hundreds of step relays, the same switches that powered telephone exchanges. Scott set these switches in different patterns to trigger sounds from several Clavivoxes and other instruments. It was, in effect, the first programmable sound sequencer; a machine that, once you told it what to do, played itself.

Scott went on to use these machines to create some of the first commercial recordings of electronic music—some unsuccessful, like the eerie 1963 album *Soothing Sounds for Baby*; some profitable, like jingles for General Motors, IBM, Bendix, and the cosmetics company Lightworks.

What is the magic that makes one's eyes / sparkle and gleam, light up the skies? singer Dorothy Collins asked, as Scott's machines gurgled a gentle, computerized arpeggio. *The name of the game is Lightworks.* Though Scott was a trained musician and traditional bandleader—he'd composed much of the *Looney Tunes* and *Merrie Melodies* music for Warner Bros.—his recorded efforts made him something else: one of the first professional electronic producer-composers.

The otherworldly sounds of Scott's devices were not meant to be facsimiles of traditional musical instruments. They were automatic instruments for an atomic generation who *liked* the robot's synthetic voice, who fetishized the future and all its *bleep-bloop* sounds, evoking computers, satellites, spaceships. Scott's machines made music that sounded like machines.

By the 1960s, electronic instruments had become available to both professionals and amateurs, and their use began to spread. The Wurlitzer Side Man was the first commercially produced drum machine. Scott's assistant, Bob Moog, created the pioneering synthesizer that bears his name; it ended up on the recordings of Motown artists like the Supremes and, across the Atlantic, on records by the Beatles. The Moog was limited: it was monophonic, which meant that it could generate only one note at a time—great for creating melodies, but not for playing chords. By the end of the decade, a duo of musicians—Bob Margouleff and Malcolm Cecil—would string a number of Moog modules together to create the world's first polyphonic synthesizer, TONTO. At the dawn of the 1970s, Stevie Wonder, the master of harmony, would be the first artist to create a body of work with it. Meanwhile, the funk artist Sly Stone began substituting a drum machine called the Rhythm King for traditional drums in his music. A few years later, a group of German musicians who called themselves Kraftwerk—German for "power station"—forged synthesized and human sounds into an aesthetic they dubbed "Man Machine." Kraftwerk posed as robots making music that sounded as if it were made by robots posing as men. Another producer working in Germany, Giorgio Moroder, merged disco with machines on a 1976 track for Donna Summer, "I Feel Love." Moroder fashioned almost every sound on the track with a Moog Modular synthesizer, which now had its own onboard sequencer, enabling Moroder to program the bass line into the machine and have it play back on its own with a surreal, robotic consistency.

The backlash against disco drew much of its energy from white audiences hostile to disco's Black and gay subcultures, but there was an aesthetic revolt, too. For many people weaned on classic rock and soul, the synthesizer became the object of outrage. This ire was misdirected. These same music fans often had no problem with the Who's or Stevie Wonder's use of synthesizers on their most beloved albums. What the anti-disco crowd was repelled by was not so much the sounds of the synthesizer as the unvarying, "soulless" silences of the sequencers employed to trigger them.

Despite the dissent, by the end of the 1970s the sound of popular music was on the precipice of an electronic transformation because of these two futuristic innovations—the synthesizer that generated tones and percussion, and the sequencer that ordered those synthetic events in time. And behind the synthesizer and sequencer were the same two elements that composed the ancient ancestors of these music machines: the thing that gets struck, and the clock that times the strike.

Detroiters had a natural affinity for unnatural sounds. Berry Gordy literally composed his first songs to the rhythms of the assembly line. At the height of Motown's success, Gordy hired Raymond Scott to develop an advanced music machine called the Electronium. George Clinton and his funk futurists embraced the synthesizer, pushing its sounds squarely into American dance music. And as mechanized sounds permeated popular music in the late 1970s and early 1980s, they found a particularly enthusiastic audience in the Motor City, fostering a local underground club scene in which disc jockeys played a multigenre melange of machine music that they called "progressive dance." The community was bolstered by a number of high school social clubs, run by teens who fetishized the lives and fashions of the European jet set, their party names an alphabet soup of continental high-fashion labels, boutiques, and publications: *Arpegghio*, *Avanté*, *Charivari*, *Ciabittino*, *Courtier*, *Giavante*, *GQ*, *Reminiques*, *Schiaparelli*. Their functions started with house parties and moved into small nightclubs.

While some teenagers emphasized the flash, others perfected the footwork. This countermovement had a lot to do with Detroit geography. The path that Woodward cut into the Michigan wilderness divided Detroit into west and east sides, and many of the progressive dance social clubs and their high-fashion-loving followers came from the West Side, which, in the 1980s, signified that your family might be a little more well-off, that your house might be a little nicer, your high school a little better. These kids were called the "preps." But there were others from Detroit's East Side and deteriorating swaths west of Woodward who had a love of futuristic dance music without the pretense. The preps called them, somewhat derisively, "jits."

The name came from local dance crew the Jitterbugs. At its core were three brothers—Tracey, John, and James McGhee—who developed synchronized routines that combined constrained, fast footwork with tumbling leaps, the acrobatic, amped successor to the Motown choreography of groups like the Temptations. The Jitterbugs might have remained obscure had it not been for the kindness and encouragement of Dewitt Yancey's protégée, Kim Weston. The McGhee brothers enrolled in Weston's annual Festival of the Performing Arts in 1978, and she gave them the space and time to perfect their craft, the vision to see themselves as artists, and the connections to become paid professionals. They performed at public events and on TV shows like Nat Morris's *The Scene*, exposing the entire metroplex to their moves: the Walk, the Jazzit, the Tone, the Strike. Detroit kids condensed them into one catchall phrase: the Jit. To this arsenal of dance, the children of the city added others, composing a physical vocabulary that only Detroit spoke: the Rambisco. The Errol Flynn.

At first, the mix of west and east, prep and jit, on the progressive dance floors was fraught, but the preppy posturing dwindled as the scene focused less on fashion and more on the music, of which Detroit was now starting to produce its own, homegrown variety. In 1981, the Electrifying Mojo began playing a local record, "Sharevari," by a group called A Number of Names, and went on to champion other local records, including "Alleys of Your Mind," released in 1981 by Cybotron.

Detroit's electronic music scene had a symbiotic relationship with those of two other cities. In New York they dubbed their electronic dance music "electrofunk" or simply "electro," ignited in 1982 by Afrika Bambaataa's "Planet Rock," a drum machine–powered reworking of Kraftwerk's "Trans-Europe Express." In Chicago they called it "house," fueled by the 1984 track by Jesse Saunders, "On and On." And in Detroit, a 1984 track by Cybotron, "Techno City," would be the first mention of the word from which the local music eventually took its name. These three genres—New York electro, Chicago house, and Detroit techno—were intertwined, but the Detroit variant leaned into the ethereal, the mechanical, the political, the futuristic. The children of Motown found a soul in the machine.

In the 1980s, every kid from Detroit grew up with techno. But there was another kind of machine music—unique to New York City and made on different tools altogether—that gripped the imaginations of a select group of Detroiters.

I n 1937, the experimental composer John Cage predicted that the same machines invented for music *reproduction*—the record player and the radio—could and would actually be used for music *production*. Two years later, in 1939, Cage created a piece called *Imaginary Landscape No. 1*, in which he used three different turntables as part of a musical performance.

The idea that a disc jockey could be a musician, and that the contraptions of their trade—the turntable, the microphone—could be their instruments, only came into full fruition in the 1970s, in a place experiencing, like Detroit, a kind of deconstruction.

A young DJ from the Bronx, Clive Campbell, performing at house and park parties as Kool Herc, created a turntable technique in 1973 called the "merry-go-round," in which he would play only brief portions of funk and soul records—the "breakdown" sections that featured solely the rhythm section, the "best" parts of the records for dancers. Herc did this by using two record players and a mixer to switch from one record to the next in rapid succession. By slowing down or speeding up his turntables, he could synchronize the tempos of the two songs and "match" their beats. Other DJs throughout the borough built on Herc's techniques. Joseph Saddler, who went by Flash, developed what he called "clock theory" to use the rotation of the vinyl records to ensure precise timing; rubbing, catching, and releasing the vinyl to create percussive, melodic, and harmonic effects; and using two copies of the same record to extend the typically short "break" sections into infinite loops. The techniques spread to all five boroughs of New York City, the birth of a new culture that would later be called hip-hop. The breakbeat scene engendered its own dance culture, breakdancing or B-boying.

The street DJs of New York began a collective search for the records that had the best "breaks." They dug them out of parents' old record collections or found them in bins at local record stores. Their discoveries were assembled gradually into a canon of break records, many of them obscure to the general public but known to every DJ for the vital moments within them: The first seven seconds of the Incredible Bongo Band's 1973 remake of the Shadows' "Apache." Two minutes and thirty-eight seconds into the 45-rpm single of James Brown's "Funky Drummer (Part 2)," released in 1969. Four minutes and twenty-nine seconds into James Brown's "Give It Up or Turnit a Loose"—the faux-concert version that appears on his 1971 *Sex Machine* album, not the one released as a single two years earlier. If you were a serious DJ, you needed these records in your repertoire.

As the party DJ became an instrumentalist, busy juggling records, the work of exhorting the crowd over a microphone passed to a "master of ceremonies." The rhymed routines of the MCs became as sophisticated as those of the DJ, and the "rapping" part of this new culture soon eclipsed its musical innovations. It's not surprising that the first successful hip-hop song, released in 1979, was called "Rapper's Delight," its music a breakbeat replayed by a band of traditional musicians rather than played from the record itself. In the recording studio during hip-hop's early days, the disc jockey's turntables were mostly silent. But the drum machine made the DJ a programmer, a producer, a beatmaker. The machine's takeover of hip-hop began in 1982 with Afrika Bambaataa's "Planet Rock."

This one song marked a fork in the hip-hop family tree. Of the records that followed, the ones that skewed uptempo for dancers were called electro. Electro's pulse was more even-keeled. Electro's cousins, house and techno, emphasized a "four on the floor" feel—meaning a kick drum playing on all four beats—reminiscent of Motown and its successors, Philadelphia soul and disco. The other branch, a slower machine sound that leaned downtempo for rappers, sloped toward the One, emulating the funky feel of James Brown and George Clinton. This school of production was established in large part by the Queens programmer-musician Larry Smith in 1983 with the song "Sucker M.C.'s" by Run-DMC. The stark track contained only three musical elements—rhymes from Joseph "Run" Simmons and Darryl "DMC" McDaniels; sounds from a drum machine; and turntable rubs performed by DJ Jam Master Jay.

TRY IT YOURSELF: FUNK vs. DISCO/PROGRESSIVE DANCE

STEP ONE: Try this alternating, syncopated pulse, used in funk/hip-hop

Count	1	n	2	n	3	n	4	n	1	n	2	n	3	n	4	n
CLAP			▓				▓				▓				▓	
STOMP	▓				▓				▓				▓			

STEP TWO: Try this "four-on-the-floor" pulse, used in disco and dance

Count	1	n	2	n	3	n	4	n	1	n	2	n	3	n	4	n
CLAP			▓				▓				▓				▓	
STOMP	▓		▓		▓		▓		▓		▓		▓		▓	

Smith, the following year, would be responsible for another minimal, drum machine–driven rap song by Whodini, "Big Mouth."

Both songs riveted ten-year-old James Dewitt Yancey in Detroit, introducing him to the unfamiliar East Coast vocabularies and disciplines of the drum machine, the turntable, and the MC.

Though New York hip-hop would have a sizable impact on Detroit music, it wasn't quite seismic. Detroit's hip-hop fans remained a creative minority. Still, most of Detroit's young music-makers shared one thing—the gift of space, made possible by the sprawl of the city as it emptied out. Attics and basements became greenhouses for a new generation of musicians.

5.
Dee Jay

James Yancey walked the halls of Farwell Junior High dressed in Levi's and silk shirts. In his hand, he always carried a briefcase.

Frank Bush wondered, *What was in that thing?* After they became friends, Frank found out: Cassettes of rap albums that James had bought or mixes he'd taped off the radio. Candy he'd boosted from a convenience store on 7 Mile Road. Frank's kind of guy.

Frank was new to Farwell. He'd recently moved from southwest Detroit, where he learned to skateboard and breakdance around a bunch of older Latino kids. Practicing on a big sheet of linoleum in his basement, Frank became the crew's secret weapon. One late night after Frank helped them win a battle in the parking lot of a nearby bank, they carried him home on their shoulders. It was totally worth the whupping he got later that night from his mother. Norma Bush, a bookkeeper, moved Frank and her older children to a house off Nevada Avenue in Conant Gardens just as her youngest was starting sixth grade. For other kids, the move to a new neighborhood might have been traumatic, but at eleven years old, Frank was unafraid, unreserved, and uninhibited. He befriended Earl, a light-skinned kid with wavy hair who looked a bit like El DeBarge—in 1986, Motown's newest young heartthrob. Earl could draw like nobody he'd ever seen. And the more Frank talked, the more Earl understood that Frank was on the same wavelength as his brother, who was a year ahead of them both at Farwell.

You need to meet James, Earl said.

Frank and James both loved hip-hop. They were both dancers. They were both among the shortest boys in the school. The big difference between them was that Frank was a talker and James never spoke more than he had to. They balanced each other out.

Frank visited the Yanceys' house on Wexford, and James taught him how to do hip-hop DJ tricks like the "transformer" scratch by toggling a stereo/mono button on his parents' turntable. Frank would stay until Dewitt came home from his shift at the plant.

Turn that music off! Frank get your ass outta here! Dewitt bellowed. Maureen, at that point very pregnant with James's soon-to-be-born little brother John, shouted back: *Leave them boys alone!*

Frank soon fell in with James's friend from Atkinson Elementary School, another dancer. Derrick Harvey was the same age as Frank, but he and James both regarded Derrick as older because he was already into adult pursuits: He had girls. He smoked. But Derrick shared their obsessions with music and dancing, his favorite mixtape reflecting the binary music culture of Detroit. With hip-hop on one side, he breakdanced; with house music on the other, Derrick perfected the furious styles favored by his brother and the older guys in the neighborhood, the "Jit."

When they got a little older, Derrick, Frank, and James got Dewitt to ride them over to the Dancery, a club on Mount Elliott near downtown that hosted an afternoon disco for the teenage crowd from 3:00 p.m. to 8:00 p.m. on weekends. Even there, the duality of Detroit music was evident—techno and house and R&B in the foreground, only a bit of hip-hop thrown in. In that club, while kids strutted and talked shit, James said next to nothing. He simply sank to the floor and jitted . . . on his *knees*.

For Frank, it was the genesis of an admiration for James that would grow over the years—his realization that James was quietly excellent at almost everything, so good that Frank sometimes jokingly called him an alien. He was supersmart. He could dance, he could DJ, he could rhyme, he could sing. As short as James was, he even had a sweet jumper on the basketball court. Derrick had *been* knowing. One semester, Derrick opted to take music class instead of gym because he didn't want to take showers at school. Derrick couldn't play a lick. James taught music theory to Derrick by citing examples of the concepts within the latest hip-hop jams. To help him during tests, James would shout out references to songs: "Push It!" "My Posse's on Broadway!" Derrick mastered theory, learned cello and piano, and aced the class. That was James.

But once they got to know him, Frank and Derrick discovered other things about James: he sometimes seemed withdrawn, but he was always watching, always listening. And they found that James's reserve belied a stubborn will. James knew exactly what he wanted and pursued those things with determination. You were coming along for the ride or you weren't. And if you got in his way, you'd witness a temper that seemed to flare from out of nowhere. That, too, was James.

Frank's and Derrick's parents didn't go to church, but the two boys turned up occasionally at Vernon Chapel alongside James and the Yanceys because they were cool with the pastor's sons: fraternal twins Terrence and Tobias Wright, and their older brother Copez. Derrick took Bible class on Sundays and Frank, who lived on the same block as the Wrights, rarely missed a "shut-in"—sleepovers in the church's brown-and-beige-tiled basement, complete with a stage, kitchen, and shuffleboard court.

Making Vernon Chapel a welcome place for neighborhood kids had been a part of Pastor Alexander Wright's mission since 1983, when he first mounted the pulpit of the modern redbrick church, a concrete crucifix built into its edifice. Built before World War II when Conant Gardens was an insular Black middle-class community, Vernon Chapel packed its airy sanctuary every Sunday with over 150 faithful, worshipping under a roof of polished wood beams. Wright was a liberal pastor in a denomination where worship and expression were somewhat restrained: in his last assignment, at an AME church in Champaign, Illinois, he and his wife, Mary, scandalized the parishioners by getting up to dance at a church function. Wright had written his seminary thesis on the blues, and loved all kinds of music, religious or secular, so he welcomed his transfer to Detroit. Wright made music and dance a key part of his outreach, and that deepened his church's attraction for the children of Conant Gardens.

To kids like James, Frank, and Derrick, the Wrights—who lived in the roomy church parsonage on Shields Street—were as close as Conant Gardens got to the Huxtable family, those television paragons of Black upper-middle-class living on the 1980s *Cosby Show*. Pastor Wright had a big television and a room with a pool table. The Wright kids had a Commodore computer and a Nintendo video-game player. Copez was the DJ of the family: he had dozens of records—mostly house and early techno—and a mixer and two belt-drive turntables from Radio Shack. James spent hours in the Wrights' basement, going through records. Though James was four years younger than him, Copez came to see James as a peer in terms of DJ skills. Copez judged himself a better beat-blender, but he conceded that James was superior at scratching and cutting. James occasionally came for sleepovers in the basement. Terrence would fall asleep while James was still at the turntables, listening to music through Copez's headphones. He'd wake at 4 or 5 in the morning, and James was still listening.

The skills and wills of these kids coalesced in the chambers of Vernon Chapel. It was in the sanctuary that James sang his first solo over an uptempo, funky version of "Swing Low, Sweet Chariot." It was on the basement stage that James—that young man of few words—launched himself as a rapper, MC Silk, with Derrick dancing and Frank DJing behind him. Frank had become good enough on the turntables that he and James started hiring themselves out as a duo to play records at their friends' birthday and house parties, performing as Silk and F.O.F. (for "Fingers of Fury"), with Derrick tagging along to dance. But there were challenges. The pastor's wife, Mary Wright, worked for the Detroit Public Schools and hired James to DJ a middle school dance. When he didn't show, she got concerned. She found James at home: he hadn't thought to arrange transportation for himself.

At their gigs, James and Frank learned to navigate the differences between their increasingly sophisticated knowledge of music and their peers' more pedestrian tastes. The kids wanted to hear fast-paced dance music—Copez called Detroit a "120 beats-per-minute city"—and James and Frank loved hip-hop, which usually maintained a tempo between 85 to 95 beats per minute—so they would crank up the speed on the stuff they liked, like the breakdown from James Brown's "Funky Drummer," an old song that, as James and Frank were learning, was a vital building block of the genre they loved.

As they DJed, the sound of hip-hop records was changing. At a new label called Def Jam in New York, founder and producer Rick Rubin found ways to bring both the DJ and the sounds of the breaks back into the mix. On the rapper LL Cool J's 1985 single "Rock the Bells," Rubin used a nineteen-second excerpt from a record by the Washington, DC, group Trouble Funk, running the music from a turntable right into the mixing board and onto the multitrack tape. The next year, on the first album by Beastie Boys, 1986's *Licensed to Ill*, Rubin went further: the opening track, the aptly named "Rhymin' & Stealin'," fused breaks and sounds from the records of rock gods like Led Zeppelin, Black Sabbath, and AC/DC; the closing track, "Time to Get Ill," was composed of pieces of no fewer than fourteen songs, from artists like Barry White to Creedence Clearwater Revival, to themes from the TV shows *Green Acres* and *Mister Ed*. The process of assembling these chunks of audio in the studio was painstaking. Each record had to be cued by hand and timed perfectly. Mistakes required new takes. Timing was everything. The copyright implications were ignored.

That same year, another producer, Marlon "Marley Marl" Williams, began using a new device—a digital sampler, rather than a turntable—to record and play back pieces of audio from break records, like the sound of a kick drum or a snare. By 1986, new sampling drum machines built specifically to record and play back tiny pieces of audio began hitting the professional music market. As they gained power, these machines enabled producers like Marley Marl to take not just brief pieces, but entire break sections from records, and "loop" them in an automated facsimile of what the early hip-hop DJs did by hand. By 1987, hip-hop was bursting with these new "old" sounds of rhymes over breaks. The job of the hip-hop record producer was now about making music from pieces of music that were already made; recording new records by piecing together pieces of old records. The best producers, like Rubin and Marley Marl, became sonic collage artists.

By now, James Yancey possessed a nearly lifelong familiarity with the deep catalog of R&B, soul, funk, and disco from which the breaks were drawn. He had turntables. What he didn't have was a sampler—which cost thousands of dollars. So James adopted a technique used by countless other aspiring hip-hop producers: the pause tape. James's version was considerably more elaborate.

"What the fuck are you doing?" Frank asked one day when he visited James in the attic of the Yanceys' latest home, a small single-family house on the corner of McDougall and Berry Streets in Conant Gardens. Frank saw his alien friend deconstructing a dual cassette deck. James had removed the housing to expose the wiring of the machine. Once inside, he had located the speed adjustment screw for one of the cassette drives— so he could then speed up or slow down anything he recorded onto it. When everything was reassembled, James could record something from his Erikson turntable onto a cassette; then play it back at a slower or faster speed depending on what tempo he wanted; then record that material onto the other cassette in that deck, hit the pause button on the destination cassette, rewind the tape on the source cassette, and record that same section in succession, over and over, until he had a looped break at the right tempo that sounded as seamless as any sampling drum machine. With considerable time and effort, James could create a music bed made of looped breaks and—with a second dual cassette deck—layer vocals, scratches, or sounds from a small drum machine he'd bought, almost like a rudimentary multitrack studio.

In these early recording sessions, Frank sometimes DJed, and sometimes watched as thirteen-year-old James rhymed:

Bitches bitches bitches
For me do dishes
Later on grant my wishes
Get on your knees with the quickness
Suck the dick of a ni**a named Silk, bitch

H erman Hayes, visiting with his sister downstairs, listened in disbelief.

"You're gonna let him curse like that in your house?" he asked Maureen.

"They're just doing their music," Maureen replied.

Herm shook his head. Here was Maureen—refined Maureen, sanctified Maureen, church-every-Sunday Maureen—seemingly deaf to all kinds of profanity and impiety in her own home. She sure spoiled him. James was even on a first-name basis with his parents; not "Mommy" and "Daddy," but "Maureen" and "Dewitt."

By this time, both Maureen and Dewitt had an acute sense of their son's gift for music and his single-minded dedication to it. They began to believe that James, young as he was, might have a shot as a professional performer.

William Howard validated their notion. Howard, known as "Wee Gee," had been the lead singer of the Detroit group the Dramatics, his raspy tenor knifing through their 1971 hit "Whatcha See Is Whatcha Get" or smoothing out for "In the Rain." By the late seventies, Wee Gee had launched a floundering solo career; but he could always count on Nat Morris at WGPR-TV to give him love on *The Scene* when he returned to Detroit from his home in Northern California. Wee Gee was a friend of the Yanceys' neighbor, who hipped the singer to the whiz kid next door. After hearing James's music, Wee Gee told Dewitt and Maureen that he had started a production company, and he wanted to sign and develop James as part of a rap group. James, as Silk, would be the MC; Copez the DJ; and Frank and Derrick the dancers. For the kids, things were suddenly very exciting, and for their parents, too, as Maureen and Dewitt arranged meetings with the star to secure everyone's cooperation and ensure their confidence.

"For real, Wee Gee from the Dramatics is coming to see *me*?!" exclaimed Derrick's mother, Janice Harvey, taking extra time to put makeup on for a visit from soul royalty.

There were endless rehearsals supervised, of course, by Dewitt. James was driven, too, snapping at Frank when he felt him losing focus. There was a photo session, ostensibly for an upcoming article in *Jet* magazine.

And then, nothing. Wee Gee not only disappeared, he vanished with James's expensive new boombox, a Christmas present. James was furious. Frank, with his developing street sense, concluded that Wee Gee was a crack addict who had hustled them and all their parents for attention and a little money. Derrick was despondent: he had dreams of him and Frank becoming the next "Scoob and Scrap"—the famed backup dancers for the rap artist Big Daddy Kane. For all the kids, it was only their first taste of the particular disappointment that comes from near misses and dead ends in the music business.

One door had closed for James, but as far as Maureen was concerned, a big one had just opened.

James was finishing eighth grade at Farwell Middle when Maureen got word that he had been accepted to Benjamin O. Davis Aerospace Technical High School, one of two dozen public "schools of choice" that beckoned for Detroit parents. Davis was across town, at the city's municipal airport, a school where students learned to maintain airplanes and, for a select few, to fly them. Maureen was ecstatic: James could earn college credit. He could get a great job working for an airline. With ROTC instruction, he could enter the Air Force with valuable skills. Davis was decidedly vocational, not one of the elite high schools like Cass Tech; and for Maureen, that was part of the attraction—the world was filled with unemployed people with advanced degrees. She wanted James to have a trade, something he could bank on.

But for James, Davis meant that he would no longer be going to school with his siblings and friends. "I'll just go to Pershing," the fourteen-year-old told his mother, referring to the nearby high school on 7 Mile Road in Conant Gardens.

"Oh, no, you're going to Davis," she said, "'cause I already turned your paperwork in."

He argued, and she tried to explain: *You'll have an apprenticeship.*

You can get a job in the airport the day after you graduate. You can't just depend on music. Your father has to work a factory job, as gifted as he is. How dare you think that the door's gonna open up for you and you'll just walk right on in?!

If they had learned anything from the Wee Gee experience, Maureen figured, it should at least be that.

Go one year, she said. *See how you do. And if you really don't like it, you can go to Pershing.*

On the first day of school in the fall of 1988, James Yancey sat with the new freshman class in the auditorium of Davis Aero Tech while the principal—the aptly named Edward Rockett—the teachers, and administrators explained how the program worked. There were two training tracks at Davis: airframe and power plant. In airframe, they'd learn about the body and structure of aircraft, and avionics, working on the wings and the instrument panels. In power plant, they'd be disassembling and reassembling jet engines. Each student had to pick one of the two choices and that's what they'd be spending the rest of their high school career learning, along with some basic academic subjects.

Like James, many of the kids there seemed dazed, unsure of how they'd ended up in this bizarre place just off an airport runway, learning specializations that they didn't know existed until today, and that this path would likely be one they followed for the rest of their lives. A few of the students grumbled that, unlike other high schools, there wasn't a gym, or a pool, or any sports teams.

One boy joked: *Where are we supposed to play basketball? Over by the airplanes?*

When he wasn't being driven to the airport by Dewitt, James took a few city buses to get to school. On certain days he had to wear his blue Air Force ROTC uniform, praying that none of his friends from Conant Gardens would see him in it, and hoping none of the older kids from nearby Osborn High School would fuck with him. The cap was the worst; it fucked with his hair.

Luckily James met Charles "Chuck" Moore, a classmate in the air-frame program with him, who hated Davis and loved hip-hop as much as he did. Their first encounter played out like an eighties high school movie: James, in an asymmetrical afro called a "Gumby" for its resemblance to the head shape of the cartoon character, is challenged to a battle by Chuck, coiffed with a "high-top fade." Chuck defeats James. Cut to: The next day, Chuck closes his locker door to reveal James, who wants a rematch. James scorches Chuck, to more cheers. They become the best of friends.

They rapped together in bathrooms and in the cafeteria—Chuck as "Cooley C" and James as "Silk"—James providing the beat by knocking a fist and a pencil on the lunchroom table. They cut school together some-times and met up with girls. Chuck took long bus trips to the Yanceys' house after school, recording songs over tracks produced by James on his improvised equipment setup—which now included a tiny Casio key-board that had a few seconds of low-quality sampling time. With Frank adding scratches as "Fingers of Fury," they called themselves the Flattop Society. James rhymed over the "Funky Drummer" break, superimposed with a loop of "Inner City Blues" by Marvin Gaye:

This is serious business
Time to throw down
Fingers of Fury
Bringing the dope sound . . .

. . . making way for Chuck:

F-L-A-Double T-O-P-S
Who is the man with the *S* across his chest?

James dubbed Chuck a copy on one of his little brother John's Walt Disney cassette tapes, Mickey Mouse logo on the outside, hip-hop on the inside.

Thanks to Mary Wright, James and Frank were getting hired by the Detroit Public Schools to play records at more daytime dances at middle schools, both of them delighted by the irony of DPS cutting them a check to cut school. When they DJed house parties, Chuck performed with them, Dewitt providing transportation.

Chuck spent enough time with James to see both sides of him—the kid who covered his mouth when he laughed because he was afraid of people ragging on the size of his front teeth, and the smooth-talker who won the interest of girls. Their friendship was strong enough to withstand an argument over James getting too close to Chuck's love interest, a scrap that got them both suspended from school. At the Yancey home, when Chuck wasn't breaking up near-fights between James and Earl—James baiting his little brother for his amateur rapping and for not being able to grow his relaxed, wavy hair into any kind of shape—he ate Maureen's food and chatted with Dewitt over their mutual love of Sam Cooke. When Chuck's ailing mother died after a long struggle with lung cancer, Chuck headed straight for the Yanceys' house. He lay down on the couch as James made music, and stayed there for several days until he felt like he could function again.

At the end of his first year at Davis, with Earl now about to attend Pershing High with Frank and Derrick, James went to Maureen to redeem the guarantee she'd given him. He wanted to leave Davis and go to Pershing. Maureen refused.

"You promised!" he cried.

Maureen just couldn't honor her word. She saw it as a matter of survival for James. He had done so well at Davis. *Just one more year*, she told him, hoping that he might fall in love with some part of the curriculum there. If she had to sacrifice James liking her to keep him in that school, so be it. But, desperate to keep James as happy as she could given the situation and—vitally—keep him doing well, Maureen offered further inducement if he kept his grades up.

You know my Hudson's Department Store charge card? she said. *You can run it up every month. You can buy your Eddie Bauer corduroys and khakis. Since you're DJ Silk and doing all those parties at Davis, you can buy every color silk shirt there is.*

For real? James said.

For real, Maureen replied. *And whatever music equipment you're working to buy, I'll pay half.*

James resigned himself to Davis, resenting a course of study that he knew he'd never put to use, convinced that he was missing out on something at Pershing.

Third of his name, R. L. Altman had never been told what "R. L." stood for. He wasn't sure that it meant anything at all. It was a country name, handed down from his grandfather, R. L. Altman I; to his father, R. L. Altman II, who was never much in his life; and finally to R. L. Altman III, who simplified his history by stripping his name down to a number: three.

He was "Trace" sometimes, because it sounded like *tres,* three in Spanish. Or he was just "T." His crew at Pershing High each had a ziggurat of given names, family diminutives, street sobriquets, and stage monikers. Years later, when he and his comrades began studying with a local sect known as the Order of the Divine Reality, they all took spiritual signifiers in Arabic. For his friends, those were the names that stuck. Robert O' Bryant started Pershing as "K," then "K Dawg," but he ended up as "Waajeed," which meant "seeker." Titus Glover was "Scandalous T," but he soon dubbed himself "Baatin," meaning "the hidden, inner self." Ernest Toney was "E-Dog," but ultimately called himself "Qudduws," meaning "holy," or "Que.D" for short. And T, for a time, chose "El-Anoor," from *al-noor,* meaning "the light."

But the name never really took. For T, it was more about how words sounded than what they meant. When T started rapping, he devised his MC name by colliding that letter with the number it represented, two expressions of the same idea: "T3," sounding like a double drumbeat complete with internal rhyme.

T3's writing process reflected his mindset. While most of his friends used words as vectors for conveying information, T3 used them as vehicles for sound. He wrote rhythmically first and foremost. The pattern was paramount: He began with no words at all, just chants of nonsense syllables. The words, when they came, came later. If there wasn't a word that would fit the rhythm he sought, he'd make one up, or fill the space with some other kind of utterance—drawing a breath, sucking his teeth, tightening his throat. A rapper usually strove to be a poet. T3 was a soloist.

In middle school, T3 had lived with his mother and stepfather on the West Side. When his mother died from cancer, T's stepfather informed him that he was not going to take care of him going forward. T went to live with his grandmother, Mandy Altman, and several of his cousins in a house on Minnesota Street in Conant Gardens. His first friend in the neighborhood was Que.D, who lived down the block on Yonka Street and had a boombox and a fly Troop jogging suit like the one LL Cool J wore. Que.D found that T3 could not only dance but basically point at anything and make up a rap about it on the spot. They began walking to and from Cleveland Middle School together, careful to avoid the Buffalo Boys—a group of teenagers from Osborn High who came around to terrify and rob the younger kids—and eventually formed a crew: T3 rapping, Que.D beatboxing and dancing, performing at the Vernon Chapel talent shows. When T left for Pershing, he scooped the younger Que.D up from Cleveland whenever he could and made him part of his new crew.

John J. Pershing High School was ruled by the athletes, the Doughboys, and by the other kids on track to getting dough for real. T3 and his friends chose a third path: defiantly weird. They were like an insular cultural cell dropped from New York onto 7 Mile Road. T3 and Baatin rhymed in the hallways and the cafeteria, forming a hip-hop cipher with Waajeed, Frank Bush, and Derrick Harvey. They rocked shirts with fluorescent colors and polka dots, backpacks, baggy jeans, and Chuck Taylors, doing the "East Coast Stomp" just like Busta Rhymes and Leaders of the New School. They'd hit the Dancery on Saturday afternoons and be the hip-hop outsiders on the floor there. T3 and Que.D joined Baatin and Waajeed's crew H2O—short for "Hard 2 Oppose"—T3 and Baatin rapping, Que.D dancing, and Waajeed on the wheels of steel. Aside from DJing, Waajeed was an illustrator and painter of such remarkable gifts that his work and awards, one of them from the McDonald's Corporation, were displayed in the lobby alongside the football trophies. He'd even gotten one of his pieces featured on the sides of Detroit city buses. Thus Waajeed had much in common with another artistic Pershing student, Earl Hurst, who knew someone just as obsessive about hip-hop as his new friends at Pershing High.

Y'all really need to meet my brother James, Earl said.

They set it up as a rap battle—Silk versus T3 versus Baatin—to be convened in front of Waajeed's house near McNichols Road.*

Earl had already warned James about T3, and a particular rhyme of his that ended with the vicious punch line, "You look like Shaka Zulu!"

James walked up, baggy clothes hanging over his small frame, not saying much, letting the others spit first. T3 came with his Shaka Zulu rap, and more punch lines and cartoon references. Baatin, "The Shape Shifter," liked to rhyme in multiple voices, and worked a Sammy Davis Jr. impression into his verse. And then James began with something that sounded like a stumble; but soon his pauses revealed themselves as purposeful:

Maybe if I u . . . u . . . u . . . use
The stutter-style of . . . flowing
You could . . . under . . . stand . . .
What I be . . . knowing

Everyone fell out. T3 had never heard anybody—not even on records—rap like that. James had a way of relating to rhyme-as-rhythm that coincided with his own. From that moment it wasn't a battle. T3, James, and Baatin left and went record shopping together. They bought some albums—compilations of breakbeats by the British DJ Simon Harris—went back to James's attic, and took turns freestyling over the instrumentals. They became friends. Then T3 heard James's beats.

---

* Waajeed does not remember this event happening in front of his house, though Que.D is certain of it. In T3's version of this story, both the meeting and the "battle" happen around or in his grandmother's house.

Inspired, T3 begged his grandmother to let him call a meeting in his basement—his goal, to make a collective out of their wide, weird community of hip-hop MCs, DJs, dancers, and this great producer. James came with Frank and Earl, and Chuck Moore from Davis. Baatin, Waajeed, and Que.D were there. Together, they formed a new crew, Ssenepod—"dopeness," spelled backward.

James's music fit the group's eccentricity. He looped the first few seconds of the theme to *The Flip Wilson Show*, the 1970s TV series, so that the announcer's voice kept repeating the words "The Flip!" every two measures. They turned it into a song, "Rat-A-Tat-Tat, the Sound of the Wack." Ssenepod recorded that song at a studio on the Far West Side, the beats coming right off James's little homemade "pause tape."

T3 thought: *Imagine what he could do on some real equipment.*

When Larick Mathews walked to and from Pershing High, he noticed one house near the corner of Revere and 7 Mile Road that had a basement window out of which he always heard music being created. He could tell by the way the sounds of the instruments started and stopped: *There was a recording studio down there.*

One day Mathews, whom everyone at Pershing called "Cricket," spotted the occupant of the house in his driveway, washing his restored 1960 Ford Falcon. He was tall, dark, and bone-thin, with a huge corona of curly black hair.

"I hear you making music all the time," Cricket said. "I've got a rap group, man. Can you help us?"

The man stopped and looked at the kid in front of him. He didn't hesitate. "Sure. Come through." The man introduced himself to Cricket as "Amp."

Joseph Anthony Fiddler, in his early thirties, had lived in that house since 1978, through all the changes to the city and the neighborhood. Since his father died and his mother moved to Virginia, Fiddler remained there with his brothers—even when one of them was dealing drugs and his home became a target for thieves. His door was open because his mind was open. Amp Fiddler believed in karma and love over scarcity and fear. He got that from his hippie older sister Sandra, from fond memories of all that Detroit had been in the 1960s, and especially from the guidance of his musical mentor.

George Clinton, twenty-five years after he first came to Detroit, was still recording at United Sound Systems with his P-Funk collective when Amp Fiddler became a junior member of this extended family of musical misfits. He'd begun by playing with some of Clinton's collaborators— the singer Mallia Franklin and the guitarist Garry Shider. After Clinton heard a demo tape that Fiddler produced, he summoned him to the studio. Clinton took a liking to Amp, a wiry kid with a sonorous voice. He hired him to play keyboards at recording sessions, and Fiddler got to hear himself on the radio when Clinton's single "Do Fries Go with That Shake" hit playlists across the country in 1986.

Clinton was frank with Amp about how his contributions would be handled: *For the first songs you help with, I will give you cowriting credit, but my company will publish them, because you're new and I'm giving you an opportunity. Later on, we can renegotiate. They'll always be more songs.* Clinton flew Amp to Los Angeles, put him up in the Park Sunset Hotel and then in an apartment for close to two years while they recorded and toured. Clinton and his manager Archie Ivy brought Amp with them to business meetings. And when Amp had an idea to create a line of merchandise for Clinton's next tour, George trusted him to run it. Amp Fiddler, in turn, learned to be trusting.

It was always understood that Amp was working toward a recording career of his own, and when that opportunity finally came in 1989—in the form of an offer from Elektra Records for Amp and his brother Bubz, who together billed themselves as "Mr. Fiddler," Amp returned to Detroit with an advance check of $10,000.

Amp Fiddler knew the wisest way to spend this money was not to buy time in a recording studio, but to build his own, in the basement of his home in Conant Gardens. He went to Guitar Center and, with his advance, bought every piece of equipment he ever wanted, including a new sampling drum machine that had just hit the market, an Akai MPC60.

———

C ricket showed up at Amp's and, under his tutelage, learned over time how to use the equipment. But Cricket knew someone in his circle of neighborhood friends who was even better than him as a producer, the mad kid scientist who disassembled cassette decks and made perfect loops without a sampler or drum machine, a member of the loose group of crews who were calling themselves, collectively, "Ghost Town": there was Cricket and his partner Omar, forming a duo called Walking Dead; Hippie S and Thurm called themselves Under the Shadow; and then there was T3, Que.D, and James from Ssenepod.

Cricket brought them all over to Amp's one day. Amp wanted to give these kids a bit of what George had given him, but he also felt the need to manage their expectations.

"I would love to help you guys," Amp told them. "But right now I'm busy 'cause I'm making my album and I have to put my time into that. If one of you guys could help me by learning the equipment and making some beats yourselves, then we could really do this faster."

That would be James, they replied, pointing to the short, brown-skinned kid who hadn't yet said a word and barely made eye contact.

"Oh, you make beats?" Amp asked.

James nodded, and gave a polite, "Yes."

"How do you make the music?" Amp inquired.

"With two cassettes," James replied, his terse response belying his Byzantine studio setup.

"Tell you what," Amp said. "Bring the samples tomorrow"—he meant the raw music that James wanted to loop up. "We'll load them into the machine together and I'll show you how it works."

James returned the next day, not with the records he wanted to sample, but with second-generation copies of those music fragments already recorded on several cassettes. Amp led James down to the basement and sat down with him in front of the MPC60 drum machine. While James watched, Amp demonstrated how to load the sounds—hitting a few buttons that allowed the machine to record incoming signal from a cassette player. Amp recognized one of the drum breaks, from Sly and the Family Stone's "Sing a Simple Song."

Now that the samples were stored in the MPC's digital memory, Amp asked James how he wanted to edit them: *Where should each sample start and end?* James directed Amp on how he wanted the samples trimmed or "truncated." Amp then asked James how he envisioned the edited pieces of audio being looped and layered together. To Amp's great relief and greater astonishment, the quiet kid not only had a firm sense of how to put a digital composition together but could articulate a clear musical vocabulary. James told him how many measures or bars each section would last, labeling them as intro, verses, and chorus. The process went quickly because of it, and within a few hours, after adding a bass line from a keyboard synthesizer, they had the backing track for a song James and his friends were calling "Ghost Town to the Break of Day." They finished the vocals in another hour or so. Everyone was overjoyed with the results, but none more than James, listening back to his first production on studio-quality gear.

Amp took James aside: "You just come by here when you can, and I'll show you as much as I can about this MPC. I'll get you started, and then you can do it yourself."

James came by damn near every day, knocking at the door asking, always respectfully, if Amp had some time to give him, staying each time for a couple of hours.

At first, Amp sat with James and reviewed some of the machine's basic functions: how to record and edit sounds, how to assign each of them to one of the sixteen square finger pads on the machine, and how to program the machine's onboard clock to play them in sequence. Amp explained some of the sequencer's advanced functions:

You don't have to make every measure four beats. You can loop around every three beats, or five, or six, or seven if you want.

The sequencer has a function called "Timing Correct." It will fix any little mistakes you make when you tap the finger pads. If you hit a drum sound too late, or too early, it will automatically put the sound right on time. You can use it on all your sounds, or some of them, or none of them.

If you use Timing Correct, you can also use some other functions. You can program the machine to "swing" your beats, to make them uneven.

Amp went on, the options swimming in James's head. "I'm not going to give you a manual," Amp told him. Amp wanted James to learn like *he* had learned, by experimenting. Amp retreated to a smaller studio setup he kept upstairs while James used the basement. Occasionally, James would approach Amp with questions, like when he was having difficulty truncating samples, or stringing sequences of musical events into "song mode." Amp would do his best to answer and then leave him alone to figure things out. James never seemed to tire. Sometimes he'd call Amp downstairs, not to ask a question, but to play him what he'd created.

"Damn, you made this shit?" Amp exclaimed. "This is crazy."

Amp noticed that James had quickly evolved from simply *looping* long pieces of audio to *slicing* those loops into their constituent parts—a kick drum only, a snare only, a hi-hat only, more percussion sounds— and then sequencing them. The latter technique, "chopping," took a great deal more skill. To Amp, it was like the difference between building a house made from prefabricated panels versus laying the bricks and nailing the wood yourself, and doing it in a beautiful way. Amp had already judged James to be a natural after listening to those pause tape beats. But every day that passed and every new beat that he heard, Amp felt like he was witnessing something altogether supernatural.

This kid has some other *shit going on.*

James came around so often that Amp figured he must be skipping school. After a while, Amp went to the Yanceys' home and introduced himself to Maureen and Dewitt, to assure them that James was safe and definitely up to some kind of good in his house. Amp also showed James how to operate his reel-to-reel multitrack tape recorder, so that he could record vocals onto some tracks and the sounds from the drum machine onto others. James became the producer of all his friends' music, but focused on his partnership with T3, with his percussive delivery and quick mind; and Baatin, with his multiplicity of voices, characters, and lyrical tangents. One of the first songs they recorded at Amp's, "Drop the Drum," revealed their influences and obsessions: the jazz samples, frenetic tempos, and vocal inflections found on the albums of New York hip-hop artists like Leaders of the New School and A Tribe Called Quest. But the trio became a duo shortly after James and T3 realized that Baatin was dealing drugs. They were still living with their parents and knew where to draw the line. They gave Baatin an ultimatum: *If you're living that kind of life, then you can't be around us.* Baatin didn't want to be broke more than he wanted to be in a rap group, so he left.

Still, James and T3 continued their work with songs like "Magic Marker." The two MCs, with Waajeed positioned as the DJ and Que.D the dancer, were soon calling themselves Slum Village—a nod to Conant Gardens, diminutive and diminished.

Dewitt and Maureen moved the family again, around the block to a ranch house on the corner of McDougall and Nevada, across from a barren field and small Baptist church. When Amp's studio wasn't available, James and his friends convened in the wood-paneled basement, accessible by a side door. James filled the space with his ever-expanding record collection. He put his equipment on an old wooden bar on the north side of the room. Like his grandmother Maybeline, he tacked up the covers of his favorite albums. James didn't have full possession of the room, though. After a dispute with church leadership, Maureen had left both the day care job and Vernon Chapel, and restarted the enterprise in her home. For most of the day, the downstairs was filled with cavorting kids. After 6:00 p.m., James took over and the basement filled with friends who had become family: Frank and Derrick. T3 and Baatin and Waajeed. And Que.D—who had at one point grown fond of James's younger sister Martha, a beauty much like her mother. For a few weeks, they flirted and talked by phone; then things trailed off.

Que.D soon discovered it was for the best. One broiling summer day, he didn't feel like walking to his friend James's house and asked his mother, Brenda, for a ride. As she pulled up on McDougall to let her son out, Brenda spied a man leaving the Yanceys' house, someone she recognized, and slammed on the brakes.

"Is that Dewitt?" she asked.

"Yeah," Que.D replied. "You know him?"

"Boy, that's your *uncle!*" she yelled, leaping out of the car to embrace James's father.

"Hey, Brenda, I ain't seen you in years!" Dewitt said.

Brenda explained to her puzzled son: *Your grandmother Annabelle is Dewitt's sister. That makes Dewitt your great-uncle.*

Disoriented, Que.D made his way down the steps to the basement, where James, as usual, stood behind his turntables and tape deck setup, headphones on. He waved at James to get his attention.

James waved him off. *I'm in the middle of something.*

Que.D waved back.

James yanked his headphones off, annoyed.

"What?!" James barked.

"You know we're *cousins*, man?"

"Forreal?" James replied. "Okay."

James slid his headphones back on and resumed work. That was James.

James got his driver's license. He and Martha were night owls, and sometimes they'd sneak off to White Castle after everyone else had gone to sleep. On other nights, they'd hang upside down from their beds and whisper to each other across the hall that separated their rooms— talking for hours, mostly about their friends and love interests. Martha knew how much James hated Davis, and how serious he was about pursuing a music career, so she wasn't surprised when, after another school year came and went, James again told Maureen that he wanted to leave. Again Maureen reneged on her deal.

This time, James stopped speaking to her.

It was a stony silence familiar to Maureen in her relationship with Dewitt. But she never expected it from James, whom she had come to see as her closest ally in the family, and her best friend. In her times of conflict with Dewitt—especially over her desire to advance her career— James had always been explicit in his support. The last time Dewitt screamed at her, James laid a hand on her shoulder and told Maureen that he wouldn't allow his father to do it again. Maureen was afraid that James would confront Dewitt physically, and she was relieved that it hadn't come to that. But now she felt a decisive separation from James and that frightened her in a more visceral way than her everyday, erratic estrangement from Mr. Yancey.

One day in his third year at Davis, James let her know that he would be working a late-night session at Amp's studio.

"What are you talking about?" Maureen said. "You have labs tomorrow at Davis. You can't stay out all night."

"Maureen, I've got to do the session, and I'm doing it. And I'll just have to face the consequences."

The mother in Maureen couldn't stand that her son was speaking to her in this way, so matter-of-factly. *Like I'm just supposed to be good with it.* But the frightened part of Maureen knew her son's resolve was as strong as that of anyone she knew. If she pushed him on this, she'd push him away, maybe forever. *James knew exactly what he wanted. She was either coming along for the ride, or she wasn't.* So she agreed, finally, to let him leave Davis and attend Pershing.

James didn't last but a few months there. Chuck had switched to Pershing, too, and one morning when he swung by to scoop James up, Chuck found him in the basement, busy with his music.

"I'm not going to school anymore," James told him.

"Then I'm not going to school anymore, either," Chuck declared.

Nobody ever saw either of them at Pershing High again.

James loved making music on machines, but he understood by now that music lost something when the machines took over: the *unpredictability* of a human playing an instrument that told you it was a human being playing it. It was, after all, why producers looped breakbeats: to bring the ghosts of real drummers into their machines. There was no way a drum machine could re-create the subtle playing of Clyde Stubblefield's performance on "Funky Drummer." That wasn't going to stop James from trying. That's why, one day, James and Waajeed and T3 sat in the dark, listening to the song on loop, trying to sear the timing of each hit into their brains so they could understand both the regularities and the irregularities that made the groove sound as good as it did.

Like "Funky Drummer," another piece of music hovered before James like a Holy Grail of feeling. Not a song, really, but a moment from a film.

The Yancey family had over the years accumulated a sizable library of movies, and *A Piece of the Action*, the third installment of a trilogy of Sidney Poitier–Bill Cosby caper films from the 1970s, was a beloved favorite.

Director Poitier tapped the soul music legend Curtis Mayfield to write the theme song, with Mavis Staples singing tight gospel harmonies over uptempo funk playing out over the opening credits. In the comedy, Poitier and Cosby portray professional thieves who are blackmailed by a cop into teaching career skills to a classroom of cynical teenagers. In the end, the two con men begin to appreciate the students and decide to change their ways. The class celebrates the moment by getting a little party started. Someone produces a boombox, the play button is pressed, and the sounds of the movie's theme song fill the room. Everybody dances to Mavis Staples's "A Piece of the Action."

But *this* version of the song, James noted, the one that played as the end credits rolled, was different from the first. In this scene, the sounds of handclaps had been added. Except the claps were not quite on beat.

Sometimes they rushed ahead of it.

At other times they lagged far behind it.

The claps had been added in the film editing process to give the party a "live" feeling, as if the dancers themselves were clapping. The claps were "Foley," in the terminology of film production—sound effects added after the fact. The handclaps may have been recorded by a group of people at some postproduction facility in Hollywood as they watched a screening of the scene. Their imperfect performance may have been intentionally loose, or a result of each of the performers' different sense of timing. But it is just as likely that the imperfections are an artifact of the recording and synchronization process; as in the predigital world, it was often common for machines to drift in and out of sync with each other.

But those mistakes—man-made, machine-made mistakes—were thrilling to James. They reminded him of messy house parties, and the interminable rehearsals of his childhood, and the discord of musical devotion in the sanctuary of Vernon Chapel, the unity made from the chaos of humans *interacting*.

The sound of error stayed with him.

It remained until he found a way to make those errors on purpose.

It remained beyond that, into a future that he could scarcely imagine, a future in which much of popular music would sound uncannily like that last scene from *A Piece of the Action*—simply because musicians and composers around the world wanted to sound like James.

6.
Sample Time

Years earlier and thousands of miles away in Southern California, a bizarre recording session would change the way that musicians made music and ultimately give James the perfect tool to make his.

In 1978, a drummer named Art Wood sat in a closet, behind his kit, while his housemate, Roger Linn, shouted at him from outside the closed door.

"Play the snare!" Linn cried.

Wood then hit his snare drum over and over again—louder, then softer—as the sound was picked up by a microphone that Linn had run into the closet from a reel-to-reel tape recorder. When Linn was satisfied by what he heard, he prompted Wood to move on to another drum, and Wood repeated the process: low tom, high tom, kick, hi-hat . . .

Linn and Wood were both in their early twenties, both striving musicians in Los Angeles. Wood had recently picked up some great gigs touring with the artists Gary Wright and Peter Frampton. Linn was a songwriter and guitarist who toured and recorded with Leon and Mary Russell, playing behind them in their 1976 appearance on NBC's new sketch comedy program, *Saturday Night Live*. Roger Linn was a valuable member of Leon Russell's team not only for his musicianship, but also for his ability to tinker with electronic circuitry and his aptitude for the recording process.

That strength enabled Roger Linn to solve a problem he was having, and the recording session with Art Wood was part of the solution. As a songwriter, Linn needed to record demos of his songs to pitch to artists. He needed to make them cheaply, but they also needed to be as good as possible. And here's where the trouble lay: Linn could play guitar and a little bass and keyboard, but he couldn't play drums well. The simple solution was to use a drum machine, like the one Russell employed at his recording studio as a metronome to keep his drummers playing steady. But drum machines in the midseventies had two significant drawbacks: the synthesized drums sounded horrible, and you couldn't customize the way the machine played them; they all came with preset drum patterns with generic names like "rock," "bossa nova," "waltz," and "cha-cha." And it wasn't only the sounds that were the problem, but the mechanical, robotic consistency of the *silence* between those sounds.

Linn resolved to build his own programmable drum machine, one that sounded more human. He began his prototype by buying the best "soundboard" that the Japanese electronic-instrument company Roland would sell him—a circuit board that contained synthesized drum sounds—and then used his new personal computer, one of the first on the market, a 1977 COMPAL 80, to trigger them. The big question was how to create an *interface* so he could program the patterns that the drum sounds would play. Linn had a revelation about how to do it: a grid.

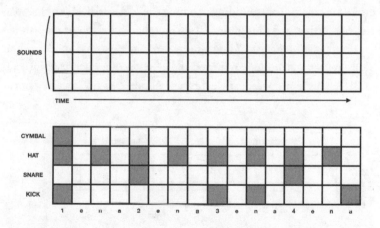

He wrote a program that displayed a visual matrix on the computer monitor, where each square going horizontally represented a sixteenth-note increment in time—one-sixteenth of a measure; and each square vertically represented a different drum sound. Then he used the computer keyboard to enter little asterisks where he wanted to hear the sounds played.

The program worked. But as happy as Linn was with his break-through, the synthesized drums still sounded artificial. Another issue presented itself when Linn found out that the pioneer of synth-driven pop music, Stevie Wonder, had been told about his drum program and wanted a demonstration.

What's a visual grid on a computer screen to a blind man? *Invisible*, Linn realized almost as soon as he set up his equipment for the legendary musician.

Roger Linn decided that if he wanted to make his programmable drum machine usable to musicians, he had to give them something to touch, almost like a miniature drum, and allow them to program the machine by playing, in real time, their preferred drum pattern on a row of pads—buttons designed to be played by the fingertips. Instead of their eyes being guided by a visual grid, their ears would be guided by a met-ronome. This idea, called real-time programming, had surfaced in em-bryonic form on a recent Roland drum machine, the CR-78. But Linn's desire for a truly great-sounding machine would necessitate pushing this concept further, and thus present its inventor with a series of challenges.

Linn realized that recording a user's real-time playing, and having it better reflect their timing, required the creation of a finer grid: instead of sixteen divisions per measure, his new number was 192 per measure.

16 PLACEMENTS PER MEASURE

192 PLACEMENTS PER MEASURE

The price of replicating the nuance of human performance was that any mistake would be replicated as well. And though those little timing errors were what made real drummers sound real, those mistakes would be looped ad infinitum on a drum machine—as most drum beats were programmed as loops of two or four measures, rather than recorded in linear fashion for the length of an entire song. For Linn, the chief purpose of making his machine was to make drumming easier for people, like him, who didn't have the reflexes and timing of a trained drummer to create a steady, predictable groove. So Linn devised the "timing correct" function, whereby the user could reduce the resolution of the grid to a sixteenth note, or an eighth note, and any errant note would be pulled onto the nearest gridline, a process later called "quantization."

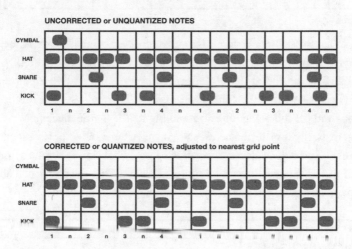

The sounds of drums placed on this timing grid, when played back, were precise. But in their precision, they had lost, again, that ineffable quality of a human playing drums. The reason was all about the difference between electromechanics and biomechanics. A simple circuit will behave with more predictability and precision than a complex organism like a human. Ask a computer to keep time and the computer will produce consistent results. Ask a human to keep time and you will get variations that, no matter how tiny, manifest obviously if not consciously. It's how we can innately tell the difference between mechanical sounds and natural ones. It's not just the genesis of the sounds, it's the *timing* of their generation that indicates their provenance.

Linn was back where he started. Then he remembered something that his mentor Leon Russell taught him during one of their many sessions together at Russell's home studio in Tulsa, Oklahoma. Russell had grown up in the music-driven worship of the Pentecostal church, and he was an observant student of drummers. *Many great drummers*, Russell said, *don't play perfectly straight. They shuffle their timing just slightly*.

By "shuffle," Linn understood that Russell was referring to a perfect triplet swing.

What Russell was saying is that great grooves come from drummers playing somewhere between perfectly straight and perfectly swung.

Roger Linn found that if he delayed every other note in a pulse of 16th notes—essentially shifting the even 50/50 ratio between the previous and the following note and making it 66/34—the machine would automatically transform the user's straight pattern into a perfect triplet shuffle. And if he reduced the ratios to, say, 58/42 or 54/46, he found that the adjustments would be more subtle, but that the patterns really *grooved*. Not straight, not swung, but somewhere in between.

NO SWING (50%)		
SUBTLE SWING (54%)		
SHUFFLE SWING (66%)		
SEVERE SWING (71%)		

After refining his machine's sequencer, the final and still unresolved challenge was improving its drum sounds. To this, Linn also found an answer. By 1979, engineers had developed digital recording techniques.

The first recordings, on Thomas Edison's phonograph, were made by transforming waves of air into waves on a foil or wax cylinder, the resulting "record" a physical imprint of sound—analogous to a handprint in cement. German scientists later found a way to cast these waves onto a strip of plastic tape coated with iron particles: magnetic tape recording. The French radio engineer Pierre Schaeffer saw that magnetic tape could be used in the same way that John Cage once envisioned using phonograph records to create and compose music. In 1948, Schaeffer recorded the sounds of a locomotive onto tape, cut it into pieces, and respliced them to create new rhythms and sounds. Another inventor, Harry Chamberlin, created a keyboard instrument that triggered tiny loops of magnetic-tape recordings of real-life instruments: the Chamberlin, later called the Mellotron. This was the ancestor of sound sampling.

In the 1970s, the invention of digital recording meant that music could be stored as a series of numbers rather than as a "physical cast" of a sound wave—which meant that audio could now be sampled, encoded, and recorded on magnetic tape and computer discs with complete fidelity.

The implication of this, for Roger Linn, was that he could record *real* drum sounds—like the strike of a snare, or a kick drum—rather than using synthesized ones, and store them on computer memory chips in his machine for users to trigger and for his sequencer to play back. The only limitation was cost; computer memory was very expensive. He could afford only a few seconds' worth for his machine to be affordable.

Luckily Linn didn't have to pay for a drummer. And that's how Art Wood ended up in his closet. Part of the task before Linn in this recording session was to keep the sounds short and sweet: kick, snare, tom-tom, conga, and so on. Cymbals were too lengthy to record because they had long decay times. He also struggled a while to find a great handclap sound. One day while Linn was engineering a recording session for the rock artist Tom Petty, he asked the singer and his band to step into the booth and clap their hands for a while, so he could record them. Linn found a moment of sound he liked, and he used it in the prototype for his new machine.

Linn now needed to raise money to put his device into production. For that, his father loaned him $20,000. For the rest, he demonstrated the prototype for every forward-thinking artist of means he could access. In the end, he took deposits of $2,500 each from around a half dozen tech-friendly customers including Leon Russell, Herbie Hancock, Herb Alpert, and—happily—Stevie Wonder. To finish delivery, Linn would be forced to barter his 1967 bathtub Porsche for a quantity of circuit boards.

In 1980, at a price of $5,000, Roger Linn's LM-1 became the first truly programmable drum machine on the market, the first to use the digitally sampled sounds of real drums, and the first to offer a more refined musical clock; it gave users sounds that were natural, not synthesized, and rhythms that were looser than perfectly straight. It's no wonder that among those users were some of the greatest musicians and composers of the early 1980s. As a result, Art Wood would unwittingly become one of the most widely heard drummers in the world.

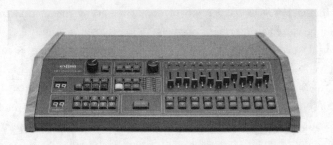

Roger Linn's LM-1 was the first of a generation of drum machines that copied his clock and digital sound innovations. But while samples of real drum sounds became ubiquitous in pop music, Linn's subtle timing functions were rarely used. One popular machine, the Roland TR-808, offered completely artificial sounds and no subtle degrees of swing. The 808 had a kick drum sound that, when detuned, shook floors and walls and tailed off for what seemed like days. That vast, detuned 808 kick became the sound of hip-hop by the mid-1980s. It came down to a matter of taste—how much did a producer or artist delight in the robotic, grid-like machine sounds and silences? For many of the early hip-hop, electro, and techno artists, the answer was "a lot."

Machine sounds and rhythms were so prevalent in the 1980s that emulating them became a fashion for traditional drummers. When Michael Jackson wasn't using drum machines for his 1982 album, *Thriller*, his studio drummers imitated the machine's unerring timing, as Ndugu Chancler did in the song "Billie Jean."

Prince's approach to the machine was different. Like Stevie Wonder, to whom he was often compared as a prodigy and multi-instrumentalist, Prince could have easily played his compositions and arrangements on traditional gear, but instead opted for a mixture of the traditional and the electronic. Prince was a dexterous drummer, but on song after song, he chose the LM-1 for its sounds and for its steady, smooth pulse.

Prince used the features of the LM-1 to make its human samples sound *less* human—doubling the tempo of hi-hats to make a phrase that would be difficult if not unplayable to mortal drummers; or detuning the clap at the maximum setting in a way that made it *his* signature sound from record to record. Few besides Roger Linn knew that when they heard that trademark "Prince clap sound," they were really hearing Tom Petty and the Heartbreakers put their hands together in slow motion.

Prince often *combined* the LM-1's sounds and fixed rhythms with those of hand-played instruments. On Prince's 1982 song "Lady Cab Driver," the LM-1 drives the tempo with a hi-hat, kick drum, and hand-claps; but Prince plays *against* the machine by skipping his sticks across the skin of a real snare drum and slapping the strings of a bass guitar. Prince often juxtaposed machine time and human time simultaneously, man engaging machine rather than emulating it.

The mix of these two ways of generating sound showed how far machines had come toward the animate realm, and yet how much distance and difference still remained between the two.

Listening To: Man-Made Rhythms

Man: "Funky Drummer" by James Brown
Drums played by Clyde Stubblefield

Man Emulates Machine: "Billie Jean" by Michael Jackson
Drums played by Ndugu Chancler, to a machine metronome

Man Engages Machine: "Lady Cab Driver" by Prince
Drums played by Prince and by the LM-1

As an amateur inventor, Roger Linn struck gold; as an amateur businessman, he lost it. Concerned that the pricey LM-1 would be undercut by copycat competitors, he toiled on a lower-priced model called the LinnDrum. Thinking that no one would want the older model once the newer one was out, Linn discontinued the LM-1. But a delay in the delivery of the LinnDrum left him with nothing to sell for six months, burning through all his LM-1 profits. And, to Linn's shock, the demand for the LM-1 remained, not just for its extra features, but because *it was Prince's drum machine*. People actually thought the machine had a soul.

Linn repeated his mistake when he released the next model, the Linn 9000, which featured a new innovation, allowing users a few seconds of sampling time to input their own customizable sounds. It was also beset with technical bugs. By 1986, Linn went out of business under the weight of debt and lack of income. Whatever spirit Linn himself had, he felt as if he had left it in his machines.

A few months later, a friend of Linn's connected him with a Japanese electronics company, Akai, that had just gotten into the professional audio market with digital tape recorders and samplers. They wanted to know if Linn would be interested in designing *their* first sampling drum machine. As it happened, Linn had been working on a product called the MidiStudio to replace his Linn 9000, to compete with the new crop of sampling drum machines. Chief among his competitors was a company called E-mu that had released a new machine, the SP-12, which gave users a full 1.2 seconds of sampling time—or five seconds with an upgrade—and copied Linn's swing function. E-mu was already developing an even more powerful model, the SP-1200.

Linn threw himself into work on a new, better machine for Akai. Unlike the E-mu machines, his would have truly touch-sensitive pads, allowing the user to add nuance to their drum tracks by recording the strength of the user's finger strike. It would have more sampling time, for recording drums with long decays like cymbals. It would have a larger screen for programming. And most important, it would conform, as Linn's last machines had done, to a vital new convention that allowed electronic instruments to talk to, synchronize with, and play each other, called Musical Instrument Data Interface, or MIDI. At the center of it all would be Linn's sequencer, capable of storing sixty thousand notes. Akai dubbed it the MIDI Production Center, or MPC60. The gleaming white chassis featured Roger Linn's signature, like a work of art.

In 1987, just after E mu rolled out its SP-1200, Linn hit the trade shows to display his MPC60. The response was enthusiastic, with a caveat. A number of people approached him and asked if they could have more sample time.

"Yes," he told one of them. "This has thirteen seconds, and you can expand it to twenty-six seconds."

"Can I get more?" the visitor asked.

"More?" Linn was puzzled. "How much more?"

"A minute?" he suggested. "Two minutes?"

Two minutes?! That's crazy, Linn thought. *What could you possibly need all that sample time for?*

———

The reason the "breaks" came back into hip-hop in the late 1980s—the reason that so few people understand even now—was as much for the silences generated by real drummers as it was for their sounds. The larger the chunk of audio you sampled, the more of the groove you imported.

The arrival of samplers—and in particular the sampling drum machine, which combined samplers with dexterous sequencers—made the process of timing and layering beats automatic. Now a producer could sample a measure or two of a favorite break like "Funky Drummer" into a drum machine, and use the machine's clock to trigger the sample at regular intervals. If the producer adjusted the tempo of the sequencer—tempo meaning speed, measured in beats per minute—to align with the natural tempo of the break, then he could duplicate the infinite loop merry-go-round of the early hip-hop DJs, but without the need to perform it manually on the turntables. Once programmed, Clyde Stubblefield would play that break ad infinitum. In the game of looping samples, just as it was with funk, the "check-in" point was the One. As long as the last beat of the loop was equidistant from the beat before it and the One of the loop after it, the groove would be seamless.

The ability for drum machines to loop larger pieces of sampled audio meant that the looser, more human groove of real-life drummers could be imported and kept in perfect time with any electronic elements. It was a way, in effect, for the machine to engage man. DJ-producers began to search not just for drum sounds, but for drum *rhythms*. Whenever you sampled and looped a large chunk of music, you were importing a particular, distinctive timing. A triggered drum loop reached back into time and made the past present. A real soul in the machine.

What hip-hop created, in the late 1980s and early '90s, was a machine-assisted collage of human music—human sound bounded by the restrictions of computer memory, human time bounded by the restrictions of machine clocks. It turned the entire history of recorded music into a deep well from which a producer/musician could draw material—both the sounds and their timing—into unprecedented combinations and compositions. And it turned the beatmaker into an alchemist of musical

DRUM SAMPLE NOT ALIGNED WITH MACHINE TEMPO

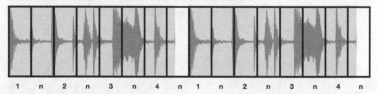

TEMPO ALIGNED by SLOWING DOWN SAMPLE

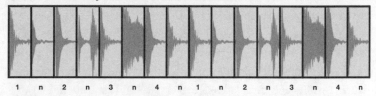

TEMPO ALIGNED by SPEEDING UP SEQUENCER

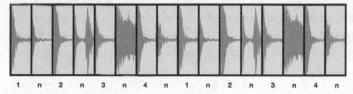

culture—whose most refined and well-crafted instruments came num-bered, not named: 12, 1200, 60.

Listening To: Machine Rhythms

Machine: "Blue Monday" by New Order
Drums on a rigid machine clock

Machine Emulates Man: "Is It Live" by Run-DMC
Drums using a "swing" function

Machine Engages Man: "I Know You Got Soul" by Eric B. and Rakim
Drums from a sample, looped every four bars

The question became: What to do with all this power? Rick Rubin had already envisioned recorded hip-hop as collage art, and more specifically a collision of sonic elements, even before the advent of the sampler/sequencer. Marley Marl was arguably the first to employ the sampling drum machine in service to that end.

From there onward, two different styles began to coalesce. Public Enemy and their production crew, the Bomb Squad, took a cue from Rick Rubin, the man who signed them to Def Jam, cultivating an aesthetic of collision, chaos, and noise, layering samples and creating jarring transitions in their song structures.

This "Beats + Noise" approach was contrasted by another one, call it "Beats + Beauty," wherein the power of the digital sampler was employed to find and recombine *harmony and melody*, not just rhythm and sonic texture. This lineage attracted beatmakers like DJ Jazzy Jeff and DJ Premier, the first to employ samples of jazz music in hip-hop.

The lines between these two approaches weren't hard and fast. The producer Prince Paul used both concord and discord in his groundbreaking production of De La Soul's 1989 debut, *3 Feet High and Rising*.

However, in the early 1990s, several hip-hop producers delved deeper into harmony.

A Tribe Called Quest—Q-Tip, Phife, and Ali Shaheed Muhammad—young associates of De La in an Afrocentric, creatively intrepid collective called the "Native Tongues," gave the hip-hop community a new vision of how the genre could sound. Their 1990 single, "Bonita Applebum," was unlike any digital production before it, looping sections of a Fender Rhodes keyboard from the 1977 jazz-soul song "Daylight," by the Roy Ayers–produced group RAMP, over a stuttering beat from the rock band Little Feat. Throughout their first three albums, A Tribe Called Quest mined jazz and seventies soul for its harmonic and melodic complexity and refined an ever-more-high-fidelity approach they branded as "precise, bass heavy, and just right." But the production credit—attributed to the entire group—deliberately blurred the relative contributions of its chief beatmakers, Q-Tip and Ali. The idea of collective credit was about unity; for Q-Tip in particular, a noble principle of sublimation to brotherhood. But the effect, for both men, would be minimum personal credit for what was essentially maximum cultural impact.

An apprentice of Marley Marl's—Peter Phillips, known as Pete Rock—took Tribe's concept even further, chopping sonic material into its constituent parts in his E-mu SP-1200 drum machine, employing subtle techniques to make these sequenced bits sound seamless, as if they were played by human hands—like using the lingering envelope of an open hi-hat instead of a sharp, closed one to relax the groove. His 1992 production, "They Reminisce Over You," melded bits of James Brown drums with a saxophone melody and ambient vocal harmonies lifted from a 1967 Tom Scott recording of the song "Today." Pete Rock was sampling jazz music, yes. But what made him jazzy was the virtuosity he developed in the art and craft of sampling.*

The work and the tools of these producers galvanized James Dewitt Yancey, primed to join the fray at this moment. Hip-hop as a genre was still a small community; and these producers, though competitive, were all friendly, seeing themselves as part of a joint quest for the sublime. James didn't know it yet, but he was family.

---

* The full complement of producers who advanced harmony in early 1990s hip-hop are too numerous to list, but also worthy of mention here are Diamond D, Large Professor, and Dr. Dre.

7.
Jay Dee

James and T3 saw commercials on WGPR-TV's *New Dance Show* in 1991 advertising Hoops, a recording studio founded by the Detroit Pistons power forward John Salley. Word spread among Detroit's aspiring musicians, singers, producers, and rappers that the basketball star was starting a label of the same name, and that he was hunting for artists.

Detroit loved Salley because Salley loved Detroit. The role of "The Spider" in the Pistons' recent championship streak aside, he made his home in the city, not the suburbs; and he invested in local businesses. Salley was convinced that even though Motown Records was long gone, the talent that made Motown possible was still here in Detroit. But Salley knew next to nothing about the music industry. For that expertise, he turned to a local producer named R. J. Rice.

Nearly everyone who came up in Detroit in James's generation had danced to "Shackles," by R. J.'s Latest Arrival, a group produced by Rice and featuring his wife, DeDe, on vocals. A progressive dance classic, "Shackles" was one of the few records out of 1980s Detroit to break nationwide, the song rising to #6 on the *Billboard* R&B chart in 1984. The road to that hit, and back from it, had been rocky. Ralph James Rice had been driving it since 1979, releasing a dozen different singles and three different albums—each titled *R. J.'s Latest Arrival*—before "Shackles" blew up. A major deal with Atlantic Records fizzled when his follow-up singles stalled just shy of the top ten; and his next relationship, with EMI Records, was plagued by corporate restructuring and the market's sharp turn toward hip-hop, from synthesized to sampled sounds. Rice had learned that a record contract was a slippery thing, the words on paper mattered less than the relationships behind them. Sometimes executives did deals just to stand next to people who made them look good. If you weren't making them money or making them look good, your deal was done.

By 1990, R. J. Rice was looking to stay closer to home. He and DeDe had a child now. He wanted to build a recording studio, but the loan officers at First Independence Bank told him that the music business was far too risky for their tastes. R. J. pondered the implications: the biggest Black-owned bank in the birthplace of Motown Records, P-Funk, and techno, declaring that Detroit music had no future. When R. J. was introduced to John Salley shortly thereafter by their mutual accountant, everything turned around. First Independence was suddenly happy to extend over a quarter-million dollars in loans. *Sometimes the money mattered less than who folks wanted to stand next to.* Salley looked at R. J.'s utilitarian Dodge Raider. *If you want to stand next to me,* Salley told him, *you need to get a new car.*

R. J. was not used to his partner's extravagance. Salley remodeled a grand old bank building in Oak Park and put a recording studio in the vault. He bought custom-made desks and chairs. He bought TV and radio spots. He brought in his childhood friend Michael Christian to scout talent. And Hoops opened its doors to a new generation of Detroit artists.

When James and T3 showed up with a tape in their hands—the rooms lit in purple and thick with the smell of air freshener—they met Christian, who called Salley down to Hoops: *You gotta hear these kids.* Salley loved the Slum Village demo on first listen. R. J. Rice didn't know what to make of them. After Salley escorted the two hopefuls back to the vault where R. J. Rice sat, Rice listened to James and T3, both of them stuttering from anxiety. Then Rice listened to their tape. They were stuttering on the tape, too. *Maybe,* Rice thought, *this is the style?*

Rice showed James their equipment—including an E-mu SP-1200 drum machine—in a studio that far surpassed anything in Amp Fiddler's basement. In short order, Slum Village became a part of Salley and Rice's Hoops roster, which came to include R&B singer-songwriter Tony Rich; local hip-hop group Dope-A-Delic; a foul-mouthed quartet of child rap-

pers called Kid Je' Not (pronounced "kid ya' not") that included Rice's
son, Young R. J.; and Rhythm Cartel, a duo of white MCs from the Detroit suburbs—one skinny, one heavy. The latter of the two, a towering,
boulder-sized teen, had acquired his own nickname, "Paul Bunyan," on
account of his resemblance to that mythical Midwestern lumberjack, but
his real name was Paul Rosenberg.

James now needed to have an uncomfortable conversation. Amp Fiddler had given him hundreds of hours of free studio time. Implicit in
their arrangement was Amp's pledge to find Slum Village a record deal. It
was a handshake agreement that James had to break.

Amp wasn't mad when James and T3 told him about their opportunity with Hoops. He ran "Camp Amp" like a community center, not
a production company. He never asked James to sign any paperwork.
James had always been respectful, and Amp wasn't really trying to be a
record mogul. Plus he knew R. J. well and had toured with R. J.'s Latest
Arrival. He was happy for them. It was all Detroit family, more than any
of them knew. James had no idea that his father's mentor, Johnnie Mae
Matthews, was also R. J. Rice's mentor. T3 didn't know that R. J. went to
high school with his father, R. L. Altman II, and with Que.D's mother.
Before James left, Amp vowed to use his connections to help him and
Slum get where they wanted to go, even though he might not be coming
with them.

James and T3 had another parley to arrange. After they signed with
Hoops, they dispatched Que.D to lure back their erstwhile partner. Que.D
had grown close to Baatin over the years and had developed an understanding of his polar nature: the mirthful guy with the bone-crushing
handshake, unattached to anything worldly, who'd give you the shoes
off his feet if it would make you happy; and the brooding kid who came
from a family troubled by mental illness. Que.D was able to convince
Baatin to return, and Slum Village became a trio of MCs once again.

———

John Salley used his celebrity and R. J. Rice his industry connections to bring the Slum Village demo to record companies in New York. Salley met with executives at Def Jam, Atlantic, and MCA, touting James as "the next Pete Rock." Within a few months Slum Village was offered a deal by a new label, Pendulum, funded by Warner Music. When it came time to negotiate, John Salley asked Rice to step aside.

"Let me do it," he said. "Nobody will lowball me."

But Pendulum's offer for the group did come in too low for John Salley, and nothing he said could get it any higher. Salley didn't want to just give Slum Village away, so he balked, and Pendulum ended up signing another offbeat rap group, Digable Planets. R. J. delivered the bad news to James and T3. They were furious with Salley for rejecting the offer without consulting them, but by now the whole Hoops situation was bad news.

The press raved about Salley's numerous business ventures: a sportswear shop, Funkee Flava, and an erotic boutique, Condomart. The TV host Robin Leach came to Hoops and to Salley's fifty-two-room mansion to film an episode of *Lifestyles of the Rich and Famous*. But Salley had a full-time job in the NBA and couldn't pay attention to the details. He discovered that the contractor they hired to build the studio had been double-ordering materials and sticking Hoops with the bill. R. J. socked the contractor in the face, but the money was gone regardless. The partners had different creative visions: Salley had no use for the older-style R&B that R. J. liked, and R. J. didn't much care for all the little rap groups that Salley was signing. He respected Slum's talent; but talent didn't sell records, hooks did. Salley and his artists got used to hearing Rice's skeptical rejoinder to any music they played for him: *But is it a* hit, *dawg?*

This wasn't a side hustle or hobby for R. J. He had a wife and a kid to support. When Rice could practically feel the creditors knocking at the door of their refurbished bank, he began quietly moving equipment out of the vault. By the time the real bank, First Independence, sued Salley and Hoops for defaulting on $325,000 in loans in 1993, Salley had been traded to the Miami Heat, and R. J. was working out of his house. Salley had guaranteed the loans personally and was stuck with the bill. He would later comment that it took him many years and a meditation retreat to Costa Rica to forgive his former accountant and erstwhile partner; but that he never regretted advocating for James. He just had a feeling that the kid was going places.

Out of high school, out of their Hoops contract, and out of money, James and T3 would often wake before dawn and drive in James's white Ford Ranger to one of the local temporary-job services located beyond 8 Mile. One day they might be sent to Technicolor to label and package VHS videotapes, and on another they might be in a warehouse assembling wood pallets with nail guns. That was their favorite job because they got to talk and listen to music—usually hard rock that the white guys who worked there played all day long—and there was a 7-Eleven around the corner where they could buy snacks. They were sent to a factory where they were given thick gloves and told to remove hot metal plates from a forge; T's gloves were too short and he seared the flesh on his forearms. T got to drive around Detroit with a lady whose job it was to go to office buildings and water plants all day long. For their efforts, the young men usually came away with around forty dollars a day. James did fly with Cricket to Atlanta in 1992 for a music industry convention called Jack the Rapper, hoping to find some kind of connection. Nothing panned out.

Perhaps it was foolish to dream of making a real career in hip-hop, especially since no one from Detroit ever had. There'd been some local rap acts in the 1980s—Felix and Jarvis, Prince Vince, Kaos and Mystro, Esham—with spotty exposure outside Detroit. By the early 1990s, only two Michigan rap acts had made anything resembling a national impact: Awesome Dre and the Hardcore Committee, the first Detroit crew to get their video on *Yo! MTV Raps*; and MC Breed, a rapper from Flint, seventy miles to the north, who scored a national radio hit with "Ain't No Future in Yo' Frontin'."

What little hip-hop community Detroit fostered was centered around a Chinese restaurant on a backstreet of the emptied New Center neighborhood where both Motown and General Motors had once made their headquarters. In a building that looked like a cross between a pagoda and an art deco drive-in diner, Stanley Hong's Mannia Cafe hosted a weekly event promoted by local hip-hop-inspired fashion designer Maurice Malone. The Rhythm Kitchen became ritual for the city's hip-hop outcasts, with MCs and DJs from the East Side and the West Side meeting in a place where conflicts were handled on the mic. Malone sold his merchandise and local rappers hawked CDs and cassettes at the tables in the front; the restaurant sold high-caliber Chinese food and low-caliber malt liquor from the take-out counter in the back; while DJs spun sophisticated fare that other clubs in Detroit ignored—indie hip-hop from New York and dancehall reggae from Kingston—on an impressive sound system.

The Conant Gardens collective came often—James and Frank, T3 and Baatin, Que.D and Waajeed. Crosstown collaborations were forged: Cricket fell in with the West Side DJ Andrés Hernández, who called himself DJ Dez. They became a duo called Rugrats, and Cricket brought Dez over to Amp Fiddler's basement to record. Crews from all over Detroit convened at Rhythm Kitchen: Triplex; former Hoops acts Dope-A-Delic and Rhythm Cartel; and the rapper Ronnie Watts, who called himself Phat Kat. But the most gregarious and relentless MC of all was DeShaun Holton, known to everyone in the room as Proof: a merciless battle rapper; an exhibitionist who'd do anything for a laugh, no matter how crazy; a people-connector weaving between crews whom everyone soon referred to as "The Mayor." After the party, the action continued in the parking lot: James playing beats for Phat Kat; Cricket jumping onto a car and challenging all comers to battle.[*]

Within a couple of years, Maurice Malone was able to open a spot of his own on 7 Mile Road, and the Rhythm Kitchen regulars relocated to Malone's new Hip Hop Shop. By then, the community had become tightly bound and interconnected. The Mayor, Proof, emceed the regular rap battles, backed by his friend from Gesu Catholic School, Kevin "DJ Head" Bell. DJ Head had dormed at Michigan State with Paul Rosenberg, who was trading his visions of a rap career for one in entertainment

---

* A moment that Paul Rosenberg would memorialize nearly a decade later in the movie he executive produced, *8 Mile*.

law. Rosenberg religiously attended the battles at the Hip Hop Shop, where he would meet the young man who would become his first client, another of Proof's protégés and, like Paul, a white rapper of some skill: Marshall Mathers, who went by the MC name "Eminem." The whole shop was managed by another Michigan State classmate of Head's and Rosenberg's, jessica Care moore, a lyricist and poet who often took to the stage to read her work.

By then, another venue downtown had opened its doors to hip-hop. On Friday nights, Saint Andrew's Hall hosted Three Floors of Fun, with different DJs on each floor—upstairs for techno, the main room for hip-hop, and the basement, nicknamed the Shelter, for alternative rock. Crossing between genres was as easy as walking up or down a flight of steps. One night, however, the hip-hop DJ punched the alternative rock DJ in the face and got ejected by security; the promoter pointed to a white kid from Lathrup Village, just north of Detroit, who'd been coming to the Hall with a crate of his own records for the past few months in hopes that he might get ten or fifteen minutes on the turntables. Michael Buchanan became Saint Andrew's resident hip-hop DJ thereafter. He took his stage name from a creature comfort of his—a pair of L.B. Evans black leather slippers with plush plaid insoles that he wore everywhere. He made a ritual performance out of it, sitting on the edge of the stage, taking his boots off and putting his slippers on like a hip-hop version of Mr. Rogers. The crowd roared.

Awww, shit! DJ House Shoes about to get on!

Within Detroit's small but thriving hip-hop scene, James Dewitt Yancey became known as "Jon Doe," producer of first-rate beats. He recorded tracks for Paul Rosenberg's Rhythm Cartel at both Amp Fiddler's and at Hoops. He helped jessica Care moore experiment with putting her poetry over beats. Cricket's pal, DJ Dez, formed a new crew, Da' Enna C (for "The Inner Circle"), and James produced the B side for their first, locally distributed single. James laid a few tracks for Proof, and together they conspired to form a new duo, Funky Cowboys; Detroit's best producer and best MC, they even got matching "FC" tattoos to seal the deal. Proof, in turn, introduced James to DJ Head, Rosenberg's and Moore's classmate at Michigan State, who had an E-mu SP-1200 drum machine that he purchased by splitting the $1,500 cost between two credit cards. James and Head became friendly and often went record shopping together—a mutual quest for the raw materials with which to make new beats—sometimes driving as far as Ann Arbor, thirty miles west of Detroit, to dig for used jazz vinyl at stores like PJ's; then driving back to Head's parents' West Side basement to put them to use.

It was there one evening that Proof, ever the competitor, got an idea: *Let's do a beat battle.* It was the producers' version of the MC battles he hosted at the Hip Hop Shop. He laid out the rules: *You get five records and twenty minutes to make your beat. Only one of them can be a "drum record"*—meaning one of the growing crop of bootleg compilations of raw breakbeats. *Your opponent picks your records, that way everyone is challenged and no one has the same music.* James reveled in these battles, spending hours upon hours in Head's basement trying to make the best beats on the fly. James and Proof became almost sanctimonious about the format's utility: *If you were going to be a professional, if you were going to work with artists in the studio for real, you had to be able to do it well and quickly and on call.* What James put himself through in Head's basement was a kind of beatmaking boot camp, during which he became so fluent and swift that his skill would seem almost miraculous even to fellow producers.

By the time James made a song with Phat Kat called "Front Street" in early 1994, recorded in part at Amp's place, his personal style had coalesced: a melodic jazz sample, the top frequencies filtered out to make the music more amorphous and gloomy, over hard drums, in the vein of A Tribe Called Quest or Pete Rock. But James's snare snapped even harder; and just as distinctive, his kick drum bounced all over the place because he didn't use timing correct on it to make the notes perfectly aligned with the grid. James played the notes freehand instead, giving the beat a looser feel. It was the first beat from James Dewitt Yancey that would sound to future listeners just like a beat from James Dewitt Yancey.

One day in early 1994, Phat Kat drove to Shantinique, a local record store, to pick up *Hard to Earn*, the new album by New York rap act Gang Starr. It just so happened that the duo themselves—Guru and

DJ Premier—were there to stop by Detroit's most important mom-and-pop record store in the midst of their promo tour. The store manager, Josie, introduced Kat to Guru and Premier as a great rapper; made him retrieve his demo from the car; and played "Front Street" for them. Impressed by the beat and the MC, Guru pressed a phone number and address into Phat Kat's hand. *Send your demo to this guy*, Guru said. *I promise he'll get back to you.* The name on the paper was Dino Delvaille, a talent executive at Payday Records, the label owned by Gang Starr's manager Patrick Moxey. They offered Phat Kat a contract and a small advance to record a single; and James got his first production credit on a nationally distributed record, as "Jon Doe." It would be a year before the single was released, under the artist name "1st Down."

In the interim, James was becoming a fixture in R. J.'s living room just as he had in Amp's and Head's basements—using R. J.'s SP-1200 to make beats and his tape machine to record vocals. He also helped on one of R. J.'s projects: an aspiring singer, a white girl from New York City, had seen R. J. Rice on John Salley's *Lifestyles of the Rich and Famous* episode and practically moved in with R. J. and DeDe to work on a demo tape. Anne Danielewski had no money; her boyfriend, the famed artist Peter Max, paid R. J. in paintings. R. J. tugged on his web again, and shook out a deal with Atlantic Records for Danielewski, performing as "Poe." With a whole album to record, R. J. rented studio space in Southfield, and he let James use a room in the back. For $1,800, he paid James for a couple of beats, one of which would end up on Poe's debut album the following year as the song "Fingertips." Poe's single "Angry Johnny" became a top ten hit on alternative rock radio, brought R. J. more production work, and launched his new studio business. R. J. gave James a programming credit on the album cover, and a new alias, "Jay Dee."

But the wheels of the record business turned too slowly for James. Between the failed Hoops deal and waiting for these records to come out, nothing ever happened when it was supposed to.

———

Amp Fiddler never forgot his pledge to James.

George Clinton brought Amp on the Lollapalooza tour with him, and through the early summer of 1994 the P-Funk All Stars toured America with rock bands Green Day and the Smashing Pumpkins, and a few hip-hop acts favored by the festival's hip crowd including Beastie Boys and A Tribe Called Quest. Over the course of the tour, Amp Fiddler needled Tribe's de facto leader, Q-Tip: *When we get to Detroit, there's this kid I want you to meet. He makes beats. He loves you, and you're gonna love him.*

Lollapalooza pulled into the Pine Knob Music Theater on July 23 for a three-day stand in the woods about halfway between Detroit and Flint. Amp came back to Conant Gardens to scoop up James and T3 in his red Ford Falcon and take them back out there, walking the two hip-hop hopefuls right onto Tribe's tour bus.

"These the guys I was telling you about," Amp told Q-Tip.

James could hardly muster anything but a smile, and his equally soft-spoken idol didn't offer much but a kind greeting and a pound. James gave him Slum Village's demo tape, with the Yanceys' phone number on the front. The two kids from Conant Gardens exited the bus, happy at least to have made a connection.

Amp made one more important introduction, joining hands between his mentor, George Clinton, and his student, James.

"I've been hearing about you," Clinton told him.

James and T3 went to watch the show, unaware that they had just become links in a long, swinging, golden chain.

The Slum Village demo was only one of countless others pressed into Q-Tip's hands since he had become a star. And it could have easily gone uncounted had Q-Tip not actually listened to the cassette.

What the fuck is this shit? he thought.

The demo featured outlandish verses and voices from T3 and Baatin— perhaps *too* out-there for Q-Tip. But the beats beguiled him. James flipped a bass line from saxophonist Mark Colby's 1978 song "Daydreamer" onto a thumping track with a curious name, "Homosexual."* In the song "Dance with Me," James displayed all the beat-chopping mastery that had long awed Amp Fiddler, slicing and dicing bits of Kool & the Gang's "Summer Madness" to create a completely different harmonic progression from the song it sampled. In other tracks—"Roxanne," "I Got Ta"—James put complex jazz harmonies over pounding rhythms that mirrored Q-Tip's own method.† After a few listens, he was no longer evaluating a submission. He was a fan.

Q-Tip shared the demo with his comrade from De La Soul, Dave "Trugoy" Jolicoeur, when they played a show together some days later.

"This is ill, right?" Tip asked Dave.

"It's like your shit," Dave replied. "But better."

t's Q-Tip!

Martha had picked up the phone in the kitchen, and hissed excitedly to James, down in the basement.

Q-Tip told James he had been playing his tape for everybody in the crew. As Tip enthused, it became clear to James that Q-Tip was more focused on him as a *producer* than Slum Village as a *group*. "Y'all are dope," Tip assured him. "But I think the road to entry is through your production skills because they're so singular."

"Damn, that's crazy," James replied. "I'm surprised." Something about this gesture didn't compute for James: a producer promoting someone who could potentially be competition. But Q-Tip was from a different school of thought: brotherhood.

"You took what I did and added sheen to it," he said. "People gotta hear your shit. We gotta figure something out. I gotta get you out here."

What that meant, as James understood it, was that Q-Tip was essentially offering to be his manager.

---

* Many J Dilla and Slum aficionados refer to this song as "The One for You," or "The One for Me," but the actual name is derived from an acronym: **Homosexual=Ho**es, I want to get **mo' sexual**. Quod erat demonstrandum.

† "I Got Ta" is the original name for "And I Go," released by Slum Village in 2017.

But what Q-Tip would really become, for the next several years, was an evangelist.

The Pharcyde, a quartet of rappers from Los Angeles, came to New York seeking beats. Their producer, J-Swift, had split from the group after their gold-certified debut album *Bizarre Ride II the Pharcyde.* On the precipice of their follow-up, they now had the clout to work with the best in the business. At the top of their list was Q-Tip. A Tribe Called Quest was the group to whom the Pharcyde was most often compared—with their bohemian clothes, twisted hair, and even more twisted sense of humor. And despite Q-Tip's noble principle of crediting his production work to the collective, he had emerged in conventional hip-hop wisdom as the locus of the group's musical genius—especially after his rare, solo-credited outside production of the rapper Nas's song "One Love." He was starting to get more offers of work than he could handle.

Members Fatlip, "Slim Kid" Tre, Imani, and Romye arrived at Q-Tip's duplex in Greenwich Village on one gloomy winter day to talk about what they needed for their new album. But Tip told the guys that it would be a while before he could get into the studio with them. He was working with another group at the moment, Mobb Deep. He suggested an alternative.

I want you to hear these beats from this new kid I'm working with, Jay Dee, he said.

Q-Tip popped in a cassette that contained a succession of thirty-second instrumental snippets: beautiful harmonies over crisp drums. They listened as each incredible track gave way to an even better one. Tre Hardson already heard a few that he knew he wanted to write to.

When can we meet him? they asked.

He's not here, Tip replied. *He's in Detroit.*

After they left Q-Tip's crib with the beat tape in hand, Tre got suspicious. *Q-Tip is pushing us onto some mysterious, new producer that nobody's ever heard of, from a city that hardly any hip-hop has come out of, but the beats are banging and sound* just *like Q-Tip's stuff?*

Tre joked with the guys when they got back to the SoHo apartment they had rented for their stay: "You know that Tip's real name is Jonathan Davis, right? I think it's him. I think Q-Tip is 'J. D.'"

Tre was disabused of this notion a few weeks later when James Dewitt Yancey, just off a plane from Detroit, showed up at their sublet—dressed fresh and clean in a blue-and-white Kangol beanie, extending a handshake and a smile.

They hung and listened to more of James's tracks, some of which had been made for Slum Village, ones that James now marked as fair game for sale to others, especially since Slum didn't have a deal on the table. It became apparent that the Pharcyde were going to take several of them. Tre was taken with one in particular, based around a Brazilian samba guitar phrase sampled from a Stan Getz and Luiz Bonfá song, "Saudade Vem Correndo," and began to write to it.

B y the time Q-Tip arrived at Unique Studios, the rapper Mad Skillz was wound up. He'd cued material from his upcoming debut album on Atlantic, hoping to impress Tip enough to get him to produce a track. The cosign from A Tribe Called Quest would be *huge*. Tip entered the control room, trailed by a short, silent kid in a fitted baseball cap emblazoned with the Old English *D* of the Detroit Tigers. Skillz played a few tracks for Tip, making his pitch.

But Tip pointed to his friend, who'd taken a seat on the couch in the back, and said, in a mellow mumble: "I want *him* to get on there. Yo, I'm telling you, he's ill."

"That's cool," Skillz offered. "But I've got to get *you* on there."

"Yeah, yeah, yeah, but I need him on there, too!" countered Tip.

If Tip was intent on making this a package deal for him and his little man, Skillz realized he had to go along.

"Yo, Jay Dee," Tip called to the kid. "Play him that *joint* joint."

James rose, handed his beat tape forward, and it went into the cassette deck.

Skillz listened to the first track. Rationally, he understood why Tip was so keen on the kid—his beats sounded a lot like A Tribe Called

Quest's stuff. Still, Skillz stared at Tip, thinking: *I don't want somebody who sounds like you. I want* you.

Then came the second track.

"What the fuck is that!?" Skillz shouted, despite himself. "I want *that*."

And Q-Tip, in that same mellow mumble, said: "Yo, I told you. He's ill, son."

Q-Tip brought James to Battery Studios, where he recorded with the Pharcyde and Mad Skillz. It was at one of Skillz's sessions that James got his first check from a major label—$9,000 for his work on three tracks. It was an entry-level fee to be sure, but it was also the most money James had ever made doing anything.

"I don't care how big I get," James told him. "If I get as big as Dr. Dre, you will always be able to get a beat from me for what you just gave me. I'll never charge any more than this."

After James flew back to Detroit, Q-Tip kept spreading the word. The producer Pete Rock was in a recording session for the rap crew InI when Q-Tip pulled him aside.

"Yo, Pete, I don't mean to interrupt," Q-Tip said. "But just listen to this right here." Into the deck went a cassette, out of the speakers came beats.

"Who made these?" Pete asked.

Q-Tip told him. *Jay Dee. A kid in Detroit I'm working with.*

Pete said: "Stop playing with me, man." And Pete thought: *I am out of a job. I'm not gonna make no more money with this guy around.*

Pete got James's number from Q-Tip, phoned him, and said: "I'm flying out there to meet you."

Among the dreamlike experiences James Yancey had since he met Q-Tip, none was so bizarre as the time that his *other* great hero spent several days at his house in Conant Gardens.

James picked the legendary producer up at the airport, and within seconds, he was hearing *brand-new Pete Rock beats.* James took Pete to record stores and friends' houses just to blow people's minds—*Look who I got with me*—and called an aspiring Detroit producer named Denaun Porter over to the basement without explanation just to see the look on his face when he entered the room. Pete sat in the kitchen at McDougall as Maureen made him food and made a place for him to spend the night. They listened to music for hours on end in the basement. They made some tracks together on James's SP-1200—not his, really, but DJ Head's: James didn't have his own machine yet and Head let James pick it up when he wasn't using it; whenever James got money, he slid Head some cash for the rental. Pete asked questions about James's techniques, and freely shared beatmaking secrets of his own.

On a whim, Pete Rock had come to meet the young producer from Detroit. He left convinced that James Yancey was from some other place.

M ike Ross, the head of Delicious Vinyl Records, had been deeply depressed about the departure of the Pharcyde's first producer, J-Swift, whose sound had been integral to their success. But Ross's mood brightened significantly once he heard the beats from Jay Dee, a complete unknown who had fallen out of the sky and right into place with the crew. Ross jumped on the phone with Tre to strategize. The group was returning to Los Angeles to mix the tracks, so maybe they could fly Jay Dee to L.A. to finish what they started. Ross got the producer's contact information—a 313 area code phone number—and ended up speaking to Maureen Yancey. Together, they arranged for James Yancey's first trip to Los Angeles.

Ross himself met James at the airport. James carried R. J. Rice's E-mu SP-1200 drum machine with him this time. As they pulled away in Ross's Lexus SC 400, James took in the Pacific breezes, the warmth of the sun, and the smell of the leather interior. The moment seemed to be the fulfillment of everything he ever hoped a career in music could be.

But then came the sessions.

The Pharcyde were holed up in Sound Castle, a studio in Silver Lake around the corner from the house they shared, the "LabCabin." Things were tense. During the creation of their first album, the guys had bickered like brothers. But a bit of success had inflated everyone's egos. Everyone was a producer now. Everyone had their own equipment. Everyone had an opinion. James had already seen them come to literal blows over the merits of different pieces of studio gear.

The day that they mixed the Brazilian track they'd worked on in New York, the song they called "Runnin'," Tre, James, Imani, and Romye went to grab some food, leaving Fatlip and the engineer Rick Clifford in the control room. When they returned, they found that Fatlip had changed James's kick drum without telling any of them what he was doing. Tre had loved the track. Now, to him, it sounded . . . stiff. Boring. And he could tell from James's expression that the quiet producer was crestfallen.

Why did you do that? Tre demanded.

It didn't sound right, Fatlip replied.

On one level, Tre understood what troubled Fatlip. Most hip-hop beats featured very predictable drum patterns, in part because they were looped, but also because they hewed to a standard time grid. But in "Runnin'," Jay Dee had flouted both these conventions. He'd programmed the kick drum not in a standard two- or four-bar loop, but in a long sequence that didn't repeat until the twentieth bar, in linear fashion, so that it did different things in every new measure of music, as a human drummer would do. And he programmed it without timing correct, increasing the sense of the unexpected. The hyperactive kick drum raced ahead of the samba sample, which in turn seemed to be racing ahead of the snare drum—which gave the paradoxical illusion that the snare was somehow *late,* making the beat feel oddly relaxed, tumbling endlessly forward.

But Fatlip had swapped the unpredictable kick drum for a very predictable one. In doing so, Tre thought he'd drained the track of its soul. Fatlip didn't hear soul. He heard chaos. It sounded wrong.

As they argued, Tre seethed. Beyond changing the very element of the song that made it so distinctive, Fatlip had disrespected their guest. Plus this wasn't the first time that Fatlip had changed shit behind their backs. Tre and Fatlip were both on their feet, and in each other's faces.

Change that shit back! Tre insisted.

Then Tre found out that Fatlip hadn't simply recorded his kick drum to a new track. He had erased Jay Dee's kick entirely. Wiped it from the tape. Tre felt the adrenaline coursing through his body. *This fool needs to get smacked.* After exchanging some "fuck yous," he invited Fatlip to step outside.

James didn't see who threw the first punch, but by the time he scrambled into the hallway, Tre and Fatlip were scuffling on the floor. To James, it was horrifying and hilarious at the same time. *All this drama over a fucking beat?*

Tre was halfway considering reaching for the knife in his back pocket when Suave, their manager, got between them.

As the two bandmates' chests heaved from exertion and fury, their hair and clothing ruffled, James tried to defuse the situation.

"Listen," he said. "Y'all my favorite crew. I'll do it however you want it."

"Fuck that," Tre replied. "That kick was perfect. We're going to redo it exactly the way it was. We're not changing it. That's your *signature*."

Tre Hardson was usually the voice of reason in a crew of knuckle-heads, but unafraid to knuckle up if need be. And so it was, in creating a song about not running away from a fight, that Tre saw something worth fighting for. He had now seen Jay Dee at work, up close. After mentioning that he'd like to do a song over a piece of Vince Guaraldi's music—made famous in the *Peanuts* children's television specials—he watched James chop up the sample, play the drums freehand, and keep pieces of noise and "air" in his drum sounds to change the timing ever so slightly. The other guys, too, were bringing James records to sample. They could have very well produced those beats themselves, but they wanted to hear what Jay Dee would do with them. When Tre told James that he had a "signature," he meant it in the same way that jazz players have distinctive approaches to their instruments, like how Grant Green has a different approach to the guitar than, say, Wes Montgomery. Tre was saying that Jay Dee had a distinctive approach to his instrument, the drum machine. And Tre put his body on the line to protect Jay Dee's rhythmic sense, a fact that was not lost on James Yancey.

James laid down the drums again, and the track stayed as he in-tended it. James would end up producing six tracks for the Pharcyde's 1995 album *Labcabincalifornia*. Some were beats he created for them on the spot, and others went as far back as the beat battles from DJ Head's basement—like the song "Drop," based on a few seconds of harp from a 1962 Dorothy Ashby record that James had sampled and Proof had pro-grammed to play backward. In the track for "She Said," James sampled a jaunty piano and shaker phrase from a Gato Barbieri record and then, in a technique he would employ regularly thereafter, slowed it down to a crawl, evoking a sense of gloom.

Of all the music he had been working on since meeting Q-Tip, these were the first to hit the market, and the most auspicious. "Runnin'" became the lead-off single and video from the album, reaching #5 on the *Billboard* rap chart.

J ames used to come to the aging Detroit City Airport every day for school. Now he came there often for Spirit Airlines' cheap, quick flights to and from New York's LaGuardia Airport. James didn't like to be away from the basement for long, not even for one night if he could help it, and would often fly out in the morning for a studio session, or to go record shopping—either at stores, or at the monthly record-trading convention at the Roosevelt Hotel where all the great DJs and producers dug for dusty records. In the evening, he'd fly back. If he sat in the window seat, he might see the silhouette of his old school as he jetted to and from work with the leaders of his new one.

Q-Tip hooked James up with a track on the upcoming solo debut of Busta Rhymes, who was so floored by James's signature spastic kick drum that Busta altered his rhyme scheme to fit its stutter step. Busta called the song "Still Shining." Tip introduced James to his friends in De La Soul, who feigned disinterest in a Jay Dee beat they loved because they feared that Q-Tip might snatch it for himself; they ended up calling the song—featuring a grand horn fanfare from Ahmad Jamal's "Swahililand"—"Stakes Is High."

The big project ahead for James was A Tribe Called Quest's upcoming album. That meant that James would have to stay for a while in New York—really New Jersey, at Tip's house in Alpine.

Q-Tip wanted everyone in a room, working together as partners. Ali Shaheed Muhammad wanted to support Q-Tip's vision and liked James's beats, but he suspected it was going to be awkward—he, Tip, and James sharing one drum machine. He and Q-Tip took their time making music, methodically going through records and experimenting with different ways to chop samples. They were deliberative, meticulous, collaborative. But when James joined their sessions, Ali saw a different way to work. One day, Ali watched James come downstairs, grab a record, and walk to their workstation, his fingers darting over the turntable and the sampler pads in a way that let Ali know James had already found some audio to manipulate and had begun chopping it. Within a few minutes, James had created an insane track—not just a beat but a completely arranged song. Then James went back upstairs, like it was nothing. Ali had never seen anything like it—James's level of freedom, the speed and beauty of his execution. It helped that James was quiet and unassuming. He never got in the way. He enhanced things. Tribe accepted him as a brother.

For James, the experience was surreal in a different way. When James had first come to New York, Tip played him a new, unreleased track, "Phony Rappers." What superfan wouldn't kill for an exclusive preview of his favorite band's album, given by the band itself? But now he was producing nearly a half dozen tracks *for* them, a group that had previously worked with only one outside producer. James holed up in Battery Studios with them and their engineer, Bob Power, helping with mixes, and bonding with Tribe MC Phife. One of his tracks, selected by Q-Tip as he paced around his basement, had become the song "1nce Again," and was a good candidate to become their first single. James could scarcely believe it was happening.

For all his work on James's behalf, Tip had never asked for nor taken a fee. But he did extend an invitation to James to be a part of a new production collective he was forming with Ali. A lot of work was coming their way, and they wanted to spread it around to collaborators like James, and to others who had different skills but a similar aesthetic. Tip and Ali had two other members in mind. The first was Raphael Saadiq, a driving force behind Oakland's Tony! Toni! Toné!, one of the few R&B groups of the early 1990s to blend soulful songwriting and hip-hop production methods in genuine and creative ways. The other was Michael Archer, a twenty-one-year-old pianist, composer, singer, and beatmaker from Virginia whose talents evoked the specter of a young Marvin Gaye, Stevie Wonder, and Prince rolled into one. He'd just been signed to EMI Records, and Ali had been enlisted alongside Bob Power to help Archer craft tracks for his debut, *Brown Sugar*, which would in 1995 launch Archer as D'Angelo.

Together—Tip, Ali, Jay Dee, plus Saadiq and D'Angelo—they'd be able to compete with the rise of powerful production teams like the Trackmasters and the Hitmen. As with A Tribe Called Quest, Q-Tip envisioned a crew in which everything they created would be credited to the collective, not to the individual. They named it after the Arabic word for "brotherhood": *The Ummah*.

Artists often create first and worry about putting things on paper later. Just as Q-Tip's management of James had been informal, the Ummah began with no official business structure. Q-Tip and Ali offloaded these concerns to their lawyer, Micheline Levine.

Micheline had met Tribe when she worked for their former lawyer, Ken Anderson, clearing samples for their second album—a laborious and expensive process of securing permission from every record company and publisher who owned the recordings and songs sampled within each of their tracks. She was good at her job: tiny in person, imposing on the phone, a protective mama bear to her young clients. And compared to other attorneys, Micheline had a bit of flavor—an Egyptian Jew raised in the Bronx and Queens who dropped out of college, moved to California, and became a polygraph operator. Having been a professional lie detector proved helpful in her career as an entertainment lawyer. When Micheline started her own practice, Tribe followed her. In the next year, Micheline became the lawyer for James as well, representing him in his first dealings with record companies. The closest thing that James had to a day-to-day manager was Maureen, and she and Micheline spoke frequently, essentially becoming teammates.

Micheline admired Tribe's integrity and parity as a group. Everything they earned from their recordings, they split evenly. Every song that was written, no matter who wrote more or less of it, was credited to "A Tribe Called Quest." Thus when it came to the Ummah partnership, she was not surprised that Q-Tip and Ali desired something similar: all songs would be credited to "The Ummah," not to the individual producers. When it came to money, however, the Ummah members who did the actual work would keep it, while contributing a small percentage to a common fund to cover overhead. But the work had already started by the time her clients asked her to "paper the deal." This was her job: *Figure out what the fuck is going on and then catch up as fast as you can.*

Micheline would end up doing a lot of catching up with James. In 1996, she took a vacation—two and a half weeks in the middle of the summer. A few months later, Micheline was astonished to find that, in her absence, James had done a copublishing deal with PolyGram—meaning that he had sold an interest in all the songs he wrote to a corporation in exchange for an advance against future royalties—and had used another attorney, a friend of hers. It wasn't the deal itself that disturbed her—it was decent, with an advance of $150,000. It wasn't the fees she would have earned for negotiating it, either. It was that her friend *knew* Jay Dee was her client, and did the work without telling her. She called him on it. The attorney claimed he thought Micheline knew.

The lie detector thought: *Bullshit.*

She also called James on his. Representing a client to the best of her ability required not only her own honesty, but his, too. *Why couldn't he wait a few weeks for her to return?*

"I don't know." James shrugged. "I just needed a deal."

Micheline Levine found that James Yancey was a very different kind of client from Tribe, because his relationship to money was *exactly the same* as it was to his drum machine: when he wanted it, he wanted it immediately, and nothing else mattered.

With James pulling down thousands of dollars per track—and with no fixed financial responsibilities—he had the kind of expendable income rivaled in Detroit only by street hustlers. He spent his money in a similar manner.

James had always loved clothes. Now he filled his closets with gear he picked up on frequent trips to Northland Mall just across 8 Mile Road, and the outlets at Birch Run, almost one hundred miles to the north.

Never again would he have to wear the same outfit twice. Some outfits he bought he never wore at all.

In 1995, he traded his Ford pickup truck for a green 325 BMW with a beige leather interior. Then James ditched his first nice car for a nicer one—a green Lexus 450 with gold trim—inspired by the Lexus he'd seen Mike Ross drive in Cali. T3 and Baatin dubbed it "the green dick," for all the women it would attract.

But what money really bought for James was the ability to create a world in which time, space, and people aligned around his primary desire: to make music. Everything else he did when he wasn't making beats served that prime directive. He'd call DJ Head or Waajeed and spend hours shopping for used records at stores like Street Corner Music in Southfield or Melodies & Memories in Eastpointe, poring over credits and liner notes, scouring for the raw materials for his next batch of music. When he didn't feel like making beats, he sometimes headed to DJ Dez's place for inspiration. The cars and the clothes were as much about putting him in an ebullient headspace for creating music as they were about looking and living large. The ritual that fed him the most, however, was the strip club.

Conant Gardens happened to be at the epicenter of a group of clubs that included Tigers, on Woodward and 7 Mile, and Chocolate City, on Conant between 7 Mile and McNichols. These clubs were designed, much like the casinos that glittered across the Detroit River in Windsor, Canada, as immersive experiences catering to the wildest fantasies of their patrons. There were practical attractions as well. By the 1990s, few fine-dining restaurants operated in the northern reaches of Detroit; the strip club was one of the few places to get a decent steak or seafood prepared with finesse. At Chocolate City, DJs and girls came and went; but the cooking of "Chef BB" was a constant.

When James started to get money, he was introduced to this circuit by Frank Bush. In high school, they'd frequented Outcast, a members-only motorcycle club on the West Side, open weekends from midnight to dawn, that hosted illicit parties where men could get lap dances and more. By the time Frank turned twenty-one, he'd decided that going to noisy nightclubs and trying to holler at girls over the din wasn't for him.

He'd rather go to the "titty bar" where he could sit down, have a drink, watch, and talk to beautiful women all night. It didn't matter to Frank that he was paying for his pleasures; in his mind, you paid for them one way or another.

Tigers was their first haunt. Sometimes they went to Chocolate City just to have dinner. They'd listen to DJs play the latest hip-hop and R&B hits—and sometimes "ghetto tech" or "booty tech," an evolving hyper-tempo blend of Miami bass and Detroit techno. They ate and drank Pepsis and watched girls shake their asses and bought dances for $10 a song and talked to pretty women. Then, buzzed from the bass vibrations and jacked on testosterone, James and Frank would drive back to the basement on McDougall and James would make beat after beat, sometimes until dawn. It was, Frank realized, all fuel for James's music.

Navigating this domain required more savoir faire than they ever needed at the biker bar. In the strip club, you were in there with the real players, real criminals, too. These men achieved their standing not just by making money, but by making it plain that they had more of it than anyone around them. Appearances were thus as valuable as currency, and the social hierarchy was vigilantly guarded. Helping James, just by whispering in his ear and being at his side from time to time, was Uncle Al.

Albert Hayes was the youngest son of Suge and Maybeline, a full thirteen years younger than his brother Herman, and only seven years older than his nephew James. When the Yancey kids came to visit Grandma Maybeline's house on Garland, Albert was the main reason why Dewitt liked to keep his kids within view. James managed to sneak off anyway, and it was with his uncle Al that he had his first sips of beer, took his first pull of a joint, saw his first pistol, and first played on a turntable setup. Al fixed cars, but he was a mechanic in his soul, pulling apart every machine he could get his hands on. It was Al who showed James how to deconstruct a cassette deck, a trick he'd learned from his older brother Terone. Years later, when James and Slum Village started doing gigs around town, Maureen asked Al to tag along, because she knew that her little brother had the street smarts and the radar for trouble that her son had never quite needed to develop. Al thus became friendly with the guys in Slum, and with Frank, with whom he went to mechanic school. Frank and James would often scoop Al up on their nightly excursions. He might have been working all day and had nothing good to wear. It didn't matter: James had already bought him a new outfit so he could get clean. It was Al who taught James some of the rules that helped him on the streets and in the clubs:

When you buy yourself a new whip, don't buy the most expensive one. Don't try to outshine the dealers. Don't make them feel threatened by you. Don't throw too much cash around at the club. Don't try to hog the prettiest dancers.

Al's presence was especially helpful if James had visits from out-of-town hip-hop dignitaries, like his friends from the Roots or De La Soul; the strip club was a chance for James to show them a good time.

Derrick Harvey, who was as much of a politician and people-connector in the street as Proof was in the hip-hop scene, occasionally came with James and Frank to the clubs and functioned as both diplomat and sentry. Another periodic Detroit-style guardian angel was Ronnie Kelly, known to all as Killa Ghanz. The word *ghanz* was local slang for marijuana, and in the 1990s Ghanz ran one of the most prosperous weed spots on the East Side; on his best days, he might gross $10,000. He'd come up with James's frequent collaborator Phat Kat and had dabbled a bit with writing rhymes, but it was only when Ghanz saw James slide his BMW up to the Hip Hop Shop that he saw evidence that a man could make a living making music. Eventually, Ghanz would form a crew called Cardi Boyz, but Ghanz made sure to keep his relationship with James strictly personal, one of the few people in James's orbit who didn't sweat him for anything. Ghanz had promised Maureen that he'd watch out for James, and the club gave him a few opportunities to do so. One evening, at Tigers, he overheard two men, one of whom he knew from the streets, plotting to rob James. Ghanz spoke up:

"That's my man," Ghanz told them. "That's not going to happen."

Gradually, as James himself became a known quantity, he received the implicit protection of the owners, the interest of the girls, and the friendship of DJs like Henhouse, who provided James with a useful laboratory for observing music in action and a vital proving ground for his new tracks.

James's personality wasn't changing so much as it was emerging. He still listened more than he talked, but his shyness had morphed into a confident attentiveness. He still kept a cloistered life, but now his cloister filled with followers who sat around him as he worked in silence, headphones over his ears, waiting for that "holy shit" moment when he'd flip the switch and audition his latest creation through the speakers. James had an aura. People were attracted to him often without knowing who he was or what he did, or without James having to expend much effort at all.

Angela Dewberry adored James before he was anyone, back when her best friend at Pershing High called him a "loser" because he was always sleeping through class. Angie was instantly curious when she saw James DJ at a high school party, but refrained when she found out he was Earl Hurst's brother—she had a crush on Earl, too. Angie was a fine artist like Earl and planned to attend the Art Institute in Atlanta. James DJed her graduation party, a surprise; they kept in touch after she moved away. Then, in her sophomore year, she came home for Christmas, invited James over while her father was out, and declared she'd been curious for far too long. *Let's go*, she said.

Angie was a beauty that a younger James might have thought unattainable—older folks claimed she favored Diana Ross, friends said she looked like Janet Jackson—with wide eyes and a vivacious demeanor. After she returned to Detroit to finish her degree at Wayne State University, she became James's first long-term adult romance just as James began his journey with Q-Tip. Angie loved music and loved James's genius; her happy place was sitting in the basement, listening to James make beats. One day he sampled a record with a sound that reminded her of water; being a swimmer, Angie felt like it was James's way of letting her in. And James showed his affection more directly with small, meaningful gifts that revealed he was paying attention to her, too. Their families loved the relationship: Maureen treated Angie like a daughter; Angie's father, Carl Dewberry, literally gave James the keys to his house on Bloom Street. James proposed to Angie, then qualified his rationale by saying, "My manager told me to, because you're the only one I can trust." Angie gave him a withering look: "That's a *horrible* reason, James."

Angie was sweet, but she was also sovereign, a kind of womanhood that James had not yet experienced in his relationships; and the kind of manhood capable of respecting it was not common in the men around him. Thus James found himself confronting intense feelings for which he was not altogether prepared. Angie was a "guy's girl"—she always had good male friends—but after she hung late into the evening with an old neighborhood buddy, James stopped talking to her for a week. Angie agreed to scale back her social activities, but also pointed out that it was she who had more reason to be jealous given James's increasing visits to the strip club and frequent out-of-town travels. It was after one of these trips that she and James had a huge argument, en route to brunch. He was in a bad mood about something, she didn't know what. He told her to shut up. And she did, out of spite, for the entire meal. By the time they got to her house he was furious at her for doing exactly as he requested. Then he slapped her.

Shocked and then furious, Angie's instinct was to fight back. And she did, kicking and scratching James until he pushed her off. Then, worried that she might not be able to really take him, Angie got scared, ran to the bathroom, and locked herself inside. James had just kicked the bathroom door in when the front door opened. Her sister entered, James fled.

Angie's sister dragged her to the police station, where Angie declined to ask for a restraining order after the cops told her that they'd visited James and that he looked to be in worse shape than she was. Angie and her sister then had to restrain Carl Dewberry from finishing the job. *James*, she told everyone, *is clearly going through something*. But after a few days, when James returned—torn up, sad, disappointed in himself— Angie refused to take him back. "I'm so sorry," she told him. "I really do love you. And I hope you do well."

Maureen was as devastated as James, and nothing she could say would change Angie's mind.

Angie, too, would be depressed for a while. The breakup was difficult in part because she and James shared so many friends. But the most difficult part was this: she really *did* love him. And drawing the line was an act of love for him, as it was for herself. In later years, she would think about the James she adored, especially whenever she'd hear that song he'd made, speaking to Angela with a voice that sounded like water.*

James spent more time in the strip club. He was spiraling. T3 had been dating Angie's best friend Tamika. Both women worked at Buddy's Pizza on McNichols and Conant; after their shift, sometimes they'd bring pies over to Que.D's house on Yonka, which he now shared with T3, and hang out. One evening, when the girls weren't there, James burst through the door, Proof at his side. They both carried pistols, and James brandished his briefly, audibly cocking the gun.

"I heard you was talking to Angie," he told Que.D.

T3 watched, dumbstruck. James and Angie hadn't been together in a while. But somehow James had gotten it into his head that Que.D and Angie were a thing and worked himself into a lather about it—probably Proof souping him up, T3 thought. *Anything for a laugh.*

Que.D kept his cool. He reminded James that he and T3 had been friendly with Angie since high school, and that they had hung out only a few times recently. He reminded James that he knew very well how he felt about Angie. And he reminded James that they were cousins. *How could you think I would do something like that to you? How could you believe someone else's word over mine?* Que.D could tell that James had come to his senses, but he was still talking tough to save face for Proof.

The two visitors left shortly thereafter. But James knew he'd fucked up in a major way. They were men now, and if James didn't make it right, he understood his cousin well enough to know that Que.D would have to. Later that night, James returned with Frank at his side to apologize. And Que.D, whose life had just been threatened in his own home, forgave him.

* The piece of music James sampled is the first few seconds of Keni Burke's "Risin' to the Top," and the song he built from it is Slum Village's "Keep It On."

F or the people in his inner circle, James's volatility had become a
normal part of dealing with him. But the way that both family and
friends indulged James's desires and tiptoed around his moods sometimes enabled his worst impulses. James would get angry, say some of the
foulest shit, and next he'd act like whatever had happened had never happened at all, offering to treat you to a meal or take you for a ride somewhere. Even before James had ever become a star producer, his friends
accepted this behavior. No one argued with James; he was the boss. For
some, their tolerance was rooted in the fear of getting cut off from the
best beats in Detroit and a possible career in music.

But others, like Que.D, had an understanding of James that tran-
scended the transactional. To know James was to experience his generosity; to catch, by proximity, his abundance mentality. To Baatin, hearing
James laugh at a joke was often funnier than the joke itself. The way
Que.D figured it, if James had never cussed you out, you weren't really
family. Despite James's rages, Que.D had an abiding sympathy for his
cousin. Those feelings came into focus for him one day when he phoned
James, wanting to hang out.

"I'm working," James said. "But if you want to come through, come
through."

When Que.D showed up at the basement, he found James, standing
immobile over his machines, his head in his hands.

"What's going on?" Que.D asked.

"I got so many fuckin' remixes to do, I don't know what I'ma do."
James gave him a list of tasks that artists and labels had contracted him
for, and the dates they were due. "Gotta get this shit done, though."

James had just put five tracks on Tribe's fourth album, *Beats, Rhymes
and Life*; it had been their first album to hit #1 on the pop charts. He had
produced the lead-off single under the aegis of the Ummah. He put a
track on Busta Rhymes's multiplatinum debut album. He had produced
the title track for De La Soul's newest album, *Stakes Is High*, which had
become an anthem about the spiritual corruption of hip-hop as it moved
toward the mainstream. Through it all, he had developed a penchant for

big, deep bass lines that carried a great deal of melody; pitting delicate harmonies against ferocious drums; and in songs like "Runnin'" and "Word Play" and "Still Shining" he continued to play with offness and error. James had found his sound. For Jay Dee the producer, 1996 had been a breakout year. He'd even received his first national press when *Vibe* magazine sent the writer Jefferson Mao to interview him while he record shopped at the Roosevelt Hotel, and ran a full-page feature on him in the June issue accompanied by a photo of James flanked by his Ummah brethren Q-Tip and Ali.

But Que.D realized that the success had brought a great weight down on James. He was carrying not only his own hopes, but those of his family and his friends, who were all proud of him and invested in his success. Dewitt had recently retired, and James's generosity made that transition easier. T3 and Baatin were still waiting for Slum Village's shot. Now Frank and Derrick were trying to rhyme, too. Meanwhile, some folks who had helped James along the way, like Cricket and Amp, felt left behind. Even Que.D had started to rap and was waiting for his turn. But in that moment, looking at James, Que.D wasn't thinking about himself. He just wished that there was something he could do to relieve the pressure. James needed help, but he rarely let anybody help him.

I t was Killa Ghanz who gave James that "baby" 9 mm pistol to carry as he moved around Detroit with his nice car and clothes and jewelry. The gun brought him protection and trouble in equal measure.

James and Frank were in the Lexus, on their way back from the car wash, when a state trooper forced them into the parking lot of a convenience store. The two cops searched the car and found James's loaded pistol in the center console. It was a Friday, and James and Frank spent the weekend together in jail. Come Monday, Frank was freed and James went to court on a charge of gun possession, accompanied by a lawyer referred by Micheline Levine. James's attorney found so many procedural errors that the judge let James off with several days' worth of community service, after which his record would be expunged. The police kept his Lexus as collateral.

Frank drove James to his service duty at a state correctional facility every day in Frank's sister's drop-top Jaguar. Inside, James didn't have to do much in the way of work, in part because he was recognized as Jay Dee. The police soon relinquished his Lexus, but James had already bought another car just to spite them: an Atlantis Blue 1998 second-generation P38A Range Rover, the Fiftieth Anniversary Limited Edition with eighteen-inch chrome rims.

Two things happened as a result of this incident: The two cops who had arrested James began stalking him, pulling up at the house on McDougall and Nevada at odd times, a pattern of harassment that would continue for years. And Frank Bush, after nearly fifteen years, finally won the respect of Dewitt Yancey.

William "Fuzzy" West met James when West promoted 1st Down's single for Payday Records, and he became James's first "industry" friend. Now that Fuzzy had a full-time job at Warner Bros. Records, he hooked James up with remixes for Warner artists, and James always showed Fuzzy a good time when he came to town. It was on one of these trips, when he took Fuzzy to Tigers, that James fixed his attention on a new dancer, who called herself Babydoll. He could not take his eyes off her thereafter.

She looks like a thick version of Tatyana Ali, James enthused to Frank, referencing the young actress from *The Fresh Prince of Bel-Air*. *You've got to see her.*

Frank came along next time. She was exactly as James described: light-skinned, petite, with big curves and round eyes that narrowed into shining slits when she smiled, which was often.

Her name was Joylette Hunter. She had grown up behind Hitsville, the old Motown headquarters, in the Northwest Goldberg neighborhood that the locals referred to as "Zone 8." Her childhood ended at the age of twelve when her mother, Sherran, died of complications from AIDS. Joylette said goodbye in a tearful homegoing service at her uncle Ricky's church in Conant Gardens, Vernon Chapel AME. Her mother's siblings swept in to care for Joylette and her older sister Janell; but Joy, a willful girl even before she entered adolescence, was the subject of many family meetings. She stayed with Ricky for a year, attending Vernon Chapel on Sundays with her cousins; but Joylette chafed under Ricky's strict house rules, so she went to live with another relative, her aunt Elaine. After Joy graduated from Northwestern High School, she stayed with her sister while she worked a series of dead-end gigs: a clothing store, a bandage factory, and a fast-food restaurant where she was fired for scrapping with a coworker who Joy thought was bullying her. She knew she didn't yet have the skills for a go-getter office job, knew she couldn't live with Janell forever, and knew she needed a path forward. Her godsister, Tiki, had been in her ear since high school, telling her to apply for financial aid so she could go to college. Joy wasn't ready for that. Another friend, who worked at Tigers, presented a quicker route to financial independence: *You're going to make money fast because you're young and cute.* Make money she did, socking it away until she could afford to rent a small apartment of her own on Log Cabin Street and McNichols.

When Joy first danced for James, he was already a "bar guy" at Tigers, known to the dancers and the DJs alike. His face was still scratched up from his fight with Angie. But Joy immediately saw that he wasn't like the rest of her clientele—mostly drug dealers and hooligans. He was nice to her. As James became a faithful customer of hers, she noticed he usually came with his boys, who wore braids and colorful jerseys and baseball caps, and all of whom, James included, drank virgin daiquiris.

"Y'all different," Joy told them as she sipped the double shot of Rémy VSOP that James bought her. "Are y'all a group or something? Y'all look like the Tribe Called Quest."

James's friends—Frank, T3, and Baatin—snickered. Joy had no idea how close to the mark she had come, no idea of who James was, and in any case, didn't care. She wasn't working at the bar to meet men. Customers often made passes at her, and she told them she was married. So when James first slid her his phone number and asked her to call, she didn't. Some weeks later, when he gave her his number again, she ignored it. The third time, however, she called.

"I can't believe it," James said, laughing. "I said, 'If this girl don't call me I ain't never giving her my number again.'" That made Joylette laugh, too.

They went on a double date, to Putt-Putt golf with Frank and one of Joy's homegirls from the Zone. James and Joy kept talking. There was something intriguing about this little guy who seemed to be the center of his crew's attention, who drove a nice car and was the only one of them who ever had any money and was always treating.

"What do you do?" Joy asked.

"I have to show you." James smiled.

"I am *not* dating a drug dealer."

"I don't deal drugs."

Later, on one of his trips to Tigers, she saw him slip a record into the hands of one of the DJs.

"So you're a DJ?" she asked.

"Yes," he said. It wasn't a lie, but it wasn't the whole story, either. By then, she had enough of a sense of the man that they were spending nights together in her barren apartment.

The first time that James brought Joy home to meet the family, his father took his son's new girlfriend into the living room and sang for her.

"DE*WITT*!!" James yelled from the kitchen, mortified.

Maureen was sweet, but somewhat less effusive. After Joy left, she collared Frank: "Where'd *she* come from?" But Maureen already knew, and she didn't like it one bit. Whatever else Joylette Hunter was beyond being a stripper didn't matter to Maureen, because Joy wasn't Angie.

Joylette sensed Maureen's chilliness almost immediately. It took Joy a while longer to understand that her connections to this odd family with the microphone stands in the living room and the kids running around in the basement went back years. She now realized that, as a child in the pews of Vernon Chapel, she'd seen the Yanceys all singing in the choir: James, Earl, and Martha, Maureen and Dewitt. She remembered giggling at Dewitt's hair, which he wore in a floppy process. Her great-aunt

Lillian Kemp Gardner, who hailed from one of Conant Gardens' founding families, had helped hire Maureen to run Vernon Chapel's day
care operation. Joy had known Earl as a kid because his birth father,
Earl Sr., had been friendly with her mother and uncles; and he'd often
bring little Earl over to visit her aunt Marilyn's house when Joy was
there with her cousins. Joy discovered that her grandmother's family
had known Dewitt and his first wife, Alice. Joy had other connections
to James's world, too. One of her best friends from the Zone, Sharonda,
was Proof's girl.

But after several months of dating, Joy still had little reference for
her new boyfriend's profession; that is, until the day she came home to
a strange message on her answering machine. She phoned Tiki: "You've
got to hear this. *Q-Tip* just called for James."

Joy's cluelessness about James's career and her indifference to his
showbiz connections were part of her appeal for James, as was his non-
chalance about her line of work for Joy. When he picked her up from
her shift at Tigers in his truck, he pointedly played D'Angelo as he sang,
"You're my lady." On nights when she wasn't working, she'd hear the
vibrations of beats and bass growing louder outside her window as he
neared her place: *There's James.* When he went to lay his head down at
night, more often it was in her bed. When he woke up in the morning,
he stayed and talked to her. He got her a cell phone, and when he went
on his way, he checked in. When they were together, he wasn't Jay Dee
and she wasn't Babydoll. She called him "Yancey." He called her "my Joy."

Detroit radio didn't play much hip-hop, and what little they did
veered toward the West Coast "G-funk" of producers like Dr. Dre.
Thus Jay Dee was unknown among Detroit's average hip-hop consumers
but a celebrity within the city's smaller, East Coast beats-and-rhymes-
oriented collective. In that community, no one did more to champion Jay
Dee's work as the pride of Detroit than DJ House Shoes.

They met in 1994 when James walked into Street Corner Music,
where Shoes worked in exchange for product. Shoes watched James
thumb through the bins with a sense of purpose, select a record, listen

to it on the store turntable, and make a quiet rhythm with his mouth, composing—Shoes realized—a beat inside his head. Shoes struck up a conversation, and James Yancey invited him into his car to hear some of his finished tracks. *Pete Rock on steroids*, Shoes thought.

They had a lot of people in common, including Proof, who was like a big brother to Shoes. Shoes already knew James's Conant Gardens crew: Baatin, the kid in the Chinese hat tearing up the dance floor at Saint Andrew's alongside James's cousin, Que.D; and Waajeed, who sometimes sat on the stage and took photos.

Shoes occasionally visited the basement on McDougall and James's tiny room in the back of R. J. Rice's recording studio, often bringing records for James to sample. He became an avid collector of James's beat tapes, and of his tracks and remixes for established hip-hop acts. With James's blessing, Shoes pressed up a vinyl EP of Jay Dee's unreleased remixes for acts like D'Angelo, De La Soul, and Busta Rhymes—the first time the name Jay Dee appeared with top billing on any release. But the collection he assembled with the greatest zeal were demos and bootlegged live performances of James's group, Slum Village. With James's busy schedule, sometimes he would perform with T3 and Baatin, and sometimes he wouldn't, but whenever Slum took the stage at the Shelter or the Hip Hop Shop, the group projected an almost punk-rock energy over James's slamming beats: Baatin and T3 bumping chests and leaping off speakers. Shoes played their songs from cassette tapes during his sets at Saint Andrew's Hall and on *Beats & Breaks*, his radio show at college station WHFR. One song, "The Look of Love," had been dubbed from tape-to-tape around Detroit. When Slum performed it months later at Saint Andrew's, a hundred people screamed every lyric along with them. Q-Tip may have overlooked Slum Village, but Shoes knew that they had a rabid base in Detroit, people who were waiting to buy something, if only there were something to buy.

When Jay Dee dropped by WHFR in late 1996, Shoes announced on air: "We've got the Ummah in the house!"—a subtle dig at the arrangement James had made with his mentor that, in Shoes's mind, shrouded the contributions of the person who actually did the bulk of the beats. James was philosophical about it: "People think I'm getting messed

around, or whatever. But everyone is all good. I'm getting a lot of work."
The conversation returned to Detroit's homegrown scene, and to Slum
Village. James announced that Slum would be releasing something on
their own in the new year, and that he was happy that hip-hop in Detroit
was "getting some unity."

James's words were barely out of his mouth when several unsigned
MCs entered behind him. As James, now Detroit's most prominent hip-
hop figure, pushed back from the microphone, he gave a supportive pound
to one of them, Proof's white buddy from the Hip Hop Shop, Eminem.

The only reason that James could promise a new release from Slum
Village is that his partners had finally lost patience with him. It had
been more than four years since the Hoops situation went south. James
had been producing for Q-Tip and the Ummah for a couple of years.
While T3 and Baatin waited, Proof had convinced his Funky Cowboys
partner James to do an album's worth of songs for his group, 5 Elementz,
and the guys in "5 Ela" were rubbing T3 and Baatin's noses in it. *Time for
FC, none for SV.*

T3 had been truly happy for James's success. But James made it hard
sometimes. Last year, he and Baatin went to the basement to visit James
just after their friend landed his publishing deal—for Ephcy Music, pronounced "FC" no less, again not enough SV. They were super broke, but
James sat on the floor counting stacks of hundred-dollar bills right in
front of them. He had taken them to the strip club later and plied them
with cash, but said: "You better tip this stripper with it. Don't put it in
your pocket!" James had been generous in giving them the experience of
having money to burn. T3 and Baatin could have used the experience
of having money, period.

T3 didn't necessarily feel entitled to a piece of James's success; but
then again, he *did* feel some kind of way about James's first big hit, "Runnin.'" T3 had found the sample and produced the first version of the beat.
James had remade it, put it on the Pharcyde record, gotten paid for his
work, but shared nothing, not even the credit. What's more, T3 was tired
of James's little power trips and dick moves. Sometimes, when James

would invite him to come through, T would arrive at the house only to have Maureen greet him at the door: *James ain't here right now.*

The person who got pissed enough to do something about James's neglect of Slum Village was Waajeed. He was studying illustration at Detroit's College for Creative Studies at the time and had no real designs on being a performer, but he felt a sense of urgency on behalf of T3 and Baatin. Like they did in the old days, Waajeed called them all to a meeting, and James finally agreed to work on their project, with a caveat: he didn't have time to sit and make an album's worth of beats for them. Whatever rhymes T3 and Baatin had, they would spit to a barren click track. With the click playing in their headphones, T3 and Baatin dumped every verse they had memorized into James's crappy microphone or—when they needed an extra one—into a pair of headphones plugged into the microphone jack.

Soon James got into the act, and the tensions they had been feeling toward each other found release in their lyrics. First, James aimed at his partners, rhyming that he was sick of them "*poppin up at my crib, all unannounced and shit.*" T3 responded in his verse with sly references to his uncredited work on James's first hit: "*Counterfeit ni**as be "Runnin'"* / *Tryin' to take shit or money that wasn't yours in the first place,*" delivered by T3 in a devil-may-care rhythmic loop-de-loop. It was an imaginative way to have an argument.

James started matching beats to their prerecorded rhymes. Phat Kat and 5 Elementz came through for some guest verses, and James gave shout-outs to House Shoes and his partner Beej in their crew 31 Flavors. He took Slum to R. J.'s studio to rerecord some songs in higher fidelity. Within a week, they'd generated almost two dozen tracks.

It was Waajeed who suggested to T3 and Baatin that they just put the album out themselves. They pooled some money, including funds from Waajeed's student loan. Waajeed took photos on a disposable camera, designed the cover, and they all went to Kinko's in the middle of the night to print up several hundred cassette labels and inserts featuring the cover art and track listing. Then they adjourned to T3 and Que.D's place to cut and peel the stickers and slide the inserts into clear jewel cases. They dubbed the cassettes, one at a time, on a high-speed deck they borrowed from James.

In early 1997, under the aegis of Waajeed's "El-Azim Waajeed Recordings" and T3's "Donut Boy Recordings"—likely a nod to the donuts from the Dutch Girl bakery on the corner of 7 Mile and Woodward that fueled their sessions—Slum Village released their first album. They called it *Fan-Tas-Tic*.

E ven the track list stuttered. The title song appeared four times, the same lyrics atop a different musical bed, reflecting James's habit of relentless revision. The album included "The Look of Love," buffered by a live recording of the song from that magic night at Saint Andrew's, plus two more remixes of the song. Some tracks were polished at R. J.'s studio, and others raw right from the basement. Some were snippets, fading up and down to capture pieces of verses that James found interesting, like "Hoc N Pucky."

Fan-Tas-Tic, the title itself broken into threes, presented Slum Village's perfect *three-ness*: James a smooth, deep baritone; T3 a slippery tenor; Baatin the acrobatic high-end. But they also had *one-ness*: while other rap groups took turns on the microphone, Slum Village often chanted in unison, staying yoked even over broken words and beats, their fused voices becoming another rhythmic element.

Four songs in particular revealed a striking evolution in technique for Jay Dee.

In "I Don't Know," T3 came up with the idea of interspersing their rhymes with little vocal samples of James Brown, a throwback to a 1988 song by DJ Jazzy Jeff & the Fresh Prince called "Brand New Funk." James lifted some of Brown's best-known ad-libbed vocalizations—"One! Two! Three! Four!" "Funky!" "Do it!" "Watch me!"—and triggered them in time with his rhyme, James Brown "finishing" each line for the three of them:

> You could ask my man, T ["THREE!"]
> I ain't the ["ONE!"] . . .
> No time for acting ["FUNKY!"] with me
> You best believe that you won't ["DO IT!"]

James set these rhymes over a sample from the Brazilian guitarist Baden Powell's "É Isso Aí." The song, in its natural state, skipped along at a brisk tempo, counted in sixes. But here's what James did: he slowed the song down to one-half of its speed. And in slowing it down, he found that the tiny imperfections in Powell's guitar playing elongated, revealing themselves. Then James jammed the sixes of the sample against the fours of the steady hip-hop beat. Last, he triggered the Brazilian sample just slightly before the downbeat of every other measure, creating a funk-like defiance of expectation. No one had ever created a groove like it.

James again decelerated elements to reveal error in "Players." He took a song from 1975 called "Clair" by Singers Unlimited—featuring the tight a cappella "vocalese" harmonies that the Yancey family practiced in his youth—and slowed it down so that the word "Clair" sounded uncannily like "Player." Beneath chopped, decelerated bits of scatting—*dooooo, dooooo, dooooo, dooooo*—foreboding where they had been gleeful at normal speed, James created a rhythm track lifted from the first seconds of one of the most recognizable songs in all of hip-hop, the very first one: "Rapper's Delight" by the Sugarhill Gang. James grabbed one hit of handclaps and a few hits of a hi-hat, slowed the audio way down, and suddenly it fanned outward in a sloppy mess. "Players" was like the nave at Vernon Chapel, like that last scene from *A Piece of the Action*, the sound of a group of people bringing their hands together but not all at the same time.

"Rock Music (Remix)" evoked James's emotional sense of harmony: two chords—the first dissonant, the second bright—cycling forth and back between melancholy and hope. Within the steady beat beneath, James triggered a subtle, quiet loop of a tambourine that came in and slightly out of alignment with the time grid.*

And in "Things U Do," beneath another bright-to-brooding duality of sampled vibraphone chords, James layered live handclaps that were so disjointed you could hear them "flamming"—different hands coming together, one after another, like a family making a joyful noise, father and daughter, mother and son.

---

* In later iterations of this album, this song is also referred to as "Forth & Back (Rock Music)" and "Forth & Back (Remix)."

L isten to this shit!"

Those were the only clear words that Ahmir "Questlove" Thompson could make out from the voice message sent to his pager by Q-Tip and D'Angelo over the distorted, thumping beats playing behind them.

On tour in Europe with his band the Roots in early 1997, Ahmir called them back at the recording studio from his hotel phone. *What the hell was that?* he asked. Tip and D'Angelo were rocking, they informed him, to the new Slum Village album.

"What's Slum Village?" Ahmir asked.

"Jay Dee's group!"

Q-Tip played the entire first side of the *Fan-Tas-Tic* cassette over the phone for Ahmir, at hotel international rates, running up a bill of more than $300 and getting Ahmir in deep trouble with the Roots' formidable manager, Richard Nichols, who docked the money from his weekly pay. Ahmir decided the expense was worth it.

Since he heard his first Jay Dee beat on tour with the Pharcyde back in 1994, Ahmir had become a superfan, collecting a library of Jay Dee tapes with dozens of tracks. His main connection to that material had been Jay Dee's partners in the Ummah, with whom Ahmir had grown close over the past couple of years as the Roots began working with Q-Tip, D'Angelo, and Raphael Saadiq. That eventually led to a friendship between Ahmir and James, whom he finally greeted at a Tribe recording session at Battery Studios. Several weeks after Ahmir's long-distance call, the Roots played a show in Detroit, and James himself came to pick Ahmir up from the airport in his Range Rover and put a cassette of *Fan-Tas-Tic* into his hand. The album stayed on repeat in Ahmir's headphones and on the Roots tour bus. He played it for everyone in his circle until his partner, Tarik "Black Thought" Trotter, walked away with the tape.

Good, Ahmir thought. *Maybe it will rub off on him.*

The Roots' two founders were in the midst of a creative conflict. When Geffen Records signed the Philadelphia crew in the mid-1990s, the label marketed them as a "hip-hop band," with Black Thought rhyming over beats played by Ahmir on a drum set, rather than breaks sampled and programmed on machines. And though Ahmir was a veritable human jukebox of classic breakbeats, live musicians could never truly replicate the specific timbres and textures of those original records. Thus the hip-hop band had a sound that didn't *sound* like hip-hop, at least to the many DJs and fans who espoused the notion first championed by Run-DMC: *DJs are better than bands. Bands are corny.* The Roots' first major release in 1995, *Do You Want More?!!!??!*, sold only around 170,000 copies, and much of the group's initial praise came from critics *outside* hip-hop's core, many of whom saw the merger of rhyming with traditional instrumentation as a sophisticated evolution from hip-hop's programmed roots. Their manager Richard Nichols and their Geffen A&R exec Wendy Goldstein informed the band that hip-hop DJs complained that the Roots' records blended poorly with the rest of their playlists. DJs wanted *bangers*, and Tarik wanted to rock over those kinds of beats. The Roots—driven by Ahmir's live drumming—sounded like a *jazz* band.

So basically, Ahmir replied, *you're telling me it's my fault.*

Simmering, Ahmir decided that if the feel of a live drummer isn't what fans wanted, then fine. He vowed to become the most rigid, machinelike drummer in response; a human drum loop. On the Roots' second album, *Illadelph Halflife*, the band ditched much of its improvisation, uncut edges, and imperfections for unvarying hip-hop heat.

But here, now, one year later, Ahmir heard Jay Dee making music—on a machine, no less—that sounded very much hip-hop but simultaneously more rhythmically free than he thought possible in the genre. "Beej N Dem" from *Fan-Tas-Tic* was a revelation: a *completely* lopsided beat, played in sixes but somehow counted in fours? Or was it played in fours and counted in sixes? He couldn't go back now, he could only go forward. The question, of course, was *how*. Ahmir "Questlove" Thompson answered that question the best way a musician could:

He sat down behind his drum kit, and he practiced.

The small run of Slum Village cassettes sold out quickly in Detroit. Waajeed designed laminated badges for the crew to carry while they marched around Saint Andrew's Hall selling the cassettes straight out of their backpacks. James sent out copies, and dubs of those made their way into the hands of some of the most influential artists and executives in hip-hop.

Q-Tip had a great deal to do with that circulation. He had initially bypassed Slum Village, the group, in his advocacy of Jay Dee, the producer. But Slum had matured, and he told James that he wanted to sign the crew to his production company, Mr. Incognito, offering to get them a major label deal with EMI Records.

"Tip's gonna call you," James told T3. "And I want you to be the one to say no."

It was a measure of James's increasingly conflicted relationship with his mentor.

James felt indebted to Q-Tip, who had plucked him from obscurity in Detroit and invited him into the inner circle of the Native Tongues collective. The mere runoff from Tip's production work was champagne to James. And yet James felt suppressed. Q-Tip had set the pace for his professional life over the last three years. When he stayed at Tip's house in Jersey, what for Tip was a pleasant cocoon felt to James like isolation, cut off from all the things that fed him at home—his ride, his boys, the strip club, the basement. And as much as James had become crew, there were ways in which he didn't want to participate.

Early in 1997, A Tribe Called Quest was nominated for a couple of Grammy Awards, one for the album and another for the single James produced. James didn't want to go to the ceremony—nothing to wear, he said, and uncomfortable in any case about appearing at a function that was far more mainstream than anything he had ever experienced.

"I don't want to go either!" Tip insisted. "But it's our first time being nominated. The other fellas think it's important. It's an album you worked on. Fuck it, go into my closet, I got fresh shit I haven't even worn!"

James went to the ceremony, hating it. Tribe lost in both categories, and James flew home. When Q-Tip called for him in the basement to smooth things over, Baatin took the phone and took up for his partner: "You be tryin' to *son* James!"

"I'm not even *talking* to you," Tip replied. "Put *him* on the phone."

"Look, *Jon*," Baatin replied, escalating things by using Q-Tip's "government" name. James grabbed the phone before things got out of hand, apologizing for his friend. But Baatin had internalized, as many of his comrades had, a bit of James's frustration with his Ummah situation.

Brotherhood, or at least Q-Tip's particular conception of it, was alien to James. For Tribe, it had been an all-encompassing ethos: transparency, togetherness, consideration, deliberation, negotiation. So when James went and did things on his own, like his publishing deal, he may not have realized that he was violating trust. And for Tip, it was about the trust, not the money.

"Why didn't you say anything?" Tip asked him when he discovered the PolyGram deal. "I'm trying to build this thing for all of us. I'm not *trying* to son you. But you put me in a position to feel like I am when you do something and you don't disclose it."

James didn't want this kind of brotherhood. He wanted control. Nothing elicited his desires and stirred his discontent more than the Janet Jackson situation.

The story began in early 1997, when Mike Ross at Delicious Vinyl sought an Ummah remix for a Brand New Heavies single, "Sometimes," hoping to get a great Jay Dee beat and a verse from Q-Tip as well. The track was an exemplar of the emergent Jay Dee sound: sampled bits of staccato Fender Rhodes from a record by the Louis Hayes Group, scrambled into a completely different harmonic progression; set against cracking drums; and propelled by a melodic bass line, played freehand and far behind the beat. The Ummah remix was so breathtaking that Ross cut a new version of the video and made that the one he promoted to radio.

Terry Lewis, one of Janet Jackson's longtime producers, heard the record as he was leaving a Timberwolves basketball game in Minneapolis. He nearly crashed his car into the guardrail when his staff producer Alex Richbourg reached suddenly from the back seat to turn up the volume. *What the fuck is this?!* Richbourg shouted. They called Ray Seville, who DJed for the station, and by the time they returned to Flyte Tyme studios they had the Ummah remix in hand. Richbourg ran the record in to Lewis's partner Jimmy Jam, who had already heard the record on the radio in Los Angeles and called in to find out what it was. Within minutes they began composing a track of their own; working, as they often did, to evoke the feel of contemporary records they liked; the mimicking method was, in fact, how they had remained relevant as producers well into the hip-hop era, while their former boss, Prince, had not. Richbourg, who began as a hip-hop producer in New York working with the Trackmasters, set Jam up with an MPC and a keyboard. The song that resulted, "Got 'Til It's Gone," built around a vocal sample of Joni Mitchell's "Big Yellow Taxi," was a conscious re-creation of Jay Dee's groove, particularly the lagging bass line. And because the connection to the Ummah was so explicit, and because Janet Jackson was friendly with Q-Tip, Jam and Lewis asked Tip to contribute a verse, just as he had for "Sometimes."

"Got 'Til It's Gone," released in the middle of 1997, became a huge critical and commercial success for Janet Jackson, and garnered her a Grammy Award for the accompanying music video. But its origin story would be debated for years thereafter. Terry Lewis and Jimmy Jam were credited as producers, but because the song featured Q-Tip and sounded like an Ummah record, many people in the hip-hop world assumed that the Ummah had produced it. And these feelings were fed in the months and years thereafter by James, who began telling friends a very different tale: that he and the Ummah had produced the track, that Jam and Lewis had bought it from them for a huge sum, and that a nondisclosure agreement prevented the Ummah from telling the truth about it. For years thereafter, Jimmy Jam explained his production process in detail, while James would remain cagey in interviews. No one on the Ummah side would contradict James's story publicly until Q-Tip's 2009 interview with Dutch music website Moovmnt: the track was simply homage to Jay Dee, with a guest spot from Tip.* However, James's work on a remix of the song, credited to The Ummah and called "Jay Dee's Revenge Mix," is not in dispute.

James's tale had the same ring of fabulousness as Dewitt's claim to

---

* Though Que.D claims to have heard this track in James's basement studio in some form, none of the people I queried in James's inner circle actually witnessed him working on it. James told T3 a modified story: that he had composed the bass line of the song, but not the whole track. Micheline Levine, who would have been involved in any Ummah business dealing, recalls no fee or nondisclosure agreement. No one whom I have interviewed who was indisputably involved in the creation of this song has contradicted Jam and Lewis's story. Q-Tip is on the record in his Moovmnt.com interview corroborating Jam and Lewis's story and denying that it is an Ummah production (for that link, and for a more detailed origin story from Jimmy Jam, please see Reporter's Notes and Sources).

have ghostwritten "It's a Shame," but both served similarly as gospel for people close to the father and the son. In both stories, for the elder and younger Yancey, there was the feeling of being at the mercy of more powerful people in the record business. James seethed at how brazen other producers could be in lifting his material, like when the Danish producers Soulshock and Karlin resampled the elements from "Y?"—one of his Pharcyde album cuts—and recombined them into a posthumous gold hit single for 2Pac, "Do for Love." Now his own partner, Q-Tip, had walked into a room with Terry Lewis and Jimmy Jam and emerged with a guest spot on a platinum hit that sounded like Jay Dee made it. And if Jay Dee had made it, what would it matter? James couldn't be "Jay Dee" anymore anyway.

The very construction of the Ummah as a noble one-for-all, all-for-one group credit situation meant that James's work and credit were essentially obscured as a matter of policy, just as Tip had long subsumed his own identity as a producer within A Tribe Called Quest. That might have worked for Tip, who was already a star, but it was an impediment to James making a name for himself. Despite the two producers sharing a soft-spoken nature, James was quiet, not humble; cynical, not noble. He was Detroit, both in terms of his artistic sophistication *and* his money mindset. He was the grandson of Thomas "Suge" Hayes and the son of Maureen; the nephew of Geno Yancey, and the son of Dewitt. He was the latest in a long line of hustlers, a son of Detroit who now looked at his own father's derailed recording career as a cautionary tale. How did all that work go unnoticed, uncredited, unpaid? *It's a shame, indeed.* That was *not* going to happen to him. He was going to get his shine *and* his money.

The person who spoke James's language in this moment was R. J. Rice.

Throughout James's rise as a producer, Rice had kept his studio open to James but professed indifference to his career. R. J. had developed a bustling production business—including hosting sessions for a local ingénue, Aaliyah Haughton, and her producer from Virginia, Timbaland. To R. J., James was still a kid. But after spying T3 and Baatin's exasperation with James, seeing James's frustration with the Ummah, and then, finally, hearing the buzz around Slum Village after the release of *Fan-Tas-Tic*, R. J. offered to find a major label deal for them. After discussing things with his wife, R. J. set aside $30,000 and began paying each of the three of them a $3,000 monthly stipend on good faith. He didn't have them sign a contract because he knew that contracts were slippery things; and he also knew how James's mind worked. He couldn't chase him.

R. J. reached out to Bert Padell, the legendary New York–based accountant and dealmaker to the rap stars, the man who matchmade Sean "Puffy" Combs's Bad Boy label with Clive Davis and Arista Records. Deputized to shop Slum Village, Padell shortly garnered real interest from a number of labels, including a solid offer from John McClain at A&M Records—the executive who had signed Janet Jackson to that label, jumped to Interscope to forge their partnership with Dr. Dre's Death Row Records, and then returned to A&M for a $1 million per year salary.

Q-Tip had a bad feeling about this arrangement, and said so in his last-minute plea to James. *If you want to go over there to A&M with R. J., fine*, he said. *But they don't know how to do hip-hop.* Nevertheless, James needed to have some part of his career outside his mentor's influence. The three members of Slum Village decided to take A&M's offer. They signed through R. J.'s imprint, Barak Records, five years after their Hoops deal fell through. Rice's nephew, Tim Maynor, became the group's manager. T3 and Baatin now had some cash of their own. And James now had a budget to record their album, new Alesis ADAT digital multitrack recorders that R. J. purchased for James's basement studio on McDougall, and his own Akai MPC3000. They celebrated, marking the first day of their recording on February 10, 1998.

J oylette's time at Tigers was relatively brief, less than a year. Maureen gave Joy a job at her day care operation, where Joy joined Martha Yancey in looking after the infants and toddlers. But that didn't last long. The money wasn't enough, and Joy didn't like being up under James's mother like that every day anyway, so she got a job selling shoes at a suburban Nordstrom, where a white coworker named John turned out to be a huge Slum Village fan. After a few months, she enrolled part-time at Wayne State University, studying computer science; and she took a job working at a nonprofit church youth program, The Safe Center.

She and James found a townhouse together just outside Detroit, on Rensselaer Street in Oak Park. Joy sensed that Maureen wasn't happy about James following her out to the suburbs. Joy wasn't stripping anymore; she figured Maureen's discomfort had to be about something else.

Still, the rest of the family seemed to warm to Joy, and the family was expanding. Martha, too, had a new relationship. She'd met a gregarious young man from the East Side, Maurice "Bobo" Lamb, a Navy veteran who performed stand-up on the small local comedy circuit. Maurice even joined the family's bowling team, playing every Sunday at the Bonanza Lanes off 10 Mile Road; and that's where he got to know James, who often stopped by to watch. James invited his sister and her boyfriend to a double date with him and Joy, out to dinner at Mountain Jack's restaurant on 16 Mile Road. Martha and Maurice both liked her— Joy was fun to be around.

Joy fell in with many of James's routines, looking for CDs while he dug through crates of vinyl at record stores, eating Mongolian barbecue, and going to movies. James could be spontaneous. In the summertime, they'd stop at roadside carnivals, hit the rides, and take pictures together in the photo booth; or spend a few hours meandering through the Detroit Zoo. Joy was teaching herself how to cook, and asked James what he wanted to eat. "Anything but chicken," is what he said, because it's what his father wanted every day from Maureen. He liked Joy's sloppy joes, and wanted them at least once a week. In their quiet times, James would talk about things that he rarely told anyone else. They talked about a future together: getting married, having kids after they turned thirty. They had lots of time.

Slum Village worked on their new album from the winter and into the spring of 1998, tracking music in the Conant Gardens basement; adding vocals and mixing at either R. J.'s studio—where Young R. J., now in high school, watched James finish some tracks in minutes while spending hours perfecting rhythms on others—or at Studio A in nearby Dearborn, where the owner and engineer Todd Fairall marveled at James's prowess behind the boards—tweaking the sounds of elements as he recorded them, running samples through sound effect devices like flangers and even a wah-wah effect, a Pete Rock trick. Usually when art- ists get a major label deal, they feel pressure to conform. James was get- ting more experimental.

It helped that their point man at A&M Records was a true fan. VP of A&R Junior Regisford, a New York native, touted them on the label's Hollywood lot as "next-level Tribe." He loved their distinctive chanting; and as a former drummer, he dug Jay Dee's "flammed" rhythms. Regis- ford also represented the rapper Kurupt—whom John McClain had plucked from Dr. Dre's camp and given a solo deal—and asked him to contribute a verse to one of Slum's songs. But Regisford realized he didn't have to make connections, because James and Slum Village already had the kind of goodwill that got them easy cameos from Busta Rhymes, Pete Rock, and, significantly, Q-Tip.

While James had been building with Slum in Detroit, things had been falling apart for his mentor. On the morning of February 9, 1998, a fire ripped through Q-Tip's home in New Jersey, destroying the re- cording studio where James collaborated with A Tribe Called Quest and decimating Q-Tip's record collection. It also erased some of the progress Tribe and James had made on their new album, *The Love Movement*, which Q-Tip declared would be their last. More than the damage, the fire confirmed Tip's sense that the first chapter of his creative life was coming to a close. Leaving Tribe, losing Slum, the blaze burned away his disap- pointments and his attachments. *I can walk away from Tribe, from music altogether, and still be happy, still be myself.* So when Q-Tip flew to De- troit to drop some beats and a verse for a Slum Village song called "Hold Tight," there was no bitterness. Instead Q-Tip offered a benediction to all his brothers: Ali and Phife, D'Angelo and Busta; and a purposeful pass- ing of the torch to a new group as he freed himself, declaring, *I'ma leave it in the hands of the Slum now.*

———

B y late 1998, A&M Records printed advance cassettes of the album Slum Village was calling *Fantastic, Vol. 2*, joining some leaked demos already circulating among the small, devout ring of Slum Village and Jay Dee fans.

But for James's peers like Questlove and D'Angelo, already adherents of Jay Dee's loose rhythmic feel, what they heard on these tracks was something altogether new, and something that would, and did, change the trajectory of their professional lives.

The music had started to limp.

8.
Dilla Time

The E-mu SP-1200 had served James well. He had launched his career and made classics on it, like "Runnin'" and "Stakes Is High." He'd done much of it on borrowed equipment. But when it came time to spend money on his own drum machine, he bought an Akai MPC3000, the update to Roger Linn's signature series.

There were a few good reasons to switch from the SP to the MPC. He'd first learned to program at Amp Fiddler's place on the earlier version, the MPC60. The MPC sampled in stereo, not mono. Its memory could be jacked up to more than five minutes of sampling time, while the SP's remained at ten seconds. It had great filtering and other ways to manipulate sound. It *looked* cooler. But most important, its clock was created by the master watchmaker of music machines.

"In my view, sequencers have evolved to a point where they are now a legitimate instrument on their own," Roger Linn wrote to his users in the owner's manual. "Many of today's musicians could be better described as sequencer players."

James may have never cracked that manual or read Linn's words, but he epitomized Linn's ideal. James was a sequencer player, playing with the idea of time in his music. He'd already cultivated several important techniques: *decelerating* samples to exaggerate their timing errors and make them lag against the other sounds that were glued to the stiff sequencer clock; or turning off that "glue," the timing correct function, and *playing freehand*, sometimes placing sounds one by one, exactly where he "felt" them; and he also began *displacing* sounds by sampling and chopping them in ways that altered their position in time.

But James's return to the MPC was significant because he realized that this machine allowed him to actually *program* that displacement and manipulate time in a way that the SP did not.

The E-mu SP-1200 copied Roger Linn's swing feature—which allowed programmers to express time in uneven intervals—except for one crucial omission. On an SP, when you applied a particular swing percentage to a segment of music, all the sounds in that sequence would be moved by that particular amount. If you chose 66 percent swing, *all* the elements—the kick, the snare, the hi-hats, the other samples—would be shifted together by 66 percent. Imagine the time grid as a rubber band, with the swung notes glued to it. As the rubber band stretches, all the elements move with it.

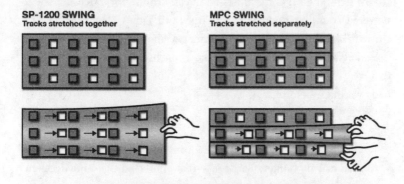

SP-1200 SWING
Tracks stretched together

MPC SWING
Tracks stretched separately

But Linn's machines were more sophisticated than that. The MPC sequencer allowed users to set the degree of swing *for each musical element individually*. For example, you could make one sound's swing barely noticeable, another a shuffle, another really severe, and another not swung at all.

Imagine now the time grid as a stack of individual rubber bands, one for each musical element—the kick drum notes on one, the snare notes on another, the hi-hats on still another. Each rubber band can be stretched a different amount, or not at all.

And Linn added another feature to give programmers even more control, the "Shift Timing" function, which allowed users to manually nudge notes either forward or backward in small fractions or "ticks" of time. Imagine those little rubber bands again, now having the ability to slightly scroll each band and the notes glued to it, forward or backward.

MPC SHIFT TIMING
Events mover earlier/later

What Linn had created on his MPC machines was a system of controlled timing that could be loosened in ways that yielded more consistent results than if, say, a programmer were simply playing patterns freehand, without the timing correct features.

By 1998, the MPC machines had been around for a decade. They'd powered countless popular songs. But until James Dewitt Yancey recorded *Fantastic, Vol. 2*, no one had tapped the true potential hidden in these key MPC features: not to make a machine beat sound more like that of a "real" drummer, but to make a kind of rhythm that no drummer had ever made before.

Fantastic, Vol. 2 began with a new song—a tribute to the neighborhood called "Conant Gardens"—that employed the same deceleration technique James had been using on *Fan-Tas-Tic*. He slowed down a guitar riff from the 1974 Little Beaver song "A Tribute to Wes," exaggerating the swing and the little timing idiosyncrasies in the hi-hat phrase behind it. So too did "Fall in Love," crafted from a decelerated piece of Gap Mangione's "Diana in the Autumn Wind," the slowed notes of its organ riff lagging behind James's drums.

But on at least six different tracks, James did something new: he shifted the timing of the snare drum, *rushed it*, so that it would hit before the actual backbeat, before the listener expected it, about sixty-five milliseconds early—more than double the "offness" of a mistake or a "flam." That small adjustment was big enough to cause a cascade of rhythmic consequences. The early snare defied the expectations set up by the pulse of the hi-hat. It was almost as if the hi-hat was saying, "We're going to go fifty-five miles per hour," and the snare came through right after and said, "No, seventy miles per hour." But the hi-hat pulse thereafter didn't speed up to the snare's pace, and neither did the kick drum. The kick and snare, usually equidistant from each other on the grid, now established a short-long-short-long pattern: *swing time*. The hi-hat, at the same time, kept even: *straight time*. So now there were two time-feels fighting each other: *straight* and *swung*.

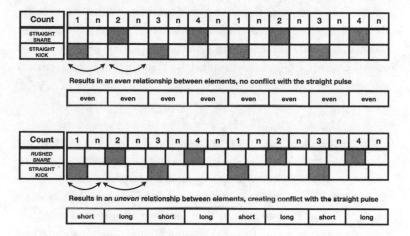

Results in an *even* relationship between elements, no conflict with the straight pulse

Results in an *uneven* relationship between elements, creating conflict with the straight pulse

The effect was disorienting in a way that listening to something simply straight or solely swung wasn't. It was *elastic*—like the feeling of going faster, then slower, then faster, then slower, but never actually varying one's speed. Because of the brain's tendency to latch on to the kick and snare as the steady bedrock of a beat, the elasticity of the snare had the effect of making the hi-hats seem swung when they weren't.

To that rushed snare, James and his collaborators added more disorientation. In "2U4U" and "Go Ladies," James, T3, and Baatin added handclaps—sometimes fighting, sometimes flamming with the swung snare. On "Get Dis Money," James sampled a piece of Herbie Hancock's "Come Running to Me," Hancock's vocoderized, cyborg melody descending through a seven-note scale over seven measures, a more severe version of the odd, three-bar loops that his mentor Q-Tip liked to use; James jammed those sevens against a beat based on fours, the result an endless downward spiral where verses and choruses started in unpredictable places. In "Once Upon a Time," featuring a verse from Pete Rock, James pitted every element against each other. The hi-hat established the pulse, the snare pushed it one way, while two other elements pulled it in other directions: a hand-played bass line and a sample of James playing a kalimba, an African finger piano—working like a music box without the wind-up sequencer—the hollow sounds of its metallic tines falling all over the place.

The final ingredients in this rhythmic commotion were the most dynamic percussive elements of all: the voices of T3, James, and Baatin—syncopating, stuttering, breathing, using their mouths to produce sounds as well as words, using rhymes as much for their rhythmic consequences as their wit.

F*antastic, Vol. 2* began a new phase and a new body of work for James Dewitt Yancey—which also included dozens upon dozens of instrumental beats circulated among friends and industry professionals in what James called "batches"—in which he used the MPC3000 to displace rhythmic elements and then set them against each other.* In these tracks some elements would be straight, some slightly swung, and some severely; some elements played freehand and others "quantized" to the grid. The rushed snare was only one of many techniques he used; in James Yancey's world, any element could be slid around to mess with time, and the degrees of that temporal sabotage varied from song to song. The new techniques represented a breakthrough, a destination at which he arrived with the aid of some important coconspirators and mentors: Amp Fiddler, his first teacher; R. J. Rice, who gave him space, tools, and time; Q-Tip, the father of James's style; Pete Rock, the soul sampler; T3 and Baatin, masters of rhythmic rhyme.

* In particular, Jay Dee's 1998 beat tape, sometimes called "Another Batch," shows a marked turn toward this new time-feel.

This approach did have a name. Between brothers, James and T3 called it "simple-complex": *If you listen to it casually, it sounds like one thing, something whole; but if you listen more carefully, you hear that it isn't whole at all—there are many different things going on at the same time. It's simple: it sounds good, and the rhythm is countable. But it's complex: it's really not a straight rhythm. It's simple-complex.*

As this predictable/unpredictable rhythm made its way outward among James's mentors, collaborators, and admirers, they started giving it their own names: that "Jay Dee swing" or "bounce" or "hump," designations that would shift to terms like "Detroit swing" a few years later when some of his protégés began using the time-feel. It was also a kind of funk: the defiance of expectation, the rigidity of the elements nailed to the grid juxtaposed with the expressiveness of the elements that weren't.

But what was actually going on in those Jay Dee tracks would continue to defy people's attempts to define it as much as the rhythms defied their expectations, because what was actually going on was more complex than simple swing.

For the last hundred years, the pulse of popular music has presented itself in two ways: even and uneven, straight and swung.

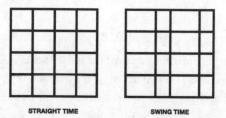

STRAIGHT TIME   SWING TIME

As we designed machines to make music and keep musical time, designers found they needed to accommodate both of these time-feels, and the continuum between the two. One machine, quite incidentally, allowed programmers to juxtapose straight and swung rhythms simultaneously, in ways that were heretofore impossible. And one programmer in particular was the first to make a body of work and a new aesthetic out of that feature, in ways that were heretofore inaccessible to the minds of other beatmakers and musicians. In doing so, James Dewitt Yancey cultivated a new time-feel, a third path in rhythm. This time-feel resulted from a machine's ability to turn grid against grid, and from James Yancey's inspiration and willingness to use that feature and nurture its fullest expression. That time-feel arose not from a musical scene, nor from the conservatory, nor from the avant-garde, but from one man using a machine in a basement in Detroit. That time-feel cannot be understood as either straight or swung time. It is not the median or midpoint or gradation between the two. It is the deliberate juxtaposition of multiple expressions of straight and swing time simultaneously, a conscious cultivation of rhythmic friction for maximum musicality and maximum surprise. It is conflicted time. It is Dilla Time.

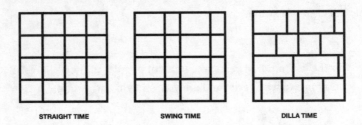

STRAIGHT TIME   SWING TIME   DILLA TIME

R hythmic conflict isn't new.

Dragging or rushing against the pulse goes at least as far back in our popular music as Louis Armstrong, the paragon of that practice. Billie Holiday, as much as if not more than any other musician, was a master of backphrasing, singing behind or ahead of the beat as she saw fit.

Straight time and swing time have indeed collided before. In a famous bit of recorded music, Little Richard's original recording of "Tutti Frutti" from 1955, Richard bangs out one pulse of straight eighth notes while the drummer, Earl Palmer, launches into a simultaneous pulse of swung eighth notes before pulling himself more in line with the piano. The conflict is brief, and subtle, but it is a microcosm of a larger transition at the time between a pop music world dominated by jazz and another that will eventually become rock music, the latter with a straighter feel.

On its own, swing evolved levels of complexity. Unsurprisingly, one of the greatest scientists of swing started his career in Detroit. The drummer Elvin Jones developed a style in the 1950s that, in one sense, reunited swing with its ancestor, polyrhythm. If polyrhythm is like keeping two rhythmic thoughts in your head at the same time, then Elvin Jones had many, many thoughts. Jones could play against one pulse with a second, expressing some or none of the first pulse, all the while keeping both in his head and making the performance as smooth as possible.

Even the elastic feel of Dilla Time has its precedents in jazz. The pianist Erroll Garner, in his 1955 song "Penthouse Serenade," rolls in his piano chords languidly behind his drummer's pulse. As Jason Moran, one of jazz's great contemporary pianists, points out, Garner's right hand would be in one place behind the beat, and his left hand would be in yet another place behind the beat. It was three-dimensional backphrasing, presaging Jay Dee / J Dilla's limping time-feel by four decades. But these moments of rhythmic conflict in traditional music-making were just that: fleeting rather than an ongoing method.

The world of machine music created opportunities for conflict prior to the rise of Jay Dee / J Dilla. In the mid-1990s, Robert Diggs, a producer from Staten Island who called himself the RZA, pioneered a more raw, rough, and low-fidelity sound in his work with the Wu-Tang Clan. Where hip-hop producers before him obsessed with aligning the junctures of loops with the time grid—making everything seamless and perfect—the RZA found charm in rhythmic imprecision; in songs like "Cuttin Heads" by Ol' Dirty Bastard, the RZA didn't seem to care that the sequencer was running too fast for the drum loop of Melvin Bliss's "Synthetic Substitution" to catch up to it. The RZA's aesthetic was more random than cultivated, an artifact of coarse looping.

Timing errors were occasionally an artifact of imperfect machine synchronization caused by tiny delays in their conversations via MIDI. The Nonce's 1995 album *World Ultimate* was filled with those errors. And other hip-hop producers had used their electronic hardware and software to displace notes before, but always for subtle effect, in ways that created rhythmic consonance rather than dissonance.* Jay Dee / J Dilla's methods of rhythmic sabotage were created by deliberate, severe displacement of elements, expressing multiple pulses of straight and swung.

The Jay Dee / J Dilla Technique: Mythology and Reality

James Yancey used a variety of techniques on his machines to achieve rhythmic friction. Yet the prevailing explanation of his methods—and the most misleading—is that his time-feel is exclusively the result of his playing freehand, without timing correct or "quantization."

A sequencer with its correction features defeated is merely a replication device. At its full resolution, it records and reproduces a programmer's input quite faithfully. At that point, a programmer becomes *just a drummer*, and a drummer is only as good as his or her sense of rhythm and reflexes. If J Dilla's methods are reduced to *good reflexes*, then anyone with a drummer's reflexes—when placed in front of a drum machine with the "quantize" function turned off—should produce beats that sound like Dilla's. That is not what happens. What actually happens is a beat that sounds like the reflexes and proclivities of that particular user. Many beatmakers before James Yancey had great reflexes. If the "J Dilla feel" could be achieved simply by turning off timing correct, it stands to reason that another producer might have arrived at that feel long before James Yancey. Nobody did.

The innovations of James Yancey bear the mark of a programmer, not a drummer. The sheer *regularity* with which elements like the rushed snare appear is not the result of error or reflex. It is the unmistakable product of his particular use—or misuse, if you prefer—of the MPC. Dilla had the compulsion to play with time. The MPC created a platform that allowed him to do it in ways not quite possible on the machines he used previously.

---

* Notably, one of the producers who regularly employed Shift Timing on the MPC was none other than Alex Richbourg, during his days with the Trackmasters. He also used it on "Got 'Til It's Gone," giving the drum track a leaning, rolling quality. Crucially, the usage of Shift Timing on this track seems to predate any use of that feature by Jay Dee. So one might envision a scenario in which Jay Dee's "revenge" merited not just a remix, but a wholesale commandeering of this feature, albeit with a more advanced technique.

James Dewitt Yancey, as the drummer Karriem Riggins has said, was the master of his instrument, and his instrument was the drum machine. And yet so much of the discourse around J Dilla heralds the MPC as his instrument while claiming that he didn't employ the very features that made it unique. They're saying, essentially: *The clock software of the MPC was so great that he didn't even use it!*

Behind the J Dilla "freehand" performance narrative, there is a fetishization of the conventional musician and a rejection of the programmer, the very person that Dilla was. There's the idea that somehow *performance* is more pure than *programming*, instinct more important than deliberation. In this view, J Dilla is likened to a musical Luke Skywalker who turns off his targeting computer in order to blow up the Death Star. But to continue the Star Wars analogy, as much as James Dewitt Yancey was a pilot, he was also the computer geek embedded somewhere deep in the Rebel command, the guy who probed the Death Star architecture to find its strengths and weaknesses in order to subvert its power. The scientist is the hero of this story.

Part of the problem with understanding how these sounds are produced and explaining what they do is that many people—musicians and beatmakers, journalists and academics—are using an old vocabulary ("pocket," "swing," "groove") to talk about something new, like trying to explain a three-dimensional object using only the language of a two-dimensional world.

From the perspective of music theory, what's going on when we hear a Jay Dee / J Dilla beat?

Why is it different than the other kinds of musical conflict that came before it? To understand that, we need to return to the concept of expectation.

To hear a rhythm at all, we must have at least two events spaced in time: like a snare hit, then a pause of any length, then another hit: *positive-negative-positive*. Once a pattern is established, it sets up an expectation. We expect to hear an event in a positive (or "strong") space, and do not expect to hear one in a negative (or "weak") space. This propensity to hear positive and negative spaces continues as rhythms become more elaborate. When those expectations get subverted, we feel disoriented.

In a two-count rhythm, we hear the first beat as the "call" and the second as the "response," "strong" and then "weak." Once that pattern is established, we expect to hear events continue along that pattern.

In a three-count, often the first beat is the call and the second and third are the responses, or strong-weak-weak.

1	2	3	1	2	3
S	w	w	S	w	w

A four-count is a multiple of the two-count, simply repeating that strong-weak polarity.

1	2	3	4	1	2	3	4
S	w	S	w	S	w	S	w

A six-count multiplies the three-count, and so on.

Why does this matter? *Because our expectations are governed by the most granular pulse in a given song*, what we call the rhythmic current.

For example, here's how a standard hip-hop beat sets up and conforms to our expectations:

In hip-hop, we expect to hear a beat counted in fours. Usually the hi-hat acts as the metronome, and because it hits two times for every one of those four beats, it sets the rhythmic current at eight. In much of hip-hop, the rhythmic current is eight pulses per measure:

Count	1	n	2	n	3	n	4	n	1	n	2	n	3	n	4	n
HAT	▓	▓	▓	▓	▓	▓	▓	▓	▓	▓	▓	▓	▓	▓	▓	▓
KICK	▓				▓				▓				▓			
SNARE			▓				▓				▓				▓	
	s	w	s	w	s	w	s	w	s	w	s	w	s	w	s	w

In that current, we expect both the kick drum (the "stomp") and the snare (the "clap") to fall on strong beats.

Because the rhythmic current—the most granular pulse—governs our expectations, changes on a microscopic level can ironically be jarring, and it is in this area, subverting the rhythmic current, that James did most of his work. In a typical Jay Dee / J Dilla beat, the rushed snare messes with our expectations by falling into a weak area of the rhythmic current and not a strong one.

Count	1	n	2	n	3	n	4	n	1	n	2	n	3	n	4	n
HAT																
KICK																
SNARE																
	S	w	S	w	S	w	S	w	S	w	S	w	S	w	S	w

Snare appears on a weak beat, rather than on a strong one, where we expect it

Crucially, the math of where Jay Dee's snare falls is so granular that it doesn't make sense with the rhythmic current of eight. Using the song "Go Ladies" as our example, we would have to divide the pulse not into eight slices per measure, but into 192 slices per measure, and shift that

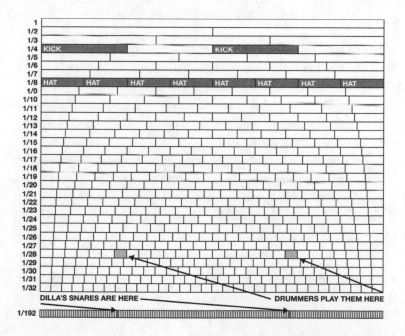

snare early by five of those slices (or five 128th-note triplets, in musical notation).

The human ear hears this as a "too-earlyness." And while it's easy to program a drum machine with this kind of fine math, a traditional musician can't count that fast. In later years, as drummers (and programmers, too) began to try this time-feel, some strained for a countable place to put the snare. Often that rushed snare falls in an "odd" place, tending to line up with a less-granular pulse where each quarter note is divided into five, six, or seven slices: twenty-eight slices per measure, each of those slices called a septuplet.*

A septuplet is a bizarre place for a musical event to be if you're thinking about a rhythmic current of straight eighth notes.

The snare's position in an odd-numbered micro-grid comes into conflict with the even-numbered macro-grid. For music nerds, this math suggests why Dilla's polyrhythm is different than a standard polyrhythm: Dilla tended to put odd rhythmic events in places that didn't make sense when heard in the context of the simple, even math of a four-count beat, or the math of two-against-three. He offset events in microscopic ways that made them instantly more complex, but musically compelling.

The hard part for musicians in thinking about these small adjustments is that they aren't momentary quirks of performance, but need to be held constant over time, and in ways that conflict with other elements. Drummers don't naturally think: "I'll keep my right leg in straight time, swing my right arm at 66 percent, and with my left, rush the snare by 1/7 of a quarter note."

Back in 1998, even without the language to express it or a theoretical framework to understand it, James Yancey's work struck the traditional musicians around him as something extraordinary. They felt the same way about the producer himself.

---

* That, for example, is how the acclaimed drummer Nate Smith sometimes "counts" his rushed snare and kick, placing them one septuplet ahead of the pulse, counting each beat quickly as *onetwothreefourfivesixseven, onetwothreefourfivesixseven, onetwothreefourfivesixseven, onetwothreefourfivesixseven*. Smith, who also came up as a beatmaker, says the technique grew out of his approximation of MPC swing. He sometimes counts his "rushedness" a different way, shooting to land his snare or kick somewhere in the "tiny gulf" between the last eighth-note triplet of a beat and the downbeat or backbeat that follows.

More Techniques

Jay Dee / J Dilla did not pioneer every practice he employed. But alongside his rhythmic innovation and experimentation with error, there are several other methods that Jay Dee / J Dilla refined or perfected, among them:

Converting time-signatures—as in his unpublished beat "Heroin Joint," where he converts a three-count song, James Brown's "King Heroin," to a four-count rhythm.

Colliding time-signatures—as in the polyrhythm he establishes in Slum Village's "I Don't Know" by setting the six-count song, Baden Powell's "É Isso Aí," against a four-count beat.

Verbal illusions—using chopping and filtering to transform words so that they say what he wants them to say, as in songs like "Players," a sample of the word "Clair"; or Chino XL's "Don't Say a Word," a chopped sample of Frankie Valli's "Grease (Is the Word)."

Odd bar loops—as when he samples a seven-bar loop, Herbie Hancock's "Come Running to Me," in Slum Village's "Get Dis Money."

Chopping to create new harmonic progressions—as he does with Dreams' "Dream Suite" in Busta Rhymes's "Enjoy Da Ride" or Brand New Heavies' "Sometimes (Remix)."

Odd entrances and off loop points—as in Common's "The Light," which does not begin on the downbeat, and which is based on a loop that starts in the middle of a phrase from Bobby Caldwell's "Open Your Eyes."

Reharmonizing existing harmonic material—as he does with a bass line and clavinet in relationship to Zapp's "More Bounce to the Ounce" in Slum Village's "Do You."

9.
Partners

D'Angelo's star rose with his first album in 1995. After three turns around the sun, his long-awaited follow-up had yet to break the horizon. He lingered in a place beyond time, searching for something that had been lost: *the sound of soul music before the machines took over.*

D'Angelo's partner Q-Tip had embarked on this quest with Tribe back in 1990, when they created "Bonita Applebum," sampling pieces of a Fender Rhodes keyboard lifted from the RAMP song "Daylight." The warm, tubular tones of the Rhodes electric piano embodied the seventies soul sound. Then, in the 1980s, they were replaced by the cooler sonics of synthesizers; and the subtle grooves of human drummers gave way to the rigid grid of machines. Just as hip-hop producers used drum breaks from the 1970s to break free of that grid and impart some human groove to their compositions, A Tribe Called Quest's great innovation was to revive the harmonic complexity and sonics of that decade by using samplers and sequencers rather than traditional instruments. D'Angelo traced his own epiphany as a programmer to Tribe's second album, *Low End Theory*: in the right hands, he realized, machines could evoke soul, too.

D'Angelo could use both traditional and digital skills in his resurrections. He thought deeply about the placements of notes—a little ahead, a little behind, what those shifts felt like—and about how humans and machines worked together. Even so, he wasn't satisfied with the sound of his first album. *Brown Sugar* felt thin compared to, say, Stevie Wonder's *Music of My Mind*. New records tended not to sound like old records, because new records were made on newer, ostensibly better equipment that didn't really *sound* better. D'Angelo had recorded his first album at the modern Battery Studios where the Ummah produced their music. For his follow-up, D'Angelo wanted a record that sounded less polished—to hear human mistakes, to hear the room itself. So he decamped in late 1996 to a neglected studio where time had stopped: Electric Lady, built by Jimi Hendrix, tucked into a tiny building on Eighth Street in Greenwich Village, on a block known for shoe shops, not show business. But Electric Lady was where many of the records that inspired the hip-hop generation were recorded.

The two biggest rooms of the three-studio complex were underground. In the control rooms, the equipment was powered by tubes and transistors rather than microchips. Walking into the control room of Studio A for the first time, D'Angelo touched the old Focusrite board and felt the spirits. Through the glass, in the spacious, oval-shaped wood-paneled live room of Studio A, sat a dusty Fender Rhodes keyboard. Not just any Fender Rhodes. *The* Fender Rhodes—the Holy of Holies, the one that created the sound of modern soul music; the same one that Stevie Wonder played on his greatest albums, the same one that RAMP employed on "Daylight," and, by extension, on "Bonita Applebum," the song that launched the aesthetic for Tribe, the Ummah, and D'Angelo himself. Electric Lady was the mother, the matron, the matrix of the very sound they sought. Deeper still, beneath the floorboards, ran the Minetta Creek, the buried watercourse of ancient Manhattan. For an old soul like D'Angelo, this was like coming home to a place he'd never been, a sacred place to commune with his ancestors.

Every evening at Electric Lady was a séance in which D'Angelo was assisted by two sonic shamans. Behind the boards sat Russ Elevado, an engineer who shared D'Angelo's aesthetic pursuits. Accompanying D'Angelo in the live room was Roots drummer Ahmir "Questlove" Thompson. They began each evening around 6:00 p.m. To charge themselves, they'd listen for hours to records, old and new, or watch Questlove's "treats"— videotapes from his collection of hundreds: old episodes of *Soul Train*, bootlegs of concerts by Marvin Gaye, Stevie Wonder, Hendrix, Al Green, Michael Jackson, and Prince. Then, as the clock nudged toward 10:00 p.m., D'Angelo and Questlove moved into Studio A's live room. Often they'd spend hours re-creating the performances they'd watched or albums they listened to. When they found a particular groove, they'd follow where it took them. Elevado and his assistant Steve Mandel recorded their jam sessions to reel after reel of two-inch multitrack tape. Sometimes they found an element or an idea that then became the germ of a song, and they'd expand it. They'd work all night and leave the studio at dawn. It was a freedom that was also deep study, deep practice, funded by the deep pockets of EMI: two years, one million dollars, and counting.

Questlove and D'Angelo were rebels against rigidity, their bond beginning on April Fools' Day in 1996 at the House of Blues in Los Angeles: Questlove onstage with the Roots, and D'Angelo in the balcony. They'd never met, but Questlove was a fan. While the drummer had been disciplining his playing into a metronomic, machinelike pulse, D'Angelo was relaxing his rhythms; songs like "Dreamin' Eyes of Mine" evoked the same feeling Questlove got when he listened to Jay Dee's beats. So the drummer sent the singer a smoke signal, launching into the drum riff of an obscure song called "Four"—penned and recorded by Prince under his jazz alias, Madhouse—elongating time, hitting the skins with a contained sloppiness. D'Angelo caught the beat, bobbing his head wildly. Their introduction after the show led to D'Angelo's first collaboration with the Roots, and to a friendship.

That evening at the House of Blues birthed another musical relationship. Next to D'Angelo sat a young performer from Dallas: Erica Wright, just signed by D'Angelo's manager Kedar Massenburg's new label. Quick-witted, with a deep gaze and an iron will, Wright was the kind of person who could be successful at anything she put her mind to doing; she'd already been a dancer, a rapper, and a comedian. What she chose, eventually, was a singing career under the name Erykah Badu. Like D'Angelo, she evoked the sounds of the past—the phrasing of Billie Holiday with the firepower of Chaka Khan; and she matched those classic aesthetics with hip-hop sensibilities. Kedar paired Badu initially with Bob Power, who coproduced what became her first successful single, "On & On," but the singer specifically requested a collaboration with the Roots. Badu flew to Philadelphia in 1996, where she and the band drifted for a couple of days before Roots manager Richard Nichols phoned a local musician who could help them figure it all out.

James Poyser arrived soon thereafter. A self-taught keyboardist who'd been mentored by the two men most responsible for creating the classic "Philly soul" sound of the 1970s, Kenny Gamble and Leon Huff, Poyser sat down, "comped" out a few chords on a Fender Rhodes, and instantly transformed the mood in the room. Within an hour they had written a ballad, "Otherside of the Game." Poyser and Erykah's chemistry, backed by Questlove's rhythmic physics, fleshed out Erykah Badu's debut album in 1997, *Baduizm*, which in turn set a sonic goalpost for D'Angelo as he recorded his second album at Electric Lady.

Neo-soul was the term Kedar Massenburg coined for the kind of music his two artists made. While much of popular R&B in the 1990s had devolved into singing over hip-hop beats, D'Angelo and Badu were among a small group of artists who strove to re-create the elements *behind* those beats—like that Electric Lady Rhodes—by using a combination of programming and traditional musicianship.* Neo-soul was a revival of soul's analog heyday by its digital children. D'Angelo and Erykah both detested the term, but neo-soul was a handy differentiator for fans and critics. Their music wasn't simply the *same* as Stevie Wonder's. The creators of neo-soul weren't just emulating old stuff, they were reckoning with new ideas as well. The emphasis, if you listened carefully, was on the "neo."

---

* Other nineties soul acts like Brand New Heavies, Meshell Ndegeocello, and Maxwell are sometimes included under the "neo-soul" umbrella for their blend of progressive and retro sensibilities, traditional and electronic music-making.

Foremost among those novel elements were the rhythms of Jay Dee. D'Angelo was an early fan, and he'd tapped James to do a remix of his single "Dreaming Eyes of Mine," one that EMI never released. But when Q-Tip played him *Fan-Tas-Tic*, D'Angelo lost his mind: Jay Dee's "pocket" was so reminiscent of his own, and he had *done it all on a machine*. He loved the way the second side of the cassette was virtually a remix of the first side. All that made *Fan-Tas-Tic* essential daily listening for D'Angelo while he recorded. Then he began listening to the tracks that would end up on *Fantastic, Vol 2*.

In the same way that they studied Prince's work and techniques, D'Angelo and Questlove analyzed the music of the electronic producer from Detroit, asking the same question they asked of any of the artists they revered: *What the fuck is he doing?* In their Electric Lady jam sessions, they re-created his uncannily disjointed machine rhythms on drums and keys, and recorded them to tape.

Playing these rhythms on traditional instruments required a new kind of musicianship. Re-creating the inner tension of a Jay Dee beat was difficult to do alone, and trickier to do in concert with others. The first time bassist Pino Palladino joined D'Angelo's sessions, D asked Pino to lag behind the beat, as he was doing on keys. The problem was that Questlove's instinct on the drums was to slide back with them. You can't play behind a beat that won't stay ahead of you, so D'Angelo told Questlove to take his headphones off—so that he couldn't hear him and Pino—and just play as straight as possible, preserving the tension. Eventually, Questlove could put his headphones on again and stay glued to the imaginary grid, even when D and Pino further exaggerated their pull against it.

Questlove developed tricks to bring more conflict into his own playing. To re-create the exaggerated "flamming" of Jay Dee's production in *Fan-Tas-Tic*, he borrowed a technique used by Prince in his song "Under the Cherry Moon" and by drummer Quinton Joseph, most prominently on Curtis Mayfield's 1974 song "Mother's Son." Instead of merely hitting the snare, Questlove angled his drumstick so that it struck the edge of the skin and then the metal rim in rapid succession. D'Angelo loved the style, and Questlove used it regularly. It even *sounded* like its namesake, the second strike hiding just behind the skirts of the first: *mother-son, mother-son, mother-son.*

To get the rushed snare of the beats from the as-yet-unreleased *Fantastic, Vol. 2*, Questlove trained himself to let his drumstick fall on the snare just slightly too soon after the kick drum. In this way, Questlove could shift the snare while the kick and hats kept the overall beat steady.

Listening To: Questlove's Techniques

"Mother's Son" Technique
> *The Model: "Mother's Son" by Curtis Mayfield (start at 1:28)*
> *Questlove: "Greatdayndamornin'/Booty" by D'Angelo*

Rushed Snare Technique
> *The Model: "Go Ladies" by Slum Village*
> *Questlove: "The Root" by D'Angelo*

Jay Dee could shift a drum's position in time by programming it, and there it would remain. But Questlove had to counteract a lifetime of physical reflexes, to retrain his body to do things and feel time differently. So much of the work was mental: playing a rhythm in 12/8 but thinking about it as 4/4; the *thought itself* could make the difference. He was grateful now for his drum teacher Jules Benner who, when Ahmir was ten years old, told him, "I'm going to teach you how to divide your mind," and then made him practice an infernal exercise—playing in fours with his feet and in threes with his hands for endless minutes while Benner read the paper and smoked his pipe. Ahmir remembered thinking it was a waste of time: *I am never going to use this in real life.* If only Benner could see him now.

The caliber of musicians that D'Angelo invited to his project was atypical for 1990s R&B: Charlie Hunter, a virtuoso of bizarre seven- and eight-stringed instruments, which allowed him to play bass and guitar parts simultaneously; Roy Hargrove, a trumpet player who'd gone to high school in Dallas with Erykah Badu and then gone on to rock the jazz world. These players came with formidable skills and experience. They understood the lexicon of swing from Louis Armstrong to Elvin Jones. But each entered new territory at the bidding of D'Angelo—inspired by Jay Dee and Slum Village—putting themselves in degrees of rhythmic conflict with each other.

As he assisted in session after endless session, the engineer Steve Mandel not only heard this alternative time-feel, he began to *see* it in the varied head-nods of the musicians. Questlove and Pino had their own distinct way of moving their heads while they played. D'Angelo's nod was so far behind the beat as to seem completely disconnected from it, a movement that Mandel ruefully compared to his own, suburban-Jewish-boy-right-on-the-beat stiff. *I'm stealing that head-nod*, Mandel thought.

The critical mass at Electric Lady continued its gravitational pull. With Questlove came the Roots and James Poyser, with Poyser came Badu. Bilal Oliver, a singer from Philadelphia who had attended jam sessions in Questlove's living room with other emerging Philly singers like Jill Scott, now lived in a dormitory across the street from Electric Lady while he studied jazz at the New School; he came through, as did art-minded New York hip-hop artists like Mos Def, Talib Kweli, and Q-Tip, who still maintained a creative connection with D'Angelo even as the singer drifted away from the Ummah. And then there was the MC from Chicago who had become an honorary member of the collective.

Lonnie Rashid Lynn was one of the few rappers to make it out of the Midwest in the early 1990s, a time when hip-hop's most important acts emerged from either the East or West Coasts. Performing as Common Sense, his demo tape had been discovered by the leading hip-hop magazine, *The Source*, and the coverage landed him a record deal from the New York–based independent label Relativity. His success was relative: though Common Sense was embraced by the Native Tongues groups, their level of record sales and tour receipts eluded him. Though he was known for skillful, candid lyrics, his biggest moment was a back-and-forth war of words with the rapper Ice Cube that ended with an armistice brokered by Nation of Islam Minister Louis Farrakhan. He even had to change his name when a band called Common Sense pursued him for trademark violation; he became thereafter simply Common. In 1997 he released an album that he believed would be his breakthrough. *One Day It'll All Make Sense* had all the ingredients for success: songs with Q-Tip and De La Soul, Questlove and the Roots, James Poyser and Erykah Badu, and a duet with Lauryn Hill. But even with name recognition, famous friends, and great singles, Common's album never cracked the top ten or merited a gold record award.

Common and his manager Derek Dudley decided that there were two things they needed to do to move his career forward. The first was to refuse to do another record for Relativity and to get him onto a major label with some promotional muscle. The second step was relocation. If they were really going to play the game, they needed to be in New York. Common and Derek settled in an apartment in the Fort Greene section of Brooklyn, the center of Black Bohemia since Spike Lee first picked up a camera. Nearby, Common browsed the stacks at Nkiru, the bookstore run and soon to be owned by fellow rappers Talib Kweli and Mos Def where another Midwestern transplant, the Detroit poet and former Hip Hop Shop manager jessica Care moore, did poetry readings. Moore had moved from Detroit to New York in 1995—James and Proof had attended her going-away party—and ended up winning amateur night at Harlem's Apollo Theater five times in a row. The moment transformed her life and gave her a career as a poet, author, and artist.

In Chicago, Common's artistic side had been something to hide; when he ventured into jazz clubs, he did so alone. But even then Common got signals that he belonged in that world. After one performance by Roy Hargrove, Common was stunned when Hargrove's drummer recognized and greeted him as a fan. The bespectacled, freckle-faced kid who introduced himself as Karriem Riggins came from Detroit; an alumnus of the famed Betty Carter Jazz Ahead band, he was a hip-hop head in equal measure. They became friends. Riggins ended up playing on Common's final Relativity album, and assembled and led the band for Common's next tour. Now, at Electric Lady, Common found himself squarely in Hargrove's circle. Or maybe Hargrove was in his? Whatever this gathering was, Common told Questlove, it was something special.

Questlove and the Roots' manager Rich Nichols saw something special in Common, too; someone who could play a greater role in *their* grand project: a commercially viable, soulful countermovement to mainstream R&B and hip-hop, which had become ever more success-oriented and aggressively consumerist, with videos full of flashy cars and shiny suits. In the same way that producer-moguls like Sean "Puffy" Combs had built stables of artists and producers who magnified each other's work—a machine wherein established artists introduced new ones—Questlove and Nichols wanted to build a similar collective around the Roots, acts that recorded and toured together. They approached Wendy Goldstein, the A&R executive who had signed them to Geffen Records, and who had recently been shifted with the Roots to sister label MCA, where the chief executive, Jay Boberg, lent Goldstein his support to build a hip-hop roster. She had already tried, at Questlove's urging, to sign Slum Village, but lost out to A&M. The idea of signing Common to MCA was seen by all as a vital step toward creating a left-of-center music machine.

Kedar Massenburg had the same idea. Tapped to revive the moribund Motown Records—generations removed from Detroit and now just a hollow brand owned by MCA's parent company, Universal Music—Kedar thought Common would be a natural complement to his roster, which included Erykah Badu.

Derek Dudley knew Kedar would market Common more aggressively, but Common knew that Kedar would begin asserting his strong will during the recording process, and ultimately what Common wanted after getting free was more freedom. He opted for Goldstein and MCA, making two requests as he began his new project. First, he asked Questlove to executive produce the album, grounding himself in the creative colony at Electric Lady. Next, he declared that, at long last, he wanted to work with Jay Dee.

Common had first met James in 1995 at Q-Tip's duplex, where he noticed him sitting shoeless and cross-legged on the floor, away from the chatter, going through records. Common was already a well-known figure in hip-hop and James was no one. But the Chicago rapper struck up a conversation and found a fellow traveler—another cat from the Midwest looking for his fortune in the East. While on tour with De La Soul the following year, they gave him a Jay Dee beat tape, and Common phoned the Detroit producer to ask if he might have a few of them. Not long thereafter, James boarded a plane to Chicago at his own expense to lay three tracks to tape at the studio where Common worked. Common didn't end up using them, but he was so touched by the gesture that he decided to stay connected with James over the years. He'd come to Detroit and visited the basement a few times. In one of those visits he introduced James to Karriem Riggins, who had been a fan of Jay Dee's and a friend of DJ House Shoes's, but whom he had never met. James invited Riggins to play drums on a track for *Fantastic, Vol. 2*, but these meetings never led to any collaboration between Jay Dee and Common. The last trip the rapper made to Detroit had been between Christmas and New Year's Eve in 1997, tagging along with Questlove and Black Thought. The Roots nabbed their first Jay Dee–produced track, "Dynamite!," for their next album. Common came away empty-handed: he was still in limbo between record deals.

Now, one year later, armed with a new recording budget, here was a chance for the crew at Electric Lady to truly partner with the producer who had become a persistent specter in their musical lives, the man whom Questlove called "The God," the unlikely digital divinity at the center of their analog sanctuary.

J ay Dee created the first beat for Common's album in the artist's absence. Questlove had come to Detroit after a Roots show in Chicago at the end of 1998. But as a huge blizzard hit Michigan on New Year's Day, shutting down the airport and canceling his flight out, Questlove settled into James's wood-paneled basement with Frank and Proof, fortified with food and drink and movies rented on videocassette by Frank's mother with her Blockbuster card. To pass the time, Frank suggested a "beat olympics," Proof explaining the game they used to play with DJ

Head back in the day, now with even more stringent rules: *Two teams have five minutes to create a beat with records selected by their opponents. Best beat wins the round.*

Questlove knew he couldn't win against James, master of records and time. But the premise of the contest was so fun that he agreed to try, with Frank as James's partner and Proof as his. By the third round, Questlove was losing badly, so he sought to even the odds: Could James make something original with a pedestrian breakbeat? Questlove chose "Ashley's Roachclip" by the Soul Searchers—overused to the point of cliché in pop songs throughout the nineties by groups like Milli Vanilli—and paired it with a record by the easy-listening crooner Johnny Mathis.

"Aw, man." James shook his head. "You might have me on this one."

James slid his headphones on, his fingers dashing across his MPC3000, chopping "Ashley's Roachclip." When he was done, James had two minutes left to attack the Johnny Mathis record. A look of panic crossed James's face as he listened for *anything* to sample. Then James stopped, committing to something. He began hitting the pads in rhythm.

"Yup," James said to himself. "Yupyupyupyup." James then listened back to what he had done, narrowed his eyes, and let out a long "Wooooooooooooooooo!"

When James played the results through the room monitors, Questlove hung his head. He'd taken a piano stab from the Johnny Mathis record and made it sound harder than an eighteen-wheeler hitting a brick wall. James had murdered him.

Final round. Questlove grabbed a record that he was *sure* had nothing worth sampling on it: Rick James's *Street Songs*, the album that featured "Super Freak," which had yielded the corniest rap song of all time, MC Hammer's "U Can't Touch This." James searched the record, sampling a piece of the song "Give It to Me Baby." As the five-minute mark neared, James narrowed his eyes again . . . "Wooooooooooooooooo!"

Questlove threw up his hands. James asked for twenty more seconds to finish up. They listened: James had deconstructed the song's bass line and replayed it so that it became an entirely new composition. And what that composition would become, once Common heard it and wrote his lyrics, was the song "Dooinit."

Snow fell hard and fast. They called it the Blizzard of '99. Detroit didn't have enough equipment to plow even the major streets, and the city was blanketed with thigh-high drifts. At the mercy of forces beyond their control, nobody was getting out for a while.

On January 21, 1999, the entire staff of A&M Records was let go and the company shuttered. Defiant employees scaled the roof of one of the buildings on the A&M lot in Hollywood, built originally to house Charlie Chaplin's movie studios, and tied a huge black band of mourning around the twirling A&M logo, a landmark above La Brea Boulevard.

Among the dismissed executives was Slum Village's A&R rep, Junior Regisford. While Slum Village were delivering *Fantastic, Vol. 2* in mid-1998, Regisford caught wind of the impending purchase of PolyGram, A&M's parent company, by Seagram, which owned Universal Music. The idea was to merge PolyGram's and Universal's music operations, the two smallest of the six "majors," to immediately become the biggest. But Regisford knew that the merger meant streamlining as well. The new company would inherit more than half a dozen labels—Interscope, MCA, and Motown on the Universal side; Island, Mercury, London, Def Jam, Geffen, and A&M from PolyGram. Some would be eliminated.

As the purchase neared, PolyGram froze all spending, which meant that Slum Village—their album completed except for photos and artwork—remained in limbo for months. Through it all, Regisford tried to keep R. J. Rice apprised. It looked like a few A&M acts would be retained by Interscope; the hope was that Slum Village would be one of them. When Regisford was laid off and both Geffen and A&M shuttered in late January, nothing had been settled. He felt like he had failed the group.

Slum Village's album ended up in a stack of CDs for review by Interscope cofounder and head Jimmy Iovine. When he finished listening, he asked his promotion people to reach out to an important Los Angeles radio DJ, Chris "C-Minus" Rivas, who also happened to be a fan and friend of Jay Dee's. Whenever James came to Los Angeles, he'd visit with C-Minus and his roommate Mr. Choc, who together cohosted radio station Power 106's *Friday Night Flavas*. When C-Minus, who served as tour DJ for the rock band Korn, came to Detroit, he'd visit James's base-ment; R. J. and Tim Maynor had brought him by the studio to solicit his advice on choices for a potential single from *Fantastic, Vol. 2*.

"I dig the record," Iovine told the DJ. "I just don't know where it can fit. Do you think they have a single? What about 'Climax'?" Here, Io-vine referenced the one song on the album that featured Baatin's sister Tina Glover singing the chorus, the most obvious melodic hook and female-friendly track on an otherwise testosterone-fueled album.

"I would play that here at Power," the DJ said.

"Yeah," Iovine said. "But where else would it get played?"

C-Minus had no ready answer. Even with the nod from established groups like A Tribe Called Quest, and even with Questlove touting them in the liner notes of the Roots' just-released album *Things Fall Apart*, Slum weren't a sure thing, stylistically different from the more popular acts of the day—Jay-Z, DMX, and the white rapper out of Detroit whom Iovine had recently signed to Interscope and paired with the producer Dr. Dre: Eminem.

Iovine assured R. J. Rice that he'd find a place for Slum on his roster. Then, weeks later, Iovine changed his tune: he'd just hired a new execu-tive in charge of Black music, Steve Stoute, and he had to defer to Stoute's take on the group.

"I don't get it," Stoute told R. J. on the phone. Stoute's sentiments be-ing what they were, R. J. asked for his album back.

"I don't know if I want to let you go just now," Stoute said. "Y'all might blow up."

Stoute's bluster aside, R. J. had a "pay or play" clause in his contract, so either Interscope had to give them a lot of money just to shelve the record, or he could pay Interscope the costs they inherited from A&M to get the record back. In the meantime, it looked like Stoute was going to make the transition as difficult as possible.

The period of limbo did result in one positive outcome for Slum Village. Karyn Rachtman, the executive responsible for supervising In-terscope's movie soundtracks, happened to be working on a new album to accompany the first theatrical feature by Mike Judge, the creator of *Beavis and Butt-Head*, MTV's hit 1990s cartoon show. *Office Space* was a satire about the lives of cubicle-dwelling tech-service employees, and Judge illuminated their suppressed rage with a rap-heavy soundtrack. Rachtman's assistant had found the Slum Village album in Iovine's pile of A&M CDs, and Rachtman seized on "Get Dis Money" as a perfect match for the movie's theme. She cleared the Herbie Hancock sample, which she loved because she'd worked previously for Hancock, and made it the second song on the album.

"Get Dis Money" was barely audible in the movie itself, ambience underneath a conversation that the protagonist and a friend are having in a bar. But it became the only record by Slum Village released by Interscope, and their first by a legitimate label. For many fans and DJs it was the first piece of vinyl by the storied group that they'd been able to get their hands on. Thus it was the first Slum Village song that played on many radio stations across the country; the first, even, on radio stations in their hometown of Detroit.

Detroiters who had loved Slum for years felt ownership of the moment. One friend, Asham Carter, was so shocked to hear the song that he phoned the crew and left a message.

He screamed: "Yo, we on the radio, baby! We on the radio!"

Common spent much of the spring and summer of 1999 waiting for James. He'd hop the shuttle from LaGuardia to Detroit City Airport, take a cab downtown to the Atheneum hotel, and sit tight. If James said he was coming at noon, Common often wouldn't see him or Frank until 3:00 p.m, or later. Some days no one would show up at all.

In the Conant Gardens basement, Common sat on the couch—talking to Frank, reading rap magazines like *The Source* or *XXL*—while James stood behind his MPC3000 with his headphones on, burning incense that he bought at the counter of Melodies & Memories record store. What Common looked for was James's head-nod. When he saw James bobbing his head, he knew something good was coming.

One day James threw an old album called *Two Rainbows Daily* onto the turntable. The project was the brainchild of Alan Gowen, a keyboard prodigy of the U.K.'s Canterbury progressive rock scene who was diagnosed with leukemia right after the album's release and spent the last year of his life composing his own epitaph, dying at the age of thirty-three. *There was something about this record.* Roused by the wobbly synthesizers and Fender Rhodes chords in the song "Morning Order," James fragmented the sounds and rearranged them rhythmically, against some offset drums and off-the-grid bass. He narrowed his eyes and began to move his head. Then came James's signature exultation: *Wooooooooooooo!*

When James finally auditioned the beat for him, Common wasn't in the basement anymore. He was inside his future, he was the artist he had hoped to become. Common began writing, James sang the hook, and they named the gentle, vibrating song after the incense smoke that drifted between them, "Nag Champa."

In his sessions, James set the rhythms, and when James felt like taking a break, Common went along. James took him to Dave & Buster's to play arcade games or to his favorite Mongolian barbecue restaurant. Sometimes Baatin or Waajeed would run Common by their favorite veggie spots. James's friends became Common's friends. They got a chance to tell Common that he had long been, for them, a source of inspiration and a bit of jealousy, too: they wanted to be the first guys coming out of the Midwest with a little East Coast flavor, and Common had beaten them to it. Conant Gardens wasn't so different than Avalon Park, the lower-middle-class Black enclave on Chicago's South Side where Common and his friends grew up—the sons of educators and civil servants with differing combinations of street smarts and intellectual and artistic sophistication; who liked rims and gold chains and who liked Thelonious Monk and Andy Warhol. Common was one of them: his musical obsessions during his Detroit sessions were Slum Village and Fela Kuti, future sounds from America and from Africa, respectively. Common felt connections, not contradictions, in this crew. Baatin practiced meditation and James's ritual was the titty bar, but that didn't mean that James was any less possessed of spirit. James's crude habits didn't diminish Common's growing awe of his abilities: as a beatmaker, MC, even a singer.

James Poyser flew out for a while from Philadelphia at Common and

Questlove's request. Poyser became a convert to Jay Dee's music when he first heard the "Sometimes" remix, rewinding it in his Walkman on a long bus ride between London and Glasgow while visiting family in the U.K. *What's wrong with the timing of these bass notes?* he thought. *And why do I love it?* The harmonies that Jay Dee constructed out of his samples were Poyser's biggest revelation. Poyser had until this trip never met the man Questlove called "The God"—never to James's face, of course—and was so intimidated that he expected a giant to answer when he knocked at the door on McDougall. The life-sized producer welcomed Poyser, showing him little things that blew his mind; for example, how he composed the song "Fantastic" not as chords but as a fugue of individual melodies. *No wonder I can't play it on the keyboard,* Poyser thought.

Common wanted to do a song with all of Slum Village, and asked the three MCs to trade rhymes with him on the song James composed with Poyser, "Funky for You." But accessing James's abilities wasn't like pushing a button and getting a predictable result. T3 and Baatin composed their verses, but James sat on his hands all night at their session. By the time James dropped him off at the Atheneum at two in the morning, Common was dejected. But he didn't say anything. There were certain people you could talk into doing things. James wasn't one of those people.

The next day, when James came to pick him up, he played Common a completely new beat, which he had somehow composed in the twelve hours since they'd last seen each other. Like "Nag Champa," it was an ethereal piece of music, slowed-down samples, swirling, whirling, drums jerking, all the elements set against each other, twos and threes at once, everything off balance. And James, knowing what Common wanted from him, had already rapped the hook: "It's the Thelonius, super microphonist / You know us, this rap shit we 'bout to own it." The song they tracked in the following days featured all four MCs tangoing with the odd rhythm, even while they were at lyrical cross-purposes: Baatin talking to God, James declaring "Bitch, I'm on some grown shit," Thelonius *and* felonious, profound *and* profane. James closed the song with his verse, each new line reversing the rhyme scheme of the last, words folding in and out like a lyrical Möbius strip . . .

> MCs they don't rhyme and ball
> They lying to y'all
> They dying to ball and rhyme
> We do all the time

This was why Common waited for James, because this is how his patience was inevitably rewarded. This was why Common didn't beef when James didn't show up for studio sessions, draining his MCA recording budget, because you couldn't put a price on what Jay Dee gave you. This was why he didn't try to convince James to do things he didn't want to do, because when James *really* wanted to do it, he'd bring you something like "Thelonius": a *perfect* song, made with you and only you in mind. It's why Common was cool with staying in the basement and writing while James hung at the strip club. Common figured if he was going to really work with James, he had to give him room to live his life. *Go, please! I'll be here when you get back.* It's why he followed when James led.

One evening James felt like catching a movie instead of working. They went to see a new action film starring Keanu Reeves and Laurence Fishburne, a science-fiction dystopia about a future in which machines declare war on humans. The concept wasn't foreign to an audience of Detroiters. In the film, a gifted computer hacker is told by strange new friends that he and all humanity are imprisoned in a grid they cannot see called the "Matrix," and that his destiny is to free everyone from it. He doesn't believe them. Their reverence for him makes him uncomfortable. They call him "The One." He replies: "I'm just another guy." The hacker acquires some skill jumping in and out of that grid, from the world of humans into the world of machines. In the end, he becomes a master: He can bend the grid to his will, everything and everyone in it. The machine world becomes just a cascade of readable ones and zeros to our hero, Neo.

When they emerged from the theater, Common could see that his friend was having a moment. James couldn't get the words out to describe how he felt.

———

J ames was a creature of habit: his long overnight hours in the studio, his frequent excursions to strip clubs with Frank and friends. But that regularity also made Joylette aware of little glitches in the grid.

One evening, James didn't come home. He wasn't answering her phone calls. After she finished work the next day, she swung by the basement. James now had the entire house on McDougall and Nevada to himself. Martha and Maurice just had a daughter, Faith; and with John now in high school, James moved them and his parents to a fancier place: the River Terrace Apartments on Jefferson Avenue, near the Detroit River. Maureen shifted her day care business to a building that James leased for her on 7 Mile Road—the old storefront from which he had once boosted candy in middle school. James now used entire rooms for his growing wardrobe.

When Joy arrived, she saw two cars parked on McDougall, James's Range Rover and another that she didn't recognize. She knocked on the side door. James opened it. Joy walked past him, upstairs, through the kitchen and into the living room, which she saw was littered with bottles.

"Oh y'all had a party last night, hunh?"

"Yeah," James said.

"I was calling your phone last night and you didn't answer. I see you're okay."

"I just stayed here," James said.

"I need to use your bathroom," she told him. Joy walked into the bathroom, quickly out of it, down the hallway to Maureen and Dewitt's old room, and pushed the door open. There, in the bed, was another woman. She closed the door.

"James, you got a bitch up in here?" she said when she returned. "I'm leaving your ass."

Joy huffed back to the side door and out onto the street, a shoeless James chasing after her. When Joy climbed into her car, James tried to stop her from going by holding the driver's-side door open. Joy threw the car into gear and drove off.

James barraged her with calls thereafter. Joy didn't take them. Then her aunt Elaine phoned. "Why is Maureen calling here looking for you?" she asked.

Over the years, Maureen had told James, "If you ever have a problem you can't solve, come to me and we'll solve it together." James had gotten girls pregnant before; it was Maureen who sometimes arranged and paid for their abortions, nearly a half dozen by her count. James, frantic at the prospect of Joy breaking up with him, asked Maureen to help him fix it. And though Maureen wasn't happy about Joy, she knew that Joy made James happy, and here was a way for Maureen to reinforce that she was the person most dedicated to his happiness.

Joy watched it happen: Maureen leaving messages on *her* house phone for James, reassuring him, knowing well that Joy herself would be listening to them.

She thinks she's slick, Joy thought.

At James's behest, Maureen bought Joy a diamond ring with a gold band, which James left in their townhouse for her.

"I don't like it," Joy told him.

Maureen had always felt slippery to Joy. Now, for the first time, James did, too. Joy bought a bed and a mattress and had it sent to her father's house, and slept there while she reckoned with James's betrayal.

I t wasn't a secret to Maureen or any of James's friends that he was sleep-ing around, and that James met many of these young women at the strip club. Monica Whitlow was nineteen years old when she began dancing at Chocolate City as "Montana," in part to save money for school. One night shortly after her hiring, Frank approached and motioned her to-ward the VIP balcony where he sat with Derrick and James.

"Dance for my boy," Frank said, gesturing to James.

As they paid her to stay with them, song after $20 song, Monica felt the other dancers' eyes burning into her. This routine resumed whenever James and his friends came to the bar, and Monica fought with her col-leagues over his attentions, getting herself ejected from the club a couple of times because of it. Monica became curious about this quiet, clean rec-ord producer who never bragged or loud-talked like the other customers. She told Frank that she wanted to go home with James, but was too shy to ask. *I don't want him to think I'm looking for money*, she explained. Frank hooked it up.

Monica knew that James had a girlfriend. She didn't care, and James didn't seem to, either. They began seeing each other. Monica liked James and learned from him. When she'd get upset about something that happened with her colleagues or friends, he counseled her to say nothing. "Just watch," he said, the technique he had perfected in his own life to navigate any social situation. She started to love him. Several months later, Monica discovered she was pregnant. This part wasn't carelessness, though: When she was sixteen, Monica had been told by a doctor that she would likely never be able to bear children. This was a cause of great sorrow for Monica, and it's why she didn't use or demand that James use birth control. The pregnancy, for her, was a miracle. She figured that once she told James about it, that would be the end of their affair. To her surprise, James was equanimous. *What do you want to do?* he asked her.

What Monica wanted was to bring her miracle baby into the world. What she didn't want, again, was for James to think she was looking for money.

But James would call, asking if she needed anything, and send cash from time to time during her pregnancy.

Though Slum Village's *Fantastic, Vol. 2* remained in limbo, a double-vinyl bootleg of the album was circulating among DJs and being sold in record stores around the world, feeding an appetite that had been stoked by prior, limited-run twelve-inch singles of the tracks from *Fan-Tas-Tic*. These pirate pressings were largely the work of one man.

Christopher Ramos, a former tour manager for Common and other rap acts, had concocted a clever hustle: selling American hip-hop tracks to independent record companies in Europe and Japan. Ramos would pay an artist like Common for a song or two and then sell it to a willing buyer for double the price. There would be no tracking of royalties or sales; it was a single cash transaction, easy money on the side for artists, especially if they were frustrated by their current contractual obligations. As the market for hip-hop vinyl singles exploded in the 1990s, and with the founding of U.S. indie record distributor Fat Beats, Ramos's new career moved into America. In a good year he could make hundreds of thousands of dollars.

Derek Dudley and Common made some money with Ramos, but Derek learned never to turn his back on him. One day Common and his manager were watching a game on TV in their Brooklyn apartment when a call came in for Derek. Common watched his partner quietly excuse himself and walk out the front door. A few minutes later, Derek returned and sat back down next to him on the couch. A second call came, this time for Common: it was Ramos, crying that Derek had just come over to his house—around the corner from theirs—and beat him down. Common looked at his partner in disbelief. Derek explained: Ramos had lifted a digital master tape from them and sold it to Fat Beats. But Derek didn't hold a grudge: he knew that Ramos meant well but didn't always do well.

Ramos met Jay Dee on one of Common's swings through Detroit, and his record hustle appealed directly to James's cash-in-hand mentality. Ramos farmed out Slum Village singles, EPs, and albums, and as particular demand grew for Slum in Europe, Ramos pitched a minitour to Slum Village's manager Tim Maynor—several dates in the U.K. and the Netherlands.

Ramos gave Maynor his hookup for quick passports for the band, none of whom had ever been outside the country. T3 and Baatin were excited to make the trip, as was Waajeed, slated to DJ. But on the day in early May 1999 they were supposed to fly out, James said he couldn't go, claiming he'd lost his passport. T3 just shook his head. *What a jerk. He just wants to stay home and make beats. Why wouldn't you want to go to Europe?!* Tim rushed over to McDougall and Nevada to reason with his client. *Think of all the women*, he told James. Then he said: *Think of the weed in Amsterdam!*

Being in the company of the hip-hop elite had finally sparked James's interest in cannabis, and after years of abstention he turned to his friend Derrick Harvey, whom James had since dubbed "Dank" for both his expertise in and redolence of marijuana. Dank taught him how to roll a blunt, and James acquired a habit. James used to order pop at the club. More often now, he popped champagne. So Maynor's words did the trick: the passport somehow materialized, and they made their way to the airport.

In Amsterdam, the group performed to a packed crowd at the Paradiso nightclub, and Ramos took James to the infamous red-light district. In London, Ramos connected James to his industry friends. Thad Baron, an executive at the U.K. branch of James's publishing company, Universal Music, began looking for ways to funnel work to the producer. Dave Laub at Source/Virgin signed Slum Village in the U.K. Gilles Peterson, a DJ who had been a fan of Jay Dee's work since "Runnin'," invited Slum onto his BBC show, where they freestyled over unreleased tracks from *Fantastic, Vol. 2* and lamented the widespread bootlegging of their music.

Of course, Ramos and James both had a lot to do with that situation. But it was also true that Ramos did for James in Europe what Q-Tip had done for him in America: he introduced him to everybody. And James found that just as New York and L.A. often gave him more love than Detroit did, Europeans revered him in ways that Americans didn't.

Still, James abandoned the tour before it was complete, leaving T3, Baatin, and Waajeed to play several shows without him. His old Detroit partners were, as ever, taking a back seat to new ones in New York.

Questlove, D'Angelo, and Poyser got giddy during James Yancey's visits to Electric Lady Studios, and the musicians around them began to understand why. Pino Palladino had received his first lessons on Jay Dee when he joined Questlove and D'Angelo in reconstructing Slum Village songs during their jam sessions. But in person, Palladino realized Jay Dee—on keyboard or MPC—was a bass player, too. He marveled at the unique sense of space in his playing and programming, with a phrasing that was almost akin to that of reggae. *The guy hears the whole band, everything. And then places his notes precisely where they need to be in relationship to everything else.*

D'Angelo had grown particularly close to James over the past year. Writing music, even for a successful professional, can be difficult and demoralizing; doing it under deadline even more so. James often called Pete Rock when he had a "beat block" and needed inspiration. D'Angelo would call James. Once, distracted by some interpersonal politics in the studio, D dialed Detroit.

"Man, what you think about that?" D'Angelo asked.

"Ehh." James shrugged. "But, maaaaan, you oughta check out *this* shit I'm workin' on, *woooooooo!*"

D'Angelo and James both cracked up. James intuited what his friend needed: *Later for that bullshit. This is what's important.* D got off the phone, charged anew, and wrote a song called "Really Love."* Moments like these confirmed for D'Angelo that they were kindred souls, and that James, on the MPC alone, was his true musical peer. D had a chance to show him what that meant.

James had come to Electric Lady with Slum Village during their A&M days, working on a track for *Fantastic, Vol. 2*. Visitors often wanted to hear a preview of D'Angelo's album, and the "showpiece" track was a rough mix of a song called "The Root." James was stunned by what he heard: Questlove's drums, sampled and programmed by D'Angelo on an MPC, the snare rushed, the guitar and bass dragging against the beat, every element unmoored from the next, yet driving forward.

James was quiet as the song ended. D studied his expression, wondering what he was thinking.

"Could you play that again?" James asked. D'Angelo recued the song. James sat again, in silence, hearing for the first time his ideas reflected back to him by a group of musicians whose skills on their instruments were commensurate with his on the machine. D could tell James wanted to hear it a third time but held himself back from asking. "The Root" stayed on repeat in his mind during James's flight back to Detroit, and he stayed up all night in the basement to re-create the song from memory on his MPC. He returned to New York, and played a stunned D'Angelo the results, D now hearing his take on Jay Dee's ideas reflected back to

---

* This song would not surface on a D'Angelo album until 2014.

him by Jay Dee himself. When Questlove heard the track over the phone, the remake was so faithful that the drummer thought James had somehow gotten possession of a cassette dub of D'Angelo's song.[*]

It was in this way that James—shuttling back and forth to Electric Lady—was gradually drawn into all the projects underway at the studio. D'Angelo's album still hadn't yielded a clear-cut single. Maybe it would be the upcoming duet with Lauryn Hill? D'Angelo had appeared on her Grammy-winning solo debut the previous year, and Questlove thought Jay Dee would be the perfect choice to produce the follow-up when she returned the favor. Meanwhile, D'Angelo had other ideas: he, Tip, and James had started a track together; and, for a different song, D seized a stuttering, polyrhythmic Jay Dee beat to write to.[†]

As the musicians bounced between Electric Lady's three studios, A, B, and C, the lines between projects—Common, D'Angelo, Erykah Badu, each paid for out of different recording budgets by different labels—were often blurred. They'd jam all day and divvy up the tracks at night. D'Angelo, Poyser, Questlove, and Pino Palladino banged out a track for Common to rap over. It was so good that D'Angelo took Questlove aside and whispered: "On Yahweh, man, you know and I know that funk belongs to me."

So they traded. The Common track became a D'Angelo song called "Chicken Grease," and D'Angelo gave up a song that became Common's "Geto Heaven, Part Two," for which D'Angelo had already sung the hook. Common now had a D'Angelo cameo on his album and D'Angelo got his groove back. Both tracks featured the same players, and the executives at MCA may have never realized that they paid for a track that ended up on an EMI album, and vice versa.

The sessions at Electric Lady also blurred lines that James had drawn in his own mind. James saw himself as a programmer, but here he found partners who saw serious programming and serious musicianship as one and the same, and thus treated him as a serious musician. Common's song "Time Travelin'" began as a bass line that James played on a Rhodes

---

[*] D'Angelo says that he still holds out hope that James's version of "The Root" exists somewhere.

[†] D'Angelo says that the first track, in which he plays a real Mellotron, is lost; the second one, which appeared on Jay Dee's "Another Batch" beat tape from 1998, is sometimes called "Marvine."

keyboard—*the* Rhodes keyboard. As James played, Questlove added a thumping kick drum to support him. Poyser conjured a moody chord from an organ, and D'Angelo threw an arpeggiated keyboard line on top. Of all the tracks that came out of the sessions at Electric Lady, this was the only one that D'Angelo, Questlove, Poyser, and Jay Dee worked on together. Yet these four began to see themselves as a unit.

One day, James overheard Questlove mention that his and Poyser's birthdays were both in late January.

"I was born February 7," James told them.

"Wait a minute," D'Angelo said, feeling the hairs rising on his skin. "I was born February 11."

James noted that all four of them were Aquarians—a star sign whose children could be inspired, creative revolutionaries or unreliable, detached enigmas, depending on one's perspective.* They began referring to themselves, jokingly, as "Soulquarians."

At first, it wasn't anything but a conversation among four friends, and the designation wasn't meant to signify something of greater import.

A ll James's partnerships were changing. James was still signed as a member of the Ummah, but his discomfort with the surrendering of personal credit and the sharing of money that it entailed had reached an apex, particularly with Q-Tip's cut of songs on which James felt he did most of the work. But thus far James had been unwilling to confront his mentor. After he began managing Slum Village, Tim Maynor volunteered to step in and speak up for James, but the phone call Maynor set up to discuss the matter with Micheline and the other producers devolved into an argument. The situation was uncomfortable for Micheline, wanting to remain an unbiased advocate for all her clients, understanding both Q-Tip's hurt feelings and James's desire to be free. The two of them needed to talk, and she told them so.

---

* Ahmir "Questlove" Thompson, born January 20, 1971, is on the cusp between this zodiac sign and the previous one, Capricorn—making him, appropriately, a "rushed" Aquarius.

Q-Tip had heard all the gossip about him trying to co-opt Jay Dee and take his money, ironic payback indeed for all his equitable intentions. Tip prided himself in being scrupulous in his business dealings. *But,* he thought, *when I have to mix the songs because Jay Dee doesn't show up to the client's sessions, am I seriously not supposed to be paid for my work?* Honesty was supposed to flow both ways in a relationship. In the end, Q-Tip had to reckon with what rankled him the most: after all Tip had done for him, James didn't want to be that closely related.

When Tip and James did speak, James finally found his words. It wasn't about the money, or lack of gratitude for his benefactor. "I just want people to know it's me," he told Tip.

That conversation essentially ended the Ummah. But, paradoxically, it released most of the tension between James and Q-Tip. Free of their obligations to each other, they could now relate more purely as friends at the precise moment that their separate journeys had become somewhat parallel: James becoming disillusioned with Slum Village, Q-Tip severing his ties to A Tribe Called Quest. Micheline concluded a protracted negotiation to release Tip from Tribe's label, Jive, and signed him to another imprint in the BMG family, Arista Records, with the help of Drew Dixon, the young A&R executive who convinced the Arista chief Clive Davis of the rapper's worth as a solo artist.

Q-Tip never wanted people to focus on him. He believed that a group is always stronger than an individual. So how did a man who loathed the spotlight embark on a solo career? Fans got a peek when Q-Tip released a single, "Vivrant Thing," built around a simple loop of a Love Unlimited Orchestra disco song. The tune was breezy, Q-Tip rapping about love and sex, not cultural politics; his manner unpretentious, like the shedding of a red, black, and green coat that had become too heavy. The black-and-white video that accompanied it, directed by Hype Williams, was similarly understated, cool, and funny, Tip finally allowing himself to be the sexy center of attention.

When James first heard the track as a demo, he and T3 phoned Tip from the car: "Ohhhhhhhh, boyyyy," James said. "You wanna *play?*" Q-Tip's solo excursion galvanized James, and he buried himself in the lab for the next couple of weeks to create beats that fit Tip's new vibe.

Frank called Tip from Detroit: "Your man has been going crazy since you sent him that shit." James began sending Q-Tip discs in the mail, and he would end up making at least nine of the dozen blistering tracks for Q-Tip's first solo album, *Amplified*, each of them credited to "Jay Dee & Q-Tip for the Ummah"—more a lingering, contractual relic than reality. The Ummah was dead. The brotherhood lived through.

James didn't much like New York, but the city invariably reminded him of how far he'd come.

Chuck Moore, his running buddy from Davis Aero Tech and rhyme partner in the Flattop Society, happened to be in town. They caught up over a meal: Chuck's singing career had recently taken off when the singer Michael Bivins, producer of the Philly pop-soul quartet Boyz II Men, signed him to his Motown-distributed label, Biv 10. Chuck now went by the stage name "Gator." On another Manhattan evening, when Proof was visiting, he and James bumped into jessica Care moore, who was then collaborating with the rap artist Nas. She set eyes on the person she had known as the shy producer "Jon Doe" for the first time since her going-away party in 1995, his short frame now swimming in a glorious, full-length black mink coat.

"You are *so* Detroit!" she shouted. It took one to know one.

James often did a little East Coast swing, dipping from Motown to Philly and back again. His relationship to the City of Brotherly Love wasn't through his comrades in the Roots, but via his unlikely friendship with one of the greatest DJs in hip-hop. "DJ Jazzy Jeff" Townes reached the pinnacle of mainstream fame a decade earlier with his partner Will "The Fresh Prince" Smith, their video for "Parents Just Don't Understand" inaugurating MTV's commitment to hip-hop in the form of *Yo! MTV Raps*. And though Will had since become a huge TV star and Jeff had tagged along, dividing his time between Philadelphia and Hollywood to guest star on *The Fresh Prince of Bel-Air*, Jazzy Jeff remained a loyal subject of hip-hop. It was on one of his excursions to L.A. in 1997 that he heard Slum Village's "I Don't Know" on the radio for the first time—played by a DJ from an L.A. crew called the Beat Junkies, who had bought dozens of Ramos's bootlegs in Japan. Jeff lost his mind, so much that he didn't realize the track was, in fact, an homage to his song "Brand New Funk." After he called the station to ask the name of the record, DJ Jazzy Jeff became a superfan of Slum Village and Jay Dee.

Several months later, Common introduced him to James by phone; several conversations later, Jeff dangled an irresistible invitation before the young producer: there was a vast used-record warehouse whose stock remained untapped by their mutual hip-hop competitors. He and a bunch of friends, including the famed DJ "Kenny Dope" Gonzalez, were going there. The only catch? It was in Pittsburgh. James flew to Philadelphia. After Jeff gave him a whirlwind tour of the city, they crashed at Jeff's house until 3:00 a.m., when they began the five-hour drive in Kenny's Lincoln Navigator.

For James—riding through the night next to someone he'd idolized since he was in middle school—it was yet another surreal moment with a hero who treated him as a respected peer. For Jeff, James represented an ideal, the person he really wanted to be and couldn't because of his own success—the kid who did nothing but stay in the studio all day making music. Pushing through the doors as soon as Jerry's Records in Pittsburgh unlocked them, Jeff felt rusty; he hadn't gone record shopping in a long time. But James and Kenny knew where the good stuff was, and they started making piles of records for Jeff. By the time the doors closed, they had bought so much vinyl that there wasn't enough room for them in the truck. James had to lie down on top of the records all the way back to Philly.

James made frequent day trips to Philadelphia thereafter. He'd call "Uncle Jeff" in the morning, and if the DJ was free to hang out, James would hop a fifty-five-dollar Spirit Airlines flight out of City Airport and be in Philly by lunch. Jeff would take him to South Street—first to Jim's or Ishkabibble's for a cheesesteak, then record shopping or to Neeve, which became James's custom jeweler of choice—and back to Jeff's crib or the new production studio complex he'd established on North Third Street, A Touch of Jazz. It was there that DJ Jazzy Jeff first got to watch Jay Dee make a beat: working the MPC, knowing intuitively what parts of records to use, rarely taking more than fifteen minutes to compose it from start to finish, evoking in Jeff the same astonishment that Q-Tip and Ali experienced years earlier.

But Jeff listened closer and watched harder: *How was James getting this humanlike rhythmic feel out of the machine?* He didn't dare ask him or crowd him. On his own time, Jeff experimented, trying to emulate Jay Dee, first by testing different quantizations for his drum sounds—sixteenth notes, sixteenth-note triplets, thirty-second notes—nothing worked. Jeff tried *not* quantizing, playing freehand—that didn't work either; what James was doing wasn't accidental, it was deliberate. Then he realized that James was using the drum machine to shift the timing of his sounds—the snare backward, so it rushed a little bit; the hi-hats forward—duplicating his patterns, modifying each of them slightly and then stringing them together to form a whole. Jeff's discovery led to a deeper realization: everyone in hip-hop had heretofore been trying to cut, splice, and jam samples to accommodate the machine's time grid, because producers were focused on mining samples for their *sounds*. But Jay Dee did the opposite: he bent the machine grid to accommodate his sample sources, because he was focused on using those samples for their rhythmic and harmonic *feel*. DJ Jazzy Jeff's fascination with Jay Dee's techniques was shared by several of the producers in Jeff's stable—many of them, like James, hip-hop heads who grew up steeped in the deep soul of church music. Soon James's ideas began to surface in their production.

James—shuttling between Detroit, Philadelphia, and New York—thus became a vital character in the tale of these three cities' role in neo-soul. While much of the recording happened in New York, a great deal of the talent came from Philadelphia, and all drew inspiration from Jay Dee's Detroit rhythms. Questlove's legendary living room jam sessions—featuring singers like Bilal Oliver and Jill Scott—morphed into a roving club called Black Lily, first in New York and then back to Philadelphia. Jill Scott had penned a hit song for the Roots, "You Got Me," but her vocals were replaced by those of Erykah Badu at the urging of MCA CEO Jay Boberg. Jazzy Jeff ended up signing Scott to A Touch of Jazz, and his producers recorded her debut album while working with another Black Lily alumnus, Taalib Johnson, performing as Musiq Soulchild.

Questlove's home in Philadelphia was a metaphor for his body: rhythm raging downstairs, a lot going on upstairs; his analytical, intellectual obsessions found an outlet in a project taking shape in his second-floor bedroom, where Angela Nissel, a recent Penn grad, assembled a team of friends to build the Roots' first website. Two decisions would make it much more than that. In an era where most band sites were nothing more than static landing pages, Questlove and Nissel envisioned their site as a space where fans would come hang with the band and talk about music. Nissel's suggestion was to create message boards for connection, discussion, and debate. And when the Roots found someone else squatting on their ideal domain name, TheRoots.com, they decided to use a neutral one based on a common Philly salutation: Okay player.com. That decision proved fateful: Nissel and the Roots' business manager Shawn Gee began selling the site as a collective home for other, like-minded artists.

Questlove brought Nissel to Electric Lady during Common's sessions to enroll artists in Okayplayer's central mission: interacting with fans online. It wasn't an easy sell. Many artists had neither email accounts nor computers. Unlike Questlove, who spent a half dozen hours each day on the message boards, Common didn't really take well to sitting in front of a keyboard and chatting with fans. But Nissel ended up hanging with him and Jay Dee, writing and performing on a skit that lampooned the rapper's "conscious" image.[*]

In the months to come, Okayplayer became the central web portal for the Roots, Common, D'Angelo, Talib Kweli, and many other neo-soul and hip-hop artists. Okayplayer also became one of the internet's first virtual communities, a way for Black bohemians, nerds of color, and their multiracial followers around the globe to circumvent the commercial musical monoculture of magazines, radio, and television, years before there was something called "social media." And even though James

---

[*] Years later, Nissel would turn those talents toward a career in comedy writing for television shows like *Scrubs* and *Mixed-ish*.

rarely logged on, he reigned as a main obsession of the people in this placeless place, unbound by geography, who called themselves "Okayplayers," who shared digital files of Slum Village's tracks and wondered whether their amazing album would ever see the light of day.

The query came to R. J. Rice as a surprise: a label in California wanted to distribute Slum Village's *Fantastic, Vol. 2*. It was a tiny imprint called Good Vibe Recordings, and the call came from its founder, Matt Kahane.

Kahane had been an aspiring rapper in his teens, signed and then shelved by Jimmy Iovine at Interscope. He created Good Vibe with some friends in part to give voice to hip-hop artists who couldn't thrive at the major labels. His successes were modest, mostly underground, eclectic West Coast hip-hop. Kahane first heard a bootleg of *Fantastic, Vol. 2* around the time he landed a funding and distribution deal with a new outfit, Atomic Pop, which aimed to be the first fully internet-native record company. C-Minus at Power 106 had hipped him to Jay Dee years before, but Kahane was equally taken with T3 and Baatin. When he heard the story about how Slum Village were shelved by Interscope, just like he had been, signing them became a crusade.

Within a few weeks, Kahane flew to Detroit to meet the group. Jay Dee was, apparently, out of town. But Kahane hung with T3 and Baatin, R. J. and Tim, and together they hammered out a deal in the low six figures—part of which included the funds that R. J.'s company, Barak, would need to buy the album back from Interscope. And because *Fantastic, Vol. 2* had already been pirated so widely, the group agreed to provide four more songs for the official release.

Kahane returned to Los Angeles to generate the paperwork, brushing back a last-minute attempt by Atomic Pop's lawyers to yank a clause that would revert ownership of the album back to Barak Records after a few years. But Kahane was adamant. *You don't pull the rug out from under your partners' feet and expect that things are gonna be cool.*

Then, after the deal was signed, R. J. and Tim Maynor pulled the rug out from under Kahane: they told him that Jay Dee was leaving the group.

T3 spent a decade mediating his two partners' moods and whims. Sometimes it felt like he had one hand on Baatin's collar, and the other on James's, and that his arms couldn't stretch any farther.

He sensed the beginning of the end for James was Slum Village's album review in *The Source*, published prematurely in the beginning of 1999 after A&M's media relations department sent out cassette advances prior to the label's closure. Everyone from the guys in Slum to the most famous artists scrutinized the album rankings in hip-hop's premier publication, the top rating of five "mics" coveted most of all. But in a small piece wedged between reviews of two lesser-known artists, Felicia A. Williams called *Fantastic, Vol. 2* "a damn good first attempt" that slipped "into moments of monotony," the album receiving only three and a half "mics." T3 could tell that James was hurt by it and wanted to move on. It was probably why James left the European tour before it ended. It was during a Slum Village photo shoot later that year that James finally called it quits.

"I don't think I'ma do this no more, T," James told him as he wiped the rims and tires of his Range Rover, not even looking him in the eye. "You're just gonna have to make it happen without me."

T3 didn't tell Baatin that day. He didn't tell anybody for a while. Unbeknownst to T3, James had already confided in R. J. and Tim that he wanted out: he didn't want to be part of a group, and certainly didn't want to be the heir to A Tribe Called Quest. He just wanted to produce. Slum always seemed to have a dark cloud following them—Hoops, A&M, Interscope—and now T3 worried that their deal with Good Vibe might be in jeopardy, too.

But T3 was surprised that Kahane took the news of James's departure in stride. In fact, Kahane seemed to value T3 and Baatin as much as he valued James. *That* was something new. James's declaration of independence seemed to soften the producer's will as well, and James vowed to his friends and Kahane that he would give whatever time he could—to appear in the videos and in several of the tour dates—as long as it made financial sense for him to do so.

Time to finish. As 1999 drew to a close, Common began mixing the album he was now calling *Like Water for Chocolate*. Jay Dee's appearances at his sessions in New York were as unpredictable as they had been in Detroit. Sometimes Common would beg James to fly out and he wouldn't show, and at others James volunteered to make the trip. When he did, Common tried his best to keep James comfortable by buying a ticket for Frank and putting them both up in a hotel.

Russ Elevado polished the songs they had tracked with the live band at Electric Lady, and Common and Jay Dee worked with Bob Power to mix the more electronic, programmed material they'd begun together in Detroit. Among those songs, the one that raised the eyebrows of manager Derek Dudley and MCA executive Wendy Goldstein as a potential single was a track called "The Light."

James took a piece of choppy piano from a ballad performed by the blue-eyed soul crooner Bobby Caldwell and set it underneath drums sliced out of an Ohio Players single, "Funky Worm."* The Caldwell piano, so rhythmically straight that it was almost cornball, contrasted with the swing and syncopation of the rhythm track. The text of the song mirrored this corny-cool incongruity: a three-verse epistolary poem, an earnest love letter written by Common to a long-distance paramour, juxtaposed with a chorus scratched in by James from a dusty piece of vinyl, composed of jagged bits of Caldwell's vocal: "*There are tiiiimes when you neeeeeed someone, I will be byyyyy your side / There is a light that shiiiiiines special for you aaaaand me.*"

It was unorthodox, but not unconventional enough for Questlove, the lone skeptic about "The Light." As the most rabid Jay Dee fan in the crew, he found it unworthy of his idol's best efforts. Questlove didn't succeed in jettisoning the song from the album, but the consensus for the

---

* The drums in this record were spliced from the Detroit Emeralds' "You're Getting a Little Too Smart."

first single shifted to "The Sixth Sense," featuring a sung chorus from Bilal Oliver and a track produced by DJ Premier, whose songs tended to be sure-shots among the hip-hop core audience. Despite being denied this first slot, Jay Dee had a hand in the creation of eleven of the album's sixteen tracks.

Meanwhile, James had committed to finishing the additional tracks for the Good Vibe release of *Fantastic, Vol. 2*. Three of the songs had been completed in Detroit: the lopsided "CB4"; the techno-inspired "Raise It Up," for which James recorded the vocals fresh out of bed to make his voice as raspy as possible; and "Untitled," a perfect example of Slum Village "three-ness," James's verses mimicking the beat, T3 slipping and stutter-stepping, Baatin's timbre dipping low and leaping high, all over Jay Dee's rushed snare.

For the fourth track, Slum Village submitted the song recorded during their pilgrimage to Electric Lady, which hadn't made it onto the A&M version of the album. Questlove had asked James: *How do you want to do this? Do you want to program a beat and me and D'Angelo will re-create it, or just do like we do for D's album and jam until we come up with something?*

James chose the latter.

The drummer had another question, an awkward one to ask. *When me and D jam, we have two "North Stars" we usually follow: Prince . . . or* you. *Which way do you want us to go?*

James paused. Then he said: *Treat it like me.*

James, T3, and Baatin adjourned to the break room to have some food while the musicians knocked around in Studio A, Questlove on drums and D'Angelo on the Fender Rhodes. After a half hour, they'd come up with nothing. But when D'Angelo began riffing on the bass line from Marvin Gaye's "Flyin' High," the groove clicked. Slum returned to the control room and, through the glass, Questlove saw Baatin jumping in the air. The groove, which James would then chop and arrange with a chorus sung by D'Angelo, became the Slum Village song "Tell Me."

And still, D'Angelo continued recording in this timeless studio as if time weren't money. He was protected in part by his new manager Dominique Trenier, who understood that D'Angelo's delays came not from dithering but from a meticulous, innate sense of when things felt and sounded *right*. Trenier insulated D'Angelo as best as he could from label pressure, but Trenier's partner, an older music business veteran named Stan Poses, seemed to relish playing bad cop with the artist, interrupting his sessions for "emergency meetings" and provoking him. *He really wants me to punch him in his face*, D'Angelo thought. D almost did, but he didn't. Desperate for progress, the EMI brass appealed to Russ Elevado, until this point a coconspirator in the artist's protracted process, to get the album delivered. As the latest deadline neared, D'Angelo told Elevado that he wanted to record a new song he'd cowritten with Raphael Saadiq. When Elevado gave him the slightest pushback, referencing the dozens of unfinished songs they could and should complete instead, D'Angelo left the studio. Thankfully, the artist prevailed: the song they tracked—"Untitled (How Does It Feel)"—became the breakout single from the project.

A few months before the release of the album, dubbed *Voodoo*, Questlove wrote a track-by-track breakdown and posted it on Okayplayer. *Voodoo*, he wrote, was born out of "a love for the dead state of black music, a love to show our idols how much they taught us," referencing Slum Village in that list of inspirations. At the end of the piece, Ahmir wrote a cryptic sentence: *"jaydee did the lauryn track."*

His words, alas, were written before *Voodoo*'s final sequencing. Lauryn Hill never did show up to Electric Lady, and according to D'Angelo, the song he intended to record with her, a remake of "Feel Like Makin' Love," was not based on a track from Jay Dee. The other tracks that Jay Dee offered for D'Angelo's album were never finished. They had simply run out of time.

O n November 30, 1999, at the Kit Kat Klub in Times Square, Arista Records and Q-Tip hosted a party celebrating the release of his first solo album, *Amplified*. The celebration ended when another rapper, Jay-Z, stabbed the artist manager Lance "Un" Rivera several times with a five-inch knife because he suspected Rivera of bootlegging his album.

The ensuing media coverage of the assault demoted Q-Tip and his album to a mere footnote in a different, sensational story about hip-hop and violence, a metaphor for how mainstream hip-hop had sidelined Native Tongues groups like A Tribe Called Quest and De La Soul, the very phenomenon they lamented in "Stakes Is High." But the fans who still needed Q-Tip to be their standard-bearer for that kind of Afrocentric and "conscious" hip-hop were shocked when they saw the video for *Amplified*'s second single.

"Breathe and Stop" had been produced by Jay Dee as a kind of amplified "Vivrant Thing." The video, directed again by Hype Williams, revisited many of the same elements that made the first clip so endearing—the head-nodding girls, the humor. But in flipping from black-and-white to Technicolor, the concept lost its artsy nuance. To some fans, this new, solo Q-Tip was as debauched as many of the "shiny suit" artists they reviled from Jay-Z or Puffy's camp. Okayplayer hosted this vigorous debate about Q-Tip's new direction; and also about Jay Dee, with some pegging the decline of Tribe and Tip to Jay Dee's involvement on *Beats, Rhymes and Life* in 1996, a charge that others called unfair.

"Breathe and Stop" stalled just below the top twenty at Black radio in the United States, a casualty of Clive Davis's flagging attention during his forced exit from Arista Records. Though it became a gold record, *Amplified* was considered a commercial failure by executives, and a creative failure by some fans—not earthy enough for old followers, and not shiny enough for new ones. As a result, the album would be somewhat overlooked as an artifact of Jay Dee's consummate production skills, at least in comparison to the outsize impact of two others that followed.

D'Angelo's *Voodoo* and Common's *Like Water for Chocolate* dropped in early 2000. Sophisticated twins from the womb of Electric Lady, praised by critics and fans, both reflected the rhythmic and aesthetic influence of Jay Dee, albeit in different ways: *Voodoo* became the first full-scale application of James Yancey's time-feel by a group of traditional musicians, and *Like Water for Chocolate* demonstrated how Jay Dee himself applied his techniques.

James had become a vital part of a new crew, but his contributions continued to be obscured. For each track that he produced on Common's album, the credit read: *Produced by the Soulquarians' Jay Dee for the Ummah.*

After a half dozen years in the music business, James's name was still smothered in brotherhood.

What hurt James more was his tangible absence from the credits of D'Angelo's album—even though none of the tracks he submitted were finished, James felt a keen sense of investment in and the presence of his influence on *Voodoo*. Back in Detroit, DJ House Shoes brought the vinyl over to the basement. James scanned the lengthy liner notes and turned to Shoes.

"Where's my name?" he asked.[*]

B ilal Oliver's work on Common's album helped land him a deal with Interscope. When the singer began recording, he made Jay Dee's Detroit basement one of his first destinations. He brought a friend with him.

Robert Glasper and Bilal met each other in 1997 on the first day of freshman orientation at the New School for Jazz and Contemporary Music, and had been inseparable thereafter. Bilal knew that Glasper, a piano prodigy, had been a fan of Jay Dee's since high school in Houston when he first heard Busta Rhymes's "Still Shining": The spastic kick drum, the patterns of clustered chords that never quite repeated themselves as they would have in most hip-hop songs. "Still Shining" seemed *composed* all the way through, different in every measure. These were the choices of a musical mind, Glasper knew.

Thus Glasper was shocked but not altogether surprised when he walked into the basement and saw another musician he respected: Karriem Riggins. His peers at the New School might have wondered what a

---

* It is worth noting that the lack of credit for influence and ideas happened a few times on James's end as well—as when T3 and Proof found samples that ended up in James's production for the Pharcyde, and also when D'Angelo and Ahmir "Questlove" Thompson helped write the music for Slum Village's "Tell Me."

great jazz drummer was doing in the basement of a hip-hop producer, but again, Glasper knew.

James, for his part, didn't know Glasper at all. The pianist, with his wild dreadlocks and tattered bell-bottom jeans, had ventured into the kitchen, come back with a butcher's cleaver, and paced casually around the basement with it.

James whispered to Karriem: "This guy's crazy."

Glasper's eyes landed on the shelves on the south side of the basement, probably the biggest and most well-kept collection of records he had ever seen. James started pulling out albums, playing them, and the hip-hop producer began schooling the pianist on the work of Herbie Hancock. Then Glasper watched, slack-jawed, as Jay Dee—in seemingly no time at all—created a composition out of sounds from three different records that became a basis for a Bilal song, "Reminisce."

T3 and Baatin came over, and they brought Bilal and Glasper along on James's Detroit circuit—to Chocolate City for dinner and dances, and roving "The Mile" in James's Range, where Glasper heard tracks from the still unreleased *Fantastic, Vol. 2* for the first time, their woozy, drunken rhythms the most aggressive rhythmic subversion he had ever heard. Then they came back to the basement and recorded another song, "Broke My Neck to Check You Out." Glasper returned the next day to his life as a sophomore studying in one of jazz's better institutions. But Glasper knew he'd just been schooled.

J ay Dee was no longer the most successful product of Detroit hip-hop. Eminem had become a multiplatinum star, and he and manager Paul Rosenberg began their own Interscope-distributed label, Shady Records. Eminem signed his mentor Proof's group—the Dirty Dozen, or D12—as Shady's first act. Maureen Yancey wondered if James resented being eclipsed. James told her: "Don't worry about that, lady. There's a time for everything."

The rise of Eminem gave more hope to Detroit hip-hop artists, and James had a long line of MCs in his camp who had been waiting for their turn. Phat Kat, who had given James his first production credit, remained at the ready whenever Jay Dee called him to lace a track. With James's blessing, DJ House Shoes pressed up three Phat Kat songs into an EP, *Dedication to the Suckers*. Shoes found a willing distributor in Fat Beats, whose head of A&R, Amir Abdullah, was a Jay Dee fan and bought all six thousand copies of Shoes's first pressing.

Ramos connected James with Abdullah and Fat Beats for the debut of two other important Jay Dee protégés, Frank-n-Dank. Frank Bush DJed with James in his youth, but now he had a day job fixing cars and installing stereos, and moonlighted as James's wingman: an official greeter and livery driver for visiting artists, and his audio-engineer-in-training. Derrick "Dank" Harvey came through less often because he was busy "on the streets," making money hustling drugs. But T3 had become a fan of Dank's constricted, high-pitched voice, and was the first to make the suggestion that he and Frank rhyme as a duo, producing their first demo, "Young Buck." The Frank-n-Dank concept languished until Dank got out of the drug game. To test his friends' stamina, James said he would help them if they did three songs without him, a "boot camp" of sorts in which they worked with T3 and Karriem Riggins. James heard the results, liked them, and produced four more tracks that he released through Fat Beats as the first two Frank-n-Dank singles, sold to Abdullah for $10,000 each.

Slowly, James made sure everyone in his Conant Gardens crew got their shot. Waajeed expressed an interest in becoming a producer. James handed him an MPC2000 that had broken when Questlove jammed a floppy disk inside it. *If you can get the disk out*, James told him, *you can keep it*. Waajeed did, and then did little else for the next year but practice, and there began his new career. Waajeed, in turn, advocated on behalf of James's cousin Que.D, who had transitioned from dancing for Slum Village to rapping. James recorded his cousin in the same brutal way that he'd tracked the first volume of *Fan-Tas-Tic*: to a simple click track, one take, no mistakes, matching the rhymes to beats later. The resulting project, a six-song EP called *Quite Delicious*, was first printed on a short run of cassette tapes, with artwork created by Waajeed. Eventually, Amir Abdullah at Fat Beats got a hold of the cassette and offered Que.D a deal to put a few of the songs on vinyl, which then led to a

deal for a second single. But once Que.D had the paperwork in hand
for James to sign, his cousin wouldn't return his calls. Desperate, Que.D
did the one thing that he knew risked pissing James off: he showed up
unannounced.

"What the fuck are you doing at my door?" James spat. "If I don't tell
you to come through, you don't just show up!"

The commotion roused Dank from his seat in the basement. Dank
told the cousins to knock it off, James calmed and signed the papers.
Ten minutes later he and Que.D were chatting about something else,
like the argument had never happened. That was James, always: he
could be super generous, but he always needed to be the one to control
time.

J oylette was doing better for herself. She got a job as a surgical tech
in the labor and delivery wing at St. Joseph's hospital in Mount Cle-
mens, far out in the suburbs. James had never stopped calling her, asking her to come back. He showed her a house Maureen had found for
him not far from their old place, a small Tudor on a quiet street, Sherwood Drive in Huntington Woods. *For the two of us*, he said. Joy tested
his commitment. She invited James to a New Year's Eve service at her
church. Common was in town to finish up his album, but James came
anyway. He listened while she got up and testified in front of the congregation, and together they brought in the new millennium.

Weeks later, Joy moved into the house on Sherwood. She made James
buy a new mattress, figuring that he had slept with other women on the
old one; Joy had a thing about mattresses. She wanted James to move his
studio to the new basement. There was no way Joy was letting that old
place continue to be a potential playhouse for James.*

---

* There is a story that Joylette relays about this particular issue, a conversation that is pivotal for her but one
that Maureen Yancey says never happened. In Joy's recollection, during a visit from James's parents, she,
James, and Maureen were talking in the kitchen. Joy says that Maureen was encouraging James to keep his
studio at the house on Nevada, while she was insistent on relocating his studio to the new house—a key point
for her given James's infidelity. According to Joy, after Maureen kept talking about it, James said, exasperated:
"MAUREEN!" Joy says it was the first time that she had seen James back his mother off. It is a fact that James
moved his studio to the house in Huntington Woods, but Maureen says that it is only because James could
not get the owner of the house on McDougall and Nevada to sell it to him at a reasonable price. James under-

The move brought another change: James now told Joy that he wanted her to have his baby. Joy was confused. *Why the sudden interest?* They had talked about waiting until she was thirty.

"Naw, I'm ready," James said.

It wasn't a lie, but it wasn't the whole story, either. What Joy didn't know, and what James didn't tell her, is that he had gotten another woman pregnant, and that she was about to give birth. Ty-Monae Paige Whitlow was born on February 13, 2000, while James was in New York. When he returned to Detroit, he came to Monica's parents' house to see his daughter.

"She looks just like my sister Martha," he said. He was too timid to hold her.

Over the next several years, James saw his daughter occasionally, bringing gifts and necessities. During those visits Monica would cook for him and fret over him as a girlfriend or a partner would. But it was not in any way an equitable relationship: James could come and go as he pleased, and give her money when he felt he needed to.

Joy remained in the dark about his first child. And James didn't make an effort to introduce his daughter to the rest of his family. Maureen would not meet Ty-Monae until she turned four.

The significant women in James's life, whether in the professional or personal realms, were more caregivers than partners. As it was for many men in his circle of family and friends, women were either objects of desire to be chased and kept, or figures to worship and protect. Women who knew James casually experienced him as shy, sweet, and polite. And he *was* shy, sweet, and polite. But in his adulthood, James's main interaction with women happened in the controlled environment of the strip club, where the relationship between men and women was strictly transactional, and the power of choice resided in the men with the most money. James leveraged his clout to maintain his control, or to escape consequences.

---

stood, Maureen says, the energetic significance of the place. Frank Bush says that, as far as he knew, "it was always the plan" to move the studio to Huntington Woods.

Hip-hop, too, was a boys' club wherein men were the power brokers, the most valued performers and producers; and where the casual misogyny of rappers and rap lyrics was often waved away as hyperbole. In the business, James rarely met women as equal collaborators.

That changed when Erykah Badu came to town; her presence short-circuited his usual order of operations, because Erykah was going to set the pace. He sent Frank to fetch her at the Westin Renaissance hotel downtown; she asked Frank to stop at a grocery store on the way. Paranoid about protecting the Grammy Award–winning artist as she walked the aisles, he watched her gather ingredients to brew a pot of special tea that would sustain her through the upcoming sessions. Back at the kitchen at the house on McDougall, Frank thought: *This is some bomb-ass tea. Probably voodoo tea.*

This is how it was for Erykah. Her new romantic relationship with Common couldn't be just a relationship. Even a pot of tea couldn't be just a pot of tea. It all had to be a bid for surreptitious control of men. She had to be "crazy." And Erykah, being nobody's fool but enjoying acting a fool, often deliberately played into those expectations.

Down in the basement James played her some beats. Badu didn't want any of them. *I want to make something together*, she said. It was a reasonable expectation, but James was now used to artists taking what he gave them. James thought: *I'm really being put to work here*, in equal parts respect and irritation. James reacted by becoming her teacher: He pointed Erykah toward the stacks and told her to pick out a record. She came back with an album, *The Very Best of Tarika Blue*, found a track she liked, "Dreamflower," and James showed her how to sample it into the MPC and loop it. James added drums and decided it needed something more. He called DJ Dez, whose father was a skilled Latin percussionist, and Dez brought his bongos and shakers to the basement and helped James complete the track. Erykah began writing the lyrics to the song that, in short order, became "Didn't Cha Know," which would itself be nominated for a Grammy the following year.

The sessions, which yielded two tracks for Erykah's album *Mama's Gun*, were short and successful. And Erykah kept James in her creative circle thereafter: on a flight with James Poyser from Atlanta to New York for a session at Electric Lady, she insisted, "I need Jay Dee." James showed

up diligently the next day with three records under his arm. He made the
track with those three records, Poyser marveled, and returned to Detroit
the same evening.

But Erykah would elicit ambivalent reactions from James in the years
to come. In interviews, James called her a "diva"; in private moments
with some people close to him, he seemed spooked by their interactions,
calling her "crazy." But that may very well have been macho bluster and
not how he really felt: as far as Frank and Poyser saw, James had great respect for the singer, and she for him. He may simply have been irritated
about having to be of service and on his best behavior. Erykah, for her
part, later relayed with relish a story about teasing James: Common had
come to Detroit while she and James were working. When Common
stepped out of the basement for a moment, Erykah snuck up behind
James and breathed into his ear: *Now, we're finally alone. You're such a
sexy guy.* When Common returned, she snapped herself away from James
as conspicuously as possible. For Erykah, an irrepressible wit, this was
typical mischief. Even if James found it amusing, it was a rare occasion
where someone made *him* the butt of a joke.

The comic tension seeped into a more serious moment. For a man
who wasn't often sick, James had two recurring issues. The first involved
his hands, and seemed related to his obsessiveness about work: Sometimes his fingers would blister and bleed after working the drum machines and records for hours on end, and he'd bandage them up so he
could keep going. More lately, his hands had begun to ache. His aunt Reta
Hayes recommended he soak them in warm paraffin wax. The second ail-
ment was migraines so painful that Joylette would occasionally see them
bring James to tears; when he got them, everything in the house had to
remain quiet. During the sessions with Erykah, James was seized by a
vicious headache. He asked Frank to take over and excused himself to go
lie down upstairs. Within a few minutes, Erykah arrived and brought him
a cup of her tea. She then began massaging his neck and head.

This part wasn't a joke for Erykah. But for James, it was another ambivalent moment. On one hand, Erykah was taking a female role he understood: caretaker; and he was grateful for the care. And yet, since it
was not only a beautiful woman straddling him, but the world-famous

Erykah Badu, it also titillated him just a bit, triggering images of the other role that women played in his life. The moment would inform a story that he later told to Gilles Peterson's BBC audience with a mischief of his own about that innocent interaction.

Erykah Badu jolted James out of his usual rhythms—the defiance of expectation, the experience of not being in control. But it was medicine nonetheless.

James honored his pledge to Slum Village and Good Vibe Recordings, flying to Los Angeles for the group's first-ever video shoot. Matt Kahane decided to film two clips, for "Climax" and "Raise It Up," booking the Universal lot because it had a decent outdoor "city" set. He even flew in Frank-n-Dank at Jay Dee's request, and spent hours before the shoot driving James from store to store to find him the "7 Up" shirt he wanted to wear—even though Kahane had made them all custom Slum jerseys. Anything to keep Jay Dee happy. He enjoyed being around the crew for a day, listening to James tell T3 how he had created a snare sound by flicking a box of raisins, hearing them freestyle together in their trailer. James turned to Kahane at one point and called him "Al Bundy," referencing the sarcastic, hand-tucked-in-his-pants patriarch of the popular eighties sitcom *Married . . . with Children*. Kahane wasn't so sure how to take this. James reassured him: "Al Bundy's the coldest white dude on the fucking planet!"

I guess that's okay, Kahane thought.

"Climax," Slum's song about convincing their girlfriends to have a ménage à trois, was Kahane's long shot at a hit. As an added incentive to programmers, Kahane thought it might be a good idea to have a comedic celebrity cameo in the video. He chose the actor Gary Coleman, from the TV sitcom *Diff'rent Strokes*. "I may be half the man," Coleman says in the clip's intro, "but I'm gonna need *twice* the ladies." Coleman ends up foiling Jay Dee's attempt at a threesome in James's brief, first, and only on-screen dramatic performance.

The shoot went well, and Questlove made a brief appearance to support his brothers. Baatin's sister, Tina Glover, who sang the hook of the song, lip-synced one of her choruses, alternating with a professional model. After Tina performed, she remarked that she wasn't feeling well. Kahane drove her back to the band's hotel on Sunset Boulevard. The next morning, before the group was scheduled to fly back to Detroit, Kahane got a distressed call from Tim Maynor that Tina was having a breakdown and wouldn't come out of her room. Kahane raced to the hotel to witness a heartbreaking scene between Tina and Baatin, who screamed at his sister as if he knew exactly what she was going through as she stared into the void: "Come back! You are not there!"

Kahane told Tim to take the group to the airport so that they wouldn't miss their flight, and that he'd stay with Tina until help came from Cedars-Sinai, the closest hospital. The episode was a frightening end to what had been one of the first things to go right for Slum Village.

As the release of *Fantastic, Vol. 2* finally approached in the spring of 2000, Slum's videos made it onto MTV and Kahane booked the group on a thirteen-stop tour. Jay Dee showed up for the Los Angeles kickoff as promised, playing beats live from two MPC machines; and again in Detroit and New York. No one on the team mentioned Jay Dee's departure, but the word was spreading anyway. Slum was about to embark on a summer tour with Good Vibe artists, was slated to open for D'Angelo in Europe, and was billed on the first Okayplayer tour with the Roots in the fall. But James declined to join. T3 couldn't understand it: *These were all James's people. Why didn't he want to go?*

But James apparently did not want to be locked in or locked down. Maybe he didn't want partners at all.

T3 and Baatin had ordered their creativity and careers around James's wishes and desires. Now James was gone. T3 had never wanted to lead. Now he was the leader.[*]

O n June 8, 2000, while Slum Village kicked off the Good Vibe Tour in San Diego, James flew in the opposite direction, to New York for a special photo shoot.

---

[*] Matt Kahane would move on from Good Vibe to become an artist and Grammy Award–winning producer. He is now known professionally as Jack Splash.

It had begun as an article for *Vibe* magazine about Questlove, whom the writer Dave Bry spied as the common thread between the latest albums by Erykah Badu, Common, D'Angelo, Bilal, and Jill Scott. But Questlove reflexively deflected to the collective: *It's bigger than me,* he said. He mentioned the portmanteau "Soulquarians" in reference to the four creatives at the heart of the activity at Electric Lady: D'Angelo, Poyser, Jay Dee, and himself. "We all share a love for 'sickness' in our work," he told Bry, "offbeat rhythms, unorthodox chords, stacks of harmony, an overall rebellious attitude to the status quo"—by this he meant the materialistic hip-hop and "shiny suit" R&B in current vogue.

But "Soulquarians" referred now to an even larger group. The aesthetic binding these people was the product of a long arc that began with Q-Tip and the Native Tongues, who provoked the birth of Questlove's and James Poyser's hip-hop-fueled musicianship; fostered the superstar careers of Erykah Badu and D'Angelo; informed the boho rhyme of Common, Talib, and Mos Def and the latter-day Philly soul of Bilal; and ran on the innovations of the Detroit rhythm scientist Jay Dee.

The *Vibe* "Soulquarians" shoot was the first time that these ten people had all been in the same room at the same time. The photographer Sacha Waldman positioned the men on either side of a radiant Badu, the colorful centerpiece of neo-soul. But squatting on the far right, as close to the edge of the frame as possible, was Neo himself.

Jay Dee was easy to miss in this crowd of celebrities, his name known mostly to hip-hop junkies. D'Angelo himself had begun to feel indignant on Jay Dee's behalf—James was everybody's best-kept secret, the rhythmic pocket in their back pocket. Yet at this very moment, James was on the precipice of his biggest commercial success. The following month, "The Light" became Common's first true hit on R&B radio. With a video featuring Erykah Badu, the song rose to #8 on *Billboard*'s R&B chart and peaked just shy of the top twenty on the pop list, but was a top-ten clip on MTV and Black Entertainment Television. "The Light" was just that—a ray of sun that outshined the shiny suits for a brief moment in the summer of 2000, a love letter to women in a musical culture that didn't always love women, ubiquitous on the airwaves and in the nightclubs, in cars and on beach boomboxes. MCA executives Wendy Goldstein and

Jay Boberg celebrated: Common had never sold more than 175,000 units of any record. *Like Water for Chocolate* soared over 500,000 and became Common's first certified gold record.

As "The Light" shined, *Vibe* magazine's September 2000 issue hit newsstands, with Eminem and Dr. Dre on the cover and the two-page Soulquarians spread on the inside. The name of the quiet man in the bottom-right corner had been buried, surrounded, and overlooked for his entire career. In the next year, the producer would morph into an artist, and the only name that would eclipse that of Jay Dee would be one of James's own choosing.

10.
Pay Jay

Welcome to Detroit. *Founded 1701.*

It was a sign of things to come as Peter Adarkwah, fresh off a plane from London, peered outside the passenger window of his friend's car.

Liquor shop, gun shop, church. Chicken joint, liquor shop, gas station. Burned house, empty lot, someone's home.

Adarkwah had been to America several times before, but the British-born son of Ghanaian immigrants had seen places like this only on television and in films. It was surreal and a bit scary.

Adarkwah ran a small label in London, BBE Music, which stood for Barely Breaking Even. The name was apt: BBE specialized in music compilations—albums pieced together by licensing songs from *other* record companies. The profit margins on these projects were thin, their sole market cachet being the names of the DJs who curated each of them, like J Dilla's record shopping buddy Kenny Dope. Adarkwah didn't own any music, but he'd decided to change that after meeting Jay Dee.

Kenny Dope had introduced them at a Slum Village show in London in 1999. Adarkwah was giddy and nervous, and accompanied James and Tim Maynor back to their hotel and proposed to release an album of original Jay Dee instrumentals. James loved the idea—his work had always been in service to others, his name appearing only adjacent or second to rappers and singers. This was the first time someone had proposed to invest in him and him alone.

The advance that Maynor later floated, $75,000, would have been a pittance for a major label, but for Adarkwah it was a sum that could have paid off his entire mortgage. He drafted the deal and funded it by securing a loan from one of his distributors. Within a few months, Maynor received a signed deal and James's check. In late 1999 Adarkwah landed in Detroit, and stepped into James's basement.

Adarkwah knew he had made the right decision when he saw that—on the wall, among dozens of other album sleeves—James had tacked up two BBE compilations; the producer had no idea that Adarkwah was the man responsible for them. Adarkwah thumbed his way through James's massive record collection, surprised to see the amount of jazz, rock, and world music. *Look at that!* Adarkwah pulled out an album by Oneness of Juju—a 1970s Afrocentric jazz-funk group from Virginia rediscovered in the late eighties by "rare groove" London DJs. Adarkwah asked James to spin the title track, "African Rhythms."

"This is the kind of stuff I want to do," James said. "I want to remake this."

"You've got carte blanche," Adarkwah replied.

Over the next few days, James realized that Adarkwah meant it. Driving in James's truck, they listened to "Think Twice," a staple hip-hop sample for the Native Tongues and neo-soul crowd from Donald Byrd—a seventies jazz-soul icon and Conant Gardens native. Adarkwah suggested that James should cover the record and have Erykah Badu sing the hook. When James suggested that enlisting Badu would be too much of a hassle, Adarkwah shrugged: "Do it yourself."

Suddenly James wasn't a producer working on an album of beats. He was an artist working on his first solo project. James's next thought was to bring some friends along for the ride.

Karriem Riggins and James Yancey were born a year apart and grew up just a few miles from each other. Both their fathers had served in the military and were jazz musicians—Emmanuel Riggins played the keys with the guitarist Grant Green while Dewitt played the upright bass on the local club circuit. Their childhoods had a jazz soundtrack, and they both fell in love with hip-hop in their adolescence. But their journeys to becoming professional musicians took them in opposite directions.

Where James mastered the drum machine, Karriem applied himself to the drum kit. In the mid-1990s, while James was becoming hip-hop's hot new producer, Riggins was making his reputation as a rising "young lion" of jazz.

Even before Riggins met Jay Dee or knew he was from Detroit, Riggins was proselytizing for him. As a returning alumnus in Betty Carter's Jazz Ahead program, he schooled a drummer and beatmaker from Virginia, Nate Smith, on the nuanced rhythms of the producer, a lesson Smith would remember. When he and James finally crossed paths, their subsequent friendship was based on both what they shared and where they differed. When James needed a skilled drummer, Karriem was eager because he was a fan. And when Karriem himself wanted to learn the drum machine after he'd bought an MPC3000 from DJ House Shoes, James was a generous teacher because he knew that Karriem was a dedicated student. Karriem's jazz eye spied James's advanced technique: his ability to alter sounds, making kick drums sound like snares, turning turntable hum into bass tones. The irony was that by the time James told Karriem about his new BBE project, they had each reversed their musical trajectories and were now moving *toward* the position of the other: Karriem wanted to produce hip-hop, and James wanted to expand into traditional instrumentation.

James asked Karriem for some tracks and Riggins gave James a cassette with one beat on it. Then another with one beat on it. Then another. James had to educate the drummer: *Make a bunch of beats and put them on one tape. A beat tape. Get it?* Riggins obliged, but when James bumped the next tape in his truck, he never made it past the first track.

"I want that one," James told Riggins. It became a song called "The Clapper," and was the first beat that Jay Dee rapped over that wasn't one of his own making. James, in turn, invited Karriem to Studio A in Dearborn to help him build his first nonelectronic production.

"Give me that bossa nova," James instructed the drummer. James laid down piano and he and Frank shouted a drunken melody over the top.

Three months after James signed the deal, Adarkwah had the finished master tape for James's album, *Welcome 2 Detroit*, in his hands.

The record contained the most severe deployments yet of James's signature time-feel: songs like "Pause" and "Come Get It" were the rhythmic equivalents of a train derailing and righting itself, repeatedly.

"COME GET IT" · J DILLA f/ ELZHI

Count	1	n	2	n	3	n	4	n	1	n	2	n	3	n	4	n	
HAT																	A
SNARE																	B
KICK																	C
BASS																	D

A. swung   B. straight + shifted   C. swung + shifted   D. straight

But James's other tracks were accompanied by striking deviations from anything he had previously produced: his faithful cover of "African Rhythms"; another track that evoked Kraftwerk and the Detroit techno of his youth, its title a grateful nod to Adarkwah, "B.B.E. (Big Booty Express)"; and his first productions with all traditional instruments, including the Brazilian jam with Riggins, "Rico Suave Bossa Nova," and James's cover of Donald Byrd's "Think Twice," keyboards and brass played by another Detroit musician, Andwele Gardner. Performing locally under the mononym Dwele, Gardner had made a name for himself as a singer at Detroit's boho nightspot Cafe Mahogany, and was introduced to James by Waajeed and Baatin.

Riggins and Dwele were just two of a half dozen Detroit artists with whom James shared his new platform. Some, like Phat Kat, were perennial collaborators. Some, like Big Tone and Ta'Raach, were local MCs with established reputations. And others, like Jason Powers, were getting their first shot. Powers was a shy kid back at the Hip Hop Shop in the 1990s. With mentorship from T3, he had become the shrewd, acrobatic MC Elzhi. Frank-n-Dank, under T3's and James's tutelage, had come to understand their voices as instruments, and rode James's broken rhythms now with ease, spelling their names in an alphabet soup of humor and confidence on "Pause." But James himself carried the most impressive vocal performances—alternating between his smooth singing voice and the rough rap persona he called, jokingly, "Ni**aman."

James's broadened musicality seeped into his work-for-hire. In London, the music publisher Thad Baron's client Steve Spacek hired Jay Dee for a remix. James did not know what to do with Spacek's song, called "Eve," especially Spacek's lilting, trilly vocal. He dragged his feet for as long as he could, even offering it to Riggins to see if he had any workable ideas. Riggins didn't. Before James missed the deadline, he finally dove in.

James called DJ House Shoes over to hear the results. First he played the dry, a cappella vocal, which sounded to Shoes something like a cross between Curtis Mayfield and Tiny Tim. Shoes fell to the floor in a fit of laughter.

"Now," James giggled. "Watch this shit." James restarted the song, but with the music he had added.

First, James's voice: *Let me fuck with it.*

Then, the beat: a lurching, stumbling rhythm. Next, a tiny organ suspended above it, a tiptoeing bass line now a perfect dance partner for Spacek's voice.

Shoes stopped laughing.

The chorus opened like a sunrise, building layers of notes and texture as James himself sang a new refrain, his words pushing ahead of the dragging beat:

IwantyouIneedyou
IwantyouIneedyou

Shoes looked at his friend, thinking: *You just had me listening to the worst shit ever. Two seconds later you made it the best shit ever.*

Shoes voiced his thoughts in a simpler way: "You're an asshole, bro."

A darkwah returned in September 2000 for the *Welcome 2 Detroit* cover shoot at Chocolate City—James, Frank, Dank, and Karriem holding fistfuls of cash toward the camera—and elicited liner notes from James for the packaging, the only extended prose about his process that he ever published.* In addition to thanking his parents and Joy, his mentors Amp Fiddler and Q-Tip, his collaborators and entities like Good Vibe and Okayplayer, James ended the album with an entire track of "shout-outs," which included one to his adoptive brother Earl, who had drifted away from the Yanceys in the 1990s after he entered the military; and an even more curious mention of the world's most popular boy band, the multimillion-record-selling *NSYNC.

The reference was not a joke. House Shoes's roommate and partner on his WHFR radio show, Aaron Halfacre—another white hip-hop head from the suburbs who had become Shoes's deputy collector of Jay Dee beats—happened to be the longtime friend of JC Chasez, the young *Mickey Mouse Club* cast member who later formed *NSYNC with his fellow Mouseketeer Justin Timberlake. Halfacre became friendly with Timberlake as *NSYNC's career took off, slid him Jay Dee beat tapes whenever he could, and Timberlake became a fan, asking Halfacre to see if Jay Dee might be interested in working together. When Halfacre visited James's new basement in Huntington Woods, James seemed keen on the idea. But on two separate occasions when *NSYNC was in Michigan, James didn't pick up his phone or return Halfacre's calls, nor his invitations to come by the arena where the band was performing, completely ghosting him. James knew he might get a huge fee. But he told friends, privately: "Man, I ain't doing that shit." Even for James, money wasn't everything.

I n a scene from *Office Space*, the movie that featured Slum Village's "Get Dis Money," a character named Michael Bolton detests that he shares his name with the famous easy-listening singer.

"Why should *I* change," Bolton seethes. "*He's* the one who sucks."

---

* "'Shake It Down' was done by mistake," James wrote of the song. "Check it. I had a beat block for a minute. I told myself, 'Get yo' ass in the basement and make some shit, if you don't, somebody will!' No lie, I looped the first thing the needle touched, some HAPPY-ASS FOLK SONG SHIT (just my luck). Trying to be funny, I filtered the loop." James was saying that he took the high frequencies out to squelch the vocals and boost the music underneath. "After passing a few blunts," he continued, "I thought of some rhymes to it so I finished it. Enjoy. Oh yeah. Beatheads, the loop unfilters at the end. What is it?" It was a 1971 song by Boz Scaggs called "Nothing Will Take Your Place."

James Dewitt Yancey had a more relaxed stance about his name. His professional alias had evolved through his years of obscurity from Silk to Jon Doe before settling on Jay Dee. But there had always been some brand confusion with a Dutch DJ and producer, also named "Jaydee." More recently, an established Atlanta-based producer, Jermaine Dupri—coincidentally a client of Common's manager, Derek Dudley—had begun to refer to *himself* as "J. D."

Since he was evolving, James decided it was time for his name to evolve again, too. The cover of *Welcome 2 Detroit* was credited to "Jay Dee aka J Dilla."

Common Sense had gone through a midcareer moniker change and thrived, so it was fitting that Common gave James his new nickname. A member of Common's band was named "J. B." Common had started calling him "J. Billa" while they were on tour. During the making of *Like Water for Chocolate*, "Jay Dee" similarly became "J Dilla."*

James liked it. Time to change everything.

A head of *Welcome 2 Detroit*'s February 2001 release, Peter Adarkwah brought James, Frank, and Dank to the Winter Music Conference in Miami, and then flew them to London, where Gilles Peterson invited James to guest-host a thirty-minute segment on his BBC Radio One show, and Ross Allen—whose record label, Blue, had hired James to remix Spacek's "Eve"—interviewed him on BBC London.[†]

Jay Dee was a hero to these DJs, who credited him as a key figure in the hip-hop soul renewal they championed on their playlists. And though James extolled the creative and spiritual connection he'd found with the Soulquarians, J Dilla now declared independence from Jay Dee:

"I don't ever want to use a Fender Rhodes again if I don't have to," he told Ross Allen.

This was surprising, Jay Dee not only changing his name, but re-

---

* Peter Adarkwah says that James told him that the moniker "J Dilla" came from Busta Rhymes. Frank Bush and Karriem Riggins confirm that the name came from Common.

† James and crew also stopped by the hip-hop DJ Tim Westwood's BBC radio show, somewhat less revelatory on the music side and more about James and his crew's porn film preferences.

nouncing his signature sound. There was a reason for this aesthetic shift that James did not articulate: Not long after James wrapped up work on *Welcome 2 Detroit*, Musiq Soulchild hit American radio with his debut single, "Just Friends (Sunny)." Over a dragged, D'Angelo-style Fender Rhodes, the song bore the unmistakable rhythmic signature of Jay Dee, *the rushed snare*. That made sense: Musiq, who once delivered pizzas to Questlove's Philly living room jam sessions, had become part of the roster of artists at Jazzy Jeff's A Touch of Jazz collective. The song, pro- duced by Jeff's associates Ivan "Orthodox" Barias and Carvin "Ransum" Haggins, was the first to drive James's rhythmic signature into the top ten of *Billboard*'s R&B chart. Around the same time, fellow Soulquarian Talib Kweli teamed up with the Cincinnati-based producer Hi-Tek on a song called "The Blast," in which every rhythmic element was set against the others—dragging shaker, rushed snare, loose bass line. The filtered and flanged loop, the vocal sample that twisted the word *body* into *Kweli*, even the sharpness of the snare all spoke to Jay Dee's influence.*

"That's *my* shit," a dumbfounded James remarked to House Shoes when he first heard it, half liking it, and half not wanting to half like it.

These new copycat productions were, for James, a reason to bet on himself. He told Gilles Peterson, "Anything I've done, I'm not about to do. That's my word."

For the stutterer, fluency often comes with confidence. In James's deep baritone, his words flowed without hesitation.

I n his interviews, James alluded to an even bigger deal in the works. The idea came from the mind of Derek Dudley as he observed James's work habits during the making of *Like Water for Chocolate*.

"You need your own studio," he told James. "Forget giving all your money to Studio A. That way you don't have to worry about budgets, you can work at home, or wherever you build it."

---

* Hi-Tek, who met James at Electric Lady and was friendly with him, states that the track's elements were as much an homage to Pete Rock and Q-Tip as they were to Jay Dee, the off-the-grid shaker being the most explicit nod to the Detroit producer. It's clear James also admired Hi-Tek's work: he remixed a song called "Secrets of the Sand" for Tek's group, Mood, and then sampled one of their tracks, "Millennium," for the Slum Village song "Climax."

"I love it," James told him. "Let's do it."

Derek Dudley knew someone who might fund the project. Derek had formed a solid relationship with Wendy Goldstein—he practically had his own desk at MCA's New York offices—and he suggested to her that MCA extend a production deal to Jay Dee. *Let's lock him down before he's got five other labels at his door*, Derek urged. For Goldstein, the move made sense in her continuing quest to grow a hip-hop roster. Derek arranged her first discussions with James, which accelerated once "The Light" became a hit.

After flying to Detroit in the summer of 2000, Goldstein proposed a three-part deal. First, James would be signed exclusively to MCA as an artist, and given an advance to create an album of his own. Second, he'd get an imprint at MCA, McNasty Records, to which he could sign any artist of his choice, with a yearly overhead payment and artist advances covered by MCA. Third, he'd have a deal to produce a set number of records for other MCA artists, like Common or the Roots, at a fixed rate. And at the core of the deal was a substantial budget to build a state-of-the-art recording studio.

The culmination of everything James had been working toward in the ten years since he'd left Davis Aero Tech, the MCA offer confirmed all the lofty sentiments his admirers and collaborators held for the quiet hip-hop virtuoso from Conant Gardens.

See that boy fly.

While Micheline Levine negotiated the terms of James's future with MCA, she also severed several of his ties to his past.

First, Micheline sent notices to labels that had already contracted with James for production work, telling them to eliminate any mention of "The Ummah," and to structure his credit as "Jay Dee for Pay Jay Productions," the new business entity through which he would furnish his services to labels and artists. Next, she fired off a letter to R. J. Rice officially ending James's business relationship with him and with Barak Records. James didn't like his current business managers—he complained that it was too hard to get cash when he wanted it, and he chafed at normal processes like withholding large portions of his incoming checks for taxes. Micheline saw it as a product of James's impatience with regard to money; still, she recommended that James move to Arthur "Arty" Erk at Wlodinguer, Erk & Chanzis. But if this were truly J Dilla's time to become a recording artist and label owner, he needed something that he never quite had: a manager.

For many years, that's what James called Q-Tip, though, in reality, Tip simply made connections for him. James's default, day-to-day handler was his mother. And though Maureen Yancey had come to enjoy doing this work for James—handling his correspondence, his travel, his banking, doing countless errands and tasks—there was much she didn't know. And it wasn't always the healthiest dynamic for her and James. Though James could be generous, he didn't officially put his mother on payroll, and he occasionally lost his temper with her. "I don't *ever* want to see a bill!" he screamed at her one day, Frank's jaw dropping as he silently determined never to have to put his own mother in that position. When James's moods turned against her, Maureen would sometimes turn to Micheline for help, and vice versa. While Micheline was in Paris attending the funeral of her sister, whom she had nursed through her losing battle with ovarian cancer, James became upset about something, called her cell phone, and cursed her out. In tears, Micheline then phoned Maureen.

"I'm sorry," Maureen commiserated. "I told him not to call you. I'm going to yell at him."

When James and Micheline spoke again, he offered an apology only as a breezy aside: "I'm sorry about that time."

What James really needed was a dedicated, professional manager. Paul Rosenberg, James's former Hoops labelmate and now manager of Eminem, had once courted Slum Village in the days before they achieved success, but he backed off after he sensed James was deliberately evading him. Tim Maynor was now Slum Village's manager and always helped James when called on, but James had just put Slum and Barak in his rearview mirror.

The present option was Derek Dudley. And for a time, Derek called himself Jay Dee's manager. After Derek brokered the MCA deal, he turned his energies to taking James's production career to the next level.

Derek thought that James could be one of the most successful producers in the game if he'd let him nurture relationships with a new echelon of pop clients. So he placed a call to Ron Fair, an A&R executive at BMG, the home of teen pop sensations Christina Aguilera, Britney Spears, and *NSYNC. Together, Derek and Fair conspired to set James up to do tracks for *NSYNC's next album, putting him in position to be on the team when Justin Timberlake began his solo project the following year. But Derek had no idea that Aaron Halfacre and Timberlake had already made one unsuccessful overture to James, and Derek was taken aback when James turned down the prospect of a session with the group.* *If all he wanted was someone to administer his work with his current friends, what was the point of taking him on as a client?* Derek had by now realized that James didn't respect things like exclusivity, and would do a side deal with another manager or lawyer as long as the cash came easy. Derek Dudley walked away, and Justin Timberlake would end up pairing with up-and-coming hip-hop producers Timbaland and the Neptunes.

Micheline suggested another route. Briant "Bee-High" Biggs currently managed one of her clients, Memphis Bleek, and was a cousin to one of the most revered and successful solo artists in hip-hop, Jay-Z. James liked Bee-High and thought he might get him some production work with his famous relative. But what Bee-High lacked, for Micheline, was a bit of business savvy and follow-through. So Micheline suggested to Bee-High that he team up with her part-time assistant and paralegal Jonathan Dworkin, who managed several fledgling rock acts. Bee-High could connect Jay Dee with Jay-Z, Dworkin would handle the p's and q's, and together they would try to manage the heretofore unmanageable.

Still, the broad and generous deal with MCA had been Derek Dudley's brainchild. And though James begrudged Derek his finder's fee, James's initial artist advances and overhead came to around three-quarters of a million dollars, an amount that made the label president, Jay Boberg, uncomfortable. But Boberg was a big fan of the Roots, and of Common, and wanted to support Goldstein's vision. In addition to the huge budget

---

* In a text message with Aaron Halfacre, Justin Timberlake says that he never knew of the second overture to J Dilla by Ron Fair on *NSYNC's behalf. "It never got to any of us at least," he wrote.

for James's new studio, the deal contained another stipulation, that MCA immediately accept a specific act James wanted to sign to McNasty, and that album needed to be released even before his own.

D errick "Dank" Harvey punched out of his shift at the Aetna steel plant in Warren, Michigan, around midnight and walked out to his car, a beat-down 1987 Toyota Cressida. Whenever he put the key in the ignition, the car grunted three times before it would start.

"Your car funny as hell," James had teased when Dank stopped by the basement earlier that night.

It was funny, but it wasn't. Dank had been on the streets for years while his friends toured the world. When he left that lifestyle to enter James's artist "boot camp," he was happy for the opportunity. But life in Detroit was getting harder. Now that he had gotten a real job, his luxuries were few. He was still living with his mother. He had children, and he was in a dispute with their mother over visitation. The police wouldn't enforce a court order on his behalf. He was praying a lot.

Bone-tired, Dank drove back to Conant Gardens, to the home studio of a friend who wanted him, as a favor, to lay a verse on a track he was producing. When Dank emerged from the vocal booth, he was surprised to see James, smiling.

"Tell them ni**as you're out," James said.

"What you mean?"

James ushered Dank out of the house and into his gleaming indigo Range Rover, parked by Dank's crappy Cressida.

"Listen, Dank," James began. "I'm ready. I already talked to Frank. Go home and tell your mom you gotta quit that job."

Dank knew what James meant. He began to sob.

"Ni**a, stop crying, we good," James said. "Just go home and tell your moms. You ain't got to worry about shit."

Frank Bush and Derrick Harvey had been his companions, his drivers, his assistants, the homies who tagged along when he and all the other artists did their thing. Now they would have their turn as the first act on McNasty/MCA.

Dank stepped out of James's truck, got inside his Cressida, and screamed: "Thank you, Lord!"

Wiping his tears, he put his key in the ignition and turned it . . .

Unnnnnnhhhhh . . .

Unnnnnnhhhhh . . .

Unnnnnnhhhhh . . .

The car started and Derrick Harvey drove home to tell his mother the news.

is friends had never seen him happier. James's score was bigger than anything his grandfather Suge Hayes had seen in his day, bigger than anything his family and friends had ever experienced, and it transformed their lives. Frank and Dank deposited their $60,000 advance check, and Dank said goodbye to his Cressida. The extended Yancey family—Maureen, Dewitt, John, Martha, Maurice, and Faith—moved into two stories of a large white three-floor, twelve-bedroom, nine-bathroom house adjacent to the tony Detroit neighborhood of Indian Village. Meanwhile, James dove into work on Frank-n-Dank's album in his basement in Huntington Woods. They would not work there for long, because James and Joy were compelled to move.

Making a home with James again and planning to start a family had been rocky for Joylette. Before the split, she hadn't minded his habit of going to the titty bar with Frank and friends—she had met James at the bar, after all. Now she found herself threatened by the frequency of his nocturnal excursions. Once, after she'd gotten pregnant, she caught him lying about going, and they'd gotten into a huge argument. She miscarried the next day. But the love Joy felt for and from James proved stronger than her suspicions. She'd been the one who insisted that he move his studio downstairs, and she got used to people coming through and loud music rattling through her home at all hours. His beats had become her lullaby.

The neighbors, however, did not feel the same way.

Joy suspected that the white man who lived next door hated them—their nice cars, their frequent visitors, the loud rap music. His wife and kids were friendly, but when he was around, they kept their heads down while he scowled. In Conant Gardens, James was frequently harassed by the Detroit police; living in the suburbs just outside the city limits provided little relief, as James dealt with frequent traffic stops from suspicious state troopers and suburban cops, one police cruiser tailing his truck right into his driveway. James channeled his rage into a song, "Fuck the Police," that drew its name from N.W.A's famed anthem. The thing that pushed James over the edge were the anonymous letters dropped on his doorstep accusing him of being a drug dealer and warning him to leave or face the consequences. He wouldn't show them to Joy. He just told her that they had to move out, had Micheline handle the details, and let Maureen find them a safer place to live.

Joy was pregnant again by the time they moved, temporarily, into her sister Janell's place. James took Joy shopping for a new ring and slid it onto her finger, Janell snapping a photo of the moment.

Maureen found her son and his fiancée a place deeper into the suburbs, a colonial home just off 16 Mile Road in Clinton Township near the hospital where Joy worked, with a bedroom for the baby and a basement big enough for the studio that MCA was buying him. All the while, James continued to hide his occasional, secret visitations with Monica and his one-year-old daughter, Ty-Monae.

When James needed equipment he most often turned to Michael "Chav" Chavarria and Johnny "Audible" Evans, who worked together at the Guitar Center in Southfield. When it came time to make his new studio, he asked them to do the work. Evans would handle the contracting, Chav the electronics.

"Blow it out," James told them. The budget for the project came to more than $450,000, with $300,000 for equipment alone.

What Chav built for James in his Clinton Township basement was a state-of-the-art digital studio, recording music onto a computer drive that would afford him unlimited tracks and time, rather than onto reels of analog tape. Chav bought him the fastest Apple computer available and created a massive, modular mixing board that allowed James to control ninety-six tracks at once. Meanwhile, Evans built a vocal booth and a drum room, which Chav outfitted with the best monitors, microphones, and stands, and a small lounge where James hung his plaques and placed a pool table that just barely fit the space.

James was the master of the drum machine, but he had never owned a computer. By midsummer 2001 Chav began training James in the software and equipment. But as he observed James's workflow, Chav gradually became the student.

James had an older version of the MPC with less memory; Chav told him he'd get him an upgrade. "Don't," James told him. "I like to keep it limited." The limitations, Chav understood, kept him resourceful. James had lots of archaic habits like that: keeping a stash of records with his favorite drum sounds nearby, marked with masking tape like clock hands so he could easily find the cue points of each sound; James was sampling his sounds anew every time. On the computer software, Chav witnessed James do esoteric things that he'd never seen before: triggering low-frequency waves to add bottom to his kick drum sounds; splitting his hi-hat sound signal in two and delaying one of them by eleven milliseconds to create a "flam" between them; using noise "gates" to alter the start and end times of drum sounds to better form the "pocket" of his grooves.

The two men became friendly. Every morning before they went downstairs, they'd share a smoke from a kitchen drawer of perfectly organized and prerolled blunts while they listened to music on James's living room stereo. Chav got comfortable enough coming around that one day, James walked downstairs to find Chav there, unannounced.

"Maaaaan," James said. "Never run up in a man's house like that."

Over the course of months, Chav continued to tweak the studio and add hardware and software. He helped James as he began to do sessions with vocalists. But the drum room never got a drum set; James filled it with records. And even though the studio did everything James wanted it to do, every day James hired a white limousine to take him to Studio A, thirty miles away in Dearborn, where he continued to pay for studio time. It wasn't the only part of James's process that would surprise his corporate funders at MCA.

Jay Dee, the producer, had been associated with politically conscious, high-minded, bohemian hip-hop. James, the person, was quite the other thing, aligned more with the material obsessions of mainstream, commercial rap—bling, cars, big booty women. For his solo album, tentatively titled *Pay Jay*, James wanted to introduce the world to who he really was.

To focus on his persona, he needed to apply himself with a singular dedication. On this album, he'd be the MC, and he would leave the beatmaking to others—whether established producers he idolized, like Pete Rock, or peers like Hi-Tek, or with pupils like Karriem Riggins, who had provided James with the first workable example of this concept on *Welcome 2 Detroit*.

Beat by beat, the producers came to work with James. "Supa Dave" West, who had been to De La Soul as a producer what James had been to A Tribe Called Quest, came from New York and stayed for several days. Hi-Tek journeyed from Cincinnati to deliver a beat CD and was so nervous about his session with James that he accidentally drove for hours in the wrong direction, to Cleveland, before he changed course. James chose another Riggins beat, and—in a first—even invited House Shoes to audition some tracks. As James listened on his stereo system, nodding to some beats, laughing at others, Shoes's emotions oscillated from hope to embarrassment. By the time the last track played, Shoes was disconsolate. James looked at him and said: "That one." James would make it the introduction to his album.

House Shoes played a key role in bringing another producer to James's project. Otis "Madlib" Jackson flew in from California, accompanied by his de facto manager, Chris "Peanut Butter Wolf" Manak, who had signed Madlib to his label, Stones Throw Records. Shoes and Wolf had been friendly for years—they'd collaborated in the 1990s to release an EP of rare Jay Dee remixes on vinyl—and they had introduced James and Madlib to each other's work. Madlib was still an obscure artist building a solo career on an underground indie label, so James's request to have him produce a couple of tracks for his major label debut sent ripples of excitement through the small Stones Throw camp, who worked and lived together in a house in Los Angeles.

James and Madlib were both men of few words; and the pace of work was slow, centered around the consumption of dozens of joints containing the weakest weed the California visitors had ever smoked. But it was the start of a creative relationship that would grow increasingly potent for both of them.

T he white neighbors were nicer in Clinton Township. They came to Joylette's baby shower and brought cakes, pies, and gifts. Joy quit her job and, throughout the summer of 2001, she furnished the house, prepared the nursery, and drove back to her old neighborhood in Detroit for weekly checkups at the Henry Ford Hospital. She was on her way one September morning when news broke that the United States was under attack. She phoned James, who was at the house with Mike Chav watching the twin towers crumble on his studio monitors. When Joy returned, she and James fretted about the world into which they were bringing their baby.

On a Friday in late September, Joy went into a labor that continued through the weekend and into the first day of October. She developed a fever. By Monday the doctors ordered an emergency C-section.

"I'm on my way," James told her before she went into the operating room, her sister Janell and her aunt Elaine beside her.

By the time he arrived, his daughter Ja'Mya Sherran Yancey had been born.

W hat's wrong with her?" James asked Joylette as Ja'Mya's cries woke them in the middle of the night.

"She's hungry, James," Joy said as she went to go feed her.

James had grown up in a house literally crawling with children, but he'd never taken responsibility for one. In part because he was with Joy and had concealed his other daughter, he hadn't invested much time in Ty-Monae's care. So he was timid about holding Ja'Mya at first, but he began to take pleasure in bottle-feeding her. He left the diaper changing to Joy, who understood that James was coming from a place where he didn't have much of an example of that kind of fatherhood. Dewitt had taught James about music. He had been supportive and ever present. But James divulged how sad he was that Dewitt had rarely been openly affectionate with him.

"I mean, I know he loves me," James told her. "But he never told me that."

James would have to teach himself to be the father he wanted to be. Joy thought maybe he could pick up some missing pieces from other men in his life, like Uncle Al, whom Joy admired because he seemed so secure in his word and deed. Time would have to do the rest.

The true gift of Common's album *Like Water for Chocolate* wasn't a gold plaque or a royalty check, but liberation. It gave James a path to become a solo artist, validated Common's instincts, and confirmed the Soulquarians' collective endeavor: to make sure that the new era of commercial plenty for Black artists also came with expanded creative horizons. So when Common's thoughts turned toward a follow-up, he decided to indulge his artistic wanderlust. He'd been listening to the progressive rock band Pink Floyd's *Dark Side of the Moon*. He asked himself: *What would my version of that album sound like?* In 2001, members of the Soulquarians returned to Jimi Hendrix's house at Electric Lady to answer that question.

The sharpness of Common's turn surprised Questlove, who found himself wanting to linger in the aesthetic they'd championed: the rushed snare, the warm Fender Rhodes keyboards. Yet James, too, was saying, *No more soul, man. Let's go electronic. Do the opposite. Let's not get comfortable.* Questlove, who considered himself a dutiful student, obliged.

One consistent critic of the experimental direction was Derek Dudley, who hated the new music and saw in Common's creative detour a bit of avoidance. His friend had just enjoyed his first hit with "The Light." It was easier for Common to pose a new question rather than answer the one that his fans and his funders were asking: *Can you make another song that shines as bright?*

Derek worried for his client, and wondered about James's fate, too. A big fat advance check from a major label isn't liberation, it's a mortgage. At some point, the bill comes due, and you either satisfy the lender or get your loan pulled.

J ames had collected dozens of alien figurines over the years and dotted his studio with them. Frank figured that James just liked to be with his kind.

James's ways continued to be alien to him, too. One day in 2001, as they were putting the finishing touches on their Frank-n-Dank MCA project, James burst into the studio and proclaimed: "We're starting from scratch."

"Hunh?" Frank said.

"We'll keep your vocals," James said. "But I'm stripping all the samples out."

Frank could hardly believe what he was hearing. They had just crafted an entire album, *48 Hours*, a lyrical ride with Slum Village's grimy street cousins over banging Jay Dee beats. They were about to deliver it to MCA. But then James paid a visit to Vanguard, the recording studio where Proof was working on D12's album. Though the project's star producer, Dr. Dre, was absent at the time, James got a look at his setup.* Dre worked differently than James did, often using live instruments to approximate samples, thus eliminating the frustrating clearance process—getting permission from the rights holders of both the sampled *song* and its *recorded performance*—in which the owners of those recordings and songs could and often did demand a huge chunk or all of a producer's

---

* There are two stories about this encounter: The first, from Frank, is that James was meeting with Proof there to squash a beef related to one of Phat Kat's lyrics on *Welcome 2 Detroit*, thought to be a diss of Eminem. The second, from Denaun Porter and Mark Hicks, is that James didn't come into the studio, but rather spent a day shopping with one of Dre's producers, Mel-Man, and the two got to talking about the expenses involved in working with samples.

royalties.* The expense and chaos of the sample clearance process led several hip-hop producers to either reduce their sampling or eliminate it altogether. To do that and retain the hip-hop aesthetic took a great deal of practice, skill, and musicality. Rising hip-hop producers from the South were adept at this: the Neptunes by being sparse, Timbaland by being hectic, and Organized Noize by being lush. But Dr. Dre, from the West, had long since set the bar for them all.

By the time James returned from his excursion, he vowed to stop sampling—a craft of which he had total mastery. James sent a flurry of orders for new keyboards and synthesizers to Mike Chav. For Frank-n-Dank, this meant dissecting their perfect album, delaying its delivery, and ending up with something that might not sound like a Jay Dee–produced album at all. Still, they accepted James's leadership as their producer and the head of the label they were signed to, McNasty. And Frank did succeed in getting James to keep one song almost as it was: "Ma Dukes," a tribute to Norma Bush and Janice Harvey over a lilting sample of the guitar intro from the Supremes' song "The Wisdom of Time." James asked Chalmers "Spanky" Alford, a guitarist in Tribe and D'Angelo's circle, to replay the guitar part faithfully to avoid the sample clearance.

But as Frank anticipated, Wendy Goldstein was puzzled by the sound of the new album, just as she had been by Common's new music. She didn't confront James or Common about their new directions, but she did ask each of them to submit an additional song—something record executives often do when they don't hear anything that they can market as a single. She and Derek Dudley paired Common with the Neptunes,

---

* Composing music made from *sampled bits and pieces* of others' songs has, since its inception, been completely unprotected by law, in contrast to the way that remaking *entire* songs written by others enjoys *complete* protection. For example, when James replayed Donald Byrd's "Think Twice" for *Welcome 2 Detroit* without sampling the audio, his cover version could be done without the performers' or the songwriters' permission because U.S. copyright law, to balance creativity and commerce, provides something called a "compulsory license" for songs. As long as James pays the song's publisher, Alruby Music, the legal rate, he can legally perform the song on his own recording. But if James had wanted to *sample* only a few seconds of Donald Byrd's *recording* of "Think Twice" for a *new* song, the law offered no compulsory process for licensing a *portion* of a song, nor any process whatsoever for licensing a *portion* of a *recorded performance* of that song. So if James sought permission for that use, the two owners of "Think Twice"—the song and the recording of it—could potentially set *any* price they wanted, or even deny James's use altogether. The record labels that released James's music throughout his career had to engage in a lengthy sample clearance process, even for the tiniest of samples. James was particularly bitter that his use of an uncleared sliver of a classic breakbeat, "UFO" by the group ESG, in the song "Let's Ride," from Q-Tip's *Amplified*, led to a six-figure lawsuit.

who had now become the go-to hitmakers of hip-hop. To assuage Goldstein's concerns about Frank-n-Dank, Jay Dee went back into the lab with his artists and came up with "Take Dem Clothes Off." If James had the skill to program without samples, he had not yet found his voice; the song sounded to Goldstein like a Neptunes knockoff.

Nobody heard back from her for a while after that.

Then they got word that Wendy Goldstein, the good shepherd of the Soulquarians, had left MCA Records.

Not long after James inked his deal with MCA, Wendy Goldstein received a life-changing job offer from a rival major, Capitol/EMI. Jay Boberg's counteroffer at MCA didn't even come close, but when Goldstein accepted the Capitol job, Boberg refused to let Goldstein out of the remaining months of her contract. First hurt, then resolute, Goldstein stopped coming to work; she vacated her New York office, moved to Los Angeles, and waited to begin her new gig.

Goldstein's departure rattled the representatives of the artists she'd signed—the Roots, Common, Mos Def—as MCA scattered their projects to other A&R executives. At first, no one on J Dilla's team, not Micheline Levine nor Jonathan Dworkin nor Bee-High, knew who their new contact would be. Eventually, the work landed on the desk of Naim Ali McNair, who had accompanied Goldstein on her first trip to Detroit. But during Goldstein's standoff with MCA, oversight of her projects had evaporated. Alarm bells were ringing about J Dilla's project in the quarterly A&R meetings: hundreds of thousands of dollars had gone out the door, and MCA had heard very little music in return.

Into this gap stepped Tim Maynor, who tried to broker a connection between McNair, who seemed to want to move things forward, and James, who seemed to be losing enthusiasm. There was only so much Maynor could do: he was busy finalizing a deal with Virgin Records for James's onetime protégé Dwele; and, in a twist, working with R. J. Rice and Wendy Goldstein to move Slum Village to her new digs at Capitol Records—with Elzhi now holding down James's MC slot next to T3 and Baatin. While James's project languished, his former collaborators ended up with a modest hit, "Tainted," written by the group with Karriem Riggins and Dwele. Slum Village had done it all without their former producer.

Frank Bush got conflicting messages about the fate of his own project. At first, it looked like Frank-n-Dank's album was moving forward. MCA flew him, Derrick, and James to New York to master the record and shoot the cover. Then, ostensibly after a meeting with the label, James told him: "MCA is cool with my record. I'm straight. But they don't know what they're gonna do with your album."

So Frank found a number for Naim Ali McNair and phoned him. From McNair he heard why MCA was perplexed. McNair thought that the Frank-n-Dank demo he'd heard back in Detroit was one of the most impressive bodies of work he'd encountered in his career as an A&R executive. *Your album isn't like the stuff James originally played us*, McNair told him.

Of course it isn't, Frank thought. *After he took the samples out, it didn't sound like a Jay Dee record.*

McNair suggested Frank-n-Dank reinstate or revise some tracks. But James now refused to work. He turned on his oldest friends in frustration.

"Y'all need to call your label and have them send some money so we can finish these songs," said the head of McNasty Records.

"Hunh?" Frank replied. "Call my *label*? So you want me to go outside and call *you*?!"

At some point, James gave the MCA executives a disc of twelve tracks meant for his album. But by the fall of 2002, James's abundance mentality and expansive vision for *Pay Jay* and *48 Hours* had come up against some hard financial realities. James had built a studio with MCA's money but spent much of his budget recording at Studio A in Dearborn. He'd contracted with nearly a dozen other producers to use their music, sometimes for up to $50,000 per track. He still owed them their back-end payments, but he had already blown through his entire recording budget. Jonathan Dworkin requested a meeting with Boberg and MCA's head of business affairs, Jeff Harleston, to ask for a "reforecast." In plain English, he was asking MCA to give J Dilla more money to deliver an album that, contractually, they had already paid for.

Boberg and Harleston were confounded by the request: *Didn't we do this entire deal to get his production? Why is he paying* other *producers? We bought him a studio. Why doesn't he just finish this album on his own?* Dworkin also got the sense that Jay Boberg's job was in jeopardy, and that the executives weren't in a position to be generous. He left the meeting with nothing. *If you weren't making them money or making them look good, your deal was done.*

The disc with the dozen Dilla tracks ended up in a drawer in the office of the marketing executive Tim Reid. On it, James had written the title of the collection of songs he'd given them: *The Middle Finger.*

James never told Joy about the withering of his project at MCA. All she knew was that he was stressed and moody. In the first years of their relationship, Joy tended to stay out of James's business—recording studios bored her, and she always kept a job and earned her own money. That had changed once they got engaged and had a child together. She was dependent now on James in ways she had never been and became more sensitive to his pressures, financial and otherwise. Joy decided that the source of their discontent was James's mother.

Maureen had always taken an important role in James's career. She was, essentially, his personal assistant, but with a kind of intimate, maternal care. And though Maureen had never taken a salary for her work on James's behalf, there was an understanding that James always took care of his family off the top. Whenever his mother cashed a check for him, he'd ask her: *Did you take something for yourself? Something for Martha? Something for John?*

Joy did not begrudge James's generosity with his family in principle, but she had come to believe that James did not have healthy boundaries when it came to Maureen, and vice versa. With Maureen visiting Clinton Township daily—to pick up and drop off things and take a list of errands to run for James—Joy felt subject to a scrutiny and judgment that made her feel like Maureen fundamentally saw her as a guest in James's home, and not the woman of the house.* James sometimes got flustered dealing with his family's financial expectations. There always seemed to be something that James was expected to pay for. When Joy stopped working, James had put her on an allowance. She asked him: Why had he not put his mother on one? *Which family*, Joy wondered, *actually came first?*

Maureen saw things differently: *James came first.* She wasn't trying to manipulate her son, she was doing the things that James wanted her to do. And Maureen was convinced Joylette wanted to usurp her role, in part because James convinced her: *Joy asked me why are you doing all my business, and Joy said she should be the one doing it.* At one point, James asked Martha to broker a peace between the two women. Martha came away from her conversation with Joy feeling like Joy was simply obsessed with her mother. To Maureen and Martha, Joy was the one with the unhealthy boundaries.

No matter what James thought or what he told his family, Joylette insisted that she wasn't interested in *running* James. She wanted *James* to run James. And she didn't want to feel like she was wrong for wanting a say in their affairs, nor did she want to compete with Maureen in her own home—about which washer/dryer set to get, or anything. She felt she had earned, at this point, the right to have expectations. Those expectations were not only monetary. After Ja'Mya's birth, Joy found herself wanting to spend more time around her people. The Hunters were a "get-together" type of family; but James, of course, would never want to go to any gatherings, as he often skipped the Yanceys' and Hayeses' holiday celebrations. That refusal was an increasing source of frustration for Joy. So too was James's choice to continue the routines of a bachelor. *I made sacrifices*, Joy fumed, *so you can work long hours in the studio with these rappers; and when you're done you want to go out with Frank and not take me to a show or something? No, you call* Frank's *ass and tell him you can't go.*

---

* There is another conversation that Joylette recalls from this time, again pivotal for Joy, but one that Maureen Yancey says never happened. Joy says that, while moving into the Clinton Township house, Maureen took exception to Joy handling some of the arrangements: "I feel like once he marries you, I'm going to be pushed aside," to which Joy says she replied, "You can never be pushed aside. I can't give him what you give him and you can't give him what I give him."

The first year of a child's life can test the best of relationships, and James and Joy's combined stresses—the dwindling of their income, James's problems with MCA, Joy losing her father to cancer, Maureen's daily presence and Joy's resentment of it, the demands of caring for a newborn, and likely James's continued concealment of his other daughter— provoked the worst quarrels they'd ever had as a couple.

Joylette was a fighter from way back. She had a mouth to match James's, and at the beginning of their relationship, she and James often tussled when they argued, pushing and shoving. But unlike his time with Angie, James never struck Joy, and she had threatened to "call her people" if he ever did. Joy believed that she had mellowed a bit over time. But James and Joy had known each other for a half-dozen years. She still knew how to push his buttons and he hers.

On the morning of March 11, 2002, the two of them got into a huge fight. Two calls from the house went out to the Clinton Township Police, one from Joy, one from James. The police arrived when things had calmed somewhat. Each claimed the other had attacked them. Neither one had marks or bruises, and neither wanted to prosecute the other. In the end, Joy left with Ja'Mya.

There are two disjointed accounts of that morning.

Joy's story was this: She threatened to leave James as she held Ja'Mya in her arms. James threw a towel at Joy. It hit the baby, who began crying. Then James pushed Joy, who lost her balance and fell. Livid, and wanting to let James know that he had gone too far, she made three phone calls: her people—sister Janell and cousin Brandon—and the police. She told Janell that James had hit her. James shouted to Janell: "She's lying!" Brandon arrived, thinking the situation was far more dire than it really was, because when Joy met him at his car outside, she discovered to her horror that her cousin had brought an AK-47 with him.

Are you crazy? Joy said. *You'd better leave before the cops come.*

She didn't want James hurt, nor did she really want him to have trouble with the cops. When the police arrived, they asked: *Do you want to press charges?* "No," Joy replied. They asked: *Do you have some place to go while things cool off?* "Yes," Joy said. She took Ja'Mya to her sister's house.

James's story was this, to the police: He argued with Joy over her leaving "for an interview" while he was supposed to be working.* She attacked him, ripped his shirt, and broke things. He did not hit her back. They both called the police. When they arrived, James wrote an account in which he added that "she always does this but this time it was [e]xtreme." Later, James told his family that Joy had trashed the house, that he hid in a room while she did so, and that the police removed Joy from the home and escorted her and Ja'Mya to the town limits.

The officers at the scene, in their report, listed James Yancey in the "victim" section, but added that "both called." They noted that the "house appeared ok," and that "Hunter left with the 5-month-old daughter." It does not support James's claim that Joy was frog-marched out of the house with their baby in her arms and then run out of town.

But the two irreconcilable narratives, Joy's and James's, would ultimately finish their relationship. James's story, and Joy's behavior in its aftermath, would confirm for the Yancey family their belief that Joy brought chaos to James's life. Joy's experience was the opposite: she had lived with James's chaos and his mother's disdain for years; she'd been called crazy, and now she felt she really was going crazy.

Joy didn't have her clothes or Ja'Mya's, and weeks went by before she could retrieve her belongings. By the time she was allowed back, she was so angry that she quietly grabbed a knife from the kitchen, went upstairs, stuck one of Ja'Mya's soiled diapers in James's mink coat, and with the knife, slashed James's mattress open. Joy had a thing about mattresses.

As soon as she was out of the house, Joy regained a sense of peace. Yet she couldn't fully disconnect. She had to speak with James regularly to arrange visitation for Ja'Mya. Even these calls would be the subject of dual narratives—James told his family that Joy called him constantly to scream at him, Joy told her people that James was beefing with her like they were still together. Moreover, Joy woke to the fact that she had nothing, and a child to raise. She told James and Maureen both that she'd have a lawyer reach out to Micheline Levine to negotiate a support agreement. Even that was a source of affirmation for the family: *All Joy wants is the money.*

---

* Joylette Hunter has no idea what this reference means: "I didn't have any interview scheduled and I would never leave the baby at home without calling Clarice," Maureen's sister, who sometimes came to watch the baby.

Maureen gave thanks that Joy was out of James's life. Meanwhile, Joy prayed that James would maintain his relationship with Ja'Mya.

F rank had access to regions of James's psyche that the women in his life did not. It was why, in Frank's opinion, he had incurred the ire of Joy and Maureen from time to time as they desired to close the space between themselves and James, the space that Frank himself occupied. But everybody was territorial about James. Everybody wanted something. Frank, being honest, put himself among them.

From Frank's perspective, James's parents' expectations had become a kind of weight on him. But Joy, too, had always taken up a lot of real estate in James's mind; she could spark his fury in ways that he'd seen no one else do. Joy wasn't his wife yet, but she exerted the pressure of one. James had explained his split with Joy to Frank this way: *I'm paying her not to live with me.*

James resumed the life of a bachelor. Frank had connections to a crew of male strippers who threw afterparties for their female clientele, and the two of them secured occasional invitations to these post-club events where the men were outnumbered by dozens of horny women. At one of these parties, James met Tia, a woman somewhat more reserved than her counterparts: pretty, nice body, her natural hair in a headwrap. They exchanged numbers and started talking regularly. He found that she had a son. But she was, in at least one way, like his first love, Angie: a college girl. As Frank put it, a "good girl."

When James brought Tia by the house, Maureen liked her immediately.

S ince Madlib and Peanut Butter Wolf left Detroit, they'd been checking in on the status of Madlib's tracks for the MCA album, in part to get paid, but also because they were fans of Dilla's. When no money or explanation was forthcoming, they began to feel ghosted. They caught James's attention another way.

On a lark, Madlib created an album's worth of rhymes over a Jay Dee

beat CD that he labeled "Jaylib"; over one of them, he rapped an interpolation of the classic rap song "The Message." Wolf wanted to play the
track at his DJ gigs, and pressed up 250 copies of the mix on vinyl. Eothen "Egon" Alapatt, Stones Throw's general manager, thought the bootleg innocent enough as bootlegs go: Jay Dee had already used the beat
for the Busta Rhymes song "Show Me What You Got," and Egon was sure
that Busta's label, Elektra, wouldn't care.

But James cared. When one of those pieces made it into James's
hands, with JAYLIB in bold type, Wolf got a call: "What's up with this
bootleg?!" Egon and the rest of the Stones Throw crew froze as James's
screaming voice bled from Wolf's phone. But in Wolf's attempts to calm
James down—*It wasn't something we made for sale*, he insisted—he realized that the producer actually *liked* the idea of working with Madlib
this way.

"If we're gonna do this," James told Wolf, "let's do it official."

Wolf assumed that the easiest way to do something "official" would
be to ask nothing more of James and simply release Madlib's "Jaylib" CD
as it was. But when he suggested this to James, Wolf got another taste of
James's temper.

"Fuck that," James spat. "That's not what we talked about."

What James envisioned was a true collaboration album—Madlib
rhyming over James's beats, and James rhyming over Madlib's. Wolf realized he'd hit a double nerve: he'd pegged James as the beatmaker when he
really wanted to be an MC; and he'd suggested releasing something old
against James's instinctive reflex to do something new. It took very little
time for James to turn around more than a dozen songs over Madlib's
tracks, one featuring Frank-n-Dank, and another with an MC whom they
had never heard of, Guilty Simpson, rapping in a relaxed rumble that
could crack concrete.

James met Byron Dwayne Simpson through a mutual friend from the
days of the now-defunct Hip Hop Shop: DJ Tony Tone, who hosted
freestyle sessions at a club called the Lush Lounge, one of the few places
in Detroit where MCs could still match wits. Simpson, a part of the local

crew Almighty Dreadnaughtz, had a voice to match his physical magnitude. A few days later, James dispatched House Shoes to summon the rapper to his studio. Thereafter, James made Simpson his new protégé, often swinging by the rapper's house in Hazel Park in his new 2002 champagne-colored Cadillac Escalade—which James had customized with metal plaques that read DILLALADE—to bring him back up to Clinton Township. With James, Guilty earned his first money for recording his rhymes, a check for $1,500.

James intended to have Simpson play a key part of his new project, *Welcome Back 2 Detroit*, the sequel album for which Peter Adarkwah at BBE was itching, especially now that James's relationship with MCA had soured. James envisioned the LP as a showcase for more of the city's talent. To A&R the project, he tapped the two most connected Detroiters he knew, House Shoes and Guilty Simpson's manager, Gene "Hex" Howell. The rotund young Hex possessed a quick mind and an even quicker punch with which he flattened anyone who annoyed him; if Proof were the mayor of Detroit hip-hop, Hex was its one-man army. Shoes and Hex together helped James coordinate a kickoff meeting at Beans & Cornbread, a restaurant on 8 Mile Road. James found his helpers too helpful: Nearly forty people showed up from crews all over the city. James was overwhelmed with the response, and the initial positive energy of the gathering quickly disintegrated into petty rivalries and jealousies, and James lost interest in this idea, too.

Another contributor to the flagging of this project was a sudden rift between James and House Shoes. James had been invited to perform a show at a small club in Toronto with Frank-n-Dank. But after two moves in the past several years, he had misplaced the vinyl for his own music. James called Shoes to ask where he could buy his own records, and Shoes offered to let James borrow his crate of Jay Dee productions on vinyl that he had painstakingly collected over the past decade.

Weeks later, Shoes texted James to get his crate back, catching the producer in the middle of the first birthday party for his daughter Ja'Mya and unwilling to interrupt his day to return it.

But Shoes insisted: "You needed something and I gave it to you, now I have to DJ *tonight*." James texted a stream of curses at House Shoes in the manner that Shoes had observed James flip on so many others in his inner circle. But as much as he idolized Jay Dee, Shoes wasn't one of James's aspiring artists.

"Motherfucker, I'm sitting right here on my porch. You can come over here right now and we can roll around in the grass."

James never came. That was the last House Shoes saw of his records, and the last time he'd speak to James for a long while.*

The Yancey family lost their lease on the big white house near the river. By the end of 2002 they had moved back up to a modest rental home a mile from Conant Gardens, on Rowe and McNichols, behind Zorba's Coney Island diner. It wasn't uncomfortable: Maurice shot hoops in the driveway with John and played horseshoes and grilled in the backyard with Dewitt. But it was a different lifestyle.

James's financial prospects were contracting. Just a few years prior, James was commanding up to $60,000 per track for his production work. Now he was lucky if he got more than $15,000. That wasn't so much a sign of James's declining worth as it was the changing economics of the industry. Compact disc sales had plummeted, and the birth of a tiny, legitimate digital download market couldn't match the profits from selling music on little pieces of plastic. Frank and James just a year earlier had been plotting to buy Chocolate City. Now they hustled small projects just to get some cash and keep their creative process going. Christopher Ramos came with a timely connection: he knew Beni B, the owner of a small hip-hop label in Oakland, California, ABB Records, and Ramos suggested that Beni put out some of the Frank-n-Dank music that had been snubbed by MCA. Beni and James spoke by phone and Ramos brokered a deal to put out a vinyl twelve-inch, downplaying the fact that, technically, MCA still owned the recordings. A few months later, James and Frank reached out to one of Ramos's European contacts: Groove Attack,

---

* On the forthcoming Jaylib album, James would take an oblique shot at his friend: "It's barefoot bullyshit, so you don't need them house shoes." Also featured on the song was Guilty Simpson who, indebted to James and Shoes both, alerted the DJ to the line before the album's release.

a distributor of dance and hip-hop vinyl based in Köln, Germany, for whom Ramos had helped start a line of twelve-inch singles featuring artists like Common and Phife, the latter of which James produced. Groove Attack had also released some of the Slum Village tracks from *Fan-Tas-Tic* under the artist name "J-88."* When the founder Frank Stratmann heard James's tales of woe with MCA, he offered him, essentially, a new home. If James and Frank could deliver the recordings, Groove Attack would create and sell the product. Frank and James quickly envisioned a new imprint, Mummy Records. They recorded a new Frank-n-Dank single, "Push," and James whipped up six brand-new tracks in the course of a week for an EP he dubbed *Ruff Draft*.

The silver lining of Frank's travails with MCA and McNasty had been an increase in his business knowledge. So he took the role of James's liaison and project manager, overseeing email communications even though he didn't have his own computer, enlisting his friend Rod to send and receive messages for him. The effort proved thankless. Early one morning, Frank's phone rang. It was James, screaming at him: "Why is everybody looking at my email?"

"What the fuck are you talking about?" Frank asked, still groggy. He quickly deduced that James was reading an email thread on his Blackberry phone in which someone had mistakenly hit "Reply All." James didn't understand how email worked, didn't understand that it wasn't Frank's fault, and didn't care. He just wanted to rage. Finally, Frank snapped:

"You know what? I don't know what the fuck you're going through, bro, but I'm about to throw on some pants and come to your house and *whoop your motherfucking ass.*"

Frank hung up the phone. By the time he made it to his driveway, Dank was pulling up; James had phoned him to intervene.

"Wait, what the fuck is going on?" Dank asked.

"I'm about to beat the brakes off your motherfucking cousin," Frank fumed. "Talking reckless, especially with some shit where he don't even

---

* "The 788" and "J-88" were two related aliases for Slum Village. The former represented the days of each of the three members' birthdays; and the latter replaced James's birthday, February 7, with his first initial.

know what the fuck he's talking about. I don't give a *fuck* about this rap shit, bro."

Dank managed to calm his partner down. At base, Frank cared deeply about his friend; he actually *did* know what James was going through, professionally and personally. He knew that James's impatience and exactitude wasn't just bile, but grew out of his own hard-won sense of self-worth, an understanding that in business, he himself was the product. And he knew the past year had been hard on James, even after Joy left. There had been a break-in at the house. A few months later, James was alone there at night when the cops came barreling through the doors. They cuffed James and put a black hood on him in his own living room. For nothing but a random complaint from a neighbor who smelled marijuana. They found a blunt and a couple of baggies and charged him with possession. Frank was the one who got the calls when James was in need or vulnerable.

But the years of subordinating himself to James Yancey had taken their toll on Frank Bush, exhausted from having his fortunes tied to his oldest friend's moods and whims. Throughout this time, with no help from James, he had been calling MCA, trying to get someone, *anyone* on the phone who could tell him what was going on with his project. Finally, his persistence paid off: he found himself in conversation with MCA's CEO, Jay Boberg. Frank was polite and measured. After a brief chat, Boberg cleared the way to release Frank-n-Dank from MCA and McNasty. Frank was now his own man.

G one were the warm bass lines and textured harmonies of old Jay Dee. Gone were the glossy pretentions of his tracks for *Pay Jay*, or the concerns about sampling that had bedeviled *48 Hours*. The songs on *Ruff Draft* were the beats James made for his own listening pleasure. They were jagged, imperfect, decidedly low-fidelity, without the pretense of commercial appeal. "Real live shit," he called it in his intro. "Sound like it's straight from the motherfuckin' cassette." *Ruff Draft* was James rubbed raw.

Ruff Draft accompanied other breaks with James's past: with Joy, with

House Shoes, with Frank. It also marked a more decisive split with MCA, which gave James a release from his contract in the final months of 2002, around the same time word came that Jay Boberg had been ousted; and that the entire label itself would likely be folded into Jimmy Iovine's Interscope, just as A&M had been years earlier.

The news coincided with the release of two MCA albums from the Soulquarian family—Common's *Electric Circus* and the Roots' *Phrenology*. With Boberg gone and his staff paralyzed, the albums limped into the marketplace. Not that any label could have saved these two baffling records: the most savage reviews came from inside the Soulquarians' virtual house, the Okayplayer message boards, where fans intuited that the musicians' nerdy cloistering had become narcissistic self-absorption.

The Soulquarians' battle against the shiny suits would end, appropriately, in a conference room. There, Boberg's former lieutenant Jeff Harleston was asked to make a last-ditch argument for the retention of each act on the MCA roster in front of a panel of disinterested Interscope executives led by Steve Stoute. Harleston would later speak of the moment as the most humiliating of his professional life. The Roots and Common ultimately made the cut, with words whispered from producer Dr. Dre into Iovine's ear. But nothing was more indicative of their diminished horizons than when Jimmy Iovine—in a meeting with Harleston, Questlove, Black Thought, and Richard Nichols—professed his admiration for the Roots by blithely suggesting that the best course of action for them would be to become the backing band behind his shiniest star: Eminem, now the leading man of an autobiographical hit movie, *8 Mile*.

The suits ran the table. The Soulquarians got the scraps.

I n the first, frigid month of 2003, James flew to Europe to pick up some more cash. James's booking agent, Asya Shein, presented Jonathan Dworkin with an opportunity: a quick DJ tour of several cities. All James had to do was show up to each venue, play some records, and make stupid money.

Frank had patched things up with James after their argument, but he was still putting some healthy distance between them, decamping

to Canada to snag a deal for Frank-n-Dank with Toronto label Needill-
works. Dank alone accompanied James on the trip. Right away, things
went awry. The airline lost James's records. Visiting Groove Attack's offices in Köln, they learned that the new *Ruff Draft* vinyl had yet to be
delivered. James and Dank hung loose and stayed high. After landing at
their next destination, Dank lost track of what country he was in, happily puffing on a joint that his host had rolled for him, referring to it as
"good German shit." He was in Finland. Their Finnish host had lost track
of something, too: he kept calling him "Frank the Dank." In the Netherlands, at Club Effenaar in Eindhoven, James borrowed some records
from DJ Lefto, a Belgian radio personality who often played James's music on his Studio Brussel show, *The Hop*. As James went through his vinyl,
Lefto noticed that many of James's fingertips were covered by bandages.

"Did you cut yourself?" Lefto asked him.

"Naw," James replied, telling him that his fingers had been raw and
sensitive lately. Lefto asked James if he was feeling okay.

"I feel like I have something going on," James replied.

James and Dank's European adventure continued with ups and
downs, perhaps mirroring the way James was feeling. At every stop,
Dank was having a difficult time getting James to eat, especially when
their road manager Hischam kept them in hotels in remote locations. At
one point in the tour, James got so furious with Hischam that he jumped
him. In Paris on January 17, the promoter of his Divan du Monde show
thought he was getting a J Dilla stage show rather than a DJ set, and after
a dispute James and Dank left the stage. The promoter dialed Dworkin
in a panic, saying that James wouldn't go back on unless he got some
"bitches and weed."

It's a weekend, I'm at home, I'm in my boxers, and I'm an ocean away,
Dworkin told him. *What do you want me to do?*

After Paris, they went to a club in London, where James was approached by a business partner whom he'd never met in person. Beni
B had just flown into town after attending the Midem record business
convention in France, heard that Jay Dee was playing at a local club, and
came through.

With Beni was another one of his artists: Taz Arnold, part of the Los

Angeles-based production trio Sa-Ra Creative Partners, who all idolized Jay Dee. Taz had just made a record with Waajeed and visited Detroit, but hadn't yet met James, who seemed to be a little under the weather— Taz couldn't put his finger on why. They took pictures together. For one photo, Beni gave James a copy of an album from a new group he had signed called Little Brother. He knew that the crew would appreciate the snapshot, because he knew their sound owed a lot to the man who now held their vinyl in his hand.

T wo years earlier, when James was in Europe promoting *Welcome 2 Detroit*, he gave two radio interviews, snapshots of a producer transitioning into an artist. On this trip he gave two more, the most comprehensive and introspective of his career. The first was conducted backstage after his show in Eindhoven by the local beat producer and blogger Frank Sens, who went by the name "Y'skid" (pronounced "wise kid"); the second during his final stop, in Sweden, by the music journalist Mats Nileskär. Both interviewers believed that James's true importance exceeded the conventional wisdom that pegged him as a great but relatively marginal beat producer. They were utterly well versed in James's work, and James responded with equal depth.

James shed light on some unanswered questions, like why he chose to leave Slum Village. "How can I fight this man I'm about to go onstage with?" he asked Y'skid rhetorically, referring to both T3 and Baatin and their creative differences. "I needed my space." He tried to explain how Common pushed him and the rest of the Soulquarians for such an unconventional album in *Electric Circus*. He announced the recent dissolution of his MCA deal, his upcoming Jaylib album with Madlib, and his work with the Detroit MC Guilty Simpson. He even talked about his new Dillalade, a gift to himself to enjoy the moment, he said, "because it can all be taken away from you."

He also spoke, for the first time, about his father's truncated career in music, about the genesis of his "loud and off-beat" time-feel, and about the soul group of musicians in which he found himself.

"I feel that we have been here before," he told Nileskär of his peers like Pete Rock, Questlove, and D'Angelo, fumbling for the words to express their collective connection to the sounds of the past. "Maybe I have the same soul of these drummers. Like a certain. I don't know. I-I can't explain it . . ." It was a mystical connection in which James's own role seemed to mystify him: "All these other cats are so talented in so many other areas, and here I come," he told Y'skid. "All I know how to do is work the MPC. Maybe I brought something different to the table."

Yet, with his answers, it was clear that James *knew* that he had brought something. The truth that rankled Y'skid was the same thing that aggrieved James: *how quickly his sonic and musical signatures had been adopted, adapted, or "cloned" by a growing number of producers.* James referred to Jimmy Jam and Terry Lewis's production of "Got 'Til It's Gone," hinting, however vaguely, that it was his own work. James mentioned Hi-Tek with both frustration and admiration. Y'skid referred to a particular song by the singer Toni Braxton that lifted James's well-crafted drum sounds, the handiwork of the producer Rodney "Darkchild" Jerkins, who had mined not only J Dilla's drum library but had used James's grid-busting techniques on a new multimillion-selling album for the singer-actress Brandy.

"I can't stand that shit," James blurted.

Unmentioned, but doubtlessly also in James's mind, was the music coming from Philadelphia's A Touch of Jazz collective, who had been the most aggressive propagators of James's time-feel, certainly due in part to James's close relationship with his "Uncle Jeff." On Musiq Soulchild's second album in 2002, Ivan Barias and Carvin Haggins continued to misalign time grids by rushing the snare on songs like "Newness." That same year, none other than Michael Jackson released a single, "Butterflies," that bore those same Dilla rhythmic signatures. It was produced by A Touch of Jazz's Andre Harris and his writing partner, a fervent Slum Village fan and transplant from England, Marsha Ambrosius. The two most prominent members of pop music's royal family—Janet and Michael—had created music using James Dewitt Yancey's rhythmic approach, without ever having met or worked with the man himself.

Something about this situation didn't compute for James. He had his own influences, and freely admitted that some of his productions were his own takes on the work of his contemporaries, like "Let's Grow," the song he recently did with Detroit's Royce da 5'9": "See, that was *my* Timbaland impression," James told Y'skid. "I get inspired, but you want to still *do you.*"

For James, "his own takes" were just that. Whatever he made, it sounded like him. It's why he called Karriem Riggins over to his house one day for a little chat after hearing some of Riggins's new beats for Slum and Dwele: *You have all this talent. You can do things I can't possibly do. Why would you want to sound just like me?*

James's question made sense coming from hip-hop, where developing one's own signature sound was vital. James thought like a beatmaker: *All I know how to do is work the MPC.*

But this was small thinking. The bigger the idea, the more people it would influence. The more people it influenced, the farther it would travel. The farther it traveled, the more impossible the idea was to own. The reason James didn't understand why all these people sounded like him is that James still didn't know that he *wasn't* simply a beatmaker, nor did he grasp how big of an idea he had cultivated.

The reason James's rhythmic ideas were pervading pop music at this particular moment was a transformation in how electronic music was being composed and recorded—not on stand-alone drum machines, but on computers using software that made sound visible and more easily manipulable—thus making the ideas of James Yancey much easier to replicate.

James *knew* why he made music, day and night, telling Nileskär: "I want people to feel what I feel."

People were feeling it now. But James wasn't sure how he was feeling about that. As he flew home, he wasn't sure how he was feeling at all.

11.
Warp Time

Back in 2000, Nicolay Rook was the new guy at Personal-Ware, a division of IBM in the Netherlands. He had never studied a lick of computer science; he'd been a musicology grad student at the University of Amsterdam. Feeling pessimistic about his prospects for a music career, Nicolay walked into a temp agency and they sent him to this godforsaken place to answer phones. Before long he was offered a position as the supervisor of the company's support team. And though he was versed enough in computers to keep up with his work, Nic couldn't shake the music thing completely, and spent much of his day lurking in the online message boards of Okayplayer.

Nicolay discovered the site after he had seen it listed in the liner notes of two of his favorite records that year: *Voodoo* and *Like Water for Chocolate*. For a musician interested less in the old European masters and more in the new American virtuosos like D'Angelo, Common, and Jay Dee, the Okayplayer community became a soul group in which he wanted to dwell. Despite the language and time differences, Nic gradually felt comfortable joining the conversation. He found his people—Questlove, posting music treatises as "Qoolquest"; a guy from Detroit, Kelly Frazier, posting as "RenaissanceSoul," who kept a running discography of all things Jay Dee; a college student in Indiana, Bill Johnson, posting as "DJ Brainchild," who seemed to have every piece of rare and unreleased music in his hard drive; and an aspiring MC from North Carolina, Phonte Coleman, who posted as "TayGravy."

That summer, Nicolay had a chance to visit this virtual world in real life when Slum Village opened for D'Angelo at a festival in neighboring

Belgium, an experience that set new song ideas swirling in his head. But
without access to expensive recording equipment, the only tool he had
to make his music was the same one he used to access Okayplayer. On
his cheap home PC, Nic downloaded a copy of free shareware, Mod-
Plug, one of several "tracking" programs that allowed users to sequence
computer-generated sounds and samples, or to trigger sounds on external
synthesizers via MIDI. ModPlug was arcane and complicated—click here
to place a drum sound, click there to create a keyboard melody. It was
completely without the real-time, record-and-playback ergonomics of a
professional drum machine or the newer, commercially available computer programs. But Nicolay found that it gave him the granular control
he needed, *especially* when it came to trying to decipher and emulate the
rhythmic quirks of Jay Dee. With just a few clicks, he could nudge a kick
drum forward, or a snare backward in time, or—in a technique he found
very effective—shifting all the hi-hats a few fractions of a quarter note
later, unmooring them from the grid and misaligning them in relation
to the other drum sounds.

Nicolay had heard these broken rhythms for years. The computer
screen enabled him to actually *see* and *create* them.

The synthesizers, sequencers, samplers, and drum machines of the
late twentieth century were all "computers" in the sense that they
used circuitry to manipulate information.

But the rise of another tool, the *personal computer*, would prove to be
more powerful and versatile than any of them for composing, playing,
and recording music. The promise of the personal computer as a music
making device had partly to do with its open-ended functionality: A
drum machine or an electronic keyboard was hardware made to do one,
specific thing. A computer, hypothetically, could be programmed using
software to do almost *anything*.

It took a great while for personal computers to gain the power and
connectivity to perform even simple musical tasks. The first software
applications turned computers into rudimentary synthesizers that generated basic tones, or into sequencers that could control external syn-

thesizers via MIDI connections—new interfaces that allowed electronic instruments to "talk" to each other. By the end of the eighties, these computer sequencers, with names like Cubase, Vision, and Performer, were in use widely by both professionals and amateurs, to employ the computer as the "master clock" of the recording studio.

These new computer programs had some clear advantages over the sequencers embedded in drum machines and synthesizers, chief among them that software sequencers took advantage of the graphical user interface of computer monitors. Where drum machines used small LED lights and tiny LCD screens to help musicians and programmers navigate, computer sequencers allowed users to visualize *everything*: to see all the instruments and notes laid out in a horizontal grid representing the passage of time.

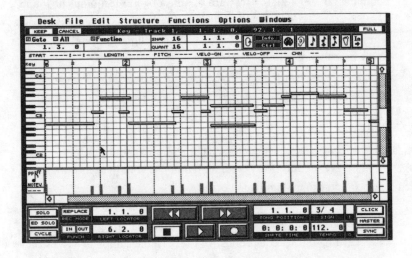

Computer sequencers soon acquired advanced timing functions like quantization and swing; and added features such as "grooves"— algorithms that could be applied to rhythm tracks to change the positions of notes to impart different rhythmic feels. Crucially, they allowed the user the freedom to manually move notes back and forth along the grid by pointing and clicking with the computer's mouse. By the early 1990s, computer sequencers essentially embodied all of Roger Linn's clock innovations.

D'Angelo, Bob Power, and Ali Shaheed Muhammad, for example, were using programs like Notator and Vision to sequence and tweak note timings on D'Angelo's 1995 debut album. But the reason that many hip-hop producers didn't simply ditch their MPCs and SP-1200s in the 1990s is that computer sequencers still performed only *half* of the function of their trusty drum machines. It took years for computers to gain the speed and memory to store and play back *samples*, and to perform the next, obvious step up from that: recording multitrack audio, replacing the role of the tape machine in the recording process.

By the year 2000, these powerful programs, collectively called "Digital Audio Workstations" or DAWs, essentially put the entire recording studio onto a computer and allowed producers to "see" sound as graphic waveforms—from professional-level software costing hundreds and sometimes thousands of dollars, like Pro Tools, Digital Performer, Studio Vision, Cubase, Reason, Logic, and Ableton; to software like Garage Band and FruityLoops for amateurs and hobbyists, wherein preset rhythms and chunky graphics gave music-making the feel of playing a video game.

And then there were the tracker programs like ModPlug for computer geeks like Nicolay, in which the timelines ran from top to bottom instead of left to right, a lo-fi version of the cascading green code of *The Matrix*.

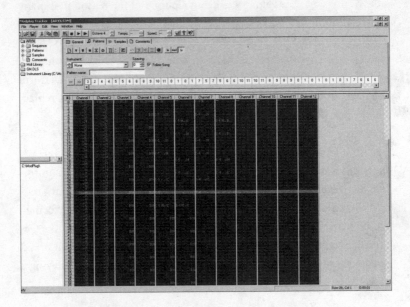

Tasks that used to take drum machine producers like Q-Tip, Pete Rock, and J Dilla hours now took computer producers seconds. New programs like ReCycle could automatically chop a drum loop into its constituent parts—kick, snare, hi-hat—and then instantly assign those to a keyboard or pad controller. With drum machines, producers had to slow samples down or speed them up to match the tempo of other elements, resulting in jarring fluctuations in pitch. But DAWs allowed users, just by dragging a waveform to make it longer or shorter, to "time stretch" or "warp" any piece of audio to a desired length *without* altering the pitch; or, conversely, to change the pitch *without* altering the time, something previously impossible without expensive outboard gear.

The limitations of the older machines provoked the innovations of the producers who used them, and cultivated character, too—patience, perseverance, focus, risk-taking. Once computers allowed a new gener-

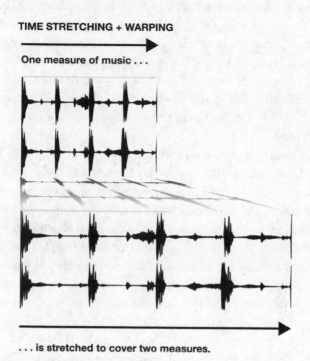

TIME STRETCHING + WARPING

One measure of music . . .

. . . is stretched to cover two measures.

ation of electronic composers to more easily replicate those hard-won techniques—especially the time-feel of James Dewitt Yancey—they became ubiquitous.

When Patrick Douthit called on Phonte Coleman at his dorm room at North Carolina Central University, he usually had some new, unreleased hip-hop in his hands. Last time it was a bootlegged Black Star album featuring Mos Def and Talib Kweli. This time, it was a cassette of incredible instrumental beats.

"Who's this?" Phonte asked.

"This is me," Patrick answered.

"This is *you*?!"

Phonte, an English major and aspiring lyricist, didn't know Patrick made beats under the alias "9th Wonder"—on his desktop computer no less. Phonte took one of them and wrote a song, "Paper Lines." Before long, they joined with Phonte's friend, Thomas "Big Pooh" Jones, to form a hip-hop trio, Little Brother. The name came from their worship of their 1990s "big brothers"—groups like De La Soul and A Tribe Called Quest who embodied that magic juxtaposition of the sublime and the rugged—and of a newer group that Phonte called "Tribe on steroids," Slum Village.

Phonte sensed something profound going on with Jay Dee's music, but he didn't quite have the language to express it until he and Pooh began skulking around the music department where, alongside jazz vocalists and musicians, the two rappers took a production course with Professor Chip Shearin. Each week, Shearin would challenge his students to bring in their favorite pieces of popular music for discussion. One of Phonte's classmates brought a contemporary R&B song by the girl group Total, produced by Timbaland. Shearin, a jazz bassist unbound by academic manners, tore it apart. "Oh my God, this ain't nothin' but three notes," he lamented. "Y'all buying this shit?!"

That attitude vanished when one of Phonte's friends played "Thelonius" by Common. As Jay Dee's drums, keyboards, and bass swirled with and against each other, Shearin's eyes widened.

"Oh, man . . . that bass line! . . . the phrasing! . . . I would have never phrased it like that . . . that's fucking crazy . . . this shit is sick!"

To hear a professional bass player extolling the virtues of a *Jay Dee* bass line was startling. Phonte's drummer friends in class broke the rhythms down to him: *The kick is late. The snare is early. As simple as the stuff sounds, it's complex.* It was the first time Phonte saw a beatmaker being held in esteem by traditional musicians. In the wake of the one-two punch of *Like Water for Chocolate* and *Fantastic, Vol. 2.*, Phonte bumped the latter album repeatedly. He told his partners in Little Brother: *This is who we've got to beat. This is the fucking bar.* To leap over it, 9th Wonder used his computer software, FruityLoops.

The program made it simple to shift elements later or earlier in time; with each shift, 9th created conflict and subverted expectations. Phonte,

as he watched 9th work, began to comprehend the power of those minute shifts, even to elements other than drums.

"It's sounding a little stiff," 9th said about one of Phonte's verses. "I'm
just gonna nudge it over a little."

Phonte watched 9th click on the block of his recorded vocal and slide
it slightly to the right in the timeline, so that each syllable and each word
landed a tiny bit later than it had in the original recorded pass. And
just like that, what had sounded stiff now sounded loose and relaxed.
Phonte discovered—as did Jay Dee and the great musicians before him
stretching all the way back to Louis Armstrong—that delay communicated "cool." *I'll get there when I get there. I'll see you when I see you. It'll
be worth the wait.* So every time that Phonte recorded a vocal thereafter,
he gave it a little digital nudge, to the right.

C omputers were changing everything about music: the way it was
created, the way it was distributed and consumed. Little Brother
made their music on a computer and found their audience on it as well.
While Phonte Coleman served as the arts and entertainment editor of
the campus newspaper, he spent most of his time on Okayplayer.com,
surveying the message boards: *Lord of the Flies* for music nerds, a cross
between a rap magazine and the Roman Colosseum. Nobody pulled any
punches, nothing was too sacred for a vigorous debate, even Jay Dee.
Okayplayers came from all over the world: One poster from the Bronx
who called himself "Desus Nice" had a way of telling stories that were
so fucked up and brilliant and funny at the same time.* Some guy from
the Netherlands of all places, "Nicolay Music," posted some of the most
amazing tracks Phonte had ever heard.

The boards were the place that Phonte posted the first Little Brother
track, "Speed." An Okayplayer from Florida posting as "Slop Funk Dust"
offered to make the group their first web page, posting four Little Brother
songs. After he launched it, the traffic crashed his server. Another Okay-

---

* He would later become a national TV host on the program *Desus & Mero.*

player, "DJ Brainchild," then posted digital copies of the songs on the boards. Phonte shot him an angry message; he didn't understand what good could come of this digital free-for-all until he got an email from Ian Davis, who worked for a small hip-hop independent label out of the Bay Area called ABB. He had passed the music to the label's owner, Beni B, who wanted to sign the group. They did the paperwork, and shortly, Phonte, 9th Wonder, and Pooh began working on their first album.

Thereafter, the Okayplayer boards remained Little Brother's ready-made core audience and resource. In late 2001, as Little Brother was recording their album for ABB, Nicolay Rook got a direct message from Phonte Coleman about his tracks: "Wanted to know if you'd be interested in doing some collabs. Read from your post that you were hungry for emcees. Little Brother and the rest of my crew would be more than happy to bless your joints." Nicolay was floored and grateful.

But Phonte's comrades in Little Brother weren't quite into Nicolay's work, being somewhat glossier than 9th's. So while Little Brother finished their album, *The Listening*, in a recording studio in Durham, North Carolina, Phonte began a new collaboration, conducted entirely computer-to-computer, a transatlantic trade of beats and vocals between him and Nicolay that they would eventually dub the Foreign Exchange.

I n late 2002, MTV began airing a video for "Floetic," a curious clip directed by Marc Klasfeld that used computer effects to convert the streets, buildings, and bridges of Philadelphia into musical instruments. The song was the product of another foreign exchange: two transplants from London, Marsha Ambrosius and Natalie Stewart, who called themselves Floetry. Ambrosius, the singer and songwriter of the duo, was an avid fan of neo-soul, and more specifically of Slum Village. She figured she had listened to the first ten seconds of "Hold Tight" more than any other piece of music in her life—something about the cheekiness of Jay Dee's pocket and Q-Tip's rap made her think: *Finally. Someone understands me.* Thus Ambrosius dove at the opportunity for Floetry to perform at the famed Black Lily in Philadelphia. In a room with people they'd only heard about—Jill Scott, Jaguar Wright, Bilal—with Questlove playing those lagging, dragging Jay Dee–type beats behind them, Ambrosius decided she wasn't going back.

Ambrosius began working with James Poyser, but ultimately she made an enduring connection with Jazzy Jeff and his team at A Touch of Jazz, six guys working in three pairs: Ivan Barias and Carvin Haggins, Andre Harris and Vidal Davis, Keith Pelzer and Darren Henson. She took every opportunity they gave her to make demos for the guys' projects, and for Floetry. One day at the studio complex on North Third Street, Jeff received a visitor: a short, quiet man in a long chinchilla coat, who cast an even longer shadow over Jeff's crew.

Oh my God! Ambrosius thought. *It's friggin Jay Dee!*

He was there and he was gone, an apparition of Detroit cool. But the man's ideas were ever-present in her creativity. Ambrosius and Andre Harris recorded a song of hers, something she had written when she was only sixteen, and set it to a limping, conflicted beat. DJ Jazzy Jeff sent the demo to John McClain, the man who had signed both Slum Village and Janet Jackson, and who now worked for one of Janet's older brothers. One day Jazzy Jeff called Marsha into his office and played her a voice message: it was Michael Jackson, saying that he wanted to record the song she had written, "Butterflies." Ambrosius spent a surreal week in New York's Hit Factory coaching Jackson through a perfect replication of her demoed vocal over her and Harris's track. It was her first songwriting credit, and would be the last single released by Michael Jackson during his lifetime, in early 2002.

By the end of the year, Floetry landed a deal with DreamWorks Records, their album preceded by that bizarre video, the places and people of the City of Brotherly Love all vibrating together and apart in Dilla Time.

The producers and songwriters of A Touch of Jazz were now bringing Jay Dee's rhythms full circle: the keyboardist Pete Kuzma, another Jay Dee fan, contributed a song to the debut album by Dwele—imparting a Detroit rhythmic feel to a Detroit artist by way of Philadelphia. By the time Dwele's album came out in 2003, the disciples of James Dewitt Yancey were churning out their own variations on James's themes.

But place mattered less now. Phonte from North Carolina and Nicolay from the Netherlands completed an entire album without having met each other; and they wouldn't until after Peter Adarkwah's BBE Music signed the Foreign Exchange. They finally shook hands when Phonte flew to Europe with Little Brother.

These ideas were everywhere now. James's sound had become central to hip-hop and R&B, even as his name and his production had moved to the fringes. With computers, everyone could warp time like James. But James would, in his final act, prove that tools were only as good as the hands that touched them.

12.
J Dilla

James felt ill when he returned to Detroit in late January 2003.

Figuring he had gotten sick from something he ate overseas, he drove to his family's home on Rowe Street and stayed the night. The next day there was blood in his urine. He called his sister Martha to the bathroom door to tell her; she joked with him that it must have been caused by some "nasty girl" he'd been with. The third day his condition worsened: he was feverish, shaking with chills, suffering from nausea and bloody diarrhea. Maureen and Dewitt took James to Bon Secours hospital in Grosse Pointe. In the emergency room, nurses and doctors examined James and gave him blood tests, and returned with blanched expressions: James's blood platelet count was well below 10,000 per microliter. The normal range, they said, was well above 150,000.

It's so low that he shouldn't even be able to walk around, they said.

Platelets play a major role in clotting the blood. Without them, the slightest injury can cause massive bleeding. The staff said that they needed to admit James and get him a blood transfusion right away.

The bigger question, for the doctors, was why James's platelet count was so low. After several tests, and after reviewing his symptoms and history, the physicians came back with a diagnosis.

Thrombotic thrombocytopenic purpura, or TTP, is a blood disease so rare that only a half dozen people per million develop it.

Blood possesses a mechanism for maintaining its volume in case of injury: the ability to clot. There are some diseases where the blood does not clot enough, like hemophilia. And there are others wherein the blood clots too much.

In TTP, an overgrowth of the stringy protein responsible for clotting attracts too many platelets, essentially making the blood "sticky," causing clots within small blood vessels and organs. The platelets block the vessels, and have the side effect of shearing the healthy red blood cells that pass through them. This causes two problems: a drastic reduction in platelets available to clot the blood elsewhere in case of an injury; and a reduction in the amount of red blood cells that carry oxygen. Those problems can cause both uncontrollable bleeding and catastrophic organ failure.

The mechanism by which TTP and its sibling disease hemolytic uremic syndrome (HUS) wreak havoc on the body wasn't truly understood until the 1990s with the discovery of the enzyme ADAMTS-13, the "scissor" that, when functioning normally, cuts all those stringy, clotting proteins. Scientists found that TTP occurred when the body produced antibodies to ADAMTS-13. Thus TTP was an autoimmune disease, in which the body attacks its own healthy cells. The few experimental drug trials based on this revelation were taking place in Europe, not America. None of the doctors who were treating James mentioned ADAMTS-13 to James or Maureen, if they knew about it at all.

Still, the question remained about why certain people developed these antibodies in the first place. The cause seemed to be genetic predisposition. Women tended to get TTP more than men; people of African descent more than European or Asian. TTP could be triggered in adulthood by substances like quinine or certain prescription drugs. It could be a secondary condition to other illnesses, like cancer or HIV. Or it could be provoked by another chronic autoimmune disorder that had an uncannily similar demographic profile to TTP, called SLE, commonly known as lupus.

With no predictable cause or cure, TTP has a 95 percent mortality rate if left untreated. And the preferred treatment at the time of James's diagnosis was plasma exchange. The thought was that if the blood were refreshed with donor plasma, the dysfunctional proteins would be removed, properly functioning proteins could be introduced, the platelet level would rise, and the clotting would stop.

The prognosis was too dire to digest. James felt tired, but he'd been sick before and always gotten well. The treatment seemed severe, especially given that he *was* lucid and mobile, defying the doctors' expectations. James didn't want the procedure, didn't want to check into the hospital, and ended up getting into an argument with one of the doctors. The physician told James: *If you don't return for treatment in the next twenty-four hours, you will likely die.*

Maureen felt she had to respect her son's decision to leave, but agreed to bring him back if James's condition didn't improve. Back at the house on Rowe, James walked into the bathroom, closed the door, and cried for a long time.

Martha knew that her brother was terrified. They all were. They begged James to return to the hospital. Maureen, needing an ally, phoned Micheline Levine. *Talk to him, please,* Maureen said. She took the phone over to James.

Your mother is distraught, Micheline told James. *You've got to take care of yourself.*

But he told them he wanted to just lie down at home and process everything. That night he crawled into his parents' bed. Martha kept a vigil until dawn, praying, standing outside the door, calling James's name regularly, waiting for his response.

The next morning, James let Maureen take him back to Bon Secours. Within minutes they had admitted James—who thankfully had a good insurance plan through AFTRA, the union for TV, radio, and recording artists—and began the plasma exchange procedure to try to get his platelet level up.

James, a needle in each arm, was hooked up to a machine called a cell separator. Over the next couple of hours all the plasma in his body was exchanged. The uncomfortable procedure often makes patients feel light-headed or numb. With TTP, this procedure has to be repeated, daily, until the platelet level stabilizes above 150,000 for 48 hours and symptoms improve. The problem with James was that his platelet levels would rise after each treatment and then dive again.

And there was another complication: the clotting had already ravaged his kidneys. The organs responsible for filtering toxins out of his blood weren't functioning, and James had to be put on regular dialysis, yet another excruciating procedure that involved installing a port on his body, being hooked up to another machine, and having his entire blood volume again circulated through it.

Maureen stayed through the first night in the visitors' lounge. James was moved to a room, where family could visit and he could watch TV. James was lucid throughout, and thoroughly frustrated that he couldn't just get up and walk out, kept alive by machines, missing the one machine that made life worth living.

D ays became weeks. Maureen updated James on business and James asked her to take care of several errands. He spent his twenty-ninth birthday in the hospital. James didn't want visitors, but the people who loved him came anyway. He was bashful when Amp Fiddler stopped by, but there wasn't any hiding from Maurice "Bobo" Lamb, who burst into the room with Martha Yancey.

"Damn, James, look at that chest!" Bobo bellowed, pointing to James's exposed torso. "For a small guy you got a lot of hair!" James laughed for the first time in a long time.

James's children and their mothers were not among his visitors. Monica was unaware of his situation; she and Maureen had yet to be introduced. Joylette missed a phone call from James before he entered the hospital. But when James didn't call for a while to speak to Ja'Mya, as was his custom, Joy reached out to Maureen to check on him and felt like she couldn't get clarity on James's situation.*

---

* Joylette insists that Maureen told her, "He's in the hospital. He was in a coma but it's all good now." Maureen rejects this account, stating that James was not in a coma or semi-comatose state during his stay at Bon Secours.

Finally, in the second week of February, James's platelet level stabilized, and he was discharged. It was only after he got out that he phoned Monica, a call in which James remained evasive about his situation, but urged her to get Ty-Monae "tested for TTP-HUS" before he brusquely hung up. And there were two caveats to his release. Almost half of TTP patients experience relapses, so James would need regular check-ins with a specialist, Dr. Jeffrey Zonder at Harper Hospital. And his kidneys weren't functioning properly, so he would need to go on thrice-weekly outpatient dialysis.

J ames found he was too weak to look after himself, so he returned to his family's home to convalesce. It was hard for James to move around, so Maureen fetched James's MPC and a turntable from his house and placed them on the dining room table so he could work.

Al Hayes was too spooked to see his nephew while he was in the hospital, but he dropped by when John had a party with some of his friends from his basketball team. Al stepped into the kitchen, saw James for the first time in six months—bloated at the time from excess fluids and steroids—and excused himself quickly, saying he forgot something in his car. Once outside and out of sight, Al wept.

Joylette, too, had to keep her composure when she visited, James walking haltingly out to greet her and his daughter.

Ja'Mya held her hands out to James as if to say, *Pick me up!*

James, obviously too weak to lift her, hesitated.

Maureen's sister Reta, who lived a few blocks away, was visiting the house as Joylette attempted this little family reunion. Reta could feel Maureen's anger with Joy was overpowering her and Dewitt's awareness of the moment. So Reta took charge.

"James," she said, "why don't you just sit on down and let the baby climb up on you?"

James sat in a chair, and daughter and daddy were reunited. Joy whispered to Reta, almost a plea: *You're going to be here the whole time, aren't you?*

Later, after Joy left and James went to lie down, Reta spoke her mind to Maureen and Dewitt: "You know I love both of y'all. But for the sake of James and the grandchildren, y'all might need to put a little curb on that attitude with Joy."

What are you talking about? they replied.

"You didn't even see he was dying to pick up his daughter?" Reta insisted. "C'mon, y'all. Feel *James*."

Dewitt said: "You're right."

J ames stayed at his family's house for weeks, until he strengthened. But it was difficult to simply resume his life and routines. He'd stopped by a Slum Village recording session briefly after leaving the hospital, leaning on a cane, receiving the well wishes of all present. But after moving back into his house in Clinton Township, he guarded his privacy.

Young R. J., who had studied James in his father's studio as a teenager, was taking on a more active role as a member of Slum Village's production team. Since last year, James had begun talking about resuming work with Slum for their second Capitol album; Young R. J. had become the conduit and courier for that collaboration. But Young R. J. was shocked that James didn't want to see him when he arrived to drop off some Pro Tools files for James. "Just leave it in the mailbox," James said. It took a few months for James to let his guard down. In May, James invited Young R. J. and T3 to his studio. They listened to James's tracks, and to *The Listening*—the debut album from Little Brother that Beni B had given to James in London. When the first snare of the first song struck just slightly early, James and T3 heard their own influence at play, half liking it, half not *wanting* to half like it. Through it all, T3 was struck by how frail his former partner looked. The great majority of Slum's album would end up being produced by Young R. J. and his partner Black Milk.

Frank and Dank returned from Toronto energized—working with a new label on a new album. With a video camera in hand, they explored the studio, recalled James's "boot camp" credo for visiting rappers— *Don't pop your ass up, don't bring no extra ni**as, and be ready to lay some hot shit*—and reminisced about how James used to jit on his knees at

John Salley's X-Spot nightclub on Livernois. James chuckled, his face bloated beneath his wave cap from immune-system suppressing steroids, sitting in front of his MPC, his languid movements contrasting with those in Frank's story.

Common, sitting behind James's vast soundboard, wasn't laughing so much. This was the first time he'd seen James since his hospitalization. He didn't know how serious it was until one day, James stopped in the middle of a session and said, "I need to rest." Common thought: *If he ain't trying to make music, then I know he ain't feeling good.* The moment stayed on Common's mind as the rapper faced a transition of his own. *Electric Circus* had tanked. His relationship with Erykah Badu had ended. He was thinking more seriously about an acting career and moving to Los Angeles, where Derek Dudley had already set up shop and Karriem Riggins had moved. He floated the idea to James: *Why don't we go out there together? We can find a place and work on my next album.* A change in scenery, the warm weather, Common thought, might be a tonic for James.

James took his friend's suggestion in, but he wasn't in shape to think about moving. During his first months home, Maureen came every day, leaving the day care in the hands of her employees. She'd drive up in the morning for breakfast, drive back to 7 Mile to check in at work, and then return. She'd cook James lunch and dinner, make sure he took his medicines—doses of prednisone, heparin, and others—and a few times a week bring him a brownie sundae from Big Boy as a splurge.

These and other new routines made returning fully to his old ones impossible.

D ialysis sucks.
       Nobody knew this better than Christopher Price, known throughout Detroit as DJ Fingers. In 1990, while playing for Mumford High School's basketball team, the sixteen-year-old Fingers went up for a jump shot and crumpled to the floor. He woke up in the hospital, where he learned that his kidneys had stopped working and that he had fainted

from toxic uremia. He'd been on outpatient dialysis three times a week since then. Fingers channeled his energies into DJing and producing, an important pioneer of "ghettotech," that hypertempo genre that fueled the city's dance and strip clubs.

Fingers knew James, crossing paths with him often at R. J. Rice's studio, sliding him the Alicia Myers record James sampled for Slum Village's *Fantastic, Vol. 2*. Fingers, of course, never got the record back. One day in early 2003, Fingers got a call from R. J., telling him that James had just gone on dialysis, and that he might need someone to talk to.

R. J. was right. When Fingers phoned, it wasn't long before James began crying. He thought his career was over. And he was worried even more about his sex life. He wondered why this was happening to him.

What did I do to deserve this? he asked.

Fingers told James: *You can't think like that. You've got to move forward. I got you.*

Fingers arranged to pick James up and go get a treatment together at a dialysis center. They sat in chairs. Technicians hooked incoming and outgoing tubes to ports that had been surgically implanted in them. Those tubes ran to hemodialysis machines that essentially acted as external kidneys, removing excess fluid and toxins from the blood, cleaning it and returning it to their bodies. Fingers tried to keep James engaged, distracting him from the side effects, like nausea and stomach cramps. Two hours later, they were done.

There and thereafter, he coached James about life on dialysis.

You can't skip a treatment.

You can't drink too much. Suck on ice if you're thirsty.

You're not going to pee anymore—the dialysis treatment, that's your pee right there.

You really shouldn't drive yourself to the dialysis center. You ever need a ride, call me. You ever have a question, call me.

James did.

"Hey man," James asked, "what is that thing where your blood pressure drops and they have to put your chair almost upside down?"

"That's called a 'drop out,'" Fingers told him. "That happens when they take too much water out of your system. They gave you saline, right?

They have to put more water in your system and get your blood pressure back up."

Fingers knew, above all, how James loved the titty bar and how much of his life was connected to sex.

"I'm not trying to scare you or nothing," Fingers said, "but you're only gonna have enough energy in your body to fuck one girl a day."

James burst out laughing.

"Try it," Fingers said.

James phoned him back. "Damn, you right, Fingers."

"I'm trying to tell you," Fingers said. "Your blood gets thin, so there's not enough good blood going to your nuts and your dick. So you better save that big ass nut for somebody you really want to fuck, 'cause you ain't gonna fuck three times a day while you're on dialysis."

Fingers made sure to keep calling James regularly, because he knew the truth about dialysis. The biggest health hazard wasn't infection, or forgetting to go, or overdoing it with fluids or alcohol or drugs. The real killer was depression; dealing with the fact that your body no longer took care of itself and that your life would never be the same again.

For James, a man who barely stopped his daily routine to eat, taking four hours every other day for an often painful procedure and more for regular doctor's appointments and blood work was the worst medicine. Every precious hour he spent, he could have been digging or making beats. Fingers could feel his friend wondering whether it was worth it.

W hen we go on tour, watch what you eat," James told Guilty Simpson. "I was over in Europe and ate something and that shit fucked me up. I've been going back and forth to the doctor since I got home."

Guilty had been working with James intermittently, filling the space in James's inner circle that Frank and Dank had vacated. James had been asked to remix an instrumental track, "As Serious as Your Life," for the British electronic artist Kieran Hebden, who recorded under the name Four Tet. James ended up using the very first track that Guilty had laced for him the previous year, adding a sung chorus. After months of waiting, what Hebden received was a completely new song, and he was astonished by it. A huge Jay Dee fan, Hebden had come to see James's ability to move rhythms around in unorthodox ways as a mastery akin to those of the greatest jazz musicians. Hebden wasn't alone in that conclusion.

James was raised by a jazz musician and had listened to jazz every day of his life. His own music was composed of jazz's bits and pieces. His record collection contained far more albums from Blue Note Records than from Def Jam. Still he was surprised when, in mid-2003, he got a call from an A&R executive at the venerated jazz label.

Eli Wolf, working under Blue Note president Bruce Lundvall, was a new kind of jazz fan. The first two records he ever bought, at the age of twelve, were *The Jazz Messengers at the Cafe Bohemia, Volume 2* and De La Soul's *3 Feet High and Rising*. Wolf knew that the greatest jazz and the best hip-hop shared similar traits: virtuosity, courage, and a sense of play. But Wolf also thought most of the previous attempts to "merge" the genres were cheesy as hell, like Blue Note's Us3—their "Cantaloop" based on a loop of Herbie Hancock's "Cantaloupe Island"; or contrived, like the *Jazzmatazz* series: *Here's hip-hop, here's jazz, let's put them together!* He'd much rather hear Jay Dee manipulate Luiz Bonfá's samba guitar from "Saudade Vem Correndo." He didn't understand why the merger of jazz and hip-hop always had to sound like insipid lounge music or be marketed like some strange crossbreeding.

So Eli Wolf was motivated to work with hip-hop producers. In 2002, Blue Note Wolf met Peanut Butter Wolf and hammered out a deal for Madlib to mine the Blue Note vaults to create an album's worth of dusty hip-hop, *Shades of Blue*. The concept worked so well that, the next year, Eli Wolf began coproducing an album to celebrate the sixty-fifth anniversary of the label, *Blue Note Revisited*, with DJs and electronic composers interpolating selections from the company's catalog.

At the top of Wolf's wish list was J Dilla. Wolf loved Dilla's remake of Donald Byrd's "Think Twice" on *Welcome 2 Detroit*—the original song had been a Blue Note release—and Wolf suspected that the producer

---

* James actually produced one track for this series, "Certified," featuring Bilal, released in 2000.

might want to remake another Byrd track. But James's response surprised him: Brother Jack McDuff's "Oblighetto," the source of the sample behind one of James's collaborators' classic hits: A Tribe Called Quest's anthemic "Scenario." It would not have surprised Wolf to know, however, that some of James's earliest memories were of listening to McDuff in his father's record collection.

Wolf sent James the "parts"—the original recorded elements on a digital file. After several weeks, Wolf received a package from Michigan, tore it open, and listened to the disc inside. If he was excited before, now he was deflated. To his ear, James had barely touched the song—just put some drums behind it and a rather unfortunate synth bass line that evoked the saddest of gangsta rap tropes. Wolf couldn't figure out if James was being too respectful of the original or had simply not cared enough about it. He phoned Jonathan Dworkin and confided in him: *This wasn't what I was expecting from the great J Dilla.* Dworkin suggested that he speak directly to the producer about it. *I don't know what he'll say,* Dworkin warned him.

You never knew with James. A few years back, James had told House Shoes a story: He had been asked by his Ummah brothers, Raphael Saadiq and Ali Shaheed Muhammad, to remix a song called "Without You" for their new group, Lucy Pearl. James had returned with a track of bashing snares and overdriven clavinet, flinty and sparse. Too sparse, apparently, for Saadiq, who—according to James—phoned him to ask for more. James said he told Saadiq to suck his dick and hung up on him. So much for brotherhood.*

Eli Wolf, anxious, rehearsed what he intended to say: *I loved how you made "Think Twice" your own. I think you can do much more with this.* But when Wolf got James on the phone, he was shocked to hear that James seemed to be nervous, too: he was stuttering.

I understand. I want you to be happy with it. I'll take another pass.

A couple of weeks later, a new package arrived from Michigan. James

---

* This story, told to House Shoes and Young R. J. and relayed to this reporter in differing ways, has not been confirmed by Raphael Saadiq after several queries, and James may have been exaggerating or boasting, as he sometimes did. For his part, Ali Shaheed Muhammad, who has no knowledge of any such exchange, says he thought the remix was brilliant.

had written on the CD in black Sharpie: *Dilla/McDuff*. Next to it, a face with a tiny, unsure half-smile. Wolf listened.

James began with a light touch: a simple kick and snare under the song's central phrase—the obbligato—a woman wailing like a ghost over McDuff's organ. Then, halfway through the song, a surprise:

The beat stopped. The wail vanished into ether.

A piano trill, evoking "Think Twice."

A new beat, a tresillo, conjuring Afro-Cuban spirits.

A keyboard line, played by James, carrying the obbligato.

A piano and bass riff, played by James, providing counterpoint.

Then chords, fading in from an organ, adding "tensions"—notes that seemed wrong, pulling against the established harmony. Then another layer of keyboards, adding still more tension. Then another.

Within a minute, James had retimed and reharmonized the song.

This was genius work. Eli Wolf felt better now for having pushed James. Of course, he had no inkling of James's harrowing health ordeal. But in making that request, Wolf joined an exclusive club of two people, just he and Erykah Badu, who dared to demand more from James and got it. And Wolf got it, in part, because he was asking James for more of himself, not less.

James Yancey, son of Dewitt, would make his debut on Blue Note Records the following year. The "Oblighetto Remix" by J Dilla was vindication for Eli Wolf, too, who saw jazz as a way musicians *thought* rather than something they *played*, and to him, J Dilla was firmly in that fraternity.

Young R. J. visited more frequently, adding some drum programming to "Oblighetto" and helping James keep up with the pace of work on some other productions. James didn't talk about his illness, but he answered a few questions that his student posed from time to time.

Young R. J. had been among the few to watch James during the making of the first Slum Village albums. James had shown Young R. J. how to use the swing and step edit functions on the MPC to craft rhythms—but his reaction to hearing James's rushed snare was much the same as many other folks: *Something sounds off.* Young R. J. wanted to know what it was all about. James told him: "This is my natural rhythm. It's how I bob my head." Young R. J. wanted to know why James changed that sound midcareer, why he wanted to rhyme over beats from other producers on his solo album. James told him: "I'm tired of making and rhyming over the same stuff. I don't want to get stuck in the same place."

Young R. J. had seen this impulse working on an almost daily level: he and T3 would pick a beat and rhyme over it; James would then give them the final mix over a different beat. Young R. J. knew that James was also trying to outrun his imitators. He, like Karriem, had gotten scolded by James about sounding too much like him. Even now, in this studio, where James was doing the best audio engineering and mixing Young R. J. had ever heard from him, James would try to hide the splash screens of his Pro Tools plug-ins so Young R. J. couldn't see his workflow. He wondered why James was so protective, and he got a puzzling answer.

James told him: "I don't want nobody to have my sounds when I'm gone."

B ack in Los Angeles, Peanut Butter Wolf and Stones Throw's general manager, Eothen "Egon" Alapatt, had been trying to schedule a photo shoot for the Jaylib album cover. Aware that James couldn't travel, they adjusted their plan—instead of getting a photo of Madlib and James together, maybe they could take them separately and combine them digitally. They decided to send a photographer to Detroit.

The man who got the call was Brian Cross. Tall, with a shock of brown hair and a soul patch below his lip, Cross was an Irish hip-hop fan who hailed from a town that could lay claim to having started this rap shit: Limerick. After studying painting in Dublin, Cross moved to Los Angeles and, camera in hand, became a fixture on the hip-hop scene known as "B+": a photographer, author, and filmmaker. Cross had been one of the first to shoot the Pharcyde, and had been in the studio with them when Jay Dee first came to L.A. Cross barely registered James, who kept quietly out of frame, focused on his SP-1200. By 1998, when Cross was hired by A&M to shoot Slum Village with his partner Eric Coleman, both of them had become huge Jay Dee fans.

Cross flew to Detroit with Coleman and drove out to Clinton Township. Cross knew that Jay Dee had some health issues—what, exactly, he didn't know—because the shoot had been postponed a couple of times. The producer, when he appeared, didn't look bad, but he looked different. They sat in the kitchen to chat. Jay Dee didn't remember either of them from the Slum shoot, but Cross was grateful to hear that the producer had actually seen their first short documentary film, *Keepintime*, a movie that collided drummers and DJs. James took interest in the food Cross had brought with him from Trader Joe's—Cross told him that he was on a restricted diet after a minor operation.

"Yo, same with me," James said. "I've got to eat healthy, too." James pointed Cross to the refrigerator, which he said was stocked with juice, offering them some. Cross looked inside, confused: the fridge was filled with fruit-flavored sugar drinks. He looked around the kitchen. He saw more sugary food, like Red Vines. His heart sank. *Maybe Jay Dee doesn't quite understand what healthy food is?*

In the basement studio, Cross framed his subject: James at the mixing board, close-ups of his spotless Timberlands. James changed clothes, donning the baseball cap of Detroit's old Negro league team, the Stars, and they went outside: James standing alone, hands in his pockets, an uneasy smile in front of his neighbor's white A-frame home. Then Cross suggested they go digging. They departed for Car City Records in Saint Clair Shores, where Cross shot James, fingertips on the discount crates, in deep concentration.

Cross returned to Los Angeles and developed the photos: serene, muted, melancholy. James was a beautiful man. But when Wolf and Egon saw the prints, they couldn't get past how puffy James's face was; he didn't look like the Jay Dee they knew. At a tense meeting to discuss the matter at Stones Throw's commune, Cross became livid, shouting, "My fuck-it meter is up to here!"

In the end, Stones Throw's designer Jeff Jank stuck a processed version of one of Cross's photos on the back of the album. The cover of Jaylib's *Champion Sound*, released in October 2003, would feature instead an illustration, something Jank thought perfectly symbolized the spiritual connection between Detroit and Los Angeles: a tire tread.

J ames had been thinking about that connection more.

Detroit made the automobile, Los Angeles showed the world how it could be a way of life. Detroit created Motown, but Motown had to move to L.A. to grow. Detroit produced Jay Dee, but while his home town virtually ignored him, Los Angeles embraced him. A trip to L.A. with Frank and Dank in late 2003 to shoot a Jaylib video confirmed his feelings.

It took years for James to get there. Detroiters take pride in the difficulty of the place, settlers making a life on treacherous terrain. Even the map made no sense: the town where parts of the East Side were west of the West Side, and parts of the West Side were east of the East Side; the only place in America where Canada lay to the south; where roads deadended, and where a train called "The People Mover" just went around in circles. James knew this place. Detroit is hard, but it's home.

But Detroit wasn't the same for him since he'd gotten sick. Frank and Dank had moved away, Karriem had too. The joys of the strip club were now reminders of his own limitations. He was embarrassed by his illness. Detroit, in the best of times a physical and psychological minefield, was a bad place to be vulnerable. Even in the suburbs there were problems: The sump pump in the basement failed and James's basement studio flooded. And James was still livid about the police raid.

For a while James considered moving to Philadelphia, Jazzy Jeff sat on the phone with him, going through the pros and cons of Philly and L.A. But in the end the latter made more sense.

James confided in Joylette when he saw her. *I can stay with Common. It would be better for my work. They have better doctors out there.*

The vitriol that passed between the two of them before James's hospital stay had subsided. He and Joy had finalized a child support agreement, which called for joint custody of Ja'Mya, and James paying $2,675 per month for her care. Joylette found a house for herself and Ja'Mya on Detroit's Far West Side, in a tiny neighborhood called Castle Rouge. Unable to look after Ja'Mya on his own, James visited with his daughter there a couple of times per week. The visits made James conciliatory.

"Dewitt is always talking about that I need to be back with you," he told her. "He said: 'All those years you been together, you got that big house and then y'all separated? It doesn't make any sense.'" Joy told James that her own grandmother had told her much the same thing.

But that reunion was not going to happen, for any number of reasons: Joy's dynamic with James's mother, James's feelings for other women, his illness, and the fact that he had never reckoned with Joy about his first child.

Even with James's inconsistent presence, three-year-old Ty-Monae had developed a bond with her father that, for Monica, approached the mystical. Out of the blue, Ty-Monae would declare, "My daddy don't feel good," or, "He got a tummy ache." James would then call, invariably confirming his daughter's feelings. So Monica was terrified when James told her he was moving.

"No the hell you're not," she told him. "Not without us." For Monica, who had made a credo out of not making demands, this was a shift.

For James, it was easier to fly away.

James was welcomed to Los Angeles by a man named New York. Dave Tobman worked for Budget Car Rental on Sunset Boulevard, specializing in luxury vehicles for visiting entertainers. A Jewish transplant from the Bronx, Tobman was extra sweet to his rap clientele, who were always grateful for his personal service and access to potent California weed. "Dave New York" is how Tobman introduced himself.

James wasn't sure about the guy—built like a construction worker gone to seed, scruffy, and gravel voiced. In the parking structure across from the terminal, they climbed into a gleaming midnight-blue Chrysler 300 truck, their drive from the airport a mirror of James's first California ride with Mike Ross.

Nosing toward Baldwin Hills, Dave handed James a blunt.

James demurred. "I don't smoke anymore," he said.

"You're coming to Cali and not *smoking*?!" Dave asked him.

James reconsidered and took it, puffing while he admired the suede interior, the TVs in the headrests.

"You like the truck?" Dave asked him.

"Yeah."

"It's yours."

"What you mean?!" Startled, James started methodically wiping down every surface he had touched, figuring the car was stolen.

It wasn't: Common and Karriem had rented it for James to use. Dave New York parked the car in front of an apartment building in Studio City, a temporary rental while Common looked for a permanent home for him and James, and handed James the keys.

"Don't be a stranger," James told him, giving him his cell phone number.

James stood alone on the balcony of Common's apartment, smoking another blunt while he gazed into the San Fernando Valley haze. On the balcony below him, a young man tapped away on his laptop computer when a gob of hot ash fell onto his fingers. Denaun Porter looked skyward and saw James.

"What the fuck you doing up there?"

James looked down to see his friend from home.

"What the fuck you doing down there?"

James walked down to Porter's apartment, and the two Detroiters caught up. Porter told James he was working with Dr. Dre on D12 and other projects. Chopping it up with his first teacher, out here in Cali working with his second, Porter realized that his mentors had never met, and vowed to make that meeting happen.

On February 18, 2004, James's oldest friend in the record business, Fuzzy, drove him to Can-Am Studios, where James helped Dr. Dre celebrate his birthday with several friends, including Porter and the producer Focus. Porter knew that James being there was a gift for Dre, who was a longtime admirer of James's technique and listened to Dilla beats while he worked out. The encounter was a gift to James as well. Between the MCA debacle and his illness, he felt he had missed a step. Dre suggested to James that the two of them do a record together. Collaborating with Dr. Dre might be the injection he needed to boost his career; in truth, the only doctor he looked forward to seeing again.

N ot more than a few years earlier, J Dilla had been the young, ascendant producer-MC from the Midwest. In the interim, another had risen.

Kanye West hailed from Chicago, a protégé of No I.D., Common's chief producer before that role passed to James. Kanye found his big break when No I.D. gave his demos to Jay-Z's Roc-A-Fella Records; and though James had been ostensibly managed by Jay-Z's cousin, it was Kanye who ended up producing tracks for the superstar rapper and signing to his label as an artist. In another turnabout, Common had now tapped Kanye to work on tracks for his next album alongside James. In close quarters, the producer was a human tornado of bluster and beats, a fan of Jay Dee and a fan of himself. James was ambivalent about Kanye in the same way he was about any of his upstart admirers: half liking him, half not wanting to half like him. In a final irony, Kanye West had produced the first single from *Detroit Deli (A Taste of Detroit)*, the forthcoming album from Slum Village.

Slum shot the video for the song "Selfish" in Los Angeles. Young R. J. invited James, who watched from the wings as his former partner T3 and onetime protégé Elzhi frolicked on the soundstage with a bevy of beautiful brown women, Slum's rough edges now smoothed with preppy polish: crisp polos, bright sweaters, and pastel blazers. Kanye took a verse for himself and gave the chorus to his discovery, the singer John Legend. The shoot was the biggest investment ever in the group by Capitol Records and Wendy Goldstein.

James sat with Young R. J. and one of Kanye's associates, Scrap Dirty, a fan of J Dilla's who nonetheless needled James about Kanye "killing him" in the production game at the moment, particularly in his use of samples from soul records.

"You think he's better than me?" James asked. It was a question, but it was also a threat. James would not forget the moment.

T3, aware of James floating around the periphery of the set, was so wrapped up in the work that he didn't find a moment to talk to his erstwhile partner. It felt weird having him there. When James left Slum Village, his star was rising, and T3 felt abandoned. Now Slum was ascendant and James was going through some rough times; by choice or by default, in retreat from the commercial side of the business. Baatin, T3's other partner, was no longer in the group. He had become unreliable and erratic as he dealt with the dual effects of schizophrenia and self-medication with recreational drugs. On tour, Slum had to hire Que.D just to come along and supervise Baatin to make sure he didn't go anywhere on his own and lose control. At a certain point, it just got to be too much. So while this moment represented the success T3 had been chasing, with no Baatin beside him and Jay Dee there-but-not-there, it wasn't what he expected.

James ultimately made two contributions to the album: The beat for "Do You" transformed a Michigan classic, MC Breed's "Ain't No Future in Your Frontin'," fragmenting the original sample, Zapp's "More Bounce to the Ounce," reharmonizing it with a new bass line and misaligned clavinet chords, "simple-complex." And James took a verse on the song "Reunion," albeit without Baatin's presence, in which James got off a trademark boast, saying he "repped more D than twelve Eminems."

James's appearance on Slum's album was momentary, as it was in the final cut of the "Selfish" video, just a nod to the camera as it dollied by. It was Kanye West now who radiated and absorbed the most energy.

I t was only in L.A. that James could walk into the biggest pop radio station in town and receive a hero's welcome. On March 28, J Dilla and Madlib came to promote the opening date of their Jaylib tour on *Friday Night Flavas*, the main mix-show on Los Angeles's Power 106, cohosted by James's friends C-Minus and Choc.

Their DJ had his own agenda. Jason Jackson, as "J-Rocc," had been hoarding Jay Dee beat tapes for years and spreading the gospel of J Dilla alongside his local comrades in the Beat Junkies, the elite Southern California DJ collective that included Choc, DJ Rhettmatic, DJ Babu, Shortkut, and Melo-D. For J Dilla's arrival, J-Rocc had prepared a surprise from his vaults.

At first, James barely registered the DJ in the booth behind him. J-Rocc played an old beat from a Jay Dee batch that circulated among artists and A&R people in the late nineties, called "E=MC2." He played "Clair" by Singers Unlimited, the basis for Slum Village's "Players"; then "Give It to Me Baby" by Rick James, deconstructing it on the spot so that it became Common's "Dooinit." Then J-Rocc played Baden Powell's "É Isso Aí."

"Wait a minute, man!" James said. James had sampled only a fraction of that Powell song for Slum's "I Don't Know." He had slowed it down to unrecognizability. But somehow J-Rocc had found where it came from.

"How di . . . How did you . . . how does," stuttered James, reduced to sentence fragments as J-Rocc skipped through his catalog and decoded it in real time. "That's IMPOSSIBLE, man! What is . . . OH MY GOD!"

"He's special, isn't he, Dilla?" Mr. Choc asked.

"I knew, but now I *know*."

Before the producer left, James gave J-Rocc his phone number and an invitation to be the DJ on Jaylib's upcoming tour dates, opening for Madlib's other duo, Madvillain, his project with the rapper MF Doom.

"This is your *home*, Dilla," Mr. Choc told him on air before they all bid goodnight to Los Angeles.

"I feel it here," James replied. "I'm here, man."

The first leg of the Madvillain/Jaylib tour began on April 2, 2004, at the Henry Fonda Theatre, with J-Rocc on the ones and twos. This was the biggest night ever for the Stones Throw crew—Peanut Butter Wolf, Eothen "Egon" Alapatt, and Jeff Jank—a coming-out party for the label. The new Madvillain album was a success. Even though the Jaylib LP had stiffed by comparison, they were ecstatic to have J Dilla as a part of their movement.

A few hours before Wolf and Egon were to begin their warm-up DJ sets, Jank walked through the backstage area and found James sitting alone, behind some boxes. He went over to say hello, and found that James was shivering, even though he was wearing a baseball cap and a thick leather jacket.

This was puzzling to Jank: *Did Dilla have stage fright? Or was something else going on?*

In any case, James was in high spirits by the time he hit the stage, and the crowd roared as soon as he appeared. From Los Angeles, they decamped to San Francisco—James had never been to the Bay Area, and the beauty of the place stunned him—then New York and Toronto. J-Rocc used his new proximity to his idol to probe J Dilla for more information about the sample sources he used in his songs. Gradually J-Rocc "geeked down," and got to know James, the person. They woke each other up with text messages, got food, and went record shopping together. There were jokes and smokes aplenty. Madlib created a litany of aliases for J Dilla, like "Dill Cosby" and "Dill Withers." James liked that last one especially.

B ack in Los Angeles, James connected with hematologists Maureen and his Detroit doctors had found for him, and James checked in with them on a regular basis for blood work. Though none of his friends ever saw him go to dialysis, he told Maureen that he was keeping up with his outpatient treatments. Common found them a permanent home— the bottom floor of a duplex on North Sycamore in the Hancock Park district of Los Angeles.

Once they were settled, James phoned and left a message on Joylette's answering machine back home.

In Detroit, Joy listened and spied on her caller ID a name she didn't recognize: *Lonnie Lynn*. Joy let James have it when she called back: "So you're staying with a woman named Lonnie?"

James was silent for a bit, and then burst out laughing.

"Joy," he said, catching his breath, "Lonnie is Common's name."

"Hunh?"

"Lonnie Rashid Lynn, that's his name."

Joy joined James in cackling at her defensiveness. "I'm not seeing anyone right now," he assured her. "I'm out here to work." Then he turned candid. After a year of draining, dreary dialysis, he told her that he didn't think he could have sex anymore. "I want you to find somebody," he told Joy.

"I'm not thinking about sex right now," she told him.

Then James asked: *Would you ever consider moving to California?*

"I guess I could," Joy replied. "I don't know what I'd do out there. Maybe I could get work at one of the hospitals."

James told her something even more surprising: "I'd really like to live in San Francisco."

For a man who had never lived more than a quick drive away from his family, these were encouraging developments. There was a big world out there. James, at last, wanted to live in it. And though it seemed like James wanted her in that world, too, Joy took it in cautiously.

This time James told the whole truth: he wasn't in L.A. to play.

He commandeered a couple of tables in Common's living room as his new home studio space for a simple setup: his MPC3000, a portable turntable. James re-created his routines in California: he kept his friends around him while making beats, Frank and Dank's loquacious and herbescent presence replaced by Dave New York and J-Rocc. Common, there day and night, thrilled to wake up hearing James making music, some of which he knew would end up on his upcoming album. And Madlib and the Beat Junkies introduced James to a cratedigger's paradise, venturing together to record stores across the area, from Record Recycler in West L.A., to Aron's Records in Hollywood, to Rockaway in Silver Lake. Generally, Madlib went for quantity, leaving stores with stacks and stacks of records; James was more selective. When he returned home, though, his methods of music-making were now showing a great deal of Madlib's influence.

Making beats is always a conversation between producers, and between the present and the past. James's tracks in the 1990s were an answer to a question posed by Tribe, Pete Rock, and DJ Premier: *Could a beat be beautiful and banging at the same time?* Now James found himself answering a new question, posed by Madlib and, in a different way, by Kanye West: *What parts of a record can you use to make a beat?*

When beatmaking began, the game was simple: find the breakdown section of a record, the "open" place where the vocals dropped out, and loop it so an MC could rhyme over it. Often beatmakers would find a great piece of music to use but find that the singer's lyrics were always in the way of a "clean" sample. Of all the producers in hip-hop, James Yancey was arguably the most dogged in finding small "open" spaces where other producers might give up looking. Questlove once observed James chop up a record by Roy Ayers that he was certain had no usable pieces on it. James found more than a dozen tiny bits—fractions of seconds of sound—to create a new track miraculously wiped clean of any vocal. It became the bed of a song for Mos Def and Talib Kweli.

Kanye West didn't care about open spaces. He sampled anything— vocals, no vocals, it didn't matter. He took dusty old soul records, like Lenny Williams's "Cause I Love You," jacked up the speed, chopped the music and vocal alike, and made a new track for the Chicago rapper Twista, "Overnight Celebrity." It was a technique presaged, just as the conflicts of Dilla Time were, by the insouciant sampling habits of Wu-Tang Clan producer the RZA. But Kanye was more deliberate and consistent in his use of vocal bits, creating an aesthetic that was part hip-hop, part the Chipmunks. Madlib, too, was creative progeny to the RZA, but with an even more profound lean into error. As such, Madlib and J Dilla were producers of the same heart.

James had for a time left sampling behind, for reasons more financial than creative, but the lure of his original craft had returned: If it were now fair game in hip-hop to use *any* part of a record—if vocals could be masticated and then regurgitated into the very fabric of the song rather than avoided—then James had some of his own ideas about that concept's potential for harmony, melody, rhythm, and meaning. You could simply take a virtual sledgehammer to the record and make a collage with the multicolored shards.

Three years after his 1972 smash "Me and Mrs. Jones," Billy Paul recorded a lesser-known song, "Let the Dollar Circulate." James zeroed in on a sliver of Paul's vocal improvisation—"Circula-ay-yay-yay-yay-yay-yay-yate"—and used it as the rhythmic frame of his track; other slivers became intros, bridges, and breakdowns, their edges jagged and misaligned. James splintered the Jackson 5's "Dancing Machine" intro into bits: Michael Jackson singing the words "move it," fragments of background harmony from his brothers. When James slowed and recombined the elements, a momentary horn swell on the Jacksons' record became a metallic drone, bits of vocals whizzing by like shrapnel. Other songs went through James's electronic blender: Smokey Robinson and the Miracles' "Much Better Off"; Brenton Wood's "Gimme Little Sign"; Mary Wells's "Two Lovers History"; the Impressions' "We Must Be in Love"; the Supremes' and the Temptations' version of "Sweet Inspiration"; "My Baby Must Be a Magician" and "You're the One" by the Marvelettes.

These new beats, mostly created from bargain-bin vinyl James bought at Aron's Records, ended up on a raw, riotous sixty-one-minute, forty-three-track recordable CD that James labeled "Dill Withers," after Madlib's appellation. It would circulate months later among fans under the nickname *The Motown Tape* for its rooting in late 1960s soul. Some of the beats James would reserve for himself, as he began to reconceive his long-awaited follow-up to *Welcome 2 Detroit* as *Welcome 2 LA*. Other beats made their way into artists' hands. Steve Spacek, visiting town to record a new album, dropped by Sycamore with the legendary Philly soul songwriter Thom Bell in tow, looking for tracks. James gave the Billy Paul–based track to him, and the artist who provided James one of his biggest remixing challenges now found himself challenged in reverse by James: *Try singing over this*. Spacek did, and the song "Dollar" ended up on his album the following year. James shared a Zip drive of beats with Q-Tip, as was his custom, and his former partner seized the shattered "Dancing Machine" interpolation for his upcoming album.

Over the past several years, Q-Tip's and James's paths remained parallel: while James made albums for BBE and MCA that highlighted his overlooked talents, Tip recorded an eclectic project called *Kamaal the Abstract* that featured more traditional instruments and songwriting, improvisational arrangements, and Tip singing instead of rapping. James's MCA project and Tip's Arista album were shelved by their respective labels at around the same time.* Still, they loved each other's work. They even talked about forming a rhyming duo together, Buddy Lee. So when James had new batches of beats to send, Tip was always on his mailing list.

Some time after sending Tip the Zip drive, James received the finished song on CD. James played it while J-Rocc listened. Q-Tip had smoothed out the roughness with a booming kick drum, a bass line, and some flanging and filtering effects, shrouding the subtle tappety-tap of the percussion carried over from the Jackson 5 song. They were tiny tweaks. But James laughed all the same, recalling Q-Tip's little additions to his beats over the years.

"Why did he do that?" James asked J-Rocc. The friends began a mocking little dance.

Q-Tip was still making things beautiful. But James had moved from beauty to the beast. This moment was the logical terminus for a journey into the realm of error that began in the nave of Vernon Chapel and the basement of McDougall, in the end credits of *A Piece of the Action* and in the middle of "Funky Drummer": finding the holy in the broken. *Break the records, break them all.*

I n May 2004, James returned to Detroit with J-Rocc and Madlib to play at Movement, the Detroit Electronic Music Festival. It was his first time back in Detroit since his move, a quick trip with some time to visit with his mother and Ja'Mya; and also time to reconcile with House Shoes, whom James shouted out from the stage during his performance.

In June he was back at his home in L.A. To others, he seemed to be feeling good: sharing a blunt with his booking agent Asya Shein, talking shit, watching the Detroit Pistons win the playoffs, sliding around in his socks on the hardwood floor every time the team scored. But privately, in the same notebook in which he had drafted the lyrics for songs like "Reunion,"

---

* Q-Tip and A&R executive Drew Dixon remained with Arista after Clive Davis left in late 1999, hoping for more aggressive promotion with the new head of Arista, L.A. Reid, who had called *Kamaal the Abstract* "genius" in a meeting with executives, according to Dixon. But Reid soon cooled to Q-Tip's album, and to other projects and prospective signings of Dixon's—like Kanye West and John Legend—an ostracism that Dixon attributes to her refusal to reciprocate Reid's sexual advances, which she details in the 2020 HBO documentary *On the Record*. In 2017, Reid exited his post atop Sony Music after the company investigated allegations of sexual harassment.

James catalogued a list of symptoms that distressed him: *Headaches. Back pain. IV pain. Trouble sleeping. Heart racing. Night sweats. Scrotum hurts. Blood rushes to jaw and cheeks when eating. Stomach feels full all the time.*

In the spring and early summer, Jaylib played a series of concerts in Europe, accompanied by Peanut Butter Wolf. They hit the Jazz Cafe in London, wound their way through several countries, climaxing with a performance onstage at the Montreux Jazz Festival in July, where they were welcomed as avant-garde artists. The Jaylib dates in 2004 composed the most extensive tour that James had ever done. And yet they came at the moment in James's life when the stresses of the road could complicate his recovery. James had been, in the previous year, on regular dialysis. None of his friends ever saw him detour for a treatment, nor did they know he may have needed them. When they got to Europe, J-Rocc noticed that on some days James appeared sluggish and disconnected.

"You okay, Dilla?" J-Rocc would ask, concerned.

"Yeah, I'm alright," James replied. "I just don't feel good."

Generally, James was stoic. Only on one morning when Wolf had urged everyone to assemble in the lobby ahead of schedule did J-Rocc see a flash of James's legendary temper.

"Maaaaaaaan," James began, hunched over in a chair. "I don't mind waiting. But don't make me hurry up to wait."

Wolf and J-Rocc apologized, and the moment passed. But James continued to suffer. His disposition would worsen, then get better. James's friends couldn't stave off some concern about their companion.

The ironic thing about James's illness for Martha Yancey was that, for one precious year in Detroit, she got her big brother back again.

For many years before that, James felt far away. His career took off, he spent more time away from home. Meanwhile, Martha had her daughter Faith and moved downtown. What changed their relationship the most was when Joy came into the picture. Martha got much less of James then. Gone were the long brother-sister talks that they used to have. And with all the tension that Martha felt Joy generated for the family, James still kept Joy in his life. She had secretly been mad at James for years about that.

But after James got sick, he began to deliberately make up for lost time. He came over to the house every Saturday for a long, lazy day where they'd watch movie after movie until bedtime. Once he even took Martha on a "date," a day for just the two of them; they drove around and ate at Steak 'n Shake. The Yanceys were not a family that expressed love by saying "I love you." They expressed love by being together. James was telling Martha that he loved her.

So Martha was looking forward to her visit to California with Faith, Maureen, and Dewitt. James was too, in his own way: he'd created a packed itinerary for his family. They only had so much time. But Martha was on *vacation*. On the first day, she was supposed to be ready by noon, and she wasn't. James started screaming at her in the car. This was also the big brother she knew: bossy, impatient. She yelled back—she was the only one in the family who ever did—while her parents and Faith listened in silence. Then Martha started crying. That ended the argument.

She was still in tears by the time they got to Shatto Lanes in Koreatown for bowling. James came over and asked her if she wanted anything, talking to her as if nothing at all had happened. James didn't ever apologize outright; this was his way of doing it. Martha took a breath and began to enjoy the day. They were joined by James's California friends—Peanut Butter Wolf, Egon, Jeff Jank, and Stones Throw artist Koushik, who grew up a few hours' drive from Detroit, in Hamilton, Ontario. Martha watched her brother handle the ball; bowling was the rare skill at which James didn't excel, but that never stopped him from trying.

"You're releasing the ball too early," Koushik called to Dilla after a bum roll. "It isn't one of your snares."

James laughed. The Stones Throw folks were grateful for a moment to do something light and fun, to see James around his people.

A few days later, James dropped his family at LAX for their flight home. Before they parted, he gave Martha an Adidas jacket and a DVD of him and Madlib performing.

She was grateful for the gifts. But she couldn't quite figure them out.

James was telling Martha that he loved her.

———

J aylib played the Rock the Bells festival in Anaheim, California, in November. Headlining was the reunited A Tribe Called Quest; beneath Jaylib on the bill was the rap group Little Brother.

The North Carolina trio had graduated to a deal with Atlantic Records, a major label. For their upcoming album, *The Minstrel Show*, they attempted to record a song with Jay Dee and Elzhi, a way to acknowledge James's and Slum Village's influence and pay it back. Jonathan Dworkin, still helping where he could as James's manager even though he had moved into the ringtone business, suggested that they'd have a better chance of getting James if they recorded in California. Little Brother couldn't make the trip. In the end, only Elzhi blessed the track, "Hiding Place." After Phonte heard that James was sick, he rued that Little Brother hadn't gotten on that plane. But now, seeing James backstage, looking better than he expected, Phonte introduced himself.

"I just want to thank you," Phonte told him. "You showed a lot of us the way."

James returned the compliment: "That shit's dope. Y'all raw."

Too diffident to join this exchange was another Dilla follower: Nicolay, partner in Phonte's other group. The Foreign Exchange had just become labelmates with James by signing with Peter Adarkwah's BBE. They delivered an album, *Connected*, that contained multiple strands of Dilla's musical DNA, and were about to shoot their first video while in town.

A Tribe Called Quest had reunited, but James wasn't feeling well enough to join the reunion; he just wanted to get home. News had come during the show of the passing of Ol' Dirty Bastard of the Wu-Tang Clan, dead from a drug overdose. It was a reminder of how fragile life could be.

J ames had done his best to live his life and remain active despite his illness. But he was pushing himself now in a way he hadn't since the days before he got sick. One evening in late 2004, James left a session at Madlib's home studio; a few hours later, as Madlib himself made to leave the house, he saw his friend's truck still parked in the driveway, James in the front seat, unable to muster the energy to make the half-hour drive back to Common's place on Sycamore.

Something was happening to him again, James felt it. He picked up the phone to call Maureen.

"I need you," he said.

"When do you want me to come?" she asked.

"I need you now," James answered.

Maureen flew out to Los Angeles and checked James into Cedars-Sinai Medical Center. After a few weeks, James's platelet count had stabilized. He'd had a fever, but it had broken. His situation had improved enough for him to be released from the hospital, and Maureen felt comfortable flying home—she needed to check on the day care and handle some things for Dewitt and John. She set James up with medicines, sorted into correct dosages on trays, and left for the airport. She was home less than twenty-four hours before she got word from Common's New York–based executive assistant, Saunte Lowe. James needed her back in California.

"I'll make the arrangements," Lowe told her. "When can you leave? Do you have somebody to cover for you at your job?"

Maureen told her that she had an administrative assistant at her day care operation who could look after things.

By dinnertime, Lowe phoned back.

"Your flight is at eleven p.m.," she said. "Can you get to the airport? We need you."

Maureen was struck by Lowe's urgency and began to worry. On the plane ride to California through the night, she looked out the window and began to see wisps of light, translucent figures that seemed to be following her. *Angels*, she thought. It was still dark when she arrived at LAX, riding down the escalator beneath a plaque that read: WELCOME TO LOS ANGELES.

Common's personal assistant in Los Angeles, Olivia Fischa, took Maureen's bag, and brought her out to a car. As they drove off, she told Maureen, "I'll take your things to the house later, unless you need to change."

Now Maureen was alarmed. *They weren't going to the house.* They were driving to Cedars-Sinai, where James had already been admitted.

H ere is what happened. It was the lull between Christmas and New Year's Eve. Common was out of town, Saunte was in New York, Maureen was in Detroit, and nobody had been able to raise James. So Olivia drove over to Sycamore in the pouring rain to see if he was there. It was very late at night. The lights inside were on. She knocked. No answer. She wasn't sure, at first, if she should use her key—she respected the privacy of her employer and his friend. *What if James were inside and in there with somebody?* Then she peeked through a window, one that gave a view down the long hallway from the living area to the bedroom. That's when she saw James's legs on the floor.

Olivia burst into the house and ran to James, who was lying facedown near the bathroom, unconscious, for how long, she didn't know. Hours? A day? She flipped him over. He was breathing, barely, very pale. There was foam coming out of his mouth, and she wondered whether he'd had a seizure. She tried to rouse him, and when she couldn't, she called 911. An ambulance came to take him, and Olivia followed him to Cedars.

James had been in L.A. for almost a year. Until that moment, Olivia didn't know how sick he really was.

J ames was experiencing a full relapse of the TTP and its symptoms: ultralow platelet count, kidneys shutting down. The doctors at Cedars-Sinai put James on daily plasma exchange and dialysis.

Maureen kept a vigil at her son's bedside in the Cedars ICU over the following weeks as James experienced cascading complications. Because his body was attacking his healthy blood enzymes, he was being given steroids to suppress his immune system. The steroids made it difficult for his body to fight off its real enemies. His dialysis port became infected and had to be moved. He was receiving large doses of intravenous antibiotics every time he had a procedure, and every time he received dialysis. The long periods of lying down, his weakened physical state, the clotting of the small blood vessels in his body, and the decimation of his red blood cells had also begun to cause cardiopulmonary problems. His ability to breathe properly plummeted, and he was given oxygen.

Friends visited when they could. J-Rocc and Madlib, Egon and Wolf, Dave New York and Karriem and Common came to lift James's spirits; or if he was sleeping, to support Maureen, whom they all had come to care for.

O ne day in late January, after James had been moved to his own room, the hospital room phone rang. Maureen picked up, and whispered to James: *It's House Shoes.*

When Shoes and James reconciled in 2004, the Detroit DJ saw no hint of James's illness. But in January 2005 he heard that James had been hospitalized in California, found the number to Cedars-Sinai, and called.

"I gotta come check on you, homie," Shoes told James.

In the first week of February, House Shoes found his way to James's bedside. He barely recognized the man he saw. Physically, James was weak, but it was his friend's energy that threw Shoes. James had always been a cocky motherfucker. That person was not in this room. It took all the strength Shoes could muster to maintain his poker face.

Over the next week, when Shoes came for daily visits, Maureen would often take a break, leaving them to catch up. He didn't ask James about his illness. They chatted about music; Shoes put James up on some new releases, and James hit Shoes with tracks he had been working on, like a track for his next BBE album featuring Pharoahe Monch. Shoes bought James a pair of speakers for the room. Sometimes, when James was undergoing treatments or oxygen therapy, they'd listen together in silence.

Shoes was grateful that James had found a new home for himself in California, in part because Detroit hadn't given James the recognition he deserved. He decided to try something to remedy that. One day, Shoes told James: "Listen to this message someone left me." Shoes played the voice mail on his cell phone speaker, a voice of support and love and well wishes for James from Detroit. And then another. And another. Some of the voices James knew: Phat Kat, Guilty Simpson, Frank, Aaron Halfacre. Others he didn't: Shoes's friends, random fans. Even Shoes's mother left her good wishes, remembering when she had brought him and her son champagne to celebrate putting out their first twelve-inch together. Shoes played two dozen messages in all. By the last one, James had completely broken, tears streaming down his face.

Shoes was there for James's birthday on February 7, when James's friends packed into the room. It was the first time Shoes met James's L.A. crew—Brian Cross and Eric Coleman, Wolf and Egon, Jank and J-Rocc. They came with balloons and a birthday cake. James wasn't hungry.

But J-Rocc knew James was feeling at least a little better because his impatience seemed to have returned. As Shoes passed out copies of his mixtape to Dilla's industry friends in his hospital room, James looked at J-Rocc and rolled his eyes, his voice rising in his signature signal of irritation.

"Maaaaaaaannnnn . . ."

On March 16, 2005, Maureen rolled James out of Cedars-Sinai in a wheelchair.

James was frail and his condition was precarious during his first days home. His health could easily deteriorate, and he might need to be rehospitalized, so Maureen decided to stay in Los Angeles indefinitely—as long as it took to make sure James was going to be okay, no matter the consequence to her day care business back home and no matter how much Dewitt complained about her being away. But Maureen, standing four feet, eleven inches, was not able to give James the physical support he needed to get around the house and to vital, regular outpatient treatments for dialysis and plasma exchange.

For help with all that, there was Maurice "Bobo" Lamb.

Bobo had moved to Los Angeles from Detroit around the same time as James, but James didn't know it until he bumped into Bobo at a gas station in West Hollywood the previous year. Maurice's relationship with

Martha had been moribund for a while, even while he lived with the Yanceys. Finally, in a desperate act of escape, Martha eloped to Las Vegas with an old high school sweetheart. Maureen then informed Maurice that he had to move out.

He married quickly, too, a woman named Eve, who had dreams of moving to California. They drove out together. Maurice hoped that he might get out from under the low ceiling of the Detroit comedy scene. He showed up for available slots at the Laugh Factory and the Comedy Store, but he soon discovered that his proximity to stardom didn't mean that he had access to it. In Los Angeles, he felt a ceiling, too: he didn't have a network, an agent.

Maurice was glad to bump into James and became a regular visitor at the house on Sycamore. Bobo Lamb could be intense: in hustle mode, relentlessly "on," hoping for connections that would take his career to the next level. Madlib lamented Bobo's litany of "doodoo" jokes. But he was a familiar face for James in a faraway place. And despite the fact that Maureen had asked Maurice just two years earlier to leave her home, now she was grateful to have his help.

Maurice now came to the house on Sycamore daily, and the three of them fell into a routine: Maurice arriving at 9:00 a.m., rolling James out to the car, lifting him into the passenger seat; buckling him in, shutting the door; folding the wheelchair, putting it in the trunk; driving to the doctor's office or to the dialysis center; opening the trunk, taking the wheelchair out, lifting James into it, rolling up to the appointment. Once James was hooked up to a machine, Maurice made sure he was comfortable and had something to read or listen to. When the appointment was done, they drove to get James something to eat and smoke, maybe get him a Slurpee from 7-Eleven as a treat and a box of Phillies Blunts. Back at the house, Maureen emptied the tobacco from the Blunts and rolled them back up again with marijuana, and Maurice rolled James to his table so he could make beats.

James had sought to keep his illness a secret. Until recently, he had told Q-Tip only that he had carpal tunnel syndrome. He could no longer play it off. Hip-hop message boards like those on Okayplayer and other websites contained posts discussing J Dilla's brush with death.* Journalists who phoned for interviews were alerted to his condition.

"He was almost outta here," Tim Maynor told a writer for *Scratch* magazine.†

The week after his discharge, James downplayed things in an interview with Anslem Samuel of *XXL* magazine, who asked James if he had been in a coma.

"Nah, man," James answered. "The rumors were like, Jay Dee is dead and all that, but I was just in the hospital for like two months. I was in ICU, with all types of tubes, man. It was crazy. I was out of it for, like, most of January."

James continued to attribute his health problems to poor eating on the road. And in response to a query about illness cutting into his production time, he mentioned that he had been working while in the hospital.

"My boy brought a sound system and some vinyl through, so I was in the hospital, making beats," James said.

In truth, he hadn't created much music at Cedars. James emerged from the hospital to find that Kanye West had done the majority of the production on Common's new album, *Be*, save two tracks that James had recorded before his long stay. But being bedridden for two months did convince him of two things: that he could use his tiny Macintosh laptop to make beats, and that he could and should use every piece of time he had to make them.

As James strengthened, he often called Peanut Butter Wolf to take him record shopping, and the owner of Stones Throw would drop whatever he was doing and go pick James up. Lately they'd been favoring Rockaway Records in Silver Lake, with their huge selection of grungy 45s. After one trip with Wolf and Madlib in the spring of 2005, sitting in

---

* Questlove posted on Okayplayer that James was near death and in a coma, followed by refutations from friends like T3. Maureen Yancey now states that James was "semi-comatose" in the intensive care unit during the hospital stay in question.

† That writer is the author of this book.

the Rockaway parking lot in Wolf's car, James played them a new CD of beats made largely from the records he had been buying there. He'd given it one of his playful titles that derived from the name of some unhealthy food that he shouldn't be eating in his condition, like *Burger King*, *Pizza Man*, or in this case, *Donuts*.

At first, Wolf wasn't sure what he was listening to. These weren't warm neo-soul Jay Dee beats, nor were they like the unstructured, raw Dill Withers tracks he'd created since his move to California. These were tiny compositions, moving from place to place, in little more than a minute each. Instead of large open spaces on which an MC might rap, these were filled with hectic scratches and stabs of vocal and instrument samples. And the manipulations themselves were of a different kind than Wolf had ever heard James do. In one track, looping part of an old Jackson 5 ballad, "All I Do Is Think of You," James suddenly halved the tempo and stretched the loop out to cover the doubled space, while keeping the pitch constant. This kind of "time stretching" wasn't possible on an MPC. He'd done all these beats right on his laptop, via his Pro Tools software, which enabled James to see the waveforms—dice and recombine them, squeeze and stretch them—in ways he'd never before attempted. Created in a burst of energy after James's discharge from Cedars-Sinai in early 2005, *Donuts* emerged as a complete thought.*

"This is blowing my mind," Wolf told him. "I think this could be an album."

"For real?" James said, surprised.

"I'd put this out as is," he said.

James handed Wolf the disc, saying that he'd flesh out the ideas a bit more anyway. Wolf quickly made copies for the crew. But while Wolf pressed the idea of releasing *Donuts* "as is," Egon countered that they should be focused on starting the next Jaylib album. It wasn't just about the commercial potential, Egon argued: James himself had told him how the Jaylib project "got him healthy again." And *Donuts* wouldn't be much of an album anyway, the twenty-seven brief tracks clocking in just shy of

---

* The recollections of the people who were closest to J Dilla and to this project, including Peanut Butter Wolf, J-Rocc, and Jeff Jank, collectively confirm that the tracks on this initial iteration of *Donuts* were created on Pro Tools, at home; not in the hospital, on another machine.

a half hour of music. But Wolf was adamant that they not ask the ailing producer for more than he had already given them. James's health was still precarious. He was now going in and out of Cedars for short, intermittent stays. He'd be in crisis for days and suddenly better, strong for weeks and suddenly worse.

A solution was proposed by Jeff Jank, who thought *Donuts* was the best beat tape that he had ever heard. *All he needs to do is create longer versions of these tracks.* Wolf and Egon's eyes widened; the mere prospect of asking J Dilla to make changes was enough to give them heart palpitations. Wolf had been reamed by James a few times, and more recently Egon got a taste of James's wrath after the producer discovered that Egon had divulged the details of his hospitalization to C-Minus. The Stones Throw crew continued this conversation during a collective visit to Cedars, huddled outside James's room.

I'll ask him, Jank offered.

A few minutes later, when Jank broached the subject, James replied, "Why don't y'all do that?"

Jank told Wolf and Egon that he could do the editing easily on his own home computer. With that, Jeff Jank became *Donuts'* designated editor.

To extend the tracks, Jank would have to work with the source material on hand—the original beat CD containing the two-channel stereo mixes—rather than the original multitrack Pro Tools sessions. This, too, was about minimizing Dilla's stress. Since he'd been in California, James had grown tired of having to explain to people who wanted to purchase his older tracks, ones he had made in Michigan, that he had left all the original multitrack files behind, the ones that would allow an engineer to, say, bring only a bass line up in volume or tweak the sound of a snare drum alone. Once, he'd gotten pissed off at J-Rocc's homie DJ Rhettmatic for querying him about one such beat, and then decided to leave an outgoing message on his answering machine: *Anybody who wants old beats? Two-track that shit!*

---

* James became infamous for his outgoing messages in this period, leaving one in response to a fellow producer, 88 Keys, whom he felt was representing himself as closer to James than he really was: "88 Keys . . . geek down!"

Out of respect for Dilla, Jank began with the notion that he'd try to be as invisible as possible—to extend the duration of the music while preserving Dilla's structures and the order in which he placed the tracks. But Jank decided to take a chance on the second and third tracks, which both sampled the same song, 10cc's "The Worst Band in the World," and seemed to Jank like they could be united into one lengthened track. To do that, Jank would have to remove a digital glitch between the two tracks and replace that section with music cut from somewhere else in the song. Jank decided to do that edit first: If Dilla liked it, the rest of the album would be easy. If Dilla winced, or worse, well, he'd figure something else out. Jank took the two tracks, each about a minute in length, turned them into one nearly three-minute song, and went to Cedars to play the result for James, who nodded his head and said: *Cool.*

Jank had extended the first part of the song by repeating the vocal phrases James had sampled: *Play me. Buy me. Workin' on it. Fade me.* Jank duplicated that final phrase as a bridge to the second half, words that were so distorted and sibilant on the original 10cc record that the word *fade* sounded like another word entirely: *save.*

Jank was just trying to solve a problem. But in doing so, he had unwittingly magnified the significance of those last two words:

Save me
Save me
Save me
Save me

James's platelet count plummeted again, and he returned to Cedars. He began experiencing high fevers that would come out of nowhere and last for days. During those periods, James would go into a delirium— eyes closed, seemingly unconscious, but often speaking in a continuous monologue that would go on for hours at a time, as if he were reading from a script, a rambling that rattled and frightened Maureen.

"Has he ever done this before?" a nurse asked her.

"No," Maureen replied. "He's never been this ill before."

The physicians pressed Maureen to let them install a breathing tube. Knowing her son's strong feelings on the matter, she refused. Alternately frustrated and empathetic, they tried to prepare her for the likelihood that James would not make it through the night.

Maureen stayed by his bedside as he babbled, as if the lifetime of words the quiet boy kept inside him were now tumbling out. After a while, she noticed that the monologue had become one side of a dialogue. James seemed to be talking to someone named "Odie."

"Oh yeah?" James said to his invisible friend. "Don't get on the red bus? Get on the white bus?"

Maureen felt goose bumps rise on her skin.

She looked at her son. His eyes were closed. No trace of awareness of his surroundings. She figured he was talking to his maker.

As James's crisis passed and he regained lucidity, Maureen asked him a question: "What is Madlib's first name?"

"Otis," James answered.

"What's his last name?"

"Jackson."

"So who is 'O.D.'?"

James looked at her: "Why you asking?"

She told James about his delirious, one-sided conversation.

James began laughing. "O.D.B.," he told her: Ol' Dirty Bastard, the rapper who died a few months ago. James gave her O.D.B.'s side of the dialogue:

O.D.B. said, "Don't get on the red bus." He said to stay where I was, and he'd come back for me. And when he came back, he said I could have any kind of ride I wanted. "Anything you want, you'll have it. Don't worry about it." He said to stay where I was.

James phoned Karriem Riggins and told him it was time to get to work on Welcome 2 LA. Riggins convened with James and J-Rocc at a studio in Silver Lake, where they jammed for hours on several different tracks. James was overjoyed to have his Minimoog keyboard synthesizer shipped to him from Detroit, using it to revamp an old beat of his that J-Rocc had played during their first meeting at Power 106, "E=MC2." James didn't have the original discs but J-Rocc, unsurprisingly, owned the Giorgio Moroder record it sampled; and James created a new, speaker-blowing version.

With James in and out of the hospital and his outpatient treatments, the work was intermittent. Eventually, James moved to the studio of Dave Cooley, Madlib's engineer, who had mastered their Jaylib album. Cooley, a former member of the alternative rock band Citizen King, had toured with the Roots and was already a fan of Dilla's when Egon introduced them; Cooley prepped for their sessions by calling Bob Power to ask for advice on how best to replicate Jay Dee's signature full-frequency sound. Cooley was shocked when James told him that he was *really* after the sound that Cooley himself had crafted with Madlib.

"Don't add all that top end," James told him, "I want this to sound like a cassette."

Cooley assumed James would have a heavy hand, like most producers. But James rarely second-guessed the members of his team. Even accomplished musicians like Riggins tended to be deferential to the producer—asking James if he wanted them to do things differently, or record another take.

"Nah," James would often say. "We got it."

James wasn't being polite. When he said "We got it," he literally knew he had every single bar that he was going to need for the final mix, and that he had already mapped it out in his head *during* people's takes. After everyone left, he would rattle off to Cooley how to compile the performance:

Use take 1 for bars 1 through 4, use take 2 for bar 5, use take 3 for bars 6 and 7, but cut away halfway through 7 and go back to take 1.

It was the most eerie thing Cooley had ever seen in a recording studio. *He's Yoda,* Cooley thought. Like the Star Wars character, James never tried things. He just *did.* Cooley never witnessed a single instance where James did anything that he didn't keep.

James was sensitive to small increments of time—how the sounds on the grid of Cooley's digital audio software should be aligned—and had a unique vocabulary to express himself: *Move it a few baby hairs back,* James would say. *Now move it one baby hair forward.* And everything would fall into place.

In June 2005, James arranged another import from Michigan: Guilty Simpson, making good on an old promise to the young rapper. Simpson was struck by the change in his mentor. He could see it in his eyes, and hear it in James's voice, which had settled into a deeper register. In James's verse for the song "Baby," over a track he had requisitioned from a Madlib beat tape, James evoked bygone days when being in his body was much easier, with a list of Detroit dances: *"Think it's a disco when I Rambisco / If you feelin' it, where your Errol Flynn at? / Cut the check; Tim, tell 'em where to send that."*

Even Dave New York got his turn at the microphone, answering James's query about the state of commercial hip-hop: "Straight-up garbage."

James hadn't cracked the charts in almost three years. But he wasn't jealous; he had simply diverged from a genre that neither progressed nor provoked as much as it used to. Cooley witnessed how dedicated James was to that path. At the beginning of one session, James was too weak to climb the stairs; Maurice carried him over his shoulder. But as soon as Maurice set James onto the studio's sofa—in front of his MPC or his Moog—Cooley was struck by the thing he always saw when James was working on music. He was smiling.

There were good days. One morning in May 2005, James joined Madlib and the Stones Throw crew for a photo shoot at Madlib's studio, funded by Tom Bacon, vice president of marketing for the consumer electronics company VTech. Bacon was a hip-hop devotee and J Dilla fan; he brought weed to the shoot, which James rolled into a joint atop a snare drum as Roger Erickson took photos. The shoot was hot and cramped, and Bacon knew Dilla was sick, but James was patient and good-natured. Only toward the end did Maureen tug at Bacon's sleeve, saying James should rest. James felt well enough to spend a couple of days holed up in the home studio of Sa-Ra Creative Partners, reconnecting with Taz Arnold, and meeting a local bassist they worked with, Steven "Thundercat" Bruner. His agent Asya Shein came back to watch the NBA playoffs again, struck by how James's appearance had changed from the previous year.

More often, there were bad days. Back in the hospital, Maureen and Maurice returned James to his grim schedule of bedside treatments. The mornings were usually reserved for dialysis. The procedure would take around three hours, sometimes four if James was dealing with port infections and thus needed extra time for antibiotics to enter his system. In the afternoons came the plasma exchange to keep his platelet count up. By the late afternoon, James's full blood volume had been circulated in and out of him twice. By the end of the day he would be exhausted, and at times angry. Dinner would arrive—light and soft, usually something James didn't care for. Then he'd try to get some rest.

In the evenings, James requested that Maureen lead them in Bible study. With everything that was going on, Maureen wasn't sure she was in a headspace to interpret God's word. But Maurice had taken them to a bookstore to get some Bibles, and the two of them sat reading and discussing passages. James was particularly interested in the Book of Job, the tale of the righteous man who has everything taken away from him, complains about it, and is then answered by God with a litany of sarcasm:

"Where wast thou when I laid the foundations of the earth?" the Lord said. "Declare, if thou hast understanding."

Where were you when I created everything? You cannot even begin to comprehend where you fit in my plan.

Maureen was concerned for her son's mental well-being as much as his physical health. She asked Maurice to bring some more of James's production equipment to use in the moments when he felt well enough. Maurice retrieved his MPC, his Moog keyboard, a turntable, a laptop computer, an audio interface, and a crate of records. He took the equipment and set it up at James's direction on several brown snack trays that could be rolled to the bed or away from it. Sometimes James would fiddle with his music while lying in bed, and at others Maurice would help James into a wheelchair, lock the wheels, and set him before the equipment. Maureen massaged James's stiff, aching fingers for hours so he could work for a few minutes. When James stabilized, Maurice would pack up the equipment and take it home; when James took a turn for the worse, usually within a week or two, they'd all ride back to Cedars-Sinai and set everything up again, the extra snack trays for James and cot for Maureen already rolled in by staff who were, by now, very familiar with James's exceptional situation.

At the head of James's team was his chief blood specialist, Dr. Aron Bick. An Israeli-born hematologist-oncologist who earned his medical degree in Paris and spoke six languages, Bick used every bit of the intellectual and interpersonal skills he possessed to treat James, who had a difficult case and a headstrong personality to match. The diminutive doctor had developed a quirky sense of humor to get himself and his patients through some tough days. James howled when Bick first entered his room with an accordion. On some days, James would let Bick listen to his beats through headphones. On others they'd "jam," Bick on accordion or harmonica, James on his keyboard.

Peanut Butter Wolf visited often, as did Egon and J-Rocc, providing vital moments of relief for Maureen. Someone from the Stones Throw camp had gifted James the just-released Roland SP-404, a portable sampler-sequencer that was an update to the one that Madlib had been using for years. J-Rocc took Maureen crate digging on her son's behalf, introducing her to a core ritual of James's life she had never experienced. She returned with a stack of 45s, and was embarrassed when James extracted only a few of the records and told her to take the rest back.

J-Rocc wondered: *Where are James's Detroit people? Where are his celebrity friends?* Some folks, he knew, couldn't handle seeing anyone this way. J-Rocc rarely stopped long enough to ponder the impact of caring for James on his own body, mind, and soul.

That's the homie, J-Rocc thought. *This is what you're supposed to do.*

When fluid began to accumulate in James's chest cavity, doctors had to install another port to drain it. More surgery, more antibiotics. His feet swelled and one became gangrenous, and the doctors scheduled a surgery to amputate it, until a physician felt a pulse and canceled the procedure provided that Maureen followed a regimen to massage the foot.

She did so, and the foot healed. There were a number of moments like this, James hanging on the precipice, then miraculously pulling back; in the hospital suddenly, and then, just as suddenly, out.

While James worked intermittently on his "real" album for BBE, Jank continued editing *Donuts*. He began to understand Dilla's methods: how he would often play a piece of an old record and then segue into his interpolation of it, almost as if he were providing a "before" and "after," like they were messages to other producers: *Here's the sample, and here's what I can do with it*. And the material Dilla sampled was interesting: an old record made by the late Raymond Scott, the guy who invented an early version of the synthesizer and the composer of music and sound effects for *Looney Tunes*. Dilla had sampled two old commercials that Scott did, one for Bendix and another for a cosmetics company—*What is the magic that makes one's eyes / sparkle and gleam, light up the skies? / The name of the game is Lightworks*. He had turned it into an incredible beat. And even though Dilla had pieced together all this music on a computer, Jank swore that he couldn't hear the machine at all.

Whenever Jank went to Cedars to play Dilla a new edit, he always found James to be polite and generous, the opposite of the temperamental producer who intimidated Wolf and Egon. They built trust. James had already asked Jank to do one of his signature illustrations for the cover of *Donuts*, and now he told Jank he wanted him to design the sleeve of his still-in-progress album for BBE, which he had renamed *The Shining*. He pointed to his plastic respirator mask, which—when James wore it—made him look something like the alien figurines that had dotted James's studios in Michigan.

"Take a picture of that for the cover," James said.

Jank became more aware of the gravity and volatility of James's condition. He'd call Maureen and ask if it was a good time to come see Dilla, and invariably she'd give him a bright "Yes!" But sometimes he'd arrive at Cedars to find that it wasn't a good time at all, that James was barely lucid, or seemingly in great pain. As Jank shuttled back and forth to the hospital, his mind drifted to old stories he'd heard of people visiting

ailing legends, like Bob Dylan going to see Woody Guthrie in the sani-
tarium.

I'm one of those people, Jank thought. *It's happening right now.*

n the summer of 2005, Brian Cross and Eric Coleman were invited
to screen their latest film at a festival in São Paulo. *Brasilintime* was a
sequel of sorts to *Keepintime,* shot during a trip to Brazil in 2002 with
Madlib, Egon, J-Rocc, and Babu. The organizers of the festival wanted
Madlib to perform as part of their upcoming event, an easy sell for the
rapper-producer: Brazil had become Madlib's record shopping paradise.
But as he and the filmmakers discussed the trip over tacos and burritos
at Señor Fish, Cross and Coleman schemed to get someone else to join
them on the weeklong trip.

"You could bring a DJ . . . You should bring Dilla!"

Cross blurted this out as if he and Coleman had just conceived the
idea on the spot. But it had been brewing for a while, not only because
J Dilla was hip-hop's Brazilophile Number One—the man who sampled
"Saudade Vem Correndo" for the Pharcyde, the author of "Rico Suave
Bossa Nova"—but because Dilla himself had told them it was his dream
to go there. The conversation happened a half year prior, when they were
visiting him at the hospital. At Egon's suggestion, Cross had framed some
photographs to enliven Dilla's bare, white hospital walls. The thought
was: *When Dilla opens his eyes, he'll see all the great musicians he loves
to sample—David Axelrod, Lalo Schifrin.* Then Cross selected another
photo, one he'd taken years back in Havana of a brown-skinned boy leaping off the Malecón seawall and into the harbor. Cross had triggered the
lens at just the right moment: the kid airborne, frozen, no longer touching land but not yet in the water. The photo was colorful, joyous and yet,
just before he handed it to Egon, Cross had the briefest moment of pause.
This was a portrait of a person, like Dilla had been at the time, suspended
between two states.

James loved the photo and told them so, and the discussion of the
crew's travels to Central and South America prompted his comment
about Brazil. With James's exit from the hospital, this seemed to be the

opportunity of a lifetime. Madlib made a quick phone call to James—
"He's with it," Madlib reported—and Cross booked the trip.

What Cross didn't know was how sick J Dilla still was.

When Cross pulled his minivan up to the house on Sycamore, he was
shocked at how frail James looked. James climbed carefully into the van,
his baggy clothes hanging off his body, wearing too-large, unlaced gray
Jordans because his feet had become swollen. They shut the door and
drove off to LAX.

Maureen's anxiety for her son's physical health was offset by James's
excitement—he was finally making a trip to a place he had been a million
times in his musical mind. James recorded a new outgoing voice mail
message to commemorate the occasion:

". . . and I'm out, Brazilian style!"

James's right hand started to swell on the flight to Panama City.
"Yeah," he joked when Cross noticed it, "I've got the Hulk Hand."

Cross was concerned, but more so with the revelation that James had
half an ounce of marijuana taped to his leg.

"You have *what*?!" Brian whispered as they changed planes for Brazil.
"Oh my *God*, dude. They're gonna put us *under* the jail in Brazil, bro."

Cross, Coleman, J Dilla, and Madlib somehow made it past customs
unbothered, and within a few hours they had stashed their luggage in
the hotel and were walking the streets, en route to a record store. James
breathed in the mixture of subtropical breezes and car exhaust, the endless broken grid of buildings, and the crush of beautiful brown and black
people everywhere—the place in the New World that had collected the
culture of the Indigenous, the African, the European, and the African
American and created a music of maximum rhythmic and harmonic
complexity. He didn't have words for what it truly meant for him to be
here. He just said: "Brazil, man!"

But despite the world outside, James mostly stayed in his room. He
and Madlib made beats. The two had a way of communicating now that
was almost nonverbal. James would say: *Wooooooo!* Madlib would reply:
Yeeeeaaahh. James smoked weed and had Eric Coleman, who spoke a lit-

tle Portuguese, order pizzas for him. After a couple of days, Madlib told Cross that James's "Hulk Hand" had grown to a grotesque size.

They all went to dinner at the nearby restaurant Planeta's, James's ball cap riding low on his head. James ordered shrimp in the shell, and Coleman, sitting next to him, warned that it might be hard for him to eat with his hand so swollen. James dismissed his concern, but when the shrimp arrived, James realized he couldn't manipulate them. Coleman began to take the shells off.

"What the fuck are you doing?" James said. "Don't touch my food, man!"

"Dude, you're not going to be able to eat if I don't do this," Coleman replied.

Coleman didn't want to humiliate his friend, but he had already seen how James was putting himself in danger with his pride. Earlier, as they walked through a rough area of São Paulo, Coleman begged Dilla to tuck his Neeve diamond chain inside his shirt. "You can't fight. You can't run," Coleman said. "We will get murdered."

James replied: "Nah, man. I'm Dilla. I'm from Detroit."

After visiting James's room to check on him several times, one of the event producers, Suemyra Shah, began to sense that James was putting up a front for his friends and hiding how badly he really felt. Seeing his lethargy and his swelling worsen, she quietly but firmly suggested James see a doctor. When he agreed, she phoned Cross to tell him that she was taking James to the emergency room.

As Shah sat with James in the waiting area of Hospital Sirio Libanes, he began to tell her how much he had been looking forward to this trip, how much he'd been influenced by Brazilian music. Shah, a Berkeley grad, was an "Okayplayer." She already knew. It made sense to her why Dilla was in denial: he just wanted so badly to be here.

Cross and Madlib cut a television interview short and raced to meet them when they got Suemyra's call. Dilla greeted them with a sheepish grin.

"I'm cool, man," he said. Then, conspiratorially: "*Just get me my weed.*"

The Brazilian doctor, however, was disturbed. He couldn't understand how his patient was traveling while he was this ill. He lectured

Dilla, calling him "James" in a way that made Cross and Madlib stifle giggles. Nobody in their L.A. circle ever called him that.

"James?" the doctor said, exasperated. "You are going to *die*. You're going to die because you're not looking after this problem."

Cross went cold, hearing the term "TTP" for the first time, and understanding in that moment not only how serious Dilla's condition was, but how much he, Brian, had put his friend's life in danger. He'd thought it would be a great idea to bring J Dilla to Brazil. But "J Dilla" was just an idea, too. Here, in this hospital, was James.

We see TTP a lot, the doctor told him. *My colleague is an expert. He works at the hospital across the street. I don't think you're getting the care you need. He can treat you.*

The American music producer refused. He didn't want to lie supine in a strange hospital in a foreign country. He didn't want to re-create hell in paradise. He just wanted to get his weed at the hotel and fly home. Cross and Madlib begged him to reconsider: *Dude, let's just get your mother down here. We're in Brazil, man, we'll stay with you, just get better!*

"Man, I don't even know if this dude speaks English well enough," James said.

The doctor practically speaks better English than all of us, Cross thought.

"No," James said. "I need my weed."

The doctor refused to discharge James unless he booked a medical flight back to the United States. Cross and Madlib pooled several thousand dollars—basically all the money they had been paid for their gig in Brazil—and bought a ticket home for James. They fetched his belongings at the hotel, including his weed, and they asked the taxi driver's permission for James to smoke en route to the airport, to the flight that was to be met in Los Angeles by an ambulance, which would then take him to Cedars-Sinai.

After James left, they kept thinking about what the doctor said: *James, you are going to die.*

His words were sobering. Something needed to be done about that. They found Coleman—himself just recovered from alcohol poisoning the previous night—went to a bar, and got hammered. Anything to dull the thought of their friend, at this very moment, airborne, suspended between two states.

B ack in the hospital, more complications. In one moment of crisis, James was quiet, breathing erratically beneath his clear mask, his limbs jerking oddly. Maurice held James's hand, trying his best to restrain his emotions for Maureen's sake.

A nurse entered and informed them that James was breathing at 8 percent of his normal capacity. *If something doesn't change in the next few minutes*, she said, *we're going to have to put a tube in.*

Maureen shook her head, wearying of the fight, and now Maurice felt the need to support her: "No, you're not gonna put nothing in his throat," he told the nurse.

Then Maurice felt James *squeeze his hand.*

As if to support him. As if to say, *Don't let her put that damn thing in.* The nurse left. James kept squeezing Maurice's hand.

James's breathing improved markedly. The next day, he was off the respirator. He ate. He talked. He rose from his bed and, with the aid of a walker, started moving around. When Maurice saw James, he ducked out into the hallway and burst into tears.

M aureen had been in Los Angeles for nearly a year and James was not improving. She urged Dewitt to fly out again, which he did.

Long ago, James had confided in Joylette that his father had rarely been affectionate with him. But Dewitt Yancey loved James. His son's success had been, quiet as kept, his greatest source of pride and personal fulfillment.

Beverly Dewitt and James Dewitt were taciturn men who channeled their deepest feelings into their work. Still, the musical language that James spoke was his father's. He couldn't remember sitting on Dewitt's knee, his father's fingers plucking his belly, but the notes were still coming out of him.

Dewitt had overcome some of his own phobias to fly to the freeway capital of the world, twice. He visited with his son in the hospital for a few days. When it was time to go, he leaned down and kissed James on the forehead.

J oylette and Ja'Mya, too, flew out to California to see James. They did so twice: The first was after he got out of the hospital in the spring of 2005. He took the two of them to Roscoe's Chicken and Waffles and Universal Studios, and they hung out at Common's place. James was still trying to be strong for her and his three-year-old daughter, but when they were out somewhere, Joy could feel other people's eyes on James, seeing his frailty.

By their second visit, in the late summer, his physical deterioration was more evident. A photographer from Australia, Raph Rashid, was taking portraits of hip-hop producers in their home studios, and Egon and Jeff Jank arranged for him to visit Madlib and Dilla. Rashid snapped some photos of a rail-thin James, at his MPC, and standing behind Ja'Mya, holding each of her tiny hands in his own.*

James phoned Joy more frequently after she and Ja'Mya returned to Detroit, after he went back into the hospital again. Joy told James that she had snagged a small role in a locally produced movie, *Project 313*. She enthused to James that Ja'Mya had learned her consonants, after which Ja'Mya chattered away to her father. James stayed mostly silent.

"Why you call and don't say nothing?" Joy asked him.

"Maybe 'cause I don't feel like talking?" he replied.

Joy gradually understood that James was actually having trouble speaking. In the absence of reliable information from either James or Maureen, Joy had to fight to get to some kind of light on his situation.

"What are the doctors saying?" she asked him on one call.

"It's all good," he told her.

---

* Joy's visits to California are also a subject of contention for the family. Maureen and Martha Yancey insist that James did not really want to see Joy, but did so because it was the only way he could see his daughter Ja'Mya.

For Joylette, prayer was a daily habit. But in the fall of 2005, she began to have intense and specific visions of a world without James in it. She became convinced that God was preparing her: *James was going to die*. In the wake of her realization, Joy's fears weren't for herself, but for their daughter.

"You know I love you forever, James," she told him the next time they spoke. "And I know you're really not telling me what's going on. But I hope you have everything set up to give some kind of security for Ja'Mya in case something happens."

The next time Joy phoned James, she queried him again.

"It's all taken care of," he told her.

"How?" Joylette asked. "Is it a will?"

"Don't worry," he insisted. "It's all taken care of."

It wasn't a lie, but it wasn't the whole story, either.

There is a will.

It was made from a three-page blank template downloaded from the internet and printed on September 7, 2005.

It was filled out in longhand and signed with a date of September 8, 2005.

For James's personal effects, including things like his car and clothes, one beneficiary is listed: Maureen Yancey.

For James's real property and other assets—including his production company, Pay Jay, the repository of his intellectual property—four beneficiaries are listed: his mother, Maureen; his two daughters, Ja'Mya Yancey and Ty-Monae Whitlow; and his little brother, John Yancey.

As guardian of James's children should their mothers die before they came of age, one name is listed: Maureen Yancey.

And as executor of James's will and the custodian of his children's share of his assets until they turned twenty-five years old, a first choice is listed: James's accountant and de facto business manager, Arty Erk, with Micheline Levine as a second choice, and Maureen Yancey as third.

There are also the signatures of two witnesses—Maureen Yancey and Gerald Maurice Lamb Jr.—and the signature of a notary, Alfred L.

Mitchell, also dated September 8, 2005, and stamped with his commission locale, Oakland County, Michigan.*

The team at Cedars-Sinai began to suspect that something else was afoot. Though incurable and chronic, when treated TTP is not usually degenerative; in other words, it's episodic, going up and down rather than steadily deteriorating. The antibodies, the fatigue, the fevers, the inflammation, the kidney problems—along with James's history of chronic headaches and the problems in his joints—all pointed the physicians to an additional diagnosis.

He could have lupus, they told Maureen. *It's much more common in women than men. But when it hits men, it can hit hard.*

Maureen called Dewitt, and her sisters Reta and Clarice in Detroit to share the news. The family was outraged. It had been nearly two years since James had been diagnosed with TTP at Bon Secours. *Why hadn't anyone caught this?*

The new diagnosis had little bearing on James's current treatment. But it did give some clues about why he wasn't getting better.†

The mastering session for *Donuts* was nearing, and the album was still a little short on runtime, so Jank asked James for a few more tracks. James gave him a CD containing nine beats.‡ Jank placed most of them at the tail end of the sequence; to close the album, Jank decided to reprise the introduction. With that, *Donuts* came to thirty-one tracks and forty-three minutes, now a full-length LP. Jank had to name each of these tiny songs, and when he couldn't find a suitable word from the

---

* Several aspects of the will's creation story are misaligned, and thus make the truth about that creation difficult to discern. For more on this, see the Reporter's Notes and Sources section.

† Doctors know more about the family of diseases called *thrombotic microangiopathy* now, and James's case history indicates that there is a possibility that his illness may have been TTP's "sister" disease, the ultra-rare aHUS, or atypical hemolytic uremic syndrome. TTP tends to be intermittent and episodic, while aHUS tends to get progressively worse, as James did. TTP responds well to plasma exchange, aHUS responds poorly. By 2012, effective drug treatments were developed for aHUS, enabling patients to eventually discontinue dialysis.

‡ Those tracks were eventually named "Stepson," "Geek Down," "Gobstopper," "One for Ghost," "U-Love," "Hi," "Bye," "Last Donut of the Night," and "Welcome to the Show."

actual track—"Workinonit," "Light It," "Lightworks," "People"—he concocted one that sounded appropriate: "The Factory" for a particularly
industrial-sounding electronic beat; "Waves" for a track with an undu-
lating vocal sample. Jank ran the printed list of names to Dilla during a
mix session for *The Shining* at Dave Cooley's place. As Maureen sat by
her son's side, James looked them over, laughed at a couple, and handed
the list back to Jank.

"Yeah, cool," James said.

The album art proved a bit more difficult. Brian Cross had offered to
take photos of Dilla for the *Donuts* cover while they were in Brazil, but
James's premature departure nixed that. In the VTech photo shoot for
Stones Throw, James looked emaciated. Jank came up with another idea:
Dilla had appeared the previous year in a video for the Stones Throw
artist MED. Jank found an interesting freeze frame—James smiling, the
brim of his baseball cap hiding his eyes—and grabbed it for the cover.

It was hard for Wolf to convince their distributor, Caroline/EMI, to
even release the glorified beat CD; and when Stones Throw missed the
production deadline for an October release, Caroline told them to push
it into the first quarter of 2006. Wolf decided to release *Donuts* on February 7. It would be a birthday present for Dilla.

Jank understood that *Donuts* was a trifle in the eyes of many people around Dilla, and perhaps to James himself, a secondary project to
The Shining. There were no guest appearances from rappers, no lyrics at
all, yet Jank still felt the finished album he held in his hands was saying
something.

James had been offered a European tour. He wanted to go, and asked
Frank-n-Dank and Phat Kat to accompany him. With his repeated
hospitalizations, he kept postponing. Finally, in late 2005, James decided
he was ready. In many ways, he was more debilitated than he had been
in South America, as now he was pretty much bound to a wheelchair.
Jeff Jank was certain that they'd have to cancel the trip, and Egon begged
Maureen not to let James go. Maureen, again, chose not to defy her son's
wishes. She would come along to take care of him, bringing Dave New

York to give them both physical and emotional support. Their strategy was to have James rest during the day so that they could roll him on-stage at night for a brief performance. From Detroit came Phat Kat and Tim Maynor, who reached out to Peter Adarkwah at BBE to find James some places along their travel route where he could get dialysis. J-Rocc was booked on another tour, so James invited J-Rocc's fellow Beat Junkie Rhettmatic to DJ.

Frank and Derrick hadn't seen James since the previous year, when the two of them flew to California to do something unprecedented: hand a check to James, for production work on their new album. It was an er-rand filled with symbolism for Frank—a way for him to thank his friend, and a sign that he himself was ready to chart his own path as an artist. But when James rolled off the airplane in London in late November, the two of them were shocked by how much their friend had deteriorated. For a man who had taken pains to hide his illness from the world, the tour was complete exposure. James, his head covered with a green hoodie and ball cap, his body wrapped in a matching parka, took the stage at London's Jazz Cafe to cheers, which only increased when the crowd began to un-derstand that Jay Dee had endured quite a bit more than a long flight to see them. His voice was strong, and he ripped through two Jaylib songs, "McNasty Filth" and "The Official." Phat Kat watched him, thinking: *A fucking soldier.*

They flew to Oslo, then to Helsinki, then to Paris, where Dave New York pushed James down the center aisle of the Nouveau Casino, and together the men lifted his wheelchair to the stage. Grabbing the micro-phone with his long, thin fingers, James gave his French audience that most affectionate of all greetings from *le Détroit*.

"Whatupdoe?!" he laughed. "It's a blessing to be out here right now, bringing you this celebration. I'm like 'Fuck it, I want to see my peoples!' Make some noise if you're feeling me out there!"

At the end, as James thanked the crowd, he saw something he'd never seen before: a forest of hands in the air, all with fingers raised in the shape of a J.

"Whoa," James said, patting his heart. "Love y'all, man. Thank you."

James was moved by another act of love from a fan. Even before the tour reached the Unique Club in Düsseldorf, word had spread online about J Dilla's condition, with some hip-hop fans questioning the producer and his team's judgment about him traveling in his vulnerable state. The opening act for the night, the German DJ Deckstarr, felt the chatter devoid of compassion. So the DJ printed a T-shirt to wear onstage, black with white block lettering that read: J DILLA SAVED MY LIFE.

When James reached Ghent on December 8, his friend DJ Lefto came to James's hotel room to loan him an MPC. The last time he had seen James was almost two years earlier, in Eindhoven. James had hinted back then that he was feeling a little off. Lefto knew now that it was more than that.

The show that night at De Centrale wasn't packed. Even with the support from his mother and friends, the tour had exhausted James, and the audience heard the weakness in his voice.

It was time to go home.

Unhook me from this shit, Bobo," James said. "Let's go."

It wasn't the first time James had asked Maurice to cut his treatment short. James hated dialysis. It was like torture to see James so uncomfortable. But Maurice just couldn't do it. So he played it off.

"Aw, man, you only got forty more minutes on there," Maurice replied. "I'ma go outside."

While James suffered, Maurice stood in the glare of the Southern California sun and its bright indifference to his mood.

When Maurice first came to Los Angeles, he came in search of his big break. Even in his reunion with James, Maurice hoped that he and Dilla could collaborate on a comedy album. And though he remained with Eve, and though Martha had made it clear to him that a reunion with her was impossible despite the fact that she had annulled her own marriage, Maurice still harbored a belief, however naive: *If I can make it out here, I can fix everything. I can go back. I can marry Martha, I can be with Faith, I can fix my family. If I make it, I can fix it.*

Bobo's life was no longer about his career, or fixing anything back home. He'd been with James now almost every day for more than a year.

He lived now to keep James alive. He felt that God had chosen him to be there. Maurice's reflex to take up space had been blunted. With James, he had learned now to make space. *Make sure he's comfortable, make sure he's got everything he needs. Make sure he's in good spirits, tell him a joke, clown on shit. But when James needs to make beats, or when he just needs his headspace, give him a pound, give him silence, get out of the way.*

After the treatment, Maurice rolled James to the truck, rolled the truck to Sycamore, and rolled James inside. Maurice lifted him to the couch.

If Maurice had learned anything in his year with James, it was this: some things could be fixed, some things couldn't, and some things had never been broken in the first place.

"I love you, Bobo," James said as Maurice set him down.

"I love you, too," Maurice replied.

I n late 2005, Questlove drove through Los Angeles listening to J Dilla's *Motown Tape*. When he stopped at the Ralph's supermarket on Sunset Boulevard, he texted James.

"I got a theory," Questlove wrote.

James texted his reply: "?"

Questlove continued: "I think you're trying to send a message to someone. You're just basically trying to nudge the current leader of soul sample chops, aren't you?" It was a veiled reference to Kanye West.

"Yup," James wrote.

I knew it, Questlove thought.

And then: "What are you doing this evening?" James wrote.

"Gonna go to Will Smith's house for a meeting about some music," Questlove typed.

"Aiight," came the response from James. "Make sure you come see the boy."

Questlove and James Poyser had dinner with Smith; the former Fresh Prince told his Philadelphia brethren that he wanted to do a project with them that evoked their Soulquarian vibe. Later, as they drove to Common and James's place, Questlove and Poyser decided that the person they were going to see next would be perfect to have on the team. But they were not prepared for what they saw when they knocked on the front door and Maureen let them inside. James was in the living room, slumped over in a wheelchair. Questlove now engaged in the calculus that so many friends and family members did when they saw James in his enfeebled state. *Do I acknowledge this and make him feel awkward? James hates any kind of attention. I don't want to make this about me. I'll act normal.*

But Poyser froze. The producer called to him from his wheelchair: "Come over here."

Poyser approached. James's breathing was labored and shallow, and he was having trouble speaking.

It's been this way for a while, Maureen told Questlove. *Thank you so much for coming. You just raised his spirits.*

The body was sluggish, but the mind was still moving. James played Questlove a quick snippet of a new track, then gestured to a record on the floor.

"Yo . . . h-hand me that record right there," James muttered.

Questlove bent down and retrieved it: an odd Brazilian release, labeled in Portuguese, an extended play of Stevie Wonder tracks from the 1971 Motown album *Where I'm Coming From.*

"Track one," James said. "Use that."

"Use it for us?" Did James mean for him to sample the song for the Roots?

"Fuck . . . fuck around with that first track, that's the one," James confirmed. "I want you to have that."

Questlove and James Poyser looked at each other for the briefest of moments, and then looked at the floor, unwilling to let their shared, unspoken thought play itself out. Unbeknownst to them, James had been doing this for the past few months—giving little gifts to his friends. Sometimes they were promises: he pledged to produce a new track for Jazzy Jeff's next BBE album; that made Jeff happy. Sometimes they were apologies: he called Q-Tip from his hospital bed and told him that he regretted his occasionally ungrateful and petulant behavior during their Ummah partnership; that made Tip happy. Sometimes they were reconciliations: he called Cricket, who had relocated to Atlanta, to tell him that his *Donuts* promotional tour would be taking him there, and he wanted to meet because he knew Cricket might have some hard feelings about being left behind in the wake of James's climb; that made Cricket happy. Sometimes they were requests: he called Karriem and told him that he needed his help to finish *The Shining*; that made Karriem happy. Sometimes they were simple acts of reassurance: backstage in Helsinki, he had turned to Phat Kat and said, "You know you're gonna be good, right?"—and that made Kat happy.

Questlove and Poyser left without seeing Common, who spent more of his days and nights elsewhere, because he, too, wasn't prepared for his friend's long struggle and slow decline. He simply let Maureen and James have his space, and tried his best to keep his own life on track.

When Common did come, though it was painful to watch, he saw something sublime: James in his wheelchair, Maureen feeding him. James in the bathroom, his mother bathing him. James lying on the couch, head in Maureen's lap, Maureen stroking him.

Mother son, mother son, mother son.

O n February 6, Maureen and Maurice took James to see Dr. Bick, who scolded his patient.

"You're not eating enough," he said. The doctor asked James if he would take an intravenous feeding tube. James refused. He hated tubes.

"You have to eat," the doctor repeated.

They went home. On the next day, February 7, there were two big reasons to celebrate. It was James's thirty-second birthday, his first outside the hospital in a couple of years. And it was the retail day of *Donuts*. His friends from Stones Throw planned a little party for Dilla. Egon ordered a donut-shaped chocolate cake and went to pick it up. Meanwhile Wolf, J-Rocc, and Madlib assembled at the house on Sycamore. James was in his wheelchair, barely able to lift his head.

"Maaaaaaaaaan," James said softly, alerting everybody who knew him that he meant what he was about to say. "Y'all shouldn't be here right now."

It's all good, Dilla, J-Rocc and the others said.

"Seriously, y'all gotta leave man. Y'all shouldn't see me like this."

Aww, man, that's okay, Dilla, don't trip. Look, Otis brought a bunch of records for you.

"That's dope, but, maaaaaaaan, y'all gotta leave."

The friends all looked at each other, resigned. They left quickly, extending their cheeriest birthday wishes, J-Rocc calling out that he'd see James later in the week. They walked out just as Egon pulled up for the gathering, cake in hand. Madlib shook his head, and Wolf told his partner that there would be no party. Things were that bad.

Egon, holding the cake, was overcome. He felt a pain inside his chest.

"I think I'm having a heart attack," he said.

Wolf insisted on driving Egon to the emergency room, where he was diagnosed with a panic attack.

They left the cake at the door.

O n days when James had his treatments, he would put his hand up and Maureen would give him a high five. This was one of their rituals, steeling himself for the ordeal ahead. As if to say: *We're in this together.*

But on Thursday, February 9, James had a free day ahead, no doctor's appointments, no dialysis. Maureen was surprised when James put his hand up for her. She hesitated. But he kept his hand aloft until she slapped it.

"That's what I'm talking about," he said. "You're gonna be alright. I promise you."

That's when Maureen realized the high five wasn't for his benefit. It was for hers.

T hat evening, James made a beat.

In Funkadelic's 1972 song *"America Eats Its Young,"* George Clinton likens the country to a whore *"sucking the brains"* of her grandchildren in a *"neurotic attempt to be Queen of the Universe,"* over a woman's cries of sexual ecstasy.

James placed the needle of his turntable at a point almost four minutes into the song, sampled a few bars into his MPC3000, chopped it into pieces, programmed the pads to trigger those bits, and sequenced them into a new instrumental . . .

The next morning James woke early for his doctor's appointment.

"You want to leave now and get there twenty minutes early, or you want to rest a bit more?"

James didn't mind hurrying, but hated hurrying up to wait. He settled in for a nap on the couch, Maureen sitting beside him, Maurice in a chair nearby, the two of them watching TV.

When it was time to go, Maureen touched James to wake him. He didn't wake.

She called to him: "James!" She shook him.

Maurice now stood. He hustled to the couch and scooped James up in his arms. He felt James aspirate—one broken breath, in. Then nothing. Knowing, without saying, what he had really just heard.

Carrying James, Maurice raced out to the car, Maureen behind him, calling Dr. Bick's number. "Bring him right to the emergency room," Bick told her. James's team would be there to meet him.

No time for the wheelchair. Maurice slipped James into the passenger seat and Maureen put the seat belt on him. Maureen got into the back, Maurice into the driver's seat, backing out, tires squealing. Maurice called to him: "Dilla! Dilla!" Maureen trying to support James's body from behind.

She felt a breath. Then she didn't.

Maurice ran all the lights, careening down Beverly Boulevard toward Cedars-Sinai.

That's not it, Maureen repeated to herself. *It isn't time.*

. . . The woman is now gasping for breath, gasping and sobbing, her child is dying, while the drums and bass lean forward, tripping an organ, which stutters, comes in too early, or too late, or, in any case, not when it is supposed to happen.

James saved the beat to a disc. Then he went to sleep.

13.
Zealots

John Yancey was driving to the bowling alley to practice for a tournament when Ashley rang his cell.

"Come home," she said. "There's something I need to tell you."

Never the line you want to hear from your girl.

John turned his car around. He'd been living in Mount Pleasant, a small college town right in the palm of the Michigan mitten, since he enrolled the previous year at Central Michigan University. He wasn't prepared for the massive lectures. John was shy, he stuttered like his father and older brother did, and lived in daily fear of being called on. He started skipping classes, and by the end of his freshman year he was flunking out. But he'd made some good friends at school. He was in a relationship. And he'd joined a bowling league. So for his sophomore year he decided he'd stay in town and attend a less intense community college about twenty minutes away.

He had a life.

Then, when John got home, Ashley told him that James had died.

John was twelve years younger than James, an interval that put a distance in their proximity at the cramped house in Conant Gardens, and a longing in John's connection with his big brother. In middle school, John wrote an essay about his two heroes, Michael Jordan and James, whom he noted both shared a strong work ethic. But while John admired James's success, he also understood that his entire family was hard at work: Dewitt, singing, rehearsing, performing; Maureen, hustling, growing her business; Martha, writing prose and poetry; Earl, drawing. Music, too, was something that everyone in the family just did; John grew up knowing how to harmonize. To be a Yancey was to be good at stuff. You worked hard, you got better.

John's thing was basketball. He'd grown taller than James and had developed into a real player, handy as either point or shooting guard. By the time John was in high school, playing for the team at Notre Dame in Harper Woods, he'd moved downtown with the family, and his sister Martha's boyfriend was the one who spent time mentoring John on the basketball court. For a comedian, Maurice was no joke: a lefty, with crazy-ass spin on his ball, hitting threes from anywhere on the court. But when James wasn't working or traveling, sometimes he would swing by in one of his trucks to scoop John up after school. Music was always the way to be closer to his older brother. When he told James he wanted to DJ, James put John in front of his turntables and said, "Practice." When John started writing rhymes, he had to muster all the confidence he felt on the basketball court to spit them in front of John and Earl both:

I'm real nice, real ice
Real dice, real spice
Every time I shoot, all net

John felt like James took him seriously. Once, James even sent a limousine to take John to the recording studio, an envelope of cash and a new notebook on the seat beside him.

Then James got sick and moved to California. John's high school graduation present was a trip to Los Angeles—John and his friend Nick together, staying with James at Common's house, and then at a hotel room he'd rented for them. They saw I, Robot at Grauman's Chinese Theatre and had In-N-Out burgers. When John started DJing college parties, James and J-Rocc went shopping at Fat Beats and shipped him a bunch of records.

After James relapsed, John flew out to see him, this time at James's bedside at Cedars-Sinai. John understood that James's condition was serious, but even then, he was optimistic that his big brother would get better. There was a part of him unprepared for the news that Ashley gave him on that Friday in February.

Nick and the rest of John's friends came to get him off the floor. They sat with John and they drank. They all had plans to go see a movie that evening, *Final Destination 3*, but they figured John wouldn't want to go. John went anyway, to take his mind off things. When he emerged from the theater, he felt a weird kind of strength wash over him.

After the tournament the next day, Nick drove John to Detroit to be with his father and sister. The ride was long, through the wintry Michigan peninsula, and John decided to listen to his brother's new album for the first time. *Donuts* was dense and eerie. Then, in the third track, John swore he heard his brother—in the same playful voice that James used long ago in the basement while John worked on his homemade book of basketball statistics and James made beats—calling out to him:

JOHNNnnnnnny . . .

n Los Angeles, Eothen found out when Maureen called him from Cedars, sobbing. Egon fetched Wolf and they drove to the hospital, comforting Maureen while Maurice sat in silence with James's body. Then J-Rocc called and Egon gave him the news. J-Rocc cried: "But I'm supposed to go over there and see him today!" Later, they all met back up at the house on Sycamore. With Common bereft, Derek Dudley helped Maureen make plans for the memorial service and burial, driving her to the funeral home and anywhere else she needed to go.

In Hawaii with the Roots, Ahmir "Questlove" Thompson had just checked into a hotel room when Common rang. "Yo, man. The greatest has left us." Ahmir couldn't breathe. He descended to the lobby and saw the band gathering around their fifteen-passenger van, there to take them to sound check. He didn't want Tarik to see him crying, so he turned, walking away from the hotel, then running through the streets of Honolulu, all 290 pounds of him, until he found himself on a beach, far enough away that he could scream. "FUUUUUUUUCK!" He caught his breath and went back to tell his brothers.

In Toronto, Frank took the call from Maureen. To Frank, she, too, was "Ma Dukes," a woman he'd known since he was himself a child, the heartbreak in her voice breaking his own. He and Derrick cried, Frank more angry than sad. Frank's thoughts returned to the basement, where James would stay tapping the drum machine so long that he'd get blisters on his fingers. They'd pop, and then he'd wrap them in bandages and keep going. *Just like James. Not even slowing down to think about his health.* Frank now felt an overwhelming need to get to Los Angeles. His friend in Cali, the comedian Russell Peters, told him: *Take my credit card number. Buy your ticket. Stay with me.*

In New York, House Shoes was visiting with fellow Detroiters Big Tone and his fiancée, Kindra, in town for the *Donuts* release party at Joe's Pub where Waajeed had just spun. Shoes disliked the record. *It sounds like Madlib, not Jay Dee.* Still, the next morning Shoes and Tone made the pilgrimage to Fat Beats to get the new vinyl. He had it under his arm when Waajeed hit his cell. Shoes couldn't process the information, so Waajeed had to yell it: "SHOES, HE'S GONE!" Shoes and Tone sat on the curb, on Sixth Avenue, and bawled. They retreated to Tone's apartment, mourning while Kindra booked the men their flights to California.

In Chicago, Tim Maynor was driving with Dwele when Maureen called. Maynor held himself together until he dropped Dwele off, and then, tears flowing, started driving aimlessly, from downtown into the deep South Side of his youth and back again. When he collected himself, it was time to make a phone call of his own.

In Fribourg, Switzerland, Slum Village was on the first stop of their European tour. T3 and Elzhi were having dinner backstage at the venue with DJ Dez, their road manager Hex, and tour manager Howi when Maynor reached T3. His comrades read his expression. They were from Detroit. They knew that look.

"Who the fuck got killed *this* time?" Hex yelled.

"Dilla died," he said.

Less than an hour later, they were onstage. After the second song, T3 paused to announce the passing of his friend.

In that moment of silence, he remembered seeing James at the "Selfish" video shoot, but not having a chance to talk to him. He remembered Shoes telling him a few months back: "You gotta come out here, man. I don't know how long Dilla's gonna be around." And he remembered, just yesterday, when they were in London, Dez said: "Ain't nobody gonna realize how sweet Dilla is until he's gone." He and James had left a bunch of things unsaid. Now he wouldn't be able to say them.

"J DILLA IS A GOD!" someone shouted from the audience.

Now he had to go. Slum would have to tour without him while he made his way to California.

And in Detroit, Monica Whitlow found out when she called Martha Yancey, with whom she had become friendly since they met two years earlier at Ty-Monae's fourth birthday party. Monica was driving home from work, wanting to hang out. "Call me when you get somewhere safe," Martha said, before she hung up. When Monica got home and phoned again, Martha was overcome and passed the phone to her cousin Rashonda Hayes to say the words. Monica exploded, in anger and grief, crippled by the most horrifying question: *How am I going to tell Ty-Monae?*

No one from the family called Joylette. Instead, a complete stranger, Peanut Butter Wolf, phoned on Maureen's behalf to deliver the news.[*]

On February 13, holding James's four-year-old daughter's hand and with her sister Janell by her side, Joylette boarded a plane to say goodbye to James. On the flight, she became aware of a young woman stealing glances at her. And when Dave New York came to pick them up at the airport, it was this same woman whom Dave placed in the passenger seat.

"So who are you?" Joylette asked her on the ride to Common's house, where they'd be staying.

"My name is Tia," she replied.

---

[*] There is another conversation that Joylette remembers that Maureen Yancey says did not happen. Janell Hunter says that after James's death she made contact with Maureen and got her sister and Maureen on the phone together. Joy says that when she inquired about the funeral arrangements, wanting to come with Ja'Mya, Maureen said to her, "I didn't think you would want to go through all that."

"So you were . . . James's *girlfriend*? Because he never said nothing about having no woman. You lived with him?"

"No," she replied. "We were just friends. We would have been together, but . . ." Her voice trailed off.

Joylette thought: *This is some Maureen shit. She invites this girl, but she didn't want me and her granddaughter to be there.* She shook her head as Dave New York nosed the car toward Hollywood.

Joylette didn't know that there was a viewing that evening, and in any case arrived too late to attend. But the next morning, February 14, before they left for the funeral, Joy, Ja'Mya, and Janell joined hands with Maureen and her sister Clarice, Common, and other friends in a circle in the living room on Sycamore. To the wonder of all present, Ja'Mya insisted on leading the prayer.

"Bless my daddy's soul. Thank you for my daddy. I know he's with you. May we all be happy in this circle."

Dewitt, Martha, and John stayed in Detroit, as did Monica and Ty-Monae; there would be a memorial service there. But in the Church of the Recessional at Forest Lawn Memorial Park in Glendale, California, James was remembered by a mixture of friends from across the world, some of whom had been in town for the Grammy Awards and ended up staying for the service. Ahmir and Erykah and James Poyser. Frank and T3 and Waajeed. House Shoes and Henhouse. Dave New York and J-Rocc and Wolf and Egon. Wendy Goldstein and Jeff Harleston. Bilal and Pino Palladino. Dwele and Karriem Riggins. Pete Rock and Q-Tip. Common's DJ, Dummy, had assembled a mixtape of James's beats and friends' remembrances, collected and recorded via telephone. As the music played, it imparted to the service its mysterious mixture of melancholy and buoyancy—dozens of people, crying and bobbing their heads at the same time. Poyser sat at the keyboard for the entire service. He had grown up in the church, played at many funerals, and knew the hymns by heart. But as the congregation walked by the casket to say goodbye, he found himself forming the chords to "Fall in Love," a sacrament to this congregation. In another moment Poyser huddled before the casket with Ahmir, Common, Erykah, and the keyboardist Omar Edwards in a weepy group embrace. Poyser whispered a prayer and the group exploded in laughter and tears both, as the congregation watched, mystified.*

Joylette could barely process any of it. She had finally been handed one of the programs printed up for the service. There, in the last paragraph of a section called "His Story," it read: "He is survived by his Mom and Dad, three sisters, four brothers, two daughters, Ja'Mya Yancey and Ty-Monae Whitlow . . ."

A half dozen disconnected memories came rushing back to Joylette in a thunderclap, moments that now made sense when joined together: James, at Clinton Township, saying "I need to tell you something," and then getting cold feet. Common cryptically asking her over the phone before her arrival: "Joy, did you know?" Tim Maynor and his wife, Shamika, on the flight over, urging her to apply for social security benefits for Ja'Mya "before the shit hits the fan." Maureen's evasiveness on the phone and her protectiveness of the memorial programs printed up for the funeral.

After the service, Joylette, Ja'Mya, and Janell packed into the limousine on the way to the gravesite with Maureen and Clarice.

"Maureen, James had another *daughter*?" Joylette asked. "Why didn't you say anything?"

"I thought you knew," Maureen replied.

Little Ja'Mya detected the tension in the ensuing back-and-forth: "We don't talk about this right now, because this is a celebration for my daddy."

In the silence that followed, more memories came back to Joy: The time, back at Clinton Township, that Micheline Levine asked her directly if James had another child. The time a friend surfaced a rumor about it, and Joy snapped: "Tell that person to mind their business." Even *Donuts* made more sense to her. Her godsister Tiki had told her: "You know James put your name on there." She listened and sure enough, there it was, at the beginning of the song "Don't Cry," a quick vocal sample from

---

* The prayer that broke the tension was: "Dear Lord, if it's your will to leave us here with just Ahmir, then so be it. I guess we're stuck with Afro now."

the Temptations and George Kirby. There was no apparent reason for
James to use the bit of stage dialogue that ended with the words "Ok,
George," the end of the name garbled, except that they sounded just like
Ok, Joy . . . followed by the words *I can't stand to see you cry.* His song
"Two Can Win" had a different resonance now that she knew that there
had been another woman in the picture. But who?

They buried James on Valentine's Day, at the top of the same mountain where Nat King Cole and Walt Disney were laid to rest, his body
borne by his brothers in spirit: Q-Tip, Maurice, Karriem, Common, and
Dave New York. At the gravesite, Common, Maurice, and Frank flanked
Maureen while Joy held Ja'Mya's hand. It was sunny and clear, and at one
point Joy felt Ja'Mya tug her arm.

"Mama, look!"

She pointed upward: two hearts, seemingly written by an airplane
above them. But there was no plane in sight. For many who weren't already crying, that was the cue. Brian Cross stood back from the congregation, freezing the moment in one final photograph.

What that picture didn't capture was the view from the grave itself,
the grassy hill ahead of them sloping so steeply upward that it seemed
you could step right into heaven.

The word *grieve* comes from a Latin root that signifies a heavy burden. After the funeral everyone carried that burden in their own
way. During the repast at the house on Sycamore, they listened to beats
and chatted as a videographer recorded their remembrances. Ahmir
guarded his emotions; Common broke down, comforted by his girlfriend Taraji Henson. C-Minus stepped out for some air with J-Rocc,
and found Pete Rock, standing alone, breaking his silence only to say:
"The king is dead."

There was joy in the togetherness, but also a certain alienation: between the Detroiters and the Angelenos; between the friends who spent
the past two years trying to keep James alive and the people who showed

up only after he had passed; between James's celebrity friends and the people who remained outside that circle. On both sides, there were suspicions about who was there to mourn, and who was there to be seen; who was there to take the weight, and who was there to hitch a ride. Because things were feeling a little too "Hollywood," some people skipped the repast altogether. For Egon and Wolf, their unease began to set in on the day that Dilla died, returning from the hospital to find the comedian Dave Chappelle sitting on the Sycamore front stoop. Chappelle, who was in the midst of producing his popular and innovative sketch TV series for Comedy Central, had liked James and wanted him to contribute music for the show. Later, as Maurice "Bobo" Lamb sobbed, Chappelle clasped his fellow comedian's shoulder and asked if there was anything he could do for him and the family. Maurice looked at Chappelle hopefully: "You can let me open up for you on tour." The weirdness continued at the service, when the rapper MF Doom declared aloud that Dilla had come to him in a dream about a posthumous collaboration, and that Dilla insisted that Doom have the lion's share of the royalties.

While some people swore James was talking to them, others kept their dialogue with him private. Q-Tip felt eyes on him all day as he dealt with the death of his brother. He suspected some of these people still thought that he had tried to suppress James, or coveted his money or credit. They were wrong. Q-Tip had foresworn *his* personal credit, too, to the noble principle of *ummah*.

It would take him years to grapple with the folly of his nobility: Q-Tip was one of the greatest beatmakers of all time, and he wasn't mentioned half as much as his contemporaries because his name wasn't on most of his work.* But for the shine that Q-Tip had himself sacrificed, he still felt the brotherhood was worth it, even if sometimes his brothers didn't. That was what it meant to be a brother: sometimes you had to take the weight. Tip carried James's body to the grave today, and would carry some other things to his own, for brotherhood's sake. He had paid for the funeral; he didn't care about the credit. His burden was light. On DJ Dummy's mixtape, he told James so, leaving a message for him, until there was nothing left to say.

* Q-Tip would begin to stake a claim to his personal credits in the 2009 Moovmnt.com interview.

Hey
What's going on
James
I know you hear me, Jay
This the Abstract, as you called me
It's your man
I know you hear me, dog
Yo, James, I got you
I got you
Yo, Jay
It's your man, Kamaal
I got you
You know I got you, boy
Yo, Buddy Lee
The bullshittinest
Yo, Dilla
James
You know I got you, boy.
I got you.
It's your man
I got you, man.

On the day that James's biggest secret had finally been exposed, Maureen apologized to Joy for coming between her and James. The two women were sitting in James's bedroom with Clarice when Maureen vowed to make amends: "I'm going to do right by his kids," she said. Then she turned to Clarice. "I'm gonna even do better with Andre," she added, referring to her estranged eldest son. "I'm going to reach out to him and make things right."*

Joylette's head spun. Trying to make sense of everything, she approached Tia, the girl who introduced herself as James's friend.

"So, are *you* the baby's mama?" Joy asked.

---

* This conversation was confirmed by Clarice Hayes.

"No," replied Tia.

Joy would stay a few extra days to attend the Los Angeles premiere of her movie, *Project 313*. Her question wouldn't be answered until she attended James's memorial service in Detroit the following week, when she, Janell, and Ja'Mya met Monica and Ty-Monae.

A fter the repast, James's people went off to their lives, carrying him or letting him go.

House Shoes's mood had soured by the time that he and Waajeed met up with Brian Cross and Eric Coleman at a bar called Little Temple. Shoes downed double Hennessys and cringed as Coleman spun tracks from *Donuts* on the sound system. So much of who Shoes had become as a DJ arose from his personal friendship with James and his professional investment in J Dilla. Now James was dead—gone before the world even knew how great he was—and all they would remember of J Dilla was this *Donuts* shit. Shoes went across the street for cigarettes and came back with packets of Hostess donuts and began pelting everyone with them. *You want fucking donuts?! Here!* Finally, Shoes shoved Coleman aside.

"Jay wants me to DJ!" he shouted. He didn't remember anything that happened after that. But everybody who watched House Shoes tear through James's body of work certainly did.

Across town, Questlove, Erykah, and James Poyser convened in a recording studio, a session booked ostensibly for their new supergroup, Edith Funker. Ahmir wasn't feeling funky. His teacher was gone. He turned the lights down and lit candles. Poyser started playing the Fender Rhodes: a two-chord figure, bright-to-somber. Ahmir unlatched the chain of his snare and started playing with mallets on the drums for a softer sound. Erykah began singing an impromptu lyric, prompted by a story Maureen had told her at the repast, about the time that James returned from the brink of death . . .

Telephone.
It's Old Dirty.
He wants to give you directions home.

Oh, God, come on, Erykah, Ahmir thought. *I can't right now. I'll start crying.* He reached for the headphone mixer and turned her vocals down as she continued, mentioning the two hearts she had seen in the sky above his gravesite . . .

Fly away to heaven, brother
Save a place for me

They went on for forty minutes, working through the transitions. The song surfaced two years later as "Telephone," on Erykah's next album. Mixed and edited by Mike Chav, the man who had built James's studio back in Michigan, he preserved the final moment of the take: Erykah's stuttered, shivering "thank you," a release.*

J ames's friends knew that Maureen Yancey had carried the most, and so they carried her, too. In the back of the funeral program, there had been a plea for direct donations to her. The year she spent in Los Angeles had killed her day care business back home and decimated the Yanceys' finances.

Not long after Dilla's death, DJ Spinna and Waajeed threw a party at the New York City club APT; when the evening was done, they were able to cut a check for $1,000 and send it off to Maureen with a signed card. Back in Detroit, House Shoes channeled his Dilla fervor into answering that call. Speaking at James's Detroit memorial, Shoes had pledged that he would do everything he could to uphold the legacy of J Dilla, saying, "I'll carry it on my back if I have to." That work included fundraising for James's mother. When the Yancey family came to "Shoes' House," his weekly hip-hop night at the club Northern Lights, he put an empty champagne bucket

---

* Chav states that Erykah delayed delivery of her album so she could re-cut her vocals on the anniversary of James's death in February 2008. James's collaborators and friends would grapple with their loss in song over the next decade, some of the most prominent examples being J-Rocc's "Thank You Jay Dee" (Acts 1, 2, and 3) (2006, 2007, and 2008), Q-Tip's "Shaka" (2008), The Roots' "Dilltastic Vol Won(derful)" and "Can't Stop This" (2006), and their album of interpretations of his beats called *Dilla Joints* (2010); De La Soul's *Smell the D.A.I.S.Y.* mixtape (2014); Phife's "Dear Dilla" (2014); Common's "Rewind That" (2016); Dwele's "Workin on It" (2008); Elzhi's "February" (2016); and Madlib's *Beat Konducta 5-6: A Tribute to Dilla* (2009).

in front of Maureen and Dewitt—who was particularly fond of Shoes—and told the crowd: "Fill it with cash." On other occasions, Shoes and his friend Roy would run envelopes of money they raised over to the Yanceys' place.

But no one was feeling settled. Maureen's time in Los Angeles ended in sorrow, yet in that community she felt so supported. Now she had returned to her unhappy marriage. James had been a huge part of her life's work, and that work seemed to be over.

Her youngest son was restless, too: John's basketball dreams faded as his interest in college dwindled. He was thinking about a career in music now that his brother had passed. He'd even performed for the first time as an MC at Shoes' House. John could no longer be close to James physically, but he felt compelled now to go to the place where his brother had last been at peace.

House Shoes's night at Little Temple had been his entry to James's circle of friends in L.A.; he'd planted a seed, Waajeed told him, and he'd be foolish not to grow it. When Shoes told his mentor Proof that he had decided to move to California, they argued bitterly.

"You can't leave Detroit!" the mayor ordered.

Not long thereafter, on the evening of April 11, 2006, at a pool hall on 8 Mile Road, Proof got into a fight and was shot three times, once in the head and twice in the chest. The homegoing for DeShaun Holton, attended by thousands of people including Dr. Dre, Eminem, and 50 Cent, was as close to a state funeral as it got in Detroit. His death, just two months following that of his fellow Funky Cowboy J Dilla, marked the end of the city's first hip-hop era.

By July, House Shoes was living in a little apartment on Barham Boulevard in Hollywood. John Yancey arrived shortly thereafter, sleeping on Shoes's living room couch.

S tones Throw Records teetered on the brink of insolvency before James died. But the death of J Dilla just days after the release of *Donuts* earned it mentions in *The New York Times* and other publications that might have otherwise ignored the bizarre instrumental record from an independent label. With stories of James's intermittent hospitalization and reports of sampling equipment in his room, the coverage spread a dramatic creation story for the album—namely that *Donuts* had been largely composed bedside while James was being treated at Cedars-Sinai. It was a romantic narrative if not altogether true, but one that Stones Throw didn't go out of their way to refute. The record began to sell. Those sales sent a cash infusion to Stones Throw, and also to Maureen Yancey, who had essentially been James's manager on the project and who now began receiving advances on sales directly from the label at a time of great financial need.

The dozens of promotional events planned for the release in early 2006 went forward with Maureen Yancey's blessing and became impromptu celebrations of J Dilla's life, with *Donuts* as the centerpiece. But the album alienated many of James's biggest fans and closest collaborators, who felt like the frenetic, low-fidelity beats didn't sound anything like him. It was hard enough letting James go; it was harder to have James's last beat tape eclipse the body of work they knew.

Ahmir "Questlove" Thompson, however, had made peace with James's sharp musical turns and saw a clear intention in *Donuts* as he dwelled with the album in the weeks following his teacher's death. Ahmir caught the reference to John Yancey in the song "Waves"—"Johnnnny, do it!"—convinced it was deliberate because James had sampled the words "Johnny, *don't* do it" from a song by the British band 10cc and specifically removed the word "don't." Sampled lyrics like "broken and blue" and "you're gonna want me back" seemed to reference James's pain and grief; others, like "I can't stand to see you cry" and "just because I really love you," appeared directed at his family; the clever flips of phrases, like "Is dat real?" sounding just like "Is death real?"; the dramatization of his own twilight bus-stop encounter with Ol' Dirty Bastard in the song "Hi"; and the cultivation of melancholy source material like the Isley Brothers' "Don't Say Goodnight" and Motherlode's "When I Die," in which James plumbed the song's refrain: *When I die I hope to be a better man than you thought I'd be.*

Ahmir thought: *This is his goodbye letter.*

On the message boards of Okayplayer and the Stones Throw website,

Jeff Jank read theories about hidden messages in the songs, the idea that the sequence itself, starting and ending with the same track, was a meditation on the cycle of life. *Could Dilla have intended some deeper meaning?* Jank asked himself. *Sure.* Dilla had always toyed with verbal illusion and allusion in his music, like when he made the word "Clair" sound like "Players" on *Fan-Tas-Tic*. Still, Jank never detected any implicit messages while he was editing. He himself had titled the songs and sequenced the album without any meta-intention. Egon gave Jank some perspective: *Art is a process, not a product. The full dimensions of a work, even your own, aren't always apparent on the first viewing or listening. It takes other people's reactions for you to see it fully.*

The reactions to *Donuts* would be immediate, the reverberations long. Though it was not the first widely acclaimed conceptual instrumental hip-hop album, *Donuts'* influence could be felt in Onra & Quetzal's *Tribute* in 2006, would find a perch in the work of Stones Throw intern and producer Flying Lotus, and would go on to inspire much of what in later years came to be called the "lo-fi hip-hop" movement.

The irony of *Donuts'* reception as a deliberate final statement from James Dewitt Yancey is how little time he put into it in the last year of his life when compared to his other project, *The Shining*. After a burst of work together in the spring of 2005, James's hospitalizations and Karriem Riggins's tour schedule staggered the progress on the BBE album. In the fall, James's calls stopped coming. Then, in early 2006, Riggins came home to a brief voice message from James: *I want you to help me finish the album.* When James died a few days thereafter, Riggins realized that James must have given him a posthumous charge. Maureen Yancey agreed with that conclusion, as did BBE's Peter Adarkwah.

There were several mixed songs and pieces of others—jam sessions, beat snippets. Reeling himself from James's death, Riggins prayed: *How am I going to do this?* He began by reaching out to people he knew James loved: Guilty Simpson, MED, and Tarik "Black Thought" Trotter from the Roots. Common wrote verses to an extended version of the Isley Brothers–based track that had also ended up on *Donuts*. Riggins then reached D'Angelo to write and sing the chorus of the song, called "So Far to Go," and D added a gorgeous piano solo that went on for one, two, three minutes. Riggins could not bring himself to cut any of it, because he couldn't imagine that James would have either.

Karriem rounded out the album with two tracks, perfect stereo mixes that James had played for him while he was still living in Clinton Township. The first was a throwback to James's classic Fender Rhodes sound, a hypnotic instrumental on which Karriem asked Dwele to contribute vocals; they named it "Dime Piece." The other was a completely finished song, "Won't Do," that for Karriem was the epitome of what James *could* do as a producer, an engineer, an MC, a singer, and a songwriter; a snapshot of his sacred contradictions, as personal as anything on *Donuts*: a majestic, effervescent composition that was also a paean to James's highest libidinous aspiration.

Adarkwah and Karriem kept in touch with Maureen Yancey about major decisions as they finished the album, including what song they would promote as a single. Maureen queried her son John, who preferred "Won't Do" because it showcased James's singing voice. Then John Yancey fielded an unusual request from BBE: *Would he stand in for his brother in the music video?*

It would be John Yancey's first film shoot. He was nervous. In a loft space in Venice Beach, the director Mazik Saevitz took him through several wardrobe changes and setups—in front of a green screen; in a bedroom set with several beautiful young women; on the rooftop, flanked by a platoon of James's friends: Frank and Dank; Common and Talib Kweli; Karriem Riggins and Tarik; Rhettmatic and J-Rocc and House Shoes; and Will.I.Am from the rap group Black Eyed Peas. After several takes, John began to relax into his role, becoming more himself and more his brother at the same time.

In the final cut, it was easy to mistake him for James incarnate, easy to forget that James was gone at all. "Won't Do" also marked the video debut for Maureen Yancey, as she joined the cast in a bubbly, computer-generated dreamworld reminiscent of Japanese anime, gazing upward to a heaven filled with fireworks and spotlights and doves and a pastel-colored zeppelin that read: *SOMEONE YOU KNOW HAS LUPUS.*

———

H erman Hayes was touched when he heard that his nephew's final act had been to make an album called *Donuts*. That had been their connection, long ago. Now working as the food and beverage manager at the Buckhead Marriott in Atlanta, Herm decided that he wanted to do something in return. He remembered a conversation he'd had the previous year with a nice lady from the Alliance for Lupus Research, which threw its annual banquet at the hotel; he'd told her that his nephew was struggling with the disease. Herm found her card—Stephanie Chapman, the Southeastern Regional Walk Coordinator—and called her.

"My nephew died," Herm told Chapman. "I'd like to donate some money."

Instead, Chapman convinced Herm to start his own team for the upcoming September lupus walk in Atlanta. Herm had never organized or promoted anything like this before. His niece Rashonda, Reta Hayes's daughter, designed some flyers for him. Herm called his team the "Jay Walkers."

The night before the walk, Herm took himself to Atlanta's Tabernacle theater to pass out flyers prior to a show by A Tribe Called Quest, figuring he might find a receptive audience. He found more than that—a fan wearing a "Dilla Lives" T-shirt who was more than willing to help him spread the word, and an introduction to the group backstage, where he was embraced by Phife and given a VIP balcony seat. Phife announced the lupus walk from the stage, urging the crowd of more than two thousand people to show up for J Dilla.

Thirty-five people turned up the next morning, September 25, 2006, to march with the Jay Walkers. In the months thereafter, Herm and Rashonda organized and deputized Jay Walker teams in lupus fundraisers around the country, from New York to Los Angeles; from Chicago to Raleigh; and back to Detroit. These walks were often attended by James's friends like House Shoes and DJ Spinna, and members of the Yancey and Hayes families. It was the start of a new tradition that grew over the next several years and the beginning of a newfound purpose for Herman Hayes.

T he depth and scope of the mourning for J Dilla baffled Jefferson Mao, the journalist who had written the first article on Jay Dee for *Vibe* in 1996. Not long after James died, Mao was in Melbourne, Australia, for the annual Red Bull Music Academy convention, where he heard the sounds of *Donuts* spilling out of cars and cafes, J Dilla's name on the tongues of conference attendees and panelists. One woman had knitted her own J Dilla sweater. Mao had seen and covered outpourings of grief and remembrance following the deaths of the genre's most popular figures, like Tupac and the Notorious B.I.G. But he'd never seen anything like this, certainly not for a relatively obscure beat producer. *Why was this happening? And where did all these J Dilla fans come from?*

Many of the Dilla-related tributes the year following his death were impromptu acts of creation without commercial pretense: fan-painted portraits crying for him in splashes of color, songs and mixtapes shouting him out and answering his ideas, T-shirts proclaiming him, spontaneous gatherings of hip-hop fans and DJs seeking each other out to grieve and process the passing of someone whose death hit them harder than they expected. A few days after Dilla's death, Tara Duvivier and several of her comrades gathered at a small club on New York's Lower East Side. They were hip-hop nerds who met in the 1990s on the Okayplayer message boards and became real-life friends: Duvivier's username had been "T510," Derreck Johnson was "Dee Phunk," Eric Raphael was "Shinobi Shaw." Some Okayplayers had moved to New York, like Bill "Brainchild" Johnson, all the way from Kokomo, Indiana. The old friends commiserated and played records, both Dilla's and the ones he loved. Driving home, they agreed that they should make it a yearly celebration of Dilla's music on his birthday.

Thus "Donuts Are Forever" was born, which Duvivier and her partners planned for February 2007. They secured a venue, Galapagos Art Space in Brooklyn; a roster of DJs; and an appearance by the rapper Pharoahe Monch. They also wanted to use the tribute as an opportunity to raise money for Maureen Yancey, and Stones Throw Records assured the organizers that they would funnel whatever cash they raised to the woman people were now calling "Ma Dukes."

Hundreds of people lined up in the frigid February air. Some early arrivals brought dozens of donuts; Duvivier and crew handed them to the freezing fans. Inside it was warm, a packed party of people singing along to Slum Village jams like "Players" or Common's "The Light," hands in the air . . .

There are times when you need someone
I will be by your side

The first Donuts Are Forever netted only around $2,000, but its good feelings were part of a larger movement happening synchronistically around the world: in Los Angeles, in London, in Paris, in Amsterdam. February had become a time to remember James Dewitt Yancey, to dance to his music, and to reaffirm a fellowship that hip-hop lost in its climb to commercial success, a community for whom J Dilla had quickly become a patron saint.

Duvivier and her partners began planning for the following year at a bigger venue. Seeking to make their donation process more formal, they followed the lead of Herman Hayes's Jay Walkers and arranged to grant all profits to the Alliance for Lupus Research. They enlisted House Shoes and Phonte Coleman from Little Brother, among a slate of DJs and MCs. They printed flyers that read "Donuts Are Forever 2."

Then, the week before their party in February 2008—like the scrape of a needle across a record—they got a "cease and desist" letter from someone named Arthur Erk.

When his executorship of the estate of James Dewitt Yancey was approved by the Los Angeles County probate court in late 2006, Arthur Erk was charged with tallying the estate's assets and debts, and with paying off those debts before the remainder could be distributed equitably to its four heirs: Maureen Yancey, John Yancey, Ja'Mya Yancey, and Ty-Monae Whitlow.

Erk reviewed his late client's finances and saw a real problem. James had a tax debt that approached $750,000.* He had little cash, no houses to sell, no cars. James's only real asset was his production company, Pay Jay, which remained the recipient of all his royalties and owned all the copyrights to any music that had not yet been sold. In the last year of James's life, Pay Jay logged an annual income of only $13,000. Erk could not imagine that the company would make much more than that in the years to follow. Yet he was duty bound to try.

First, Erk resolved to collect and inventory all the music that had yet to be sold, and then market it. Second, he would crack down on any unauthorized uses of James's music and brand, so that the estate could maximize what little they had. To facilitate those two tasks, he hired Micheline Levine. Third, he sent the IRS a letter requesting a payment plan and permission to distribute some of the estate's income to the heirs, especially James's two dependent children. Without this explicit permission, Erk's probate court attorneys told him that he couldn't pay any money to the family. He waited for months and heard nothing from the IRS.

Meanwhile, Arty and Micheline saw the proliferation of J Dilla tributes, and viewed them not as acts of celebration or expressions of grief, but as careless infringement at best and opportunistic profiteering at worst. Even for the artists involved, the line could be blurry. DJ Spinna re-chopped a classic Dilla sample and emailed the beat to Phonte Coleman, who sang a medley of Dilla refrains over it. The resulting track, "Dillagence," circulated online. But not long thereafter, the song was pressed on a vinyl 45-rpm single. And then it appeared as the title track of an entire album-length mixtape by Busta Rhymes. Spinna knew about the 45—he saw it as a way to acknowledge Dilla while putting his own creative stamp on something cool. But he was taken aback by the Busta release; no one had asked him or acknowledged his work on the track. Phonte wasn't upset; he had recorded the track as an act of love. But the sudden surfacing of the song for sale left him feeling like

---

* According to a consultant for the estate, James Dewitt Yancey had tax liens against him for every single year of his professional career, in which time he worked with several different accountants and business managers. Though the amount due to the IRS was later revised downward toward $500,000, the debt was significant. For a man who once declared, "I don't ever want to see a bill," this was a foreseeable result. When James's final bill arrived, it was his heirs who had to pay it.

he'd been drawn into something that exploited the memory of J Dilla for commercial gain.*

For the estate, Busta Rhymes's release was one among many copyright violations. Micheline hired Jonathan Dworkin to help her track the pirates down and a litigator to fight them. But what they discovered in Busta's case, and in others—with outfits like Babygrande Records and Giant Peach merchandise—is that these would-be licensors thought they already *had* secured permission, from Maureen Yancey, and in some cases had cut checks directly to her. Even Stones Throw was bypassing the estate and sending money directly to Maureen. Micheline called Eothen "Egon" Alapatt and ordered him to stop.

Maureen is the person who we've been dealing with all along, even when James was alive, Egon explained. *Nobody ever told us to do anything different.*

I'm telling you now, Micheline said. *James has debts that need to be paid and he has three other heirs. You have to pay the estate.*

Egon knew that Stones Throw's money had been a lifeline for Maureen. So thereafter he suggested something outrageous to his partner Peanut Butter Wolf: *Pay double. Pay the estate and Maureen. It's what Dilla would want.* Thus began a clash of wills: the letter of James's legal will against what his mother and her allies believed James's actual will might be.

Maureen believed that James wanted her to continue to help his friends, and to give his gift back to the world. She started the J Dilla Foundation with the help of Karriem Riggins's manager Jae Barber. When people contacted her to arrange tribute events and donate money, she approved and accepted them. When James's friends like Busta Rhymes, who had supported her son in health and in sickness, asked for her permission to use the tracks that James had given them, she gave it. As far as Maureen knew, none of these folks were getting the time of day from the estate, who didn't seem to be initiating many deals. All she heard about were lawsuits and cease and desist orders, and the estate never

---

* Phonte Coleman's tribute to J Dilla would instead be through his own music with Little Brother, and also with the Foreign Exchange, who were nominated for a Grammy Award in 2009.

contacted her unless they were telling her to stop doing things, like when they asked her to take her foundation website down.* To Maureen, Arty and Micheline simply didn't have a clue about the true value of what they held, nor how to do business on Dilla's behalf.

She had worked unofficially for James for years, and in the wake of his death the estate had actively sought to choke off every bit of income that had been coming to her. She knew there was money coming in to the estate. *Where was it all going?* The breaking point for Maureen came when she began dealing squarely with her own health issues. Not long after her return to Detroit, she suffered a heart attack, and received her own lupus diagnosis. She received expensive infusions of chemotherapy for rheumatoid arthritis. She phoned Arty Erk to see if he could help her with the cost of medication. Erk told her that he couldn't, chiding her for expecting a "windfall" from her son's denuded estate. Then he suggested that she apply for aid from the State of Michigan. Livid, Maureen called her old ally, Micheline Levine. *Arty just told me to get on welfare! He never would have said that if I were the white mother of a white client!*

Arty shouldn't have said that, Micheline said. But there was now a limit to Micheline's sympathies. She had been the one to urge Maureen to have James sign a will so that her son could ensure she wouldn't end up with nothing. But Micheline also knew that Arthur Erk, under court order, couldn't just look the other way while Maureen took money in her son's name, because there were other heirs. The way Micheline saw it, Maureen just didn't want to hear that every time she took a check for something Dilla-related, she was taking money from her grandchildren. But that wasn't exactly true: without IRS permission to disburse funds to the family, the only money that the estate could legitimately spend was on taxes, and the fees for the lawyers and accountants who kept it running.

For the estate's main job, Micheline reached out on the recommendation of Jonathan Dworkin and Q-Tip to Egon Alapatt to help the estate collect and inventory James's music. Egon had the knowledge to find the

---

* Micheline Levine says that the estate had several serious concerns about the foundation: It was trading on J Dilla's name and likeness without their knowledge or permission. It called itself a foundation but had no tax-exempt status. It was selling J Dilla merchandise, and they were hearing reports of customers complaining about orders not being fulfilled. And the estate had no clarity in what the foundation was doing with its proceeds.

material, the expertise to convert the various discs into usable masters, and the contacts to market them. With Maureen's blessing, Egon accepted the gig as a consultant. But Egon was not prepared for the difficulty of the task of finding all of James's music, and the work took him much longer than expected. And, as he worked, Egon became hesitant about what he had agreed to do, fearful that the estate was going to take J Dilla's music and quickly sell off the masters to the highest bidder, without regard for creative considerations or his legacy, leaving the heirs without their best properties. In Micheline's thinking, that was *exactly* what her fiduciary duty compelled her to do: start a bidding war and get the best deal possible so that the taxes could get paid and the heirs could start seeing money. Several of the dates that Egon set for delivery came and went, making it impossible for Arty to deliver the required inventory to the court. Arty and Micheline began to feel like Egon was playing them. A few days before Egon was due to deliver the inventory and masters on February 1, 2008, Micheline fired him without explanation, sent him a check, and demanded he turn over his work.

Egon had already decided he wasn't just giving James's gems to these people. He was convinced that Stones Throw understood J Dilla's music better than any other entity, and that he had to save as much of it as possible from the same corporate oblivion James himself had experienced with MCA. James had asked Egon, in the hospital, to recover that MCA album, and release an expanded *Ruff Draft*. So Egon proposed a compromise that he thought would be best for Dilla's music and best for the heirs: *Let Stones Throw release two of the albums and donate the royalties directly to the family*. Micheline saw the proposal in exactly the opposite way: as an ultimatum to withhold Dilla's crown jewels unless the estate agreed to give them to the small, independent label that their consultant worked for; a situation that, in her view, screwed the family out of the hundreds of thousands of dollars in advances that Micheline believed she could get for a major deal. Furious, Micheline refused, and Egon turned over the masters in the condition he received them, with no decoding and no inventory, and didn't cash the check. The estate then sued Egon to compel him to deliver what he had originally promised.

It was around this time, amid another February awash with unauthorized Dilla tributes and parties and merchandise and fundraising events, that Tara Duvivier of Donuts Are Forever found herself on the phone with Erk and Dworkin, who issued a demand: *Give us the money or cancel your party.*

Duvivier refused. They were donating the money to a legitimate nonprofit. Erk wasn't satisfied. *If you go ahead with the party, we'll send people to audit your books.*

Duvivier thought the threat was ridiculous. She asked DJ House Shoes what he thought. *Fuck them*, he said. Shoes knew that the estate wasn't giving any money to the family. Donuts Are Forever 2 went ahead as planned. It was packed. The profits went to the lupus charity. The auditors never came.

The confrontation revealed the siege mentality and desperation of the professionals who ran the estate: they saw Maureen Yancey running her own operation, representing herself as the authority, taking checks; and whatever she was doing with the proceeds, they weren't paying down Dilla's debt, nor were they being funneled to all the heirs James had named. Other family members, too, were raising money for charities using Dilla's name. They saw employees of Stones Throw conspiring with Maureen to bypass the estate. They discovered record albums in the works—with titles like *Jay Stay Paid* and *Jay Love Japan*—for which they had no paperwork. So, in March 2008, Arthur Erk ran a full-page advertisement in *Billboard*. The text—beneath one of Brian Cross's photos of J Dilla, ironically unlicensed—read in part:

Since his passing, there has been an unimaginable amount of unauthorized use of Dilla material. The beneficiaries of the Estate include Dilla's 2 toddler children Ja'Mya and Ty-Monae. When you circumvent the Estate, you deny Dilla's children their rightful inheritance.[*]

Referencing "foundations" and "walk-a-thons" in the fine print, the ad publicly pitted the estate of James Dewitt Yancey against two family members of James Dewitt Yancey.

---

[*] The text continued: THE ONLY PERSON LEGALLY AUTHORIZED TO EXECUTE TRANSACTIONS OR MAKE ANY DECISIONS WHATSOEVER REGARDING THE COMMERCIAL USE OF DILLA'S NAME, MUSIC, MERCHANDISE, PHOTOGRAPHS, VIDEO APPEARANCES, ARTWORK, ETC., IS THE EXECUTOR OF J DILLA'S ESTATE, ARTHUR ERK. NO OTHER PERSON, INCLUDING FRIENDS OR FAMILY MEMBERS OF DILLA'S ARE ENTITLED TO DO SO.

Egon secured himself a lawyer, and he and Madlib pooled $8,000 to retain an attorney for Maureen, urging her to assert her rights in court as an heir to compel Erk to deliver some kind of accounting for the inner workings of the estate.

One of the few posthumous musical projects approved by the estate was secured with a check from Mike Ross of Delicious Vinyl, who still had more than a dozen unused beats from James's work with the Pharcyde and the Brand New Heavies in the mid-1990s. With Maureen's blessing, Ross planned a compilation album featuring different MCs rocking over a dozen Jay Dee tracks. And he wanted one of those people to be John Yancey. John had moved to Hollywood, just around the corner from him, to start a rap career. He and Ross became friendly, not in the least because John was a gentle, quiet kid like the older brother whom he so remarkably favored.

On what would have been James's thirty-fourth birthday, Ross arranged for John to perform at a celebration at L.A.'s Club 86. After John got offstage, Ross took him aside:

"Why don't you just do the whole album?"

Shortly thereafter, John Yancey—as Illa J—began work on a collaboration of fourteen songs with his brother, who was around John's age when he made the beats. He'd call it *Yancey Boys*. The cover featured a tight photo of John's face; the glimmer in his eye revealing itself to be a tiny image of James. On the album, Frank Bush introduces John to the world as a member of the Yancey clan, that alien family of unearthly talents: "Like they the Jackson 5, from Mars." In the accompanying videos, James's brother is again surrounded by James's brothers: Dave New York and House Shoes, Frank and Guilty Simpson, Rhettmatic and J-Rocc, with Maureen as the den mother. Their hands are on John, an anointment.

Not everyone thought the album was a good idea. When John first arrived in L.A. and stayed with House Shoes, the DJ preached the importance of John being careful to establish his own identity outside his brother's long shadow. When John presented Shoes with the CD as a fait accompli, the DJ saw yet another problem.

"John, these beats are all fucked up," he said. He'd heard these same tracks back in the 1990s and was convinced that these were remarkably slower than James intended them to be. But the album was, alas, complete; and in any case John was listening to other, more encouraging voices.

When *Yancey Boys* debuted in late 2008, for nearly everyone but House Shoes, the beats were a crystal clear time capsule of Jay Dee's classic sound. But Shoes was right to worry about the posthumous collaboration, because for many J Dilla fans there was only one Yancey boy worth their attention. Some music critics sniffed at John's contributions to the album—*HipHopDX* claimed he showed "potential"—while others savaged him. Tom Breihan, in a review for *Pitchfork*, wrote that "his familial connection to a great dead producer appears to be Illa's chief qualification to release an album," comparing his voice to "a seriously stoned and vaguely bored Q-Tip."

The reception deflated John. He understood where folks were coming from: *Here's an album of beats from the best producer ever with someone they don't know rhyming over them.* They all figured he was riding his brother's coattails. He wished they understood: *These beats were given to me; I didn't ask for them. I was producing before this. The whole family is talented.*

But they didn't understand. And John was sure that he'd failed.

John Yancey joined his mother's lawsuit to replace Erk as executor of James's estate, as did Monica Whitlow. Joylette Hunter, representing Ja'Mya, retained her own counsel. She didn't trust anyone at this point, especially Maureen who, Joy observed, seemingly approved the solicitation of donations for herself in James's funeral program but ensured no such plea for James's children.* And when Joy's lawyer argued for a monthly allowance for Ja'Mya from the court, he found that Maureen

---

* Joylette Hunter claims that when she inquired about the existence of a will shortly after James's death, Maureen Yancey told her there wasn't one. Maureen rejects this claim, saying she never had a conversation about the will with Joylette. Frank Bush recalls that when he arrived in California for the memorial, the talk was that not only had Joylette called Maureen about the will, but it was the first thing she asked about. Joylette maintains that her first question to Maureen was about plans for the funeral.

Yancey had received almost $10,000 from Arty before the estate went into probate; while Ja'Mya, via Joylette, received only $800. Joy was so furious that she couldn't breathe.*

After the estate's *Billboard* ad, Maureen had gone public with her struggle against its executor, giving interviews to Jeff Weiss at the *LA Weekly*, and to Kelley Louise Carter, a former high school classmate of House Shoes's who'd done the first extensive interview with "Ma Dukes" for the *Detroit Free Press* in the wake of James's death; and now she wrote a multipage feature on the heirs' troubles for *Vibe* magazine. Tellingly, the piece gave J Dilla more ink than he had ever seen in his lifetime.

By the time that the article, "Dollars to Donuts," hit newsstands in January 2008, events had veered in the heirs' favor. Maureen's attorney discovered that Erk had paid his firm and his lawyers around $150,000 since the beginning of their administration of the estate, declaring it "plunder" in his petition to have Erk removed as executor. And though many of these fees were governed by statute and not exorbitant in the broader context of legal work, the implication was that Erk's confrontational policies had essentially turned Pay Jay into a self-fulfilling litigation machine, a company whose main business was suing artists and other potential partners rather than doing deals with them, and whose proceeds in turn funded more lawsuits instead of the family. Erk countered that the actions of Maureen Yancey and Eothen Alapatt had prompted much of that expense while devaluing the estate. But in a hearing on February 9, 2009, Erk offered his resignation. Micheline Levine—second in line as executor of James Yancey's will—resigned as well. They'd both been exhausted by three years of fighting the beneficiaries they had been trying to protect. Erk's final accounting showed that he had vastly underestimated the potential of Pay Jay, which had earned seven times more per year than he initially projected, nearly $600,000 during his tenure. But of the $400,000 he spent, 3 percent went to the family, 32 percent went to the IRS, and the rest—65 percent—went to

---

* It should be noted that in her filing, Joylette Hunter suggested that James's eldest daughter might also be entitled to a similar allowance; and that Arthur Erk filed a brief in support of an allowance for both children. This allowance was not paid for nine years, until Joylette Hunter reached a settlement with the estate in 2017, when Ja'Mya was sixteen years old.

fees for accountants, lawyers, consultants, managers, and other professionals and their expenses.

In the aftermath of Erk and Levine's exit, the lawyers for the heirs—
Maureen, John, and Monica on one side, Joy on the other—deliberated
over a new administrator for the estate. They collectively nominated the
attorney Alex Borden, and also agreed that Eothen Alapatt should be
rehired as the estate's creative director, with the notion that the estate
would have a more constructive and less contentious relationship with
its beneficiaries and the larger community of J Dilla fans.

Two weeks after Maureen Yancey won her battle to change the leadership of her son's estate, she and James were celebrated in an extraordinary musical event that would have been inconceivable to either
of them while he was alive. On February 22, 2009, the composer, con-
ductor, and violinist Miguel Atwood-Ferguson convened a sixty-piece
orchestra in front of an audience to perform a series of compositions
based on the music of James Dewitt Yancey.

Like many fans of Dilla's music, Miguel didn't know some of his favorite records were made by the producer until he was schooled in 2004
by a friend, the L.A. journalist, radio host, and record producer Carlos
Niño. Together they schemed to approach Dilla about Miguel orchestrat-
ing an album's worth of his beats. James died before Carlos had a chance to
reach out. Miguel and Carlos vowed to move forward with a posthumous
tribute to the producer. Miguel would take one song, Common's "Nag
Champa," and do an orchestral arrangement around it in the same tempo,
so that if both recordings were played at the same time, they'd line up perfectly. The resulting piece would play well as a stand-alone composition
or as an accompaniment to the original song. They recorded the work in
Carlos's living room and posted their "cosmic conversation" with J Dilla
online for his birthday in 2007. They didn't expect the emotional response
the work elicited from fans and friends; Ahmir "Questlove" Thompson
emailed Carlos to tell him that the piece had brought him to tears.

Brian Cross and Eric Coleman were moved by the "Nag Champa"
arrangement, too, and jumped at an offer from Miguel and Carlos to

release an EP of several more Dilla orchestrations through their production company, Mochilla. But they faced a real obstacle: a record released for sale would require legal clearances for the use of J Dilla's name and likeness, which were controlled by the estate of James Yancey. Everyone close to Maureen knew that she and the estate had a tense relationship, and that neither she nor the other beneficiaries would see money from any deal until the tax bill was paid. So Cross and Coleman proposed a title for the project that avoided the clearance issue altogether, and would at the same time allow them to donate their profits directly to J Dilla's heirs. The name was a double entendre, referring to the sweet feelings and protectiveness that Dilla's friends had developed for Maureen, and to the collection of pieces made for her benefit: *Suite for Ma Dukes*.

While they planned the record, Tom Bacon—the hip-hop-friendly executive at VTech—offered Mochilla funding to stage and film a live concert of the Suite. The event would require Miguel Atwood-Ferguson to expand it, composing and rehearsing more than a dozen new interpretations of Dilla beats in less than three months. Miguel began by listening to every single recording of J Dilla's that he could get his hands on, and then pared that oeuvre down to its best contenders. He sat at his keyboard, sometimes twenty hours a day, working out the score. His method for many of the pieces was to establish Dilla's original harmonies, the "O.G." version, and then take it a bunch of different places from there. His mind fraying from lack of sleep, Miguel meditated and found solace in his computer's screen saver, into which he had loaded 150 separate photographs of people who inspired him. Only ten of those photos were of James. But every time he felt a moment of self-doubt, he'd look up and see J Dilla. Like James was saying: *Keep on going*.

Brian Cross fretted about expenses—the project was already $5,000 over budget and they still had to rent a large glockenspiel for an additional $1,000—but he, Eric, and Carlos tried to support Miguel during his process, as did Karriem Riggins, who had been enlisted to play the drum kit behind the orchestra.

"You can't ever be Dilla," Riggins told him, speaking from experience. "Just be you."

The moment of truth came during the first run-throughs in a large rehearsal space in Los Angeles, filled with scores of musicians hand-picked by Miguel, attended by the producers and by Ma Dukes herself. Miguel Atwood-Ferguson picked up his baton and raised his hand.

After the funeral, many of James's friends and family busied themselves so as not to grieve. Many didn't realize what they were still carrying. But when Miguel's orchestra fired up, something tore loose. Cross was overcome with emotion. He looked for Maureen. He found her outside, steadying herself. "He's here," she told him.

T he musicians wore white.

Miguel Atwood-Ferguson regaled them backstage as J-Rocc and House Shoes warmed up the crowd of more than a thousand people at the Luckman Fine Arts Complex on the campus of California State University, Los Angeles.

"Many of you did not even know who Dilla was when I called you to play in this orchestra," he said. "You have totally given your whole life and heart and intimate self to celebrate this, and I can't thank you enough."

Miguel had divided the Suite in two—the first half without drums, instead centering on the colors of several J Dilla sample sources and tracks, like "Morning Order," which provided the melody for Common's "Nag Champa." The opening strains of Slum Village's "Untitled" brought forth a roar of recognition from the crowd, but Cross observed that the Suite was losing some people. During the intermission, he caught a few friends preparing to leave the auditorium.

Stay, he begged them. *The drums are coming.*

Karriem Riggins opened the second act, rumbling through the intro to *Welcome 2 Detroit*, the album on which he received his first producer credit. Carlos Niño told the crowd: "Ma Dukes told us earlier that J Dilla used to play the cello." And now Miguel reentered from the wings holding the instrument aloft like a holy sacrament, laying it against an empty chair.

Now Atwood-Ferguson reversed the flow of his compositions, beginning with his unfamiliar variation and working toward the familiar,

Bill Evans's version of "Are You All the Things" suddenly resolving into the Slum Village song that sampled it, "Jealousy," Miguel gesticulating maniacally beneath a halo of curly blond hair. At the end of the fourth measure, Miguel pulled his hands back and the entire sixty-piece orchestra stopped dead for a beat—complete silence—and then resumed.

The crowd exploded, hooting and whistling, realizing that Atwood-Ferguson and his orchestra had just replicated the "board mute" from the original Slum record: a split second where James switched off all the music underneath the vocals for rhythmic effect. This kind of DJ trick was typical in hip-hop, but not something that traditional musicians did. Yet here was the classical symphony orchestra, perhaps for the first time in history, talking back to the DJ.

The conversation continued. Violinists and horn players, some in sneakers and baseball caps, bobbed their heads as Riggins and the bass player Steven "Thundercat" Bruner drove the rhythm. Dwele and Bilal took turns singing over orchestral versions of their songs, "Angel" and "Reminisce." For the finale, Miguel saved two evocative tunes. The performance of De La Soul's "Stakes Is High" caused a cascade of reactions—the crowd's first recognition of the melody; the strings swelling; the beat crashing in; and then, from the wings, Posdnuos of De La Soul and Talib Kweli entering to perform the verses. The audience leaped to their feet as the MCs chanted: *Love! Vibration!* The stage filled with James's friends and family, many of them tearful. They passed a microphone around. There, amid the throng, stood Amp Fiddler, singing for his fallen protégé. For an encore, the orchestra played Slum Village's "Fall in Love," sung by the crowd almost like a national anthem, with John Yancey singing his brother's refrain.

Tom Bacon, in the front row with Maureen Yancey, coaxed her to take the stage and speak to the audience. In these final minutes, Coleman's camera captured Maureen: five decades after she attended her first symphony at Detroit's Ford Auditorium, now at a symphony created in her name; white pantsuit, hair perfectly coiffed, looking younger than she had in years; strolling to the apron, holding the microphone toward audience members, mother to everyone; then, head turned, her attention caught by something to her left side.

The final edit of the film would cut to the object of her gaze: the empty chair, cello lying against it.

B aatin continued his battle with mental illness and addiction in the years after James's death, drifting out and back into the Slum Village fold as his condition fluctuated. On the way to a gig at the Rock the Bells festival in New York in the summer of 2009, Baatin broke down, pledging to his bandmates to do everything he could to stay in recovery. In early August, Baatin had a problem making it through immigration en route to a gig in Toronto, so he remained in Detroit as T3 and Elzhi performed. While Slum were in Canada, Tim Maynor called them with the news: Baatin had been found by an associate of theirs dead on the front lawn of a drug house, likely dragged outside after an overdose. Titus "Baatin" Glover was thirty-five years old.

Around the time of Baatin's death, Beverly Dewitt Yancey began showing signs of dementia: leaving for an errand, staying out for hours, and returning having forgotten the reason for his excursion. After he totaled his car on 7 Mile Road, Dewitt's condition worsened. Maureen checked him into Henry Ford Hospital where doctors concluded that he had suffered a series of ministrokes. He began having cardiopulmonary and kidney problems; and when he was stabilized, Maureen put her husband in a long-term care facility.

Maureen was ambivalent about Dewitt's decline. Their marriage had been chilly. But he had been the best father to his children. Maureen met Dewitt's decline by fighting the doctors, facilities, and insurance companies for the best care possible; she had plenty of experience now. The end came after Dewitt required a tracheotomy. Maureen observed: for a man who'd lived to run his mouth, whether to tell dirty jokes or sing, it was a spiritual death. The body hung on until September 2012, when Dewitt joined his son in the ether.

E arlier that year, on the evening of February 10, 2012, thousands of pilgrims from all over the country converged on Detroit in the midst of a blizzard. A long line snaked from the side streets around the corner to Woodward and up toward the 2,100-seat Fillmore auditorium, beneath a marquee that read DILLA DAY DETROIT | HOMETOWN HERO FROM CONANT GARDENS.

For six years, New York and Los Angeles, London and Paris had all hosted regular celebrations of J Dilla. Now Detroit boasted its own world-class event, the largest ever. Inside, Dilla Day Detroit was packed and joyous. Amp Fiddler offered a benediction from the stage, his hand raised, palm toward the audience: "All blessings to the spirit of J Dilla in the house tonight." Despite the absence of the scheduled headliners—Busta Rhymes, Phife, and Jay Electronica—the crowd enjoyed performances by the rapper Danny Brown, the Nick Speed Orchestra, and by J Dilla's core group of collaborators including Que.D, Phat Kat, Guilty Simpson, and Slum Village—now featuring a new member. John "Illa J" Yancey had been following his brother's footsteps since he left Mount Pleasant. Now he took James's place in his former group, sharing the stage and trading lines with T3 in the same way James once had. James's friends and family voiced a mixture of wonder, disbelief, and pride that their city had turned out for him in death in a way it had never quite shown up for him in life. "I know if he were here," Phat Kat told the audience, "he would be tripping."

This landmark event would not have happened without Maureen Yancey, who since her son's death had cultivated a new vocation, traveling the world furthering his legacy. Her tireless work, her gentle demeanor, and her story—caring for James in sickness, mourning his death, and battling his estate in its aftermath—had elicited from his legions of fans and friends something akin to a beatification. She had a public persona: "Ma Dukes," the mother of his followers' burgeoning faith. Thus they cheered the news that the estate's new leadership had her blessing. But, for most people, it did not matter what the estate was, or who was running it. "Estate" is abstract. "Mother" is not. *If Mother is okay, we are okay.*

The glitch in this public ordination was that it wasn't actually ordained by the will of James Dewitt Yancey. There were, under law, still four people who needed to be okay with things, who had the equal right to determine and benefit from the legacy of J Dilla. Maureen Yancey was only one of those four people.

The other three heirs could not fill Maureen's public role. John Yancey was creating a music career. The mothers of James's daughters, Joylette Hunter and Monica Whitlow, were raising school-age children; they had no relationship with Dilla fans, and had never been a part of his public narrative. Maureen was the storyteller, the witness to his life, the one whom his friends knew and trusted. She was not only fit to do the work, she was adept at it. Of that, there was no dispute.

But conflicts arose again in part because Maureen Yancey largely worked outside the structure of the estate, the entity established by the court to administer the collective will of the four heirs. Dilla Day Detroit was promoted by two organizations founded by Maureen in the wake of the estate's leadership change: the revived J Dilla Foundation, a nonprofit that opened a seemingly legitimate way for fans and friends to determine whether tributes and events were doing the right thing with the money they raised in Dilla's name; and the Yancey Media Group, a for-profit company for her own creative projects, but inexorably tied to her late son's music. In contrast to the previous regime, the estate's new leaders—Alex Borden, Egon Alapatt, and attorney Sheila Bowers—actually supported Maureen's idea for a foundation, and decided on principle that they would grant Maureen's charity the right to use her son's name and likeness for live events, and to sell merchandise at them. It was partly an act of empathy: they knew that connecting with people who loved James was a means for Maureen to work through her grief. And it was also realpolitik, a sanctioned carve-out: a way for "Ma Dukes" to take a degree of independence, agency, and even income, which they assumed would be shared with the other heirs, especially since the estate couldn't give anyone money until the tax bill was paid. But the Yancey Media Group, which emerged a couple of years later, was something different: a company set up in direct competition with the estate's media company, Pay Jay, selling material that was legally owned by Pay Jay. The Yancey Media Group had no accountability for the funds they raised to the estate or the other

heirs, including his two children, still under the care of their mothers—
one of whom, Joylette Hunter, had longstanding issues of trust with
Maureen, something that the estate's second regime didn't at first grasp.

Whether sanctioned or unsanctioned, the mere existence of these
two independent organizations created confusion about the legitimacy
of the estate. And the way the J Dilla Foundation and the Yancey Media
Group managed their affairs caused a drama that continued to pull the
story away from J Dilla's music, and drove or scared away many people
who wanted to participate in its promotion.

Maureen Yancey revived the J Dilla Foundation in 2009 with a con-
ciliatory gesture: she invited Joylette Hunter to be her partner. Joylette
accepted, hoping their relationship might turn a corner, and wanting,
like Maureen, to do good things in James's name. To run the foundation, Maureen enlisted the help of a woman she had only recently met,
not because she had experience at a nonprofit, but because she felt close
to home: Kindra Parker, godsister and childhood chum of Dwele, and
friend to House Shoes. Kindra studied the regulations, drafted the documents, and secured tax-exempt status for the J Dilla Foundation.

But almost immediately, Kindra realized she was in a toxic dynamic
between Maureen and Joylette, and became troubled by Maureen's behavior around money. Kindra secured a $50,000 donation from Tom Ba-
con at VTech, the same executive who had funded *Suite for Ma Dukes*,
only to have Bacon withdraw the offer, spooked after Maureen told him
not to give Kindra the funds. When Kindra confronted Maureen about
it, Maureen professed cluelessness.* After a few more disputes about the
use of money and resources, Kindra became concerned that foundation
funds were being used for personal purposes, transactions that could
jeopardize their tax-exempt status. Tiring of Joylette's pushiness and convinced that Maureen was not being forthright with her, Kindra resigned.
She hadn't lasted a year at the foundation she founded. Joylette withdrew
later, after an event in New York for which there weren't enough funds in
the foundation's accounts to cover their commitments; Joylette blamed

---

* There are a tangle of conflicting stories about this incident. Tom Bacon, who suggested the amount of the
donation to Kindra after she initially asked for much less, says that when he called Maureen Yancey, he got
the sense that she was having some misgivings about Kindra, the details of which Maureen did not articulate

Maureen, Maureen blamed Joylette. The foundation's tax-exempt status would be revoked in 2012 after it failed to file a tax return for three consecutive years. But the foundation's continued solicitation of donations under those circumstances would damage its reputation in the years to come, with events like Donuts Are Forever refusing to deal with it. Maureen Yancey subsequently withheld her support from the annual party.

As with the foundation, Maureen Yancey chose someone she had only recently met to run her Yancey Media Group. Jonathon "JT" Taylor had never worked at a music or media company. He was a union executive who had clawed his way up from an hourly-wage job on the Ford line after his drug rehab business imploded in the 1990s. His sole connection to J Dilla had come through his unlikely friendship with the much younger DJ House Shoes; Taylor had taken Shoes as his housemate in the 1990s and funded Shoes's first record, a compilation of unreleased Jay Dee remixes. Introduced in 2011 to Maureen by Shoes's and James's comrade Beej Brooks, Taylor saw an opportunity to do work that had gravitas, to assume the role of protector for J Dilla's legacy and, soon, for "Mrs. Yancey" herself. He took a buyout at Ford and put his own money into the business. In addition to the Dilla Day Detroit event and several sequels in the years to follow, Maureen and Jonathon Taylor produced record albums—a compilation called *Rebirth of Detroit*, pairing established and fledgling local MCs with unreleased J Dilla beats; and a series of collections of raw J Dilla demos—cassette tapes unearthed along with James's record library from a local storage unit by the owner of a record shop, who then donated the contents to Maureen.*

---

to him. Maureen recalls that she was concerned that Kindra had solicited a large sum of money from Tom Bacon without telling her. Kindra Parker says that Maureen had to know she was soliciting donations because it was Maureen herself who had provided Bacon's information for this very purpose. Maureen also says that there were people close to her telling her not to trust Kindra's motivations.

* Jeff Bubeck, the owner of UHF Records, emailed Maureen Yancey when he realized that the records and tapes were part of J Dilla's collection, but he didn't hear back from her immediately and proceeded to put the records on sale with special "J Dilla" labels. Many Detroit DJs and friends of Dilla's were outraged when they found out—Aaron Halface called Questlove and urged him to buy the collection whole in order to save it. The sell-off became a local and then a national news story. Bubeck was approached by a "lawyer from California" (likely Sheila Bowers from the estate) claiming possession of both the record collection and the original music, and soon by Maureen Yancey and Jonathon Taylor. Ultimately, Bubeck did what he had originally intended to do: he donated the original music to Maureen; gifted her the most valuable-looking records from the collection, like test-pressings; and made the rest available to her for an internet auction, a portion of the proceeds going to cover the $6,000 he paid to buy the contents of the storage locker and to the record store for covering the fulfillment costs.

But the Yancey Media Group's projects were controversial among
Dilla fans. The top three headliners didn't show up to the first Dilla Day
Detroit because they hadn't actually been booked. The release of the
twenty-one-track *Rebirth of Detroit* album later that year was greeted
with derision. "A piñata that has finally been bashed open, only to find
three pieces of the good candy," wrote Ryan Staskel of the website *Consequence of Sound*. The verdict was much the same on the product culled
from the trove of materials unearthed from storage, with names like *The
Lost Scrolls, Vol. 1*, striking many J Dilla fans as a scattershot blot on his
creative legacy. Jesse Fairfax, a writer for the website *HipHopDX*, wrote
in 2013 that the Yancey Media Group was "seen by some to be scrap-
ing the bins to cash in on the already exhausted trend of posthumous
merchandise." A similar scorn greeted the announcement that Maureen
Yancey would be selling off her son's record collection, item by item,
on the internet auction site eBay, each with a certificate of authenticity,
signed by Maureen as "Official Ma Dukes."

But these were all debatable aesthetic questions. The more problem-
atic product of the Yancey Media Group, like that of the J Dilla Foundation, was a trail of burned relationships. An activist, Piper Carter, had
promoted an annual Dilla Youth Day for several years, bringing electronic music education to Detroit children, and had grown it in size until she got a commitment from the Charles Wright Museum of African
American History to host it. Carter thought she had Maureen's blessing;
Taylor was doing Maureen's bidding when he intervened and pushed her
out; the squabbling struck the exasperated museum administrator, Drake
Phifer, as unprofessional. Jocelyne Ninneman had created the very first
Dilla youth event and served in some capacity for every iteration of Maureen's efforts since Dilla's death. She believed that Jonathon Taylor was
trying to do the right thing in creating a for-profit company that could
raise the money to resolve the foundation's tax issues and put Maureen
on solid financial footing. But the chaos and a creeping feeling that the
foundation had strayed from its stated purpose soon drove Ninneman
away. Taylor sparred with one of James's oldest friends when Waajeed
posted a series of elegant black-and-white videos on the internet, each
featuring a deconstruction of a different Dilla beat. But the most public

rupture was with DJ House Shoes, who had been since James's death one of the staunchest allies of "Ma Dukes," whether policing promoters of J Dilla parties to make sure they donated money directly to her, or battling pirates of Dilla material on the message boards of Okayplayer.

It started at the kickoff gathering for *Rebirth of Detroit* in 2011, when one of House Shoes's oldest friends, Orlando "V-Stylez" Vesey, questioned why Jonathon Taylor was involved, but not Shoes—the man who had introduced Taylor to Dilla and the most dedicated collector of Dilla beats. The answer Vesey got from Maureen Yancey stunned him: *House Shoes has been using his DJ gigs to enrich himself in my son's name and has never given me any money.* Vesey wondered if Mrs. Yancey was having problems with her memory: he had *seen* House Shoes give money to her on several occasions. Vesey knew that Shoes's strident positioning of himself as a guardian of J Dilla's legacy often took on a righteous intensity that veered into self-righteousness. *But theft?* Vesey thought. *That's not Mike.*

House Shoes was knocked sideways by the news when Vesey told him, and knocked back when his old housemate JT then phoned to *request* his help in locating unused Dilla beats. *I'm about to be a millionaire off of this shit and you need to come over here and be a millionaire with me too.* It gave Shoes whiplash: accused of being a mercenary, then pitched in mercenary terms on behalf of his accuser by a man who had never been much interested in Dilla when they lived together. Though Shoes had no idea about the genesis of Maureen's accusations—and though Taylor denied Shoes's demand to select the beats and the MCs for the project—he sent Taylor a folder of pristine Dilla beats anyway, if only to help the album be better than it could have been without them, and he personally vouched for Taylor with Vesey, Phat Kat, and others who queried him about the projects.* But when *Rebirth* landed, despite being

---

* Maureen Yancey and Jonathon Taylor each maintain that they had no problem with House Shoes prior to the *Rebirth* project. But Taylor says that Maureen at their first meeting ordered him to "get House Shoes out of my family business"; he says he did not believe that Shoes had done anything wrong, and wanted him involved. Maureen denies she had any issue with the DJ before his back-and-forth with Taylor. After speaking to many of the people involved, this reporter has not found any evidence nor confirmed any specific stories that House Shoes took more than his fair share of fees from his DJ gigs or, in another allegation, "sold" Dilla beats to people. My own sense is that the accusations about DJ House Shoes are the result of a virtual game of "telephone" in which jealousies about House Shoes's perennial presence and offense at his high-handed

thanked in the credits as a "moral compass" and having a song named after him, House Shoes was mortified to be associated with the project, convinced that J Dilla would have never worked with half of the people on the record, that the album itself sounded like a mediocre mixtape and looked like shit. On social media, he laid the blame at Jonathon Taylor's feet.

"You are a laughingstock," Shoes wrote. "None of the cats that actually fucked with Jay want anything to do with you . . . I will FOREVER be the ambassador because of the quality work I have put in for Dilla and the City of Detroit for 20 YEARS . . . You failed Dilla, Ma Dukes, and Detroit. I have never failed any of the 3."

Some of Shoes's friends on the project—like Phat Kat and Killa Ghanz—were taken aback by the DJ's vitriol. In private texts and on social media, they either appealed to Shoes's sense of loyalty or pegged him as a jealous fool. Jonathon Taylor rubbed Phat Kat the wrong way on their very first phone call, and Kat certainly didn't agree with a lot of the decisions made about the project. But he accepted them, and advised Shoes that he needed to swallow his pride, because it was Mrs. Yancey's project and everything was up to her.

But now, even though Shoes had fought blindly for Maureen Yancey as a beneficiary of her son's legacy, he began to cast aspersions on her ability to administer it: "My mother knows I make music, but she don't know a damn thing else besides that," he told *HipHopDX*, the website that had become the main venue for the controversy. "I don't want her in charge of any of that shit, I want all my boys who I fucked with on a regular basis and my core circle to be in charge."

Even before the conflict, some of Shoes's friends, like DJ Tony Tone, tried to nudge him gently away from Dilla affairs, seeing his genuine love and grief metastasizing into something toxic for him. Now Phat Kat rang the alarm: "That's his mother. Shut the fuck up."

But Michael "House Shoes" Buchanan had put himself on a collision

---

manner became suspicions about his motivations and actions. Those suspicions became rumor, and rumor became accepted truth. Those accusations often conflated *collecting* Dilla beats with *owning* Dilla beats; *sending* people Dilla beats with *selling* people Dilla beats; and getting paid to work *while* raising money for a cause with getting paid to work *from* money raised for a cause.

course with Maureen Yancey since James's death, because the way Shoes and Maureen each carried J Dilla as their life's work had brought them to stake out similar posthumous territory: to be the person empowered to make decisions about James's music. Shoes had expertise about Dilla's body of work, but scant moral and zero legal authority to wield it. The more he sniped from the sidelines, the less of it he had. But even being mother, manager, and heir to James, the irony was that Maureen's moral and legal standing, too, was insufficient when it came to J Dilla's music.

The people with that legal authority worked for the estate. Eothen "Egon" Alapatt had once been the zealot for Maureen Yancey: he got Stones Throw to keep paying her in defiance of the estate, got himself sued by the estate in part because he wanted to support her, and helped her overthrow the leadership of Arthur Erk. So he understood why people conferred upon her the right to direct the legacy of her dead son. *If Mother is okay, we are okay.* He understood why nobody wanted to hear otherwise, and why Maureen sometimes didn't either. He knew how little she had received for how much she had given James. He understood her sense of entitlement, why she might not want to share equal status with the mothers of her son's daughters. He acknowledged, too, that Maureen had become a brilliant promoter of her son's work. As it had been with James, many people loved Maureen Yancey and wanted to help her. Many tried, and many—like Micheline, Shoes, Kindra, JT, Jocelyne, and Egon—would leave her orbit feeling like they had failed. In so many ways, Maureen was very much her son's mother, as he was his mother's son.

Now that Egon worked for the estate, he saw clearly what Arthur Erk and Micheline Levine had been up against: no matter what the court said, no matter how many times he and Alex Borden and their attorney Sheila Bowers talked to Maureen, she was going to keep doing her own thing. They decided not to go to war with her over the Yancey Media Group's Detroit compilation album, or Dilla's record collection, or those hundreds of raw beats and demos, either. As far as Egon was concerned, if Dilla himself hadn't seen fit to release them or charge him with doing so, then he wasn't interested. And when they discovered Maureen had initiated deals that had the potential to be high-profile or lucrative, they would quietly remind those prospective partners that only the estate had the legal right to sell or license the properties they sought.[*]

Arty and Micheline had always remained assertive about those rights, and though Alex, Egon, and Sheila were somewhat less so, their rationale was identical: only the estate was bound to make sure that James's daughters, in particular, could inherit a legacy that was actually *worth* something. So Egon and Sheila kept their eyes on the central mission, which was to build Pay Jay into a profitable company that the estate could hand over to all four heirs once James's debts had been paid. Their core philosophy was to keep the copyrights to Dilla's work so that the kids would have a lifelong income stream; thus in their deals they licensed Dilla's music rather than selling it outright. They chased payments from music distributors, brokered marketing deals with companies like Stüssy, and created a line of J Dilla merchandise, even though Maureen had opened her own, separate online store and continued to issue music under her own imprint.

That profusion and confusion had now become a part of the culture of Dilla: the posthumous projects and parties; the Dilla Day celebrations in Detroit that became "Dilla Weekend," a multiday festival in Miami; the waves of tributes and the bootleg beats; the clamor for unreleased music—much of it was a way for people who had been connected to Dilla to keep him alive. It brought out the best and the worst in folks, induced generosity and selfishness, provoked both great art and avaricious crap. Egon's friend, the journalist Oliver Wang, called it the "Dilla Industrial Complex."[†] Sometimes grief was indeed a mask for the greedy. But sometimes what looked like greed was just grief.

Behind the commotion was a sad truth: there weren't any secret troves of Dilla tracks. James wasn't making any more. Egon persisted, in

---

[*] It is notable that some of the most compelling tribute and derivative work around J Dilla has come from outside "official" channels, among them: *Suite for Ma Dukes* (2009); the Roots' *Dilla Joints* (2010), instrumental re-creations of J Dilla beats; Bowls' *The Token Jazz Hour* (2013), a mixtape of J Dilla's sample sources; Bullion's *Pet Sounds in the Key of Dee* (2011), a mash-up of songs from the Beach Boys' *Pet Sounds* with J Dilla tracks; and Waajeed's Bling 47 Dilla Edition videos (2012, 2013).

[†] This notion also referred to the posthumous fans whose Dilla journey began only with *Donuts*, whose connection seemed more about conforming to a trend, and who wore their fandom like a T-shirt, sometimes literally. One widely circulated internet meme, over a stock photo of a fresh-faced collegiate white boy, lampooned them: "J Dilla Saved My Life. Who's Slum Village?"

part because he was paid to do so, but also because he was now a zealot for an expanded cause: both of James's now-teenage children deserved, every bit as much as their grandmother did, more than the scraps of this public scrap. But it was a lonely crusade. People outside the family saw his mother's abundant care for her son; few had ever seen evidence of James's care for his daughters. Some of them claimed to know J Dilla's personal will; few had ever seen his legal will. And none of them had to look Ja'Mya and Ty-Monae in the eyes.

E very year, the media coverage of J Dilla grew and the Dilla tribute events got bigger. The 9th Annual DC Loves Dilla event in 2014 nearly sold out the 1,200-seat Howard Theatre, with proceeds donated to the J Dilla Foundation. And on that July evening, Maureen Yancey invited a friend onstage.

"My name is Timothy Anne Burnside and I am from the National Museum of African American History and Culture, currently being built just down the street," she told the audience, the opening date of the Smithsonian's "final jewel in the crown" projected for 2016.

Burnside, a curatorial specialist and the Smithsonian's first large-scale collector of hip-hop artifacts, had been cultivating a relationship with Maureen Yancey since 2010. The following year, when she first visited the Yancey family's old house on Wexford in Conant Gardens, into which Maureen had moved again, she found her living in a virtual museum: platinum plaques for Busta Rhymes, Common, and Roots albums; a framed, gentle portrait of James taken in a supply closet at A&M by Brian Cross; another of a grade-school James sitting in a wicker chair; and dozens of pieces of fan art given to Ma Dukes in her world travels: watercolors, oil paintings, collages, and graphic design depicting James in settings from the real to the surreal. Burnside mustered the nerve to ask whether Maureen might consider donating her son's most precious possession, the item depicted in many of the photos and paintings around her: his Akai MPC3000 drum machine. But Maureen wasn't ready to let go. It took several more years for Maureen to make the decision to donate two pieces of equipment: the MPC and Dilla's cherished

Minimoog. When Burnside returned to Detroit to pick them up, she had no idea what Maureen and Jonathon Taylor went through to get them: John Yancey had left the equipment in the home of an ex-girlfriend, who then put them in a storage facility in San Diego, and Frank was dispatched with a blank check to reimburse her and retrieve James's equipment.

Burnside continued, telling the crowd: "This museum will celebrate African American culture through every possible lens. And I am here to announce today that also there when you walk through those doors will be Dilla."

The theater erupted. The global community of J Dilla followers, fans, and worshippers had been a fringe cultural phenomenon. This kind of institutional recognition was startling. The next day the Smithsonian posted their own announcement with photos of a beaming Maureen Yancey behind her son's equipment, and the news spread across music websites and social media that J Dilla's MPC and Moog would be displayed alongside artifacts from Louis Armstrong, Ella Fitzgerald, Lena Horne, Chuck Berry, and George Clinton. Burnside had to sell her superiors, including museum director Lonnie Bunch, on the idea; but now the press and social media staff were shocked by the public reaction, a kind of pop culture resonance the likes of which they'd never seen.

Bunch told Burnside: "Good job, kid."

I t didn't matter to DJ House Shoes that Maureen Yancey and Jonathon Taylor had handled the Ark of James's Covenant in one of the most dignified ways imaginable. He remained focused on what he felt was the latest obscenity from the Yancey Media Group—a limited-edition vinyl box set shaped like an E-mu SP-1200 sampling drum machine, repackaging many previously released tracks for a price of $207.74.* Shoes responded with obscenities of his own, this time blasting Maureen Yancey directly.

"If you were curious about how I feel about this, it's a piece of shit. How many times can you dig him up and fuck him in the ass? Necro-

---

* Jonathon Taylor explains the symbolism of the number: 2/07/74, James's birthday. He says he remains proud of this product.

philia is not the move. Selling him off piece by piece by piece. It's unbelievable that his MPC made it [to] the Smithsonian and wasn't sold off on eBay like his records were. Gotta be a sad life to only be able to support yourself by exploiting your dead son."

The reaction from the extended community of Dilla family and friends was swift and unanimous in its condemnation. House Shoes had crossed a line, done something that even some of his longtime comrades declared unforgivable. That's his *mother*, they said.

"The next time U go on social media & slander Ma Dukes/Dilla I'm not sayin shit I'm fucking y'all up we clear?" Dave New York wrote on Twitter. In the light of the next day, when House Shoes realized that he'd essentially turned everyone against him, he apologized:

"ONCE AGAIN. The shit I said the other day was completely out of line. I want, need and am trying to make amends. PERIOD."

Back in Detroit, several of House Shoes's onetime associates decided that the white kid from beyond 8 Mile needed to be reminded that he had always operated in the city by their good graces; and that his friendship with Dilla didn't mean he'd been appointed as the guardian of his legacy, nor did it give him the right to disrespect Dilla's flesh and blood, a Black woman and an elder at that. Shoes flew back to Detroit to do a show at the Music Hall downtown. Phat Kat warned the DJ not to come. Shoes came anyway. J Dilla's old protector Killa Ghanz took it upon himself to mete out justice. He waited backstage until Shoes finished his set, approached the DJ, and slapped him hard across the face. Shoes's cigarette flew out of his mouth as a dozen people watched. When Shoes began to speak, Ghanz silenced him.

"You have five minutes to get out of here and get on a plane or I'm fucking you up."

Shoes packed up his records and left.

The next day, Ghanz phoned Shoes to clarify his intentions. His assault wasn't a declaration of war. It wasn't permanent exile. It was discipline.

Throughout James Dewitt Yancey's ascension to hip-hop sainthood, his brother John had remained his designated doppelgänger. Taking Dilla's place in Slum Village alongside T3 and Elzhi, performing with his brother's closest friends and collaborators gave John a sense of profound connection to James, and it made him grateful to be accepted as their peer. He understood that his appearances were comforting to the legions of fans who could feel James's living presence because of him. And it had been, in a real way, his own ticket to fame.

But it could be hard for some people who were close to James to deal with the emotions they felt when they saw or spoke to John. He remembered the first time that Dave New York picked him up from the airport, on his first trip to L.A. after James died. "I can't even look at you right now," Dave told him.

The saddest part for John was that he felt that he truly had a spiritual, musical connection to his brother. People always wanted to know why James sampled this or James did that. John *knew* why: *We're weird, and we like shit that sounds funny*. People wanted to know the secret to James's rhythms. John *knew* it: *It's how we move. It's a physics of movement*.

But no one ever asked him. And several of James's close collaborators didn't seem to want to be close to him. So his role as James's proxy could be confusing and confining, a box that felt increasingly like a coffin to John's soul. The constant comparisons to his brother, both positive and negative, corroded his confidence; and he had grown uncomfortable with the way people both inside and outside Dilla's circle staked their claims to his legacy. *Everybody heard James's voice. Everybody knew what he meant, or what he would have wanted.* He didn't want to be on the receiving end of their disingenuousness, nor did he want to be one of them. Nobody would ever see him as his own man if he didn't do something.

So in 2013, John Yancey quit Slum Village, left Detroit, and moved to Montreal. He met a new girlfriend, found new creative partners, and began work on a project that would bear his own music and his name alone, *Illa J*. He released it in 2015 on a Brooklyn-based indie label. From the very first song, "She Burned My Art," John experimented, bouncing from hip-hop to house and back again. On the last track, "Never Left," he said his piece about the "hidden agendas" of people using the name of "'Big Dill' when they need a big deal."

John rapped to his brother: "I will never let somebody taint your truth / Cause tainted love is all around and the shit ain't cool."

He was still a Yancey boy. He still felt his brother talking to him. But John was starting to feel like himself again.

14.
Micro Time

The moment a musician decides to forgo a career in music can be painful. But that time came for Anne Danielsen because she couldn't find the funk.

In the 1980s, the spiky-haired Danielsen fronted a couple of bands in her native Oslo. The first, called Ung Pike Forsvunnet—meaning "Young Girl Disappeared"—became well known in Norway, but their global appeal was limited by the fact that all their lyrics were in Norwegian. In her next band, Duck Spin, she sang in English. But for Danielsen, language wasn't the insurmountable issue. Mostly, she despaired that the grooves she and her fellow musicians created didn't quite match up to the ones she heard on her favorite records. Whatever that magic was, Danielsen felt like they were missing the last 20 percent of it.

Danielsen decided that she might instead find what she was missing via inquiry and analysis. In the 1990s, she enrolled in graduate musicology studies at the University of Oslo to answer a simple question: *What makes a groove work? What makes some rhythms feel stiff and others entice the body to move, often involuntarily?* She wrote her master's thesis on Prince's *Diamonds and Pearls* album; her doctoral dissertation, *Presence and Pleasure: The Funk Grooves of James Brown and Parliament*, was picked up by an American publisher.

Danielsen found the missing 20 percent of her own career after she heard D'Angelo's *Voodoo*. She would later describe her reaction to it as *shock*: disturbed, pleasured, fascinated by the extremity of the wobbling, seasick grooves. She watched her musician friends in Norway's jazz scene, a community obsessed with accuracy and perfection, grimace as they grappled with these new rhythms.

Danielsen began to hear these broken grooves in other places and pieces in popular music in the early 2000s. And she observed that most of them were either byproducts or imitations of digital music-making. Thus her analyses became less philosophical and more mathematical. She spent hours examining the digital waveforms of popular songs in her Logic and Amadeus software, deciphering the placement of sounds and their effects on listeners, both in mind and body.

Danielsen won a grant and in 2004 used the funding to begin a five-year research project—Rhythm in the Age of Digital Reproduction (RADR)—to answer two further questions: *How has the coming of digital instruments, signal processing, and recording affected musical rhythm? What is the nature of these new, disorienting grooves and why do they make us feel and move the way they do?*

The work of Danielsen and her colleagues marked the first time that the academy took notice of the change in rhythm that had begun over the last decade.

The academic study of musical time, like many things in the Western world, was a Eurocentric enterprise, training its analysis mostly on European classical music. Thus it was also platonic, meaning that, like many things in the European approach to study, it tended to look at pristine ideals rather than practices. Time was represented as a kind of celestial clock, an ideal musicians either conformed to or deviated from.

Non-Western music and performance, and particularly African and African American genres and practices, posed challenges for this worldview. The very concept of syncopation—the idea that musical events were not located in time where they were "supposed" to be—was itself prejudicial, based on a Eurocentric perspective. The practice of swing literally fell outside the conventions of European musical notation. Musicologists developed and deployed a lexicon to account for and in some ways *discount* the subtleties of African American–derived musical expression.

In the twentieth century, the idea of "expressive timing" was born as a way to comprehend the minute shifts in the placement of musical notes and events by musicians. Here, too, these shifts were often represented as anomalies of individual performances, artifacts of the imperfections of the human body, falling short of a platonic ideal.

Gradually, the Eurocentric view was disputed and replaced with an Afrocentric one. In the 1960s and '70s, Black thinkers and academics LeRoi Jones (later known as Amiri Baraka) and Olly Wilson and white musicologist Charles Keil created new rubrics by which to understand African and African American music, and proposed that these art forms evidenced a more fluid and nuanced musical intelligence. Wilson, at Oberlin College, was also one of the first to establish the study of electronic music in academia.

In 1998, a doctoral candidate at the University of California, Berkeley, named Vijay Iyer published a dissertation—influenced in part by Olly Wilson's ideas—in which he pilloried the platonic conceit at the heart of European musicology. The body could not be divorced from the mind, Iyer argued, and thus rhythm could only truly be understood as a function and byproduct of human physical movement. "Musical motion," he wrote, "is audible human motion." Our musical clocks are not celestial, they are biological; and bodily actions like breathing, walking, and talking all have their musical correlations. This had great implications for how we make and experience rhythms. Microscopic shifts in timing weren't *deviations* or *inaccuracies*, they were *intentions*. To account for those intentions, Iyer argued the need for a more granular theoretical framework, inventing two terms to frame them: *microtiming* and *microrhythmic*.

These microrhythmic shifts, measured in milliseconds, could convey a universe of emotion, and were indeed the things that made certain rhythms compelling. The "flam," for example, even when performed by one musician on one instrument, signified collective participation and community because its dual or multiple attacks approximated the feel of human convergence around a pulse. Little timing variations, conversely, allowed individual musicians to stand out and express themselves *apart* from the collective. "Swing," the unequal division of pulse at the heart of African American music, was "grounded in the locomotive channel of human motion," meaning, essentially, that swing approximated the rhythm of walking, or running, or skipping, a "body-based" approach to making music. And the concept of "pocket," what he calls the "microscopic lopsidedness of the backbeat in the best drummers," was itself an artifact of the drum kit, and the different physical responsiveness of the arms and legs in playing it. Iyer used the music of Thelonious Monk to illustrate how playing "behind the beat" conveyed both physical and thus emotional relaxation. *A physics of movement.*

Vijay Iyer came to these observations as a byproduct of his own musical journey—a child of Indian immigrants who aborted his graduate studies in physics to play jazz piano and get a PhD in music and cognition. His music career would soon take precedence: Iyer rose to become one of the most lauded pianist-composers in the world. But Iyer's observations as a student would help ignite the deeper study of what came to be called *microrhythm.*

Some musicologists, like Fernando Benadon, went on to explore these ideas in relationship to jazz. But hip-hop—whose production methods had not been rigorously analyzed in academia until the ethnomusicologist Joe Schloss released his book *Making Beats* in 2004—would be left out of those analyses until Anne Danielsen began her exploration of digital beatmaking's uncanny movement into microrhythm.

The results of Danielsen and her colleagues' research came out in a 2010 book of essays, *Musical Rhythm in the Age of Digital Reproduction.* Danielsen proclaimed that a new body of machine-made popular music countered the notion that only traditional musicians could produce the kind of timing nuances that created compelling grooves. Moreover, because machines allowed programmers to precisely manipulate sound on a microscopic level, they had created "entirely new rhythmic feels," songs that had "overlapping layers of rhythms with multiple locations of their basic pulses at a microrhythmic level" that not only evoked earlier kinds of analog, seventies funk imprecision, but exaggerated and multiplied them, creating a sonic vertigo in the listener. Danielsen located this revolution in the act of programming, not performance: "Real musicians would probably have trouble producing truly multiple locations of a basic pulse." And yet the examples that she and her colleagues cited showed that traditional musicians were already emulating this machine-born feel.

Danielsen began at the point of her own epiphany, with D'Angelo's *Voodoo*, deconstructing the opening bars of the song "Left and Right," looking specifically at the way they oriented, disoriented, and reoriented the listener in a succession of three "situations": First, the shaker and guitar established a tempo. Second, Questlove's drums (really a looped four-bar sample of his playing) rushed in, implying a second pulse occurring slightly earlier. Third, the remainder of the song saw these two pulses—separated by approximately eighty-five milliseconds—fighting for the listener's attention. Danielsen asked: *How does a listener arrive at an acceptance and enjoyment of the conflict?* She concluded that the idea of a beat as a "point in time" was an old way of thinking, and that humans could develop a kind of "rhythmic tolerance"—a term coined by musicologist Mats Johansson—that allowed disparate events to fall within a longer "bin" of time.

Danielsen's colleagues made other interesting observations. Kristoffer Bjerke analyzed two Soulquarians songs: D'Angelo's "Untitled" and Common's "The Hustle" from *Electric Circus*—the former played by musicians, the latter programmed on machine by Karriem Riggins—in an effort to understand how timbre affects our perceptions of rhythmic conflict. Kristoffer Carlsen and Maria A. G. Witek looked at two songs with digitally created microscopic rhythmic conflicts: the Roots' "Rock You" and Brandy's "What About Us?," produced by Rodney Jerkins—finding in Jerkins's production three distinct pulses fighting with each other. Carlsen and Witek asked: *How does the human mind reconcile these differences?* Taking cues from Danielsen's idea that humans had a more dynamic and fluid way of making sense of musical events as they occurred, they referenced a theory called "dynamic attending" created by

Mari Reiss Jones: the relationship between time and our minds was bidirectional. Programmers and musicians had birthed a new kind of elastic musical time; and as it turns out, our listening minds were elastic, too.

Danielsen and her colleagues deconstructed the new, conflicted

"WHAT ABOUT US?" · BRANDY

Count	1	n	2	n	3	n	4	n	1	n	2	n	3	n	4	n	
HAT																	A
SHAKER																	B
SNARE																	C
KICK																	D
VOCAL																	E

A. straight + shifted early   B. swung   C. straight   D. straight + shifted early   E. straight + shifted late

time-feel in popular music; in so doing, they attacked the idea of static time itself and proposed a new way of thinking about musical attention. But of all the minute details that held their *own* attention, one thing escaped them. The artists and producers who created the music they examined—D'Angelo, Common and Karriem Riggins, the Roots, even Rodney Jerkins—all had one common influence. But that influencer was mentioned only in passing, in a quote from Questlove, the name "Jay Dee" confined to a footnote in Danielsen's essay.

Microrhythm's shift from the fringes of musicology took more than a few milliseconds. A few years later, Anne Danielsen completed a research project to see how drummers communicated their sense of timing to fellow musicians and their audiences. When she submitted her papers to academic journals, one reviewer replied that he couldn't read more than one paragraph because he couldn't see the rationale for the study. *Who could possibly care about these tiny, meaningless differences? What was the point?*

In 2015, Danielsen began a project called "TIME: Timing and Sound in Musical Microrhythm," created to look at four different genres: jazz, electronic dance, R&B and hip-hop, and Scandinavian fiddle music. Danielsen then launched the RITMO Centre for Interdisciplinary Studies in Rhythm, Time and Motion, which looked at rhythm as a central human activity and examined its role in all parts of human life. The study of microrhythm was both a means and a metaphor for looking more closely at places and spaces, and the people within them; how the perception of musical time is linked to one's cultural background—*who* you were, *where* you were, and *with whom* you dwelled.*

The new microrhythmic, conflicted R&B and hip-hop of the 2000s came from a place and from a people. It was created by Black Americans, in Black spaces, primarily with Black audiences in mind. And it referenced a Black perspective of that particular era. For years, people had been thinking and writing about how Black people bent sound, time, and space in their lives and expressions. Around the time that James Yancey first learned how to work an MPC, one man shared his thoughts about what happens when that expression encounters the machine.

In 1992, the filmmaker Arthur Jafa—who had just won the Best Cinematography award at Sundance for his work on *Daughters of the Dust*—addressed an audience during a conference at the DIA:Beacon museum in New York. In his speech, Jafa professed his curiosity about why people of African descent found particular pleasure in what he called "polyventiality," the impulse to deal with multiplicities: multiple rhythms, multiple tones, multiple perspectives simultaneously. Whence came the impulse to play behind the beat, or ahead of it; or to "worry the note," as he explained, "to treat notes as indeterminate inherently unstable frequencies rather than the standard Western treatment of notes as fixed phenomena"? He conjured for his audience the visual experience of the silent film, which he claimed was so transfixing because the way it replicated time was so unstable, shot on hand-cranked cameras, moved by human physiology. This was, he implied, the visual equivalent of "worrying the note." And the response of the human nervous system to that instability—constantly trying to reconcile pictures coming slightly before or slightly after we expect them to—is why we're mesmerized.

---

* Musicology's recognition of J Dilla's particular role in both the surge of and interest in microrhythms in popular music would take even more time. During the writing of this book, two papers emerged: a 2017 study by Daniel Akira Stadnicki of J Dilla's effect on traditional drummers in the *Journal of Popular Music Education*, and a dissertation by doctoral student Sean Peterson at the University of Oregon in 2018 on the Soulquarians that recognized some of the theoretical implications and mechanics of J Dilla's work.

He wondered aloud: "How do we make . . . Black images vibrate in accordance with certain frequential values that exist in Black music?" Jafa continued: "I'm developing an idea that I call Black visual intonation . . . the use of irregular, nontempered (nonmetronomic) camera rates and frame replication to prompt filmic movement to function in a manner that approximates Black vocal intonation."

Jafa was relaying a couple of notions at once. First, he was saying that the standard frame rates of film—the sixteen or twenty-four or thirty frames per second that gave the human eye the *illusion* of movement— were still not fine or frequent enough to convey the subtleties of Black cultural expression. Indeed, the standard frame rates of film remain far too coarse to deal with the fine nuances of the sound synchronized to it. Second, he was arguing that the idea of constant, linear, metronomic time was not sufficient to convey the more elastic Black time-sense. Jafa declared that he had developed 372 distinct approaches to frame rates and rhythms to do just that.

Arthur Jafa thought this way about technology because filmmakers were forced to grapple with the grid, the "sampling" of images to re-create reality and express emotion, long before musicians had to contend with it. So Jafa's feelings of confinement would in some ways predict those of James Dewitt Yanccy, who was just becoming an artist at the time that Jafa spoke, and would find ways of expressing his own "polyventiality" through a digital machine, multiple pulses and rhythms offset by minute amounts of time in ways that only a machine could maintain, making time itself feel elastic. In so doing, J Dilla made the grid's limitations his liberation, and made the machine itself sing a new song.

"A Non-Complacent Entity": Jafa on Dilla

Thirty years after his talk at DIA:Beacon, Arthur Jafa—now a lauded visual artist—sees J Dilla as a compatriot in subverting the grid: "Way ahead of the curve," he says, calling him one of the most sophisticated practitioners of a lineage of "deformation" in response to the Western musical framework and the machine. Jafa points to one precedent, in Black Americans' encounter with the piano: "The first rigid system that Black musicians in some ways were confronted with because . . . the European understanding of the sound spectrum is built into the instrument itself." He counts Monk's technique of playing flub notes, with his fingers flat, as a way of "misusing the equipment" that parallels J Dilla's use of the MPC's timing functions, and the exaggerated use of auto-tune in more recent popular music. All are indications of subversions of systems that "weren't designed to constrain a non-complacent entity." Jafa likens the effect of J Dilla's time-feel to that of the woozy irregularity of silent film and attributes Dilla's abilities to a sensitive nervous system that registered micro-differences in rhythms as distinct events where others might just hear noise: "Dilla is one of the few cats in hip-hop that I would put next to Charlie Parker, John Coltrane, and Miles Davis in terms of technical, formal sophistication."

These rhythmic events happened on a microscopic level, too fine and nuanced for the coarse measurements of notation and its digital cousin, quantization. Too fine, even, for some people to feel. Those who could were often tempted to reduce these sounds to simple feeling, pure emotion, and leave it at that; but others—like Danielsen, Iyer, and Jafa—understood the value of looking closer at a phenomenon to see how it worked, because it is on the micro level that the most powerful forces in the universe operate. These three thinkers shared a sense that these tiny things were a huge development.

As the academy started taking microrhythm seriously, a new generation of players, brought up on hip-hop but trained in classical and jazz, began thinking about and working with J Dilla's ideas—not just his rhythms but his approach to harmony and sound, and brought his provocations straight into their music. No small thing.

15.
Descendants/Disciples

D'Angelo's star hit its apex with *Voodoo* in 2000. After thirteen more turns around the sun, his long-awaited third album had yet to break the horizon. This time, D'Angelo's long hiatus was less musical quest and more personal struggle with the kind of stardom his music had wrought. A camera revolved around his bare chest and torso in the video for *Voodoo*'s breakout song, "Untitled (How Does It Feel)," the clip stimulating fans' eyes rather than their ears in ways that made the singer feel truly naked. D'Angelo stopped performing and recording for many years and struggled with substance abuse.

Then, in 2006, the day before D'Angelo's birthday, J Dilla died. It scared the shit out of him. *I'm next,* D'Angelo thought. And he heard James's voice. *It's all right,* James told him. D'Angelo called the guitarist Eric Clapton. *I know you have a spot in Antigua,* D said, referring to the Crossroads rehabilitation center. *I need to go.*

D'Angelo's recovery was, like all things in D's world, something that took time. The recording process that followed was intermittent, broken up by occasional stretches of touring, in which he often made Dilla beats a part of his set. D'Angelo learned from Dilla that he did not have all the time in the world, but what time D did have belonged to him, and he alone had the right to measure it. *I'll get there when I get there. I'll see you when I see you. It'll be worth the wait.*

And so, in August 2013, when D'Angelo was set to play a concert with Erykah Badu and Common at Detroit's Chene Park, an open-air band shell on the Detroit River, it did not shock his tourmates when he didn't show. Perhaps some in the audience thought the prospect was too good to be true—D'Angelo gig, new album just around the corner—but bought tickets anyway. One person in the wings, however, began to panic.

Her name was Naomi "Nai Palm" Saalfield, the lead singer, guitarist, and songwriter for a four-piece band, Hiatus Kaiyote. Strange name, strange looking, strange sounding, they had come all the way from Melbourne, Australia, to join this tour as an opening act. The stop in Detroit was among the most significant for them, the locus of so many of their musical influences, not the least of which was J Dilla—Nai was thrilled to have just been introduced to Maureen Yancey backstage. But Hiatus Kaiyote were unknown to this audience. They didn't have a hit single, they were only there because their music was a modern echo of the headliners' neo-soul harmonies and Dilla's rhythms. Thus Nai's joy turned to dread when she heard the master of ceremonies' announcement from the stage, which was, essentially: *D'Angelo ain't coming, but here are four white people from Australia you don't know.* The most selective audience in the world just had their hearts broken, and now she had to go out and play for them. *Kaiyote, thrown to the wolves.*

Hiatus Kaiyote's first, fated trip to Detroit was a milestone in a journey, a homecoming of sorts, the closing of a circle—not for the band, but for an idea.

James Dewitt Yancey, like many Detroiters, did not grow up with travel as something that felt safe or possible. His earliest journeys to New York and Los Angeles induced more anxiety than exhilaration. He had to be cajoled into his first European tour, preferring to remain in his underground abode in Conant Gardens. By the time he developed a true desire for changes in scenery, he was dying. But even before his death, J Dilla's rhythmic feel began to circumnavigate the globe. In the years after his passing, a new generation of artists who worked on both traditional and electronic instruments were making music in response to those ideas. These efforts weren't mere tributes to J Dilla, though there was in most of them a consciousness of their source. Rather, these musicians, working in genres from serious jazz to pop, were creating something new with the tools and techniques that he pioneered.

As a jazz student in the early 2000s, Robert Glasper's trip to the Conant Gardens basement altered his musical trajectory. You could hear it in the performances he gave just a few years later on Wednesday nights at the Up Over Jazz Cafe on Flatbush Avenue in Brooklyn. A casual observer might be forgiven for mistaking these events for hip-hop gigs: a young, mostly Black audience in sneakers, jeans, and fitted baseball caps, vocalists like Q-Tip or Mos Def or Bilal or Common on the microphone. But behind them onstage, a trio of musicians pushed and pulled on the pulse and one another like three disconnected musical magnets: Vicente Archer on bass, Damion Reid on drums, and Glasper on keyboards.

One night after a gig, Glasper walked offstage, made his way to the bar, and met James Spaulding, a respected alto saxophonist—*the* alto sax dude to call on in the 1960s—who had played and recorded with Miles Davis and Wayne Shorter. Glasper greeted his elder with all requisite enthusiasm and respect. Spaulding returned the good cheer, but something was bothering him.

"Hey man," Spaulding began. "I saw what you was doing up there but, you know, the funk is not *tight* enough."

Glasper listened with all the restraint he could muster as Spaulding gave him an impromptu lecture in rhythm: counting, slapping his hands together, and tapping his foot.

"Y'all gotta get the One together. Y'all was never *on* it. You gotta be *on* it."

Spaulding was listening to the rhythms and thinking: *Wrong.* Glasper tried to explain to Spaulding: *It's intentional. We're doing a different style. Drunk funk. Everything is lagging on purpose. You know what I mean?*

Spaulding didn't.

He never would. Jazz had seen generational divides before—as Dixieland gave way to big band swing in the 1930s, then as swing gave way to bebop in the late 1940s. Some musicians, like Duke Ellington, could make the transition; others, like Louis Armstrong, couldn't. When jazz merged with popular styles like funk and rock and soul in the 1960s, some fans and players saw this "jazz fusion" as heresy. When Herbie Hancock began using samplers and drum machines in the 1980s, jazz purists crucified him. *To dilute jazz to make it more palatable, to fuse it to the latest fad, whether for funds or fame, was to degrade it.*

"The jazz police," Robert Glasper called them. They were everywhere, standing upon the genre's ramparts, guarding against invasion from outside and revolution from within. To Glasper and like-minded comrades, the very act of "guarding" jazz to keep it pure was like using a chastity belt. Jazz was born in the whorehouses of New Orleans, after all. *Fucking around is the whole point.* Glasper imagined John Coltrane returning to the earthly plane decades after his death, walking into a jazz club to witness a bunch of musicians, all playing like John Coltrane, and saying: *I did all my work and died for this?*

Glasper knew that what he and his trio were doing was in some ways even harder to digest for the jazz community than what Herbie Hancock had done with *Future Shock* in 1983. This wasn't some *wikka-wikka* turntable scratching, or a bunch of rappers rappity-rapping over chord changes. This was a fundamental change in jazz's approach to rhythm and harmony, inspired ultimately by one person fucking around on one drum machine. He'd borne witness to it. Robert Glasper was an unabashed disciple of J Dilla. That discipline was now a part of his muscle memory as a jazz player and composer, indivisible from the more classic elements of his training. Glasper didn't feel he had to choose between his influences to be a jazz artist. But if he wanted to be *seen* as one, taken seriously by the guardians at the gates—the people who booked the clubs and the tours, the critics who wrote for the newspapers and magazines— he had to play their game. Thus Glasper split himself into two people. His trio did two shows a week at the Up Over, a hip-hop night and a straight jazz night. And when Glasper's then-manager, Nicole Hegeman, shopped his music to record labels, it was only his pure jazz stuff.

Hegeman understood her client's wariness. She saw the way the old heads just barely tolerated Robert, the way they made fun of his clothes and comportment: T-shirts and baggy jeans, pierced eyebrow, messy dreadlocks long and wild and free, just like him. They resented him not only because he broke their codes, but because he didn't care about following them at all. The only thing that kept him on their stages was his talent. When Robert Glasper's independent debut album, *Mood*, was released in 2004, Hegeman approached the jazz world's three big booking agencies on his behalf. They all turned her down. *I don't like that guy. I don't get him.*

Luckily, one record executive did, the same one who had seen J Dilla himself as a jazz artist. Eli Wolf at Blue Note Records saw Glasper's traditional mastery clearly—his "chops" or ability to play; the lyrical, melodic sense of his compositions. But he detected something else in Glasper, meaningless to Wolf's colleagues at Blue Note but electrifying to Eli: the integration of hip-hop influences in organic ways. On *Mood*, Glasper and his trio covered Irving Berlin's "Blue Skies," and it could have been like any of the thousands of jazz covers of Tin Pan Alley standards. The trio cracked the song open, trying different grooves on like so many changes of clothes. But did Glasper's phrasing, at times, almost sound like a sampled loop? The song faded out. And then, Wolf heard that phrasing again, fading in through a filter against a steady hip-hop rhythm, almost as if Glasper had become a beatmaker and was sampling himself on a drum machine. Glasper had answered his question: *Yes, motherfucker*. This wasn't the typical, corny "Reese's Peanut Butter Cup" collision of two different tastes that tasted great together. It was a reunion of musical kin and a convergence of bloodlines.

But for all his hip-hop proclivities, Glasper remained circumspect about integrating them explicitly. Upon his first Blue Note release, *Canvas*, in 2005, he told Nate Chinen at *JazzTimes*: "I keep those worlds separate, because they are two separate things . . . I don't want to sound like I'm playing at jazz, or playing at hip-hop." Glasper won his jazz accolades, and seemed loath to let them slip away by making any sudden moves.

Then J Dilla died, and things began to shift. Glasper recorded "J Dillalude"—his trio playing a four-minute quartet of four Dilla beats, "Thelonius," "Antiquity," "Fall in Love," "Stakes Is High"—and stuck it right in the middle of his 2007 album *In My Element*, prefaced by a voice mail from Q-Tip making the suggestion that he do so. In his 2009 album *Double Booked*, Glasper segregated the album into jazz and hip-hop/electronic halves, the latter with another quartet, the Robert Glasper Experiment, both anchored by his Houston comrade Chris Dave on drums. Glasper counted Dave among the select group of drummers who possessed the mix of dexterity and knowledge required to do the Dilla feel, a cohort that began with Questlove and included Karriem Riggins and Mark Colenburg from Common's stage band. If you asked Glasper, Chris Dave was the best of them all.

After three successful albums, Glasper stopped worrying about partitioning his influences. The result was an album, released in 2012, *Black Radio*, which wasn't a merger of genres as much it was an expression of what it was to be a Black American musician immersed in *all* Black musical forms. Singers like Erykah Badu and Musiq joined Glasper's Experiment band for twelve boundary-free tracks that included originals and songs plumbed from acts like Sade and Nirvana. *Black Radio* became Robert Glasper's bestselling project by an order of magnitude, and won a Grammy Award—albeit for best R&B album. A remix album the following year featured Glasper's second paean to J Dilla, featuring interpretations of four more beats: "E=MC2," "Fantastic," "Show Me What You Got," and "The Look of Love."

Now the agents who had rejected Glasper were swarming Nicole Hegeman, who told them: *I'm having trouble understanding what you see in Robert now that you didn't see then.* She turned them all down. And when the jazz police came for Robert, mostly in the form of backbiting posts on social media, Glasper was ready. He read some words by the respected pianist Eric Reed that went something like: *What Robert Glasper has done is every bit as bad for jazz as what Herbie Hancock did in making his crossover record.* Other musicians commiserated with Reed in that online thread: *Glasper just did it for the money. He's ignoring the heritage. I don't hear the history in this music.* Glasper fumed: *No history in the music? This album combined all the threads of Black music history!* Glasper shot back at Reed personally, with all the braggadocio of an MC: *When was the last time anybody cared this much about you to talk about you online?* But when he eventually calmed down, Glasper realized that he no longer needed to have the debate. *Fuck the jazz police.*

What felt for Robert Glasper like a revolution, others in jazz felt as a logical evolution. Jason Moran had a lot in common with Glasper. They were both pianists, both from Houston, both signed to Blue Note. They both grew up on jazz and hip-hop. They both became Jay Dee fans upon

listening to Busta Rhymes's song "Still Shining," and for the same reason: its ever-shifting harmonic changes and rhythmic freedom; that it
was so obviously composed in linear fashion—even though they both
considered the four-bar loop to be as valid a song form as the twelve-
bar blues progression or the thirty-two-bar standard. J Dilla's music, too,
had influenced Moran's jazz, but perhaps in subtler ways. On his debut
album for Blue Note Records in 1999, Moran's song "Retrograde" was a
conscious nod to Jay Dee's harmonic fascination with "common tone"
in songs like "Still Shining" and "Runnin'"—one note held constant as
chords shifted in permutations around it.

So Moran tilted his head toward anything J Dilla did, much in the
same way he would Thelonious Monk, the man whose playing set Moran on a course to be a professional pianist; and he took Dilla's ideas as
seriously as that of any jazz artist, each of them worthy of examination.

First, there was what Moran called "the lope." He'd heard it before, in
Count Basie's band from the 1930s and '40s, and especially in the playing of Erroll Garner from the '50s. These rhythms and Dilla's conjured
an image for Moran—a man, shades on, hat on, walking around a street
corner, the rhythm of his step not only measured by the simple left-right
of his feet, but broken down into smaller, constituent parts: the bend
of a knee, a shoulder dip. The beat that leered, the beat that had an attitude, the beat that was more corporeal than theoretical. *A physics of
movement.* That microscopic texture of rhythm was so subtle that most
musicians didn't pay attention to it. J Dilla had made it his main musical
ingredient. Dilla asked the question: What if a bass line had a lope? What
if the sample had a lope? What if the vocals, the keys, every element had
its own different lope? He'd taken that lope and exaggerated it, extended
it into an aesthetic, refined it into a language that other people could
learn and speak. Another thing that Moran learned from Dilla was that
a downbeat or a backbeat wasn't simply a point in time; Dilla made it
wide. Each beat had a front, a middle, and a back. Each held a universe
of space within it.

Moran also observed how J Dilla resolved harmony. Much of the
sweetness in J Dilla's work, the *love* movement, came from his obsession
with common tone, a harmonic metaphor for constancy amid change,

the act of love in musical form. But he made other interesting choices: J Dilla preferred to keep his voicings spare. Where many musicians used tones to color in every available space, Dilla took shards of sounds and often left only a dotted line rather than something solid. In that impulse to say less, to leave incomplete, Jason Moran saw the mark of a fellow Aquarian. *An Aquarius won't fill in everything for you.* The artists who worked the most comfortably with Dilla weren't intimidated by the empty spaces and the disconnections, nor the feeling of uneasiness, that the ground could shift beneath their feet at any moment. Some musicians couldn't relate to these ideas; they sounded unmusical, they sounded *wrong*.

This was the way music evolved; old rules need to get broken so new things can rise. It happened when Duke Ellington added notes to chords that would have sounded "illegal" to the European ear, and thus invented a new, American kind of harmony. It happened again when Monk jammed his hands onto the keyboard to bring forth the sounds of notes *in between* the ones that were actually there. The *wrongness* of J Dilla's ideas was a similar provocation.

Jason Moran looked back over music history and saw that, in each generation, the nature of syncopation changed. J Dilla created this generation's change. But why? What did his rhythms say about this time and place? Moran thought about Detroit, its singular place as an incubator of American music. Motown was the musical result of the Great Migration. Twenty years later, techno was Detroit's response to deindustrialization. And how, nearly twenty years after that, James Yancey—son of Motown, little brother of techno—arrived in an emptied city whose roads and streets had once been etched to accommodate millions. What was it like to grow up in a place that forces you to take inexplicable turns that lead to nowhere? Where you find yourself almost always in some really ugly corners? How do you make sense of that map? J Dilla took all the pieces of the city's history, put them into his machine, and—as one can do only with a machine—slammed them against one another. Grid against grid.

In Moran's world, all conflict worked toward resolution. Sometimes those resolutions were immediate and predictable—like a cheerful pop song in a major key—but other music forced you to linger in uncertainty. Even when tones and rhythms misaligned, Monk always brought you back into alignment at some point. The genius of Dilla was that you never knew when that resolution would come. For Moran, and for many in his generation of jazz like Glasper, that sensation felt good.

The questions Dilla's machine rhythms raised reminded Moran of the movie *The Matrix*, which provoked its audience to think about its own disposition to programming. *Technology is doing something strange to human beings. As we move further into the Machine Age, we'll continue to have to find our humanity within it, to find a way to maximize its potential for the positive. Are you punching through the grid or are you trapped in it?* J Dilla was his generation's first great grid jumper, master of mazes, navigator of crossroads. His music reflected the ability to live in discomfort, the certainty of uncertainty, the ease of unease, and the suspense in waiting for a resolution that may or may not come when you expect it.

As with all shifts in music, heresy gradually becomes gospel. James Dewitt Yancey's ideas created a new canon of rhythm. He had his work interpreted symphonically. The jazz guitarist Dave "Fuze" Fiuczynski, a professor at Boston's Berklee College of Music, won a Guggenheim Fellowship for which he created the piece *Flam! Blam! Pan-Asian MicroJam! for J Dilla and Olivier Messiaen*, which blended microtonal melodies inspired by birdsong with the microrhythmic beats of J Dilla. When Moran visited the great American music conservatories, musicians and composers used the hip-hop producer's name in the same way they would the great drummers of jazz to denote a particular approach to rhythm: A "Tony Williams feel." An "Elvin Jones feel."

And now, a "Dilla feel."

In 2009, another instructor at the Berklee College of Music, its pedagogy steeped in jazz fundamentals, began offering a workshop called "Dilla Ensemble." Brian "Raydar" Ellis had weathered some of the institution's own bias against hip-hop as a student—Berklee's version of the jazz police—to create a space as a professor for a growing segment of student musicians, both traditional and electronic, who had become J Dilla nerds, itching to reverse engineer his beats and the music of artists influenced by him, including Robert Glasper.

The challenging part for Ellis was answering this question: *How do I teach what Dilla does?* To replicate the conflicted Dilla "feel"—locking in a pocket that was loose but still on time—Ellis had to figure out which player was going to stay on top of the pulse and which was going to drag behind it; who was going to impart that machinelike feel and who was going to slide around. This became a big part of their workshop discussion. In a class full of Glasper fans, Ellis often found that the action of the keyboard player was more important than that of the drummer in setting the global pulse and bridging the relationships between the other instruments—a counterintuitive notion. So they'd often begin the arrangement keys first, adding in guitar and bass, and then the drums, building the songs section by section.

The more seasoned and classically trained musicians had the most difficulty letting go of their polish and their impulse toward precision. Cultivating deliberate *imprecision* became the great gift of the course. In deconstructing how instruments rhythmically interact on the subtlest level, students developed an X-ray rhythmic vision they could then use to create their own arrangements, compositions, and performances. Their learning wasn't all about maintaining dissonance. Ellis and his students spent a lot of time discussing the phases of J Dilla's creative output; how he equalized or shaped the sound envelope on different samples and drum sounds so they *didn't* conflict, and that informed the way the members of the ensemble had to make room for each other—the keyboardist, for example, not playing a bottom note to make room for the bass. They talked a lot about Jay Dee's ability to take sonic material in a major key and extract the elements with a minor tonality, giving a more nuanced, teetering kind of harmony. And they discussed J Dilla's virtuosity as a rapper: how he slowly dripped his words on top of a song like "Give It Up"; and in others evinced a sly, mathematical humor, like how he ended every line of "Climax," a song about a threesome, with a triplet. This was a course for the thinking musician.

Raydar Ellis—the first to formally teach the work of J Dilla in a conservatory setting—had the pleasure of seeing his scholars use what they learned. Roused by their experiences in the ensemble, two of his students came back to him with a new group of songs they had put together. Dane Orr and Anna Wise were calling themselves Sonnymoon, and in their demos, Ellis heard so many of the ideas they had studied being put to work.

He wondered where his students might take them.

A creative and commercial depression settled over Los Angeles hip-hop after J Dilla's death in 2006. L.A. had once been the genre's ascendant scene; the rise of gangsta rap, G-funk, and in particular, the producer Dr. Dre and his label Death Row Records captured the momentum from New York hip-hop in the early 1990s. In that era, some young Angelenos developed a rejoinder to the dominant gangster sound and ethos, a small community of lyricists and producers centered around weekly open-mic events at a cafe on Crenshaw Boulevard called the Good Life. This alternative scene made room for the emergence of groups like the Pharcyde.

But the moderate success of the Pharcyde and other crews, like Freestyle Fellowship, couldn't match the commercial power of Death Row. And Death Row itself imploded after the murder of their prince, Tupac Shakur, in 1996. The rise in popularity of new East Coast icons like Jay-Z and the ascendance of Southern hip-hop artists and styles all turned the focus away from L.A. in the 2000s. Dr. Dre's next label, Aftermath Entertainment, was less a movement and more a vehicle for Dre's corporate priorities— Eminem, 50 Cent, and the Compton rapper the Game. The alternative, artsy aesthetic was kept alive in the fringes by DJs like the Beat Junkies, crews like Sa-Ra Creative Partners, record stores like Fat Beats and Aron's, labels like Stones Throw, auteurs like Madlib, and by parties like Sketchbook, a regular gathering of beatmakers and beat lovers promoted by Eric Coleman and a DJ named Kutmah, a place for producers to hear each other's work in progress. Dilla's presence in L.A. had been fuel for this scene. His death was a gut punch. *Donuts* his parting gift, the Detroit demigod rested now in the soil of Southern California. Within a couple of years, Los Angeles began to see a new crop of artists and producers rising from the underground, all nourished by what James Yancey left behind.

Steven Ellison, a Stones Throw intern, an unabashed Dilla fan, and the grandnephew of Alice Coltrane, had begun producing his own music under the moniker Flying Lotus; he released his first album less than a year after Dilla's death. In 2006, Stones Throw signed a young vocalist and producer nurtured in part by Sa-Ra, Georgia Anne Muldrow. Sa-Ra, too, released their first full-length album the next year. This music, much of it steeped in Dilla's ideas about rhythm and harmony, texture and arrangement, was absent from the airwaves and lived mostly on CD and in digital files shared and streamed online. But the virtual subculture became a tangible scene with a new weekly gathering at Los Angeles nightclub the Airliner.

The party was called "Low End Theory"—an homage to the Tribe Called Quest album whose vibe it sought to evoke; and the heir to Sketchbook, the original party founded as a gathering for producers rather than MCs, a place to revel in beats rather than lyrics. With Flying Lotus as one of their first regular DJs, Low End Theory made a new space for Peanut Butter Wolf, Egon, and Stones Throw, for J-Rocc and the Beat Junkies, and invited House Shoes to invoke the spirit of Saint Andrew's. Rarely was there a night when a Dilla beat wasn't played. Low End Theory's "Beats" or "Future Beats" scene, as its participants came to call it, grew over the next several years, and became the launch point for new producers, including Jason Chung, performing as Nosaj Thing, and Glen Boothe, producing under the moniker Knxwledge. Artists like Thundercat and Berklee–Dilla Ensemble alumni Sonnymoon took the stage.

Within a few years, high-profile artists were making the pilgrimage to Low End Theory: Thom Yorke of Radiohead performed with Flying Lotus, Questlove spun a set of rare Dilla beats, and Erykah Badu came to DJ. Since Dilla's death, Badu's music had traced his musical footsteps, taking a sharp turn from warm neo-soul into electronic production. Badu's post-repast requiem for J Dilla, "Telephone," ended up on the 2008 album *New Amerykah Part One*, on which Erykah collaborated with a host of Dilla disciples, including Karriem Riggins, Madlib, Sa-Ra Creative Partners, Georgia Anne Muldrow, 9th Wonder, and Mike Chav. For the follow-up two years later, *New Amerykah Part Two*, virtually the same cast of characters returned with one of J Dilla's *Welcome 2 Detroit* comrades, Ta'Raach. Dilla was present in spirit, with Badu and Chav adding elements to one of his previously unreleased beats.

Though Low End Theory was a genuine indication of J Dilla's influence on Los Angeles, it was just half of the story. For as long as he'd been beloved by the Hollywood set, the producer from Detroit had a community of fervent followers in the hood who saw Dilla—with his chains and his cars and his rough lyrics—as one of their own; and in many ways, James's heart had always been with the music and musicians south of the 10 freeway.

After collaborating with labelmates Slum Village, former Death Row rapper Kurupt became a champion of Jay Dee's sound. James, in turn, was an admirer of Kurupt's producer Battlecat, who—like another L.A. polymath, DJ Quik—possessed a deep musical sense and played with time-shifting in ways more subtle than Jay Dee, but no less evocative of a sense of languid cool. In the next decade, an exuberant young protégé of Battlecat's named Terrace Martin would help orchestrate the ultimate Dilla-inspired convergence of beats and musicality in Los Angeles.

Martin's connections to J Dilla went back to his teenage years. The aunt who bought Martin his first drum machine, the singer Lalomie Washburn, was signed for a time to Delicious Vinyl; she brought her nephew by a session for the Pharcyde and pointed to Jay Dee as someone to watch. Years later, as Martin embarked on his music career, he met James again through an industry mentor, Naim Ali McNair; and again after Dilla moved to Los Angeles. By then, Martin saw Dilla's ideas permeating much of the hip-hop and R&B he loved.

Terrace Martin had pedigrees in both hip-hop and jazz. He connected with Battlecat the same year that he began seriously studying saxophone at Locke High School's renowned music program, alongside his cousin, Steven "Thundercat" Bruner. Martin's chops got him to a congress of all-star high school jazz bands in Colorado, where he befriended a teenage pianist from Texas named Robert Glasper. Martin continued his jazz studies at CalArts, but he put just as much work into his hip-hop production. He and Thundercat played in Snoop Dogg's backing band, the Snoopadelics, alongside Thundercat's childhood friend, the saxophonist Kamasi Washington. For most of the 2000s, Martin composed songs for his heroes, like Snoop, DJ Quik, and Kurupt; and even coproduced a solo EP for Frank Bush, now "Frank Nitt," at Delicious Vinyl.

But Terrace Martin found his ultimate creative foil in a teenage rapper from Compton.

Kendrick Lamar, like Martin, saw himself as a product of his neighborhood, but also as part of a greater community and a longer lineage. Lamar claimed Tupac Shakur himself had come to him in a dream to ask him to finish his earthly mission. Like the late rapper, Lamar contemplated the circumstances and destiny of the African diaspora; but unlike Shakur, his lyrical path was more subtle and self-reflective. He preferred to tell stories over the course of entire albums, and in multiple voices. And as he grew more confident in his abilities, he began to seek harmonies and rhythms that matched his verbal and psychological complexity. He found them primarily via a group of musicians and programmers able to access all forms and eras of Black music.

Terrace Martin produced Kendrick Lamar's first demo, put a song on his debut album, and enthused about him to his musician friends. Blown away by Kendrick's musicality, Robert Glasper asked Martin to connect him with the rapper to be a guest on his breakthrough *Black Radio* LP. Martin contributed a couple of tracks on Kendrick Lamar's second album, released on Dr. Dre's Aftermath label, *good kid, m.A.A.d city*, on which Lamar made a trusted contributor out of Sonnymoon's Anna Wise, whom he tapped to add vocals to a number of songs, including his single, "Bitch, Don't Kill My Vibe." It was the breakout project for Kendrick Lamar, earning him his first global hits and provoking thoughtful responses from music journalists and academics.

Bolstered by creative vindication and budgetary freedom, and gifted with epiphanies from a recent trip to Africa, Kendrick decided to make a more ambitious lyrical and musical statement, which he was tentatively calling *TU Pimp A Caterpillar*, the capital letters spelling the name of his fallen guru. The overarching storyline—a trip from Compton to Hollywood and back, serving as both autobiography and metaphor—needed a soundtrack that integrated both worlds.

Lamar connected with some of the producers who populated the Low End Theory. He'd worked with Nosaj Thing briefly, and bonded with Flying Lotus when the producer came on tour with him, fleshing out some ideas for the album. He'd also been listening to Knxwledge's work on Stones Throw, and selected an excessively broken beat of his to rhyme over. Taz Arnold of Sa-Ra provided the loopy, unhinged ideas for inter-ludes, the punctuation and connective tissue between songs that turned them into a cohesive whole. Lamar drew on the formidable talents of his label Top Dawg's team of producers, but as his musical mentor and most consistent collaborator, Lamar called again on Terrace Martin.

Kendrick wanted an education in jazz. Martin introduced him to John Coltrane's *A Love Supreme* because he felt that the rapper and the saxophonist had several important things in common: dedication to their craft, an abiding spirituality, and trust in their collaborators. Ken-drick was a musical sponge, and as he studied, Martin assembled his jazz-and-hip-hop dream team—Thundercat, Kamasi Washington, and Robert Glasper—to conjure new ideas and collaborate with Lamar's other producers. Thundercat was already pals with Flying Lotus, and together they created the musical base for the song "Wesley's Theory." Terrace Martin and Sounwave teamed up on several tracks, and on oth-ers Martin worked with the trumpeter and beatmaker Josef Leimberg, billing themselves together as "LoveDragon."

The sixteen songs that came out of these sessions were painted from a musical palette of funk, jazz, gospel, soul, hip-hop, bossa nova, and Afrobeat. Though they were presented as a cultural product of the streets, a message to the OGs and BGs of gangsta rap, they also car-ried the rhythmic and harmonic sophistication of the nerds who spent their time in basements, bedrooms, and attics honing their craft—virtu-osic beat producers with jazz sensibilities, and jazz musicians who had hip-hop chops, led by an ecumenical MC with broad vision. Perhaps the most audible evidence of that musical daring were the six songs that employed J Dilla's rhythmic signature, some of them moving in and out of Dilla Time in ways that the late producer himself had never executed.

One such moment happened on the song "Complexion." Terrace Martin brought Robert Glasper into Dr. Dre's studio for a session, and he and Kendrick played Glasper a succession of tracks—an opportunity to get his playing on as many songs as they could in one shot. Glasper listened and improvised ideas for each. "Complexion" began as it was originally conceived—a rigidly quantized, straight back-and-forth between kick and snare, downbeat and backbeat. But as Glasper added some keyboards to the song over what was to be Kendrick's third verse, it was clear to both Martin and Kendrick that Glasper's additions were calling for a completely new section and direction.

We want to do some Dilla shit here, they said.

In the final mix—which featured a verse from Rapsody, a North Carolina protégé of 9th Wonder—Martin and Kendrick faded the straight beat out from underneath Glasper, leaving nothing but his bare, comped chords. Seconds later, a new, offset, internally conflicted beat came limping in, making the difference between the two kinds of time-feels explicit.

Listening To:
Straight Time vs. Dilla Time

Kendrick Lamar's "Complexion" is a great example of a transition between Straight Time and Dilla Time, and a way to get a visceral sense of how difficult it is for humans to hold the tensions between the two time-feels.

At 2:10, as Kendrick begins singing "I like it, I love it," begin tapping your finger or foot along with the beat. You are in Straight Time.

At 2:30, as the beat fades out, keep tapping your finger at the same tempo. Let the rhythm of the vocals and the piano guide you.

Then, as the new, conflicted beat fades in after 2:35, try to hold the tempo with your finger.

By 2:43, you are in Dilla Time.

"I need that sloppy!" Kendrick yelled over Knxwledge's beat for "Momma"—employing the adjective as a noun, putting language to the time-feel that had become a vital part of his expression but had as yet no fixed name. The album, which had metamorphosed into *To Pimp a Butterfly* by the time of its release in the spring of 2015, marked a resurgence of that rhythm, one that had entered hip-hop and R&B more than a decade earlier. With the additions of Anna Wise and Bilal on vocals; the presence of Terrace Martin, Glasper, Thundercat, Kamasi, and Taz Arnold; Flying Lotus and Knxwledge; and Pete Rock's vocals and scratches on "Complexion," the album was the most significant reunion yet of the alumni of Dilla University.

Kendrick Lamar provided the thematic glue for the project in the form of a letter to Tupac that began with the words, "I remember you was conflicted"—a refrain that he reprised several times over the course of the album, each one expanding in length until, in the final track, he would read the entire epistle directly to Tupac. In citing that conflict, Kendrick was referring specifically to Tupac's own painful and ultimately unsuccessful attempt to reconcile his activist and intellectual pedigree with the toxic lure of street justice; but more broadly to a desire that Lamar shared with his spectral hero, to be a bridge between worlds—scarcity and plenty, art and commerce, sophistication and simple pleasures, Black and white—and not be broken.

As the album garnered Grammy Awards and acclaim, the analysis that followed missed certain subtleties. Some critics portrayed Lamar as rejecting the street for a more sophisticated worldview. For Terrace Martin, who in high school had looked up to Crips and taken part in criminal "licks" even as he practiced his musical ones, it was a false duality. Martin never felt he had to choose between hip-hop and jazz, nor did he feel tension between art and the street. They were one. The rappers who were supposedly "alternative," whether the Pharcyde or Kendrick, they all came from the same place. The idea that musical genius arose only with an antiseptic middle-class upbringing erased the very world that fostered artists like Kendrick Lamar and J Dilla and generations of Black artists before them, an attempt—as Martin phrased it—to "squeeze the ghetto" out of Black art. Writers also tended to obsess over Kendrick's lyrics: wordsmiths extolling another wordsmith's words. But no song is simple text. It is also subtext, context, and pretext. It is a communication consisting of tone and time. Yes, critics understood *To Pimp a Butterfly* was a landmark convergence of jazz and hip-hop. But did anyone notice that the album they lauded as one of the most important musical products of its time—a virtual opera about a man conflicted—used as its main musical motif the *rhythm* of conflict?

This particular rhythm had become a comfortable and common language, used regularly and in innovative ways by a new crop of musicians. That it had become so ordinary made its presence extraordinary, at home alongside the tools and tropes and thoughts gifted by other vital progenitors of African American music. One of them, George Clinton, actually made a brief appearance on the album's lead-off track. Another, Prince, had come to the studio ostensibly to sing the chorus on "Complexion," but he and Kendrick spent their time talking rather than collaborating. Yet so many other ancestors were clearly present, even if they weren't, and that is what made *To Pimp a Butterfly* so evocative.

Louis Armstrong and Billie Holiday were here, swinging. James Brown stomped on the One. Tupac Amaru Shakur lived in between the lines. And the pulse was driven by the irregular heartbeat of James Dewitt Yancey.

Several years earlier and all the way on the other side of the world in Australia, Perrin Moss sat for the final exam of his drum course at the Northern Melbourne Institute of Technical and Further Education. Sitting behind his kit, Perrin was accompanied by two of the three mates from his band Hiatus Kaiyote—Paul Bender on bass guitar and Simon Mavin on keyboards. The guitarist and singer Naomi "Nai Palm" Saalfield sat the song out, positioning herself behind the assessors' table to watch as the boys launched into a severely conflicted, stumbling groove; an original song she'd cowritten called "Swamp Thing." After a few moments Nai observed some commotion among the confounded judges.

"Why can't he stay on beat?" one of them asked Perrin's instructor.

"It's on purpose," the instructor replied. "It's a thing."

Only the teacher's explanation saved the student from failure.

This class had been Perrin's first official training on the drums. He began as a beatmaker. The reason he climbed behind the drum kit was to sample himself, as Perrin found that his computer wasn't the best tool to re-create the sounds and patterns in his head. In his twenties, living in a run-down six-bedroom share house with a bunch of talented musicians in Melbourne's Northcote district, supported by Australia's liberal Social

Security dole, Perrin made learning the drums his day job for two years, nicking the occasional tip from his housemates. A hip-hop head and fan of nineties rap like the Pharcyde and A Tribe Called Quest, Perrin began his education by trying to re-create classic breakbeats. When it came to emulating real-life drummers, he looked to Questlove and Chris Dave. He only later realized that the thread through his favorite records and the progenitor of the particular, conflicted feel he was trying to emulate was J Dilla.

In his head Perrin still saw rhythms as he did on his Cubase music software, as gridwork. But getting his body to nudge individual sounds earlier and later on real drums required a physical education. One of his housemates suggested that when he felt himself rushing the beat, to lean backward, away from the drums. Perrin found that different hand positions yielded different kinds of feels: tense would produce a straighter groove, loose would allow for more swing. Another friend suggested that Perrin develop his internal clock by walking around with a metronome on the slowest tempo, carrying on conversations and daily tasks while making sure to hit or tap something on every downbeat. By the end of his two years of practice, he had learned how to hold several time-feels at once, placing and displacing notes with precision. The TAFE course, the only way he could continue to qualify for social security, was his first formal training. But he loved the work; typical of his ambition, he told his instructor that he wanted to learn how to play four separate rhythms at the same time.

Perrin Moss was part of a new generation of musicians who had as much fluency with programming as playing; and for whom the disjointed, fractured rhythms of programmed music were native territory, even in Melbourne. Like Perrin, his bandmate Nai was a self-taught prodigy with an ear for the odd: raised in her mother's Melbourne home with music from Afrobeat to flamenco to American soul; orphaned and sent to live in the mountains with a foster family, where she learned to play guitar and discovered the broken beats of J Dilla; and finally back to Melbourne, where she began gigging and met Perrin while she played on a toy pink guitar at a local cafe. At another performance, she met Bender, who hailed from Tasmania, studied jazz at the University of Miami in

Florida, and loved hip-hop. For their first jam session, they added Simon Mavin, Perrin's housemate and Bender's occasional bandmate. Mavin, a keyboardist and Herbie Hancock fan, was the most accomplished musician of the bunch.

They worked on one of Nai's ideas, "Nakamarra." It was a sweet soul song, an affectionate ode to a friend of Nai's . . . That is, it could have been, if Perrin hadn't taken that left turn, launching into a lurching, limping beat during the chorus. Being a J Dilla fan by way of Madlib, Bender knew the feel well. He called it a "jilted" groove; he'd just never played one, and certainly never imagined it would work in this context.

Thus began a mutual education: two unrestrained, untrained autodidacts taking two seasoned pros on a challenging musical ride. Nai felt time differently, often beginning her phrases in places that seemed off and building stacks of notes that didn't match harmonic convention. Perrin could play swung-against-straight with ease, but hadn't yet mastered some simpler fundamentals. *Let's play in 12/8 time*, Simon suggested. *I don't know how to play in 12/8 time*, Perrin replied. Of course he did; he just didn't know it was 12/8 time. Bender decided that the more they did the crazier, jilted stuff, the better they sounded. The four musicians worked on a repertoire and created a sound, recording an album at Perrin and Simon's share house. The four of them hadn't given much thought to whether their music might make sense to anyone but themselves. No one dared harbor even modest expectations for their album, *Tawk Tomahawk*, released in 2012. Who would care about this little band from the bottom of the world, playing jazz chord changes over Dilla-style beats, fronted by a crazy witch woman who wanted her guitar to sound like an African kora, wrote like Stevie Wonder, and sang like Mavis Staples, Erykah Badu, and Kate Bush rolled into one?

One evening, Hiatus Kaiyote got a gig opening for the American artist Taylor McFerrin during his swing through Melbourne. McFerrin took their CDs on tour with him and gave them to everyone he could—including the London radio host Gilles Peterson. "Nakamarra" and its swerve into Dilla Time soon transmitted a sonic Bat-Signal to a particular global audience. Questlove and Erykah Badu posted and praised the song on social media. Q-Tip offered up a verse for a remix. Then came the news that Prince was a fan, too. They acquired an American manager, signed to Sony Music, and began touring the world. In 2013, "Nakamarra" was nominated for a Grammy Award.

Thus Hiatus Kaiyote began their second album, *Choose Your Weapon*, with an explicit nod to J Dilla. Nai Palm wrote in a style that was simple to her, but whose strange chords, bizarre timings, and sudden transitions on songs like "Molasses" and "Jekyll" demanded her bandmates' skills. Perrin Moss found ways to incorporate his "jilted" grooves into almost any song, shifting in and out of Dilla Time in bangers and ballads alike. In a band, this effect couldn't be achieved alone, and in particular required great focus from Perrin's rhythm section partner, Paul Bender. The more a drummer plays against the pulse, the more the bassist must work to maintain it. Bender had come to see his job as standing solidly in one place. When Perrin started playing in some weirdly swung subdivision of rhythm, Bender would aggressively propagate his own, straighter subdivision. Their rhythmic relationship often felt to Bender like they were standing on separate mountain peaks lobbing giant Dragon Balls of energy at each other. When they played live, and Perrin would peel off, change directions, do crazy fills that seemed unconnected to any part of the rhythm—something that would bewilder any other musician—Bender would rock his neck violently on the pulse, refusing to be pulled away from it, thinking:

Nope. I'm here, motherfucker. This is where it's at.

Hiatus Kaiyote's *Choose Your Weapon* in 2015 became the most audacious and extensive deployment of Dilla Time that any group of traditional musicians had yet attempted.

Few knew what to call Hiatus's music. Journalists tagged them as neo-soul and future funk. When Hiatus Kaiyote were nominated for their second Grammy Award it was in the R&B category. Then there was the dreaded "j" word, which the band members didn't much like, though they had jazz chops and jazz changes and jazz's ceaseless commitment to the new. Robert Glasper of course found them, inviting Hiatus onto his album of Miles Davis remakes. Hip-hop producers and artists began sampling them: 9th Wonder used them for the final song on Kendrick Lamar's *DAMN*, the album for which the artist would win a Pulitzer

Prize; Anderson .Paak, a former assistant to Sa-Ra Creative Partners and now a budding superstar, mined their material, as did Drake, Jay-Z, and Beyoncé. Though Hiatus Kaiyote were as ambivalent about the "neo-soul" label as the original neo-soul artists themselves, their embrace by that community is how the band found themselves onstage at Chene Park performing for a crowd of discerning Detroiters.

Nai was terrified as the band began their set. Then her eyes fixed on a young man standing in the third row. It was Dwele, dancing and clapping as if to encourage everyone behind him to do the same. *Welcome to Detroit. Welcome home.* And they played, swinging on the strait.

The four of them together had created an evolved version of the rhythmic friction begun in a basement almost seven miles from that spot, and first attempted by traditional musicians fifteen years earlier by D'Angelo, Questlove, and Pino Palladino at Electric Lady in New York. And though they counted J Dilla as a direct inspiration, they saw his work connected to something quite common in the rest of the world. Complex polyrhythm, microrhythmic conflicts . . . they were present in many musical traditions across the globe: West African drumming, Cuban guaguanco, Balinese kotekan. Colonialism and capitalism had forced a European frame on much of the world's popular music. Dilla's rhythms broke through that frame, creating a kind of reunion with the musical thinking of Africa, the Caribbean, South America, and Asia.

Hiatus Kaiyote played traditional instruments, but together, as a band, the instrument they had mastered was time itself, stretching it out and squeezing it in like the bellows of a celestial accordion.

I n the second decade after the death of J Dilla, his colleagues and disciples began claiming places and spaces of distinction in the twin worlds of popular and high culture. Wherever they went, his creative concepts went with them.

Ahmir "Questlove" Thompson, Tarik "Black Thought" Trotter, and James Poyser had become proverbial household names as the Roots played nightly on network television. Ahmir made a point to work in a half-dozen J Dilla "easter eggs" in their set every week, so many he joked that Dilla was the eleventh member of the *Tonight Show* band. Then came the evening in 2016 when the musical guest—a young pop singer from Long Island whom they had never met, Jon Bellion—re-created and name-checked an obscure J Dilla beat onstage before launching into his own song, which he then played on an MPC in front of a national audience. Ahmir caught Bellion after the show: "Dilla would have been proud," he told the young artist. Dilla would undoubtedly have been proud of his friends in the Roots, too.

D'Angelo delivered his third album in 2014. It was worth the wait. *Black Messiah* featured "Really Love," the song that James had helped inspire back when D'Angelo needed a charge. It wasn't so much what James had said but what he didn't say—the waves, not the words. When he thought of his friend now, D'Angelo's mind landed on a parable he once heard, from the Upanishads, about the beautiful blue-black boy who "spoke with a voice that sounded like many waters." That was James.

The ripples continued. In 2016, Jason Moran succeeded the pianist Billy Taylor as the Artistic Director for Jazz at the Kennedy Center in Washington, DC. As part of his tenure, Moran got Q-Tip appointed as the venerable institution's first Artistic Director for Hip-Hop Culture. The lines between genres, between traditional and electronic music-making and composition, between high and low art, had begun to truly dissolve. Nowhere was this more evident than when one of the world's most famous jazz venues hosted a tribute to J Dilla for four evenings in October 2019.

Part of a monthlong residency at the Blue Note in Manhattan's Greenwich Village, Robert Glasper, Chris Dave, and the rest of his band were joined by a special guest: T3, the soloist from Conant Gardens, performing on the same stage that Dizzy Gillespie, Sarah Vaughan, and Lionel Hampton had once graced. A radiant Maureen Yancey sat in the front row. One night, Common and Karriem Riggins dropped by, partners with Glasper now in another group they called August Greene.

"If you know me," Glasper told the audience, "you know that J Dilla's a big part of my life. The only producer that . . . changed the way I play music. He literally changed the way a whole generation plays their instruments."

For the next hour, Glasper, wearing a T-shirt that read DILLA STILL EXCITES, took the band and the audience through a range of Dilla-produced songs including "Fuck the Police," "Jealousy," "Climax," "Conant Gardens," "Raise It Up," "Get Dis Money," "Thelonius," and "Hold Tight."

T3, who spent years holding tight to James and Baatin as if to keep them in orbit, now played all three corners of the lyrical triangle, trading verses and choruses with Glasper, looking like he might be living out some kind of fantasy of being a member of Slum Village, his singing bringing peals of laughter from the audience.

It's three-quarters of the way through the set, and Glasper turns serious. He begins touching his piano keys, fingers moving with no logical relationship to each other, bringing forth a cacophony of jumbled notes. He isn't soloing, not really. This is a different kind of noise, a machine noise, seemingly scrolling forward and backward through a sequence, repeating, latching on to a series of chords, playing them, *run it back*, playing them, *run it back*. Close your eyes and Glasper isn't at the piano, he's hitting a pad on an MPC, repeatedly. *Can I find the right place? Can I find the open space? There it is,* run it back, *there it is.* We hear the melody hidden behind the chords: *Of love . . . that's in . . . your eyes . . . a look. Of love . . . that's in . . . your eyes . . . a look.* T3 flashes forward through the decades from the chanting crowd at Saint Andrew's in Detroit to the Blue Note in New York, where they still know the words to Slum Village's "The Look of Love." *Say it with me one time: You know what love is.*

They end every night the way almost all Dilla tribute events end, with the Slum Village national anthem. Again, everybody knows the refrain: *Don't sell yourself to fall in love with the things you do.* It's a curious little line from James Yancey, written in his twenties, more than twenty years prior. At the time, when T3 wrote his verse, he thought he knew exactly what James meant: *The rap game is fucked up. Don't give yourself away to it.* "Yeah, Jay Dee, man, that's true sometimes," he replied in the song. But James had never actually told him what it meant. That wasn't James's way. It could very well have meant something else. It might mean: *Don't change yourself so that people will love you.* It might mean: *Never get too comfortable with yourself,* always *change it up.*

T3 knows that it might not mean anything. It might just sound good.

16.
Fragments

When things got really bad in the Motor City, they were going to strip it and sell it for parts.

Inaugurated the same year that J Dilla was born, Mayor Coleman Young presided for five terms and twenty years over a white flight and industrial decline he couldn't control. Then Dennis Archer served six years, promising to heal the divisions between Detroit and its suburbs. It didn't work: Archer found that you can't heal a relationship with folks who don't care if you live or die. Then in 2002 came Kwame Kilpatrick, the so-called hip-hop mayor—only four years older than J Dilla and a Cass Tech High School football teammate of James's friend from Vernon Chapel, Copez Wright. Kilpatrick resigned in his second term, in 2008, after being convicted of obstruction of justice and perjury, as the region reeled under the aftermath of the subprime lending crisis and the ensuing financial crash and recession. Billionaires like Mike Ilitch and Dan Gilbert snapped up real estate at rock-bottom prices, gentrifying Detroit's downtown, but Detroit became the largest American city in history to declare bankruptcy, in 2013.

The city owed somewhere between $18 and $20 billion. Detroit's recently installed emergency manager, Kevyn Orr, pressured the city's creditors to settle for pennies on the dollar. The creditors, in turn, demanded the city sell as many of its assets as possible. The most precious of those properties was the $8 billion collection belonging to the Detroit Institute of Arts, which the Financial Guaranty Insurance Company argued was "not an essential asset . . . to the delivery of services in the city." The proposed sale of the works in the grand Beaux-Arts building on

Woodward included the collection's crown jewel: a mural painted by the Mexican artist Diego Rivera in 1933 called *Detroit Industry*.

Henry Ford's son, Edsel, commissioned the piece, wanting Rivera to glorify Detroit as the capital of mechanized manufacturing. But the twenty-seven frescoes that Rivera painted around the museum's central court were more ambiguous than his benefactor envisioned. Rivera's murals depicted men, Black and white alike, in the bowels of a factory, their faces alight in the fires of forges, their bodies in motion, under the watchful eyes of stern foremen. And though the laborers' muscles strained against metal, the real struggle portrayed by Rivera was against machine time: a line of men waiting to punch a clock for their shift, straining over moving assembly lines, trying not to fall behind, or be left behind, or crushed underneath. Other frescoes depicting Detroit's pharmaceutical and aeronautical industries were equally equivocal: helpful medicines and chemical weapons, planes for flying and planes for bombing, men in lab coats, men in gas masks, the gift and the curse of modernity. *Detroit Industry* evoked some of the great pro-worker art that preceded it, like Fritz Lang's 1927 film *Metropolis*, the first great science-fiction dystopia that depicted a world in which workers lived and labored deep within the Earth, in a subterranean hellscape where men fed and were eaten by machines, providing a template that would resonate not only in Rivera's murals but through the end of the century, ultimately informing the 1999 film *The Matrix*.

For some people, Rivera's images were too much a mirror for Detroit, which, alongside its forges and factories, literally had an entire underground industry—vast salt mines that ran underneath the city.* Capitalists called the mural communist and clergy called it sacrilege. But time had made *Detroit Industry* a beloved symbol of the beleaguered city that was worth saving. The outcry over the potential sale of Detroit's treasures was so great that the museum's leadership and sympathetic federal judges engineered a solution in 2014 called "The Grand Bargain," in

---

* These underground salt mines would be the subject of a play, "Salt City," written by James's old friend jessica Care moore and produced down the street from the DIA, at the Charles H. Wright Museum of African American History, in 2019.

which private donors extricated the DIA from the city's control, part of a larger agreement to move Detroit out of bankruptcy.

As the city recovered, the Rivera Court became a symbolic gathering place for people who loved Detroit. The DIA instituted a Friday Night Live concert series, giving visitors the feeling of being within the chambers of the city's heart. It was here, on February 22, 2019, amid the frescoes of man negotiating his relationship with the machine, that Detroit's son James Dewitt Yancey was finally embraced by the city's preeminent cultural institution, as the DIA hosted "The Music of J Dilla," where Miguel Atwood-Ferguson and a dozen humans would perform twelve songs based on Dilla's machine compositions from his *Suite for Ma Dukes*.

M aureen flew in from Puerto Rico, where she now lived with her new husband in a town called, of all things, Aguadilla. She strolled through marble halls filled with sculptures and tapestries with Martha's daughter Faith beside her. Maureen had never come to the DIA when she was young. Now she and James were both inside this place, physically and metaphorically.

A thousand people packed the floor of the Rivera Court—a diverse, lively crowd, echoing Rivera's portrayal of the "four races" in his frescoes above—as Miguel Atwood-Ferguson led a modest orchestra of local musicians through Dilla classics and obscurities, sounds bouncing sharply off the murals. Then, Atwood-Ferguson addressed the audience: "We have the great honor of Dilla's mother being here with us today. Put your hands together for Maureen Yancey."

As the crowd cheered, the tiny woman in the black turtleneck rose to speak.

"I am so honored to be here today," she began. "I am just so full right now . . ." She'd done this at countless events before, but Maureen found herself fighting back tears.

"I want to say thank you, Detroit, because Dilla was raised in Detroit . . . He went to Detroit public schools . . ." Here, she was interrupted by the raucous applause of her fellow citizens. The older Detroiters could remember a time when a Detroit education was as good as that of any city in America, boasting the robust music curriculum that produced the artists and entrepreneurs of Motown Records.

"I was born and raised in Detroit, in Black Bottom, and so was my mom. And I want you to know that you never know how something little becomes so much. Dilla did not have what other children had when he grew up. Now children are being taught with Dilla's music." Here she referred to the J Dilla Foundation's 2015 donation of nearly $10,000 in electronic equipment to Pershing High School to create the J Dilla Music Lab. Her second nonprofit—the James Dewitt Yancey Foundation—was currently partnering with the Save the Music Foundation to create J Dilla Music Tech Grants for electronic music education in forty-two schools across the country, including Detroit's Central High School.*

"And I just thank Detroit," she concluded. "I thank the struggle and strife that we went through because I think that that is part of what enriches our heritage. Around the world everywhere I go, people ask me: 'What is that magic that Detroit has?' And I tell them, 'Detroit, that's the *real* Emerald City.'"

They knew exactly what she meant, and they clapped for her, and she took a bow.

After the concert, Maureen was mobbed. A teary-eyed young woman in a Detroit sweater told Maureen that she lost it when they played "Stakes Is High."

"I cried too," Maureen replied, taking both of the woman's hands in her own.

A slender young man told her, "Thank you for everything you've done."

"It's been rough," Maureen replied with a sigh. "But I'm still fighting."

Now a couple approached her, asking Maureen to autograph their program. The man told her: "J Dilla changed my life."

"He changed mine, too," Maureen told him. "After a ten-year period,

---

* As of publication, the James Dewitt Yancey Foundation remains in good standing with the IRS as a tax-exempt nonprofit.

I am still mourning. But now I have a brand-new life, and it's all because of him. I met my current husband through his music."

So much of Maureen's life had been determined by men. Her childhood surnames changed as they walked in and out of her mother's life. She'd given herself over to Dewitt for decades. Even her relationship with her son James, driven by a mother's sense of duty, required a sublimation of her own identity that continued even after his death. She lost her son, lost her business, tried to build something that made her son her business, and found herself fighting, at every turn, with people who claimed that they, not her, had her son's will in mind, who told her the things she did were wrong. They were always saying, "No." All she wanted to do was say, "Yes."

The estate was still in probate court in California, an endless process that she hoped would end soon. But until then, Maureen would keep fulfilling the mission that her son gave to her. The girl from Black Bottom now flies around the world to represent James. She's greeted at the doors of museums and nightclubs as a VIP, even when she's not on the list. They know her name.

"Hey, Ma Dukes," they say. And she walks right in.

James had gone, but in his passing he had given her something he surely would have wanted for her: a will of her own.

Just miles from the birthplace of James's great-grandfather Red Cornish, the National Museum of African American History and Culture finally opened in Washington, DC, on September 24, 2016. The design of the museum compelled visitors to walk through history, from the basement to the upper floors, from a space that evoked the hold of a slave ship, through revolution and the Civil War, through Jim Crow and the Civil Rights and Black Power movements, spiraling toward the light. On the top floor, the Musical Crossroads exhibit unfolded centuries of Black predominance in American popular culture, composed of objects such as George Clinton's P-Funk Mothership, Bootsy Collins's star-shaped bass, and Chuck Berry's red Cadillac. For Timothy Anne Burnside, every object she collected was like a child, and she wanted the most space for every single one. Punctuating the very end of the hip-hop exhibit was a tall narrow case labeled "J Dilla."

Burnside designed the display with two intentions. The first was to highlight the idea of the power of collectives in hip-hop. Viewing the case from top to bottom, the story began with a legendary portrait taken by Janette Beckman in 1990 of some of the original Native Tongues—A Tribe Called Quest, De La Soul, the Jungle Brothers, Monie Love. Beneath it was Sacha Waldman's photo of the Native Tongues' direct descendants, the Soulquarians. Her second aim was to contrast hip-hop's humble origins with its impact on the world. For Burnside, J Dilla symbolized that more than any artist, the quiet influencer in the larger collective, Neo in their soul. Beneath Raph Rashid's black-and-white photo of a focused James working on his MPC in Common's living room sat his machine.

Over the years, on her way to and from meetings and errands in the museum, Burnside often detoured through Musical Crossroads just to watch people's reactions to the objects. Nothing there fascinated her more than visitors' encounter with the J Dilla display.

There were the pilgrims, the folks who came seeking J Dilla's MPC. When they spied it, *boom!* . . . they made a beeline for the case. Mos Def had been like that. When he arrived, he told Burnside: *I only have time to see Dilla. Where is he?*

There were the hip-hop heads who didn't know that Dilla's equipment was here, and when they stumbled upon it, turned toward each other, hands over their mouths, *Yo! Oh, shit!* . . . pointing at the drum machine, taking snapshots and selfies with their cell phones.

Then there were the devotees. When these folks saw the J Dilla display, they didn't take photos. They'd stop, put a hand over their heart, and sigh. Some of them would stand for a long while, a quiet communion. Questlove was like that when he came. 9th Wonder put his palms on the glass and closed his eyes.

Sometimes there were tears. Not just from his friends, but from strangers, people who had never touched or met or even seen the man. One day, Burnside saw a middle-aged woman staring at the case, holding her purse, wiping her eyes. *Thank you*, she repeated. *Thank you.* The woman, overcome, put her face in her handkerchief, took a moment, and began to tell her story. The whole family, despite their age differences—herself, her ex-husband, her oldest son, her youngest son—all lived by J Dilla's music. It was hard to explain.

Since his public tirade against Ma Dukes, House Shoes had taken a vow of silence in all matters related to J Dilla's posthumous legacy. When a writer from the website *HipHopDX* asked him in early 2016 to comment on an interview given by Maureen Yancey, Shoes responded, "I'm not clickbait."

The article, "J Dilla's Mother 'Ma Dukes' Yancey Finally Details House Shoes Beef," published on J Dilla's birthday, ignited Shoes's fury all over again. Maureen claimed she had never met him before he visited James in California, when he had been in her basement countless times and she'd even brought him Faygo pop from her fridge. She didn't acknowledge a penny of the thousands of dollars he had sent her way. She claimed she had no problem with him before the *Rebirth* project, yet friends he trusted told him that she had been actively trying to destroy his reputation even then. Now, in this article, she publicly issued an edict that no one who wanted her support or endorsement could work with him, ever.

Her resolve had been clear to him after he helped Eothen "Egon"

Alapatt resurrect J Dilla's "lost" MCA album, which was finally going to be released by the estate through the now-profitable Pay Jay production company.* The project had taken ten years to complete. Egon found that the master digital files from Dilla's Clinton Township studio computer were encoded by an archiving program made by a company that was no longer in business. Dave Cooley spent years trying to crack the code, even consulting with Mike Chav before he was able to locate someone with working software. When Cooley launched it, the multitrack files spooled out in the same meticulous manner in which James had organized them. To answer some questions about James's intentions and process, Egon called on House Shoes, who was present for some of the recording and had himself contributed the song that James had designated as "The Introduction." But when Maureen Yancey discovered that House Shoes had a track on the album, she demanded that Egon remove it.

To Egon and Shoes both, this album was the one remaining intact artifact of James's will, and both of them took their role as caretakers seriously. Slated to be released in April 2016 as *The Diary*, it was a vital time capsule of James Dewitt Yancey figuring out how to transform from a beatmaker into a recording artist; and songs like "The Shining Part 1," "The Creep," "Trucks," and "The Ex" all sounded like they could have, should have, and would have had a shot at being hits, if they had been released when they could have, should have, would have. Egon, risking his relationship with Maureen, refused to alter the album and sublimate Dilla's will to his mother's. Maureen was furious. She called Alex Borden, still overseeing the estate, and demanded that Egon be fired. Borden refused. Maureen, who had sat in the front row at Egon's wedding alongside his parents, stopped speaking to him.

Maureen had recently excommunicated Waajeed, too, announcing in a Facebook post, "DJ House Shoes and Waajeed are not part of the Dilla composition."

"To be frank, I don't know what the issue is," Waajeed responded on his own page. He'd run afoul of Jonathon Taylor back in 2012, and per-

---

* James Yancey's tax debt was paid by 2017 and money began to flow to the heirs of the estate thereafter.

haps Maureen still felt entitled to Waajeed's personal archives of photos, video, and music.* Waajeed suspected also that Maureen might be angry that he had reconciled with Shoes. But Waajeed refused to be written out of history: "I am very much a part of the composition. FOREVER. There is no delete button for my involvement. NO ONE is in a position to imply that I can't share the music I helped build."

And then Waajeed asked a pointed question: "Do you think James would be happy with this chaos in his name?"

In the thread beneath his post, amid dozens of sympathetic comments, one old friend in particular came to support him: Maureen Yancey's adopted son, Earl Hurst.

"We haven't spoken in years, K," he wrote, using Waajeed's childhood nickname. "But you were and always will be my friend, my mentor, my Brother. That's a fact. Stay real! Most of these folks don't know what's what, but I do . . ."

All of this was fresh in Shoes's mind when he read Maureen's last words in *HipHopDX*: "For House Shoes to fashion himself as my son's friend and to talk about his mom, you're definitely not a friend in any context and you're definitely my enemy."

Smoldering, Shoes wrote out a scroll—as Baatin might have said—an entire rebuttal to the article refuting it point by point. But this time, he counted: one . . . two . . . three . . . four . . .

By the time he got to twenty, he decided not to send it. And the world did not end. In fact, the next day, his song with Dilla, "The Introduction," dropped on the internet. Shoes thought: *Maybe the Universe does take care of shit.*

Shoes's love for Dilla had become less demonstrative and more private. But he still participated, when invited, in small Dilla retrospectives and tributes, because he would always represent for his fallen mentors: the Funky Cowboys, James Dewitt Yancey and DeShaun "Proof" Holton.

There were bigger targets for Shoes's outrage now. His rage tweets about Donald Trump earned him a visit from two Secret Service agents,

---

* Maureen Yancey states that she was upset when she heard that Waajeed had provided video and photos to a Dilla-related project that she had not approved.

who'd found a Rev. Shines and Conway single that he had distributed in 2018 with an illustrated cover that depicted Trump's assassination. The agents were tight-lipped, posing a line of serious questions. *How's your relationship with your family? Have you been to jail or prison? Have you ever been diagnosed with mental illness or been in a mental hospital? What's your educational history? What's your work history?*

House Shoes told them almost everything: How he dropped out of college and spent the rest of his tuition money on records. How he began working in a record shop and started his career as a DJ in Detroit. And how he began releasing his own records with production by J Dilla. One of the Secret Service agents put up a hand to stop Shoes.

"Waitwaitwaitwaitwaitwaitwait," the agent said. "Hold on. You put out one of *J Dilla's* first records?!"

The rest of Michael Buchanan's conversation with the Secret Service consisted of him sharing his Dilla memories and memorabilia.

The agents left without Shoes sharing the one story they might have found somewhat alarming: That the reason he had left college was that he had been kicked out for, on a drunken night in his freshman year, lighting a bulletin board on fire; and that before he had become House Shoes, his first DJ name was "The Arsonist."

He was the Arsonist still, setting fire to things. But Michael Buchanan was at peace with himself: *I might talk a lot of shit, and people might think I'm an asshole, but whenever I pop off it comes from a place of love and protection. Fuck it. There's nothing worse in this world than a liar or a thief, and there are plenty, and you have to stand up to them, no matter who they are.*

It was the most important lesson he was now trying to teach his children, especially to his young son, James DeShaun Buchanan.

H erman Hayes built his donut shop in downtown Detroit at the place where it all started, right there in Woodward's elegant, shattered grid: the old Milner Hotel, where Maureen and Dewitt ran their restaurant; where, in apartments 412 and 413, James spent the first years of his life; where, on sunny days, Dewitt would take two-year-old James to

Harmonie Park, just behind the building, to spin records. The triangle-shaped building was now remodeled as the Ashley condominiums, and Herm rented out the small space at the tip where the old Corner Pocket diner used to be, where Rosa Parks used to lunch. With increased foot traffic on Woodward and Broadway, and the Detroit Tigers playing at Comerica Park two blocks away, Herm felt he had a shot at making it work. Beneath it all was a plan to provide a place for his nieces and his own kids to work and, some day, to operate and own. He called it "Dilla's Delights," partly to remind the world about James's love for his two daughters, and partly because he worried that calling the shop "Dilla's Donuts" might put him in conflict with the folks at Stones Throw Records.

On May 3, 2016, Herman Hayes worked all night, made twenty-eight dozen donuts, and opened the doors to Dilla's Delights for the first time. Customers entered a small, tidy triangle, with a riot of Dilla memorabilia on the walls and red lighting fixtures hanging from twenty-foot-high ceilings. Wrapped around the sides of the counter was a patchwork of album covers of artists that James had sampled—Giorgio Moroder, the Jackson 5, Raymond Scott, Gap Mangione. Inside the glass cases, Herm's donuts were displayed before little, record shaped cards announcing their flavors, like Conant Gardens Glaze, McNasty Macaroon, Lightworks Lemon Glaze, Fan Tas Tic Fruit Fritters, and Cakeboy Chocolate. There was Black Bottom Blueberry to celebrate the old neighborhood and Red Cornish Cinnamon Roll to honor James's great-grandfather; Rasul Wasl Raspberry as tribute to Baatin, and of course the plain Jon Doe. Herm sold out by 10:00 a.m. and had to close. The opening was covered in the local press and by *Rolling Stone* and other music websites. Over the next year, visitors arrived from across the world to see the shop. It was humble, but—aside from a growing crop of murals going up with J Dilla's image on buildings around the city, including two in Eastern Market— it was truly Detroit's only living memorial to James Dewitt Yancey.

Building a business is easier than maintaining it. Herm didn't have the money for automated equipment, so he made every donut by hand. Herm found himself pulling six all-nighters a week at the bakehouse on the East Side, running the donuts to the shop, rushing to buy supplies, running home to get a couple hours of sleep, and starting over again. The foot traffic was undependable. His food and labor costs were too high to sell the donuts for less than two dollars each, a high price point for what he called a "fifty-cent donut town." By the end of his third year, Herm was deep in debt.

He had hoped, too, that more of James's people would visit. Artists who called J Dilla a friend would blow into town for a show and not stop by. Herm's sense of loneliness was compounded when James's friend and Herm's supporter since his first lupus walk, Phife, died of kidney failure. Herm was then diagnosed with skin cancer and had to balance his workload with trips to the VA hospital. He'd hated the idea of crowdsourcing funds using Dilla's name. It felt unseemly to him. But in late 2019, with a choice between that and closing the shop, Herm launched an internet fundraiser for $17,000. To his great relief, the call was answered with alacrity by thousands of donors. It let him know where people stood. Eothen "Egon" Alapatt kicked it off by donating the first $1,000, and DJ House Shoes's $300 put Herm over the $17,000 mark.

Then, two months later, the COVID-19 pandemic hit Detroit, forcing him to lock the doors. The unscheduled vacation did him good: He went down to Atlanta to stay with his adult children. He rested, he ran, he recovered his health. He stopped playing the role of "Uncle Herm" for the first time in years. Then, in the summer of 2020, he returned to Detroit. The shop remained closed, but Herm resumed making Dilla's Delights donuts for local outlets in his home kitchen.

The thing about making donuts by hand is that you can't overwork the flour, or the donuts get tough. You die-cut each ring by hand and you have to handle the dough gently so it retains its round shape. And once it hits the oil, you have to be really quick about it so that the donut doesn't burn: sixty seconds on one side, sixty seconds on the other, then onto a wire rack to drain and cool. Herm has to turn each of those donuts smoothly in the roiling oil so that they don't splatter. And he found the perfect tool to do it. Each and every Dilla's Delights donut since the very beginning has been made with a pair of drumsticks.

After James died, he came to Joylette in a dream. In it, she was back in Los Angeles, getting dropped off at the airport by Bobo, Maureen, and James for her return to Detroit.

James asked her: "You don't love me no more?"

Joy replied: "James, I will *always* love you."

For Joy, there had never been another man of consequence. In her brighter moments, she recalled the fun they had and was grateful for the time they spent together. But sometimes Joy would turn sad. She remembered when her father was dying, James asked her: "There's nothing they can do for him?" James got really quiet. Later, they talked, the only discussion they ever had about death. James told her: "When I die, I don't want to be in the grave, down there by myself." How lonely and frightened James must have been in his last days. How heartbroken at being so young and not being able to see his daughters grow up, both Ja'Mya *and* Ty-Monae. And Joy had wanted that for James, for him to have been able to go on in life, be his own man, enjoy his kids, and find love—whether it was with her or some other woman. All of that had been stolen from him. And of all the things that had been taken from Ja'Mya over the years, not having her father around was the worst theft of all.

Whenever Joylette brushed Ja'Mya's hair, her thoughts drifted to her own mother. It had been their ritual, too. After Sherran Hunter's struggle with AIDS weakened her, Janell tried to give her mother a break by assuming the task of grooming her younger sister, but Joylette insisted that her mother do it. Maybe Joy didn't fully understand what was happening, or maybe on some intuitive level, she understood completely, and wanted as much of her mother as she could get while she was still living.

"Mama, are *you* gonna die?" Ja'Mya asked Joylette after they buried James.

"No, I'm not gonna die," Joy answered. It wasn't a lie. But it wasn't the whole story either. Joy was an orphan. She would not let Ja'Mya be one. Through all the drama with the estate, this was the one thing that kept Joy going. *Let me be here for her*, she prayed. *Let me be here until she gets out of school, until she gets married.*

Joylette raised Ja'Mya while she worked jobs for the City of Detroit youth department and then for the Detroit Medical Center. She kept Ja'Mya in church, kept her focused on school. She kept her connected with James's family, and with her half sister, Ty-Monae, whom both Joy and Ja'Mya loved. She didn't let Ja'Mya have a boyfriend until high school, but when Ja'Mya finally met someone, Joylette made sure to do what she felt hadn't been done for her. She welcomed him. She befriended his family. After Ja'Mya was accepted into Emory University on a full scholarship, even James's people told her: *You did a great job.*

On the evening of Ja'Mya's eighteenth birthday, James visited Joy's dreams again. It was uncanny, like he was right there. She was stroking James's face, feeling the warmth of his skin. He said he'd come so that they could be together. To see that girl fly.

Reporter's Notes and Sources

Dilla Time is the product of time itself: more than four years of intensive work, including four summers in and multiple additional visits to Detroit; and also three decades of experience and relationships in hip-hop, music journalism, and the music business. This book is a work of independent journalism: I did not seek approval from any entity, but rather endeavored to build trust with individual people. It is narrative nonfiction: all detail and dialogue is based on reporting and research; none of it is invented or imagined. Where I relay quotes, those statements happened in real time; where my sources are unsure of what exactly was said, I italicize those statements. Where I portray the inner thoughts and feelings of my characters, it is because they told me about them, or told someone else.

This book comprises the stories of many people, but chiefly it attempts to inscribe the life of someone who is no longer around to speak for himself, someone whose speech was often spare when he was alive. I have most heavily relied on reporting—direct interviews with more than 190 people—supplemented by published or unpublished interviews with James Dewitt Yancey, court documents, and the mass of fine journalism and research done on J Dilla and the other characters and topics in this book, from musicology to medicine, from the history of Detroit to that of digital audio workstations, all listed on the following pages.

My interviewing process was layered. I not only gathered information but often returned for readbacks and fact-checking in an attempt to catch any mistakes, to preserve nuances that might otherwise be lost, and to reconcile conflicting stories. Where those accounts remain in conflict, I have provided context in the footnotes. Some sources were loquacious and others circumspect. Some told great stories and several did not want their stories told. Many sources asked me to keep certain things they said or did off the record, and that is a trust I hold inviolate.

One of the most challenging stories to tell was of the relationship between Maureen Yancey and Joylette Hunter, whose narratives of the same events often diverge, and who have both established credibility in different ways. Another is the relationship between James Yancey and Monica Whitlow, who was forthright about the broad points of her history with James but somewhat guarded about their times together. One result is that Ms. Whitlow's story here is not as detailed as Ms. Hunter's. I have chosen not to attempt to interview James's two daughters, partly because they were very young children when he died but also to respect their privacy. Still another challenge was establishing the creation story of the will of James Dewitt Yancey, which I detail in a separate section below.

Fans and students of J Dilla will notice in this book that there are several widely and perennially accepted truths that my reporting has revealed as dubious: Beverly Dewitt Yancey's authorship of the song "It's a Shame"; James Dewitt Yancey's authorship of the original version of "Got 'Til It's Gone"; the idea that *Donuts* was composed largely in his hospital bed; the idea that James created his signature sound by simply turning off the timing functions of his drum machine. These are tales told by many of the sources cited and in some cases by James himself; then circulated and repeated without confirmation or further inquiry. My own conclusions are the result of new reporting and research, and a judgment about the relative reliability of each source and the feasibility of each story.

With my judgment comes a certain subjectivity arising from my many positions in relationship to my subjects. Some are positions of difference: a native New Yorker writing about Detroit, a white American writing about Black people and culture, a person from a middle-class family writing about families with less wealth, a Jewish person writing about Christians and Muslims. Others are positions of similarity: I was a record producer and beatmaker in hip-hop; many of James's friends and colleagues were and are my friends and colleagues; I am one of the few to write professionally about James who actually worked with him and visited the basement on McDougall. The thing about positions is that they work both ways: similarities can often create a compromising closeness and differences can create a healthy distance. Either way, I try to lead with care and empathy for the humans in this book, and I hope to counter whatever unwitting damage I might do with the greater weight of good.

There are three strong convictions driving my work: first, that J Dilla deserved a history that was true and comprehensive; second, that Dilla's core innovation was not fully understood nor properly framed and needed a name; and third, that digital sampling is an art form that deserves and needs the full protection of the law. We are overdue for the legislation of a compulsory license for portions of compositions and recordings, as we already have for full compositions. Call it Dilla's Law.

Lastly, as this is journalism, I am concerned with balancing reporting and research with readability. Therefore I have listed my sources in the rear of the book rather than cite each piece of information with a superscript in the text, as an academic work might do. I use footnotes for supplemental information that would otherwise disrupt the flow of the narrative. I suspect, also, that a few musicologists might quibble with some of the simpler ways I have defined musical terms in the text. There are almost always more complex ways of defining a phenomenon, and I have decided—as a storyteller—where to set the point of diminishing returns.

THE WILL OF JAMES DEWITT YANCEY

Several aspects of the will's creation story are misaligned, and thus it makes the truth about that creation difficult to discern.

The memories of the creators do not line up. Micheline Levine recalls being worried about James dying intestate—without a last will and testament—which would be particularly disastrous for Maureen if James wanted to make sure that she was taken care of should he die. She remembers stepping up her efforts to get Maureen to have James create a will, and Maureen being resistant. She remembers being in Los Angeles, with James in his hospital room, taking James through his options as he filled out the will, and asking if he was sure he wanted Arty to be the executor. Micheline doesn't remember a notary being there, even though a notary stated that he witnessed the signing of the will.

Maureen Yancey says the reason that Micheline doesn't remember a notary being there is that she was not in the room at all; James didn't want her to see him in his condition. Instead, Maureen says she grabbed the blank forms from Micheline in the hospital lobby. She said that James filled out the will in his own hand, over time, and that she flew a notary from Michigan whom James trusted to observe the signing of the will at home. Maureen says that James explained to her his rationale for listing Arty and Micheline as executors thus: he didn't want his mother to have to mediate between the guardians of his children, one of whom still did not know about the other.

Even though he is listed as a witness to James's signing of the will, Maurice Lamb does not remember signing any document at the hospital. Nor does he remember signing anything while James was alive. He remembers instead, sometime *after* James's death, being asked by Maureen to sign some "lawyer papers" for the estate at Common's home on Sycamore in Los Angeles.

There are other misalignments. The presence of a notary is superfluous; California wills do not need to be notarized. The notary, Alfred L. Mitchell, was from Michigan, and had no notarial powers in the state of California. The signature of "James D. Yancey" is markedly dissimilar from his signatures on his driver's license and contracts as "James Yancey." The will was not filed with the Los Angeles County Probate Court until October 2, 2006, nearly eight months after James's death.

One reason for the delay is that in August 2006, the estate's probate attorney, Michael Foster, advised Arthur Erk and Micheline Levine that the will was likely invalid because one of the beneficiaries, Maureen Yancey, was also one of the witnesses, and thus the court might reject the will entirely. The attorney recommended that the estate ask the person who notarized the will, Alfred L. Mitchell, to file and sign an affidavit stating that he was present with James and Maurice on September 8, 2005, in Los Angeles when the will was signed, an event that Maurice does not remember happening while James was alive. That affidavit was produced and notarized in Michigan in August 2006.

The will was accepted as valid by the court.

These misalignments make it hard to tell an effective story about this will. But they are not necessarily evidence of anything nefarious. Memories are fallible, especially in high-stress, life-or-death situations. James Yancey spared no expense for the things he wanted, and trusted very few people. People's handwriting changes with age and illness. And lawyers can take forever to file papers.

THE MAKING OF "GOT 'TIL IT'S GONE"

According to Jimmy Jam, the idea of having Q-Tip as a featured guest on Janet Jackson's album *The Velvet Rope* grew out of their friendship, the two artists having appeared together in the movie *Poetic Justice*. The notion about the collaboration preceded the creation of "Got 'Til It's Gone," which, as the prose of this book details, began as a prompt from Alex Richbourg to Jimmy Jam, both of them inspired by the Ummah's remix of the Brand New Heavies' "Sometimes."

"Alex basically gave me a weekend homework assignment," Jam recalls. "I had an MPC, a Roland XP-50, and an Ensoniq MR-76 keyboard in my setup. He said, 'I'm going to hook the keyboards up to the MPC and I want you to make a song programming everything through the MPC'"—meaning that he wanted Jam to work as hip-hop producers worked, sequencing and saving the played notes to a master MIDI clock rather than recording each part separately to tape. "That was on a Friday. And I took Saturday off to be with my family. I came back in that Sunday, 'cause I knew no one would be at the studio and I could concentrate on my assignment, and turned everything on."

Jam says his intention was to create a two-bar loop to keep things simple. He began with the Rhodes keyboard sound from his Ensoniq, and then some drum sounds from the Roland XP-50 keyboard, all sequenced and quantized on the MPC. The bass line, which he also played on the Ensoniq, was sequenced via the MPC without quantization, to emulate the distinctive "drunken" behind-the-beat phrasing of the "Sometimes" remix. But on Monday, when he played the loop for Richbourg, Jam lamented that the drums sounded stiff and weren't swinging. "Oh, you just need to do this," Richbourg replied, hitting a few buttons on the MPC.

What Richbourg did, as the multitracks for the song reveal, was use the "Shift Timing" function on the MPC to push the kick drum pattern slightly later in time in relation to the snare and hi-hat, which remained locked to the grid. The new relationships between the drum parts gave the rhythm track a rolling, swinging quality without actually using the MPC's "Swing" function.

Jam triggered a sample of Joni Mitchell's "Big Yellow Taxi" into an AMS sampler next, along with some synthesized "scratching" sounds from his Ensoniq, and Jam auditioned the raw track for Jackson the next time she visited the Flyte Tyme studios in Minneapolis. Jackson liked it, and then did two things: She initiated a conversation with Mitchell to secure the artist's blessing for the sample use ("I can't wait to hear it," Mitchell replied to Jackson, according to Jam). And the track seemed to be the perfect opportunity to extend an invitation to Q-Tip to contribute vocals, which were added in a recording session with Jam and Jackson at the Hit Factory in New York on July 2, 1997.

"He and Janet, they were hilarious. They just had a great chemistry together. I put Tip and her in the studio together just to have a conversation." Other than a snippet of Jackson's laughter, the resultant banter did not make it to the final mix. But in an examination of the multitracks, one piece of unused dialogue stands out:

"I like this track," Q-Tip tells Jackson, with a degree of surprise.

"I'm glad you do," Jackson replies firmly.

Since the release of the song, Jimmy Jam has told this story in a number of forums—on Twitter, in a detailed interview with Red Bull Music Academy. But the story has not convinced many friends and fans of J Dilla, who point to comments like the one he made in the interview that Y'skid conducted with James in January 2003:

"Janet Jackson, how that whole thing worked out," James began, "It started with Tip and *Poetic Justice*, that's how they met. They became cool friends. Tip called and asked me did I have anything to give Janet. So what happened, this is the real deal, this is coming from me: Me, Tip, and Ali collaborate on this track. We made it happen. It was slotted for Janet Jackson's first single, 'Got 'Til It's Gone.' When it came out, it said produced by someone else."

During the reporting of this book, no one with Flyte Tyme or the Ummah—Jimmy Jam, Alex Richbourg, Q-Tip, Ali Shaheed Muhammad, or Micheline Levine—gave credence to James' story. At different times, Jam, Richbourg, and Tip have all flatly denied the story that the Ummah produced the original track. Despite James's assertions and the stories told by associates who admittedly did not witness James producing any track, no proof or early version has surfaced to corroborate those assertions. On the other hand, the multitracks and accompanying track sheets for the song, obtained by the author, confirm all of Jam and Richbourg's equipment details, and lend credence to the narrative that Jam and Richbourg produced the track at least several weeks prior to Q-Tip's involvement, as the session dates are listed on them. And musically, the programming and playing lack Jay Dee's signatures: James's bass lines and drum patterns had movement and variation, as with the "Sometimes" remix; the drums and bass of "Got 'Til It's Gone" are unvarying and loop-based. James never used synthesized, artificial sounds to approximate vinyl noise and "scratching"; in this song, they are used throughout.

I asked Jimmy Jam how he feels about James's claim: "I believe truth and fact mean different things so people can have different truths about the same thing depending on their perspective on the situation. I can only speak to my truth, but I'm always very analytical and curious about why somebody is saying what they are saying. 'If he thinks that, why does he think that?'" Jam recalls reaching out to Q-Tip to ask whether J Dilla had accompanied Tip to the studio when he laid his vocals, because Jam did not recall meeting anyone else. (In fact, the engineer for the New York session, Michael McCoy, recalls no one at the sessions but Jam, Jackson, Tip, Jackson's then boyfriend René Elizondo, and Jackson's dancers, who were practicing with her in the live room.)

"There's no use in trying to argue fact with someone who is not here. First of all, it's disrespectful, which is the last thing I would ever want to be to someone I revere so much. Plus I don't believe in arguing anyway. I do wish I could've had a discussion with Dilla to ask his recollection of the events and to profess my true admiration for him. My truth is the track that I did was one hundred percent mine and the masters and track sheets I have are documented fact. But as with many of the tracks I do, I'm trying to emulate whomever is inspiring me. And Dilla was definitely one hundred percent of the inspiration."

INTERVIEWS

Most of these interviews were conducted by telephone, video call, or in person. Several were conducted via text or email. Asterisks (*) denote conversations and lectures from my J Dilla course under the auspices of the Clive Davis Institute at New York University's Tisch School of the Arts.

Aaron Halfacre, February 27, 2020

Aaron McCray, July 19, 2019

Ahmir "Questlove" Thompson, May 3, 2017*; June 26, 2018; December 31, 2020; January 26, 2021

Al Hayes, July 21, 2019

Alex Borden, February 21, 2021

Alex Richbourg, February 15, 2020

Ali Shaheed Muhammad, January 9, 2020

Alice Scarbough Yancey, November 7, 2019

Alvin Blanco, October 28, 2019

Amir Abdullah, March 3, 2021

Amp Fiddler, November 24, 2018; April 12, 2021

Andrés "DJ Dez" Hernández, August 9, 2019; April 16, 2021

Angela Dewberry, July 1, 2021

Angela Nissel, March 20, 2021; June 21, 2021

Anne Danielsen, November 19, 2019

Arthur Jafa, June 2, 2021

Asya Shein, July 10, 2021

Beej Brooks, April 26, 2021

Beni B, April 15, 2020

Big Tone, April 18, 2021

Bill Johnson, February 1, 2019

Bob Power, May 3, 2017*; December 10, 2019

Brian Coleman, January 19, 2020

Brian Cross, April 19, 2017*; March 6, 2019*; January 23, 2020; June 15, 2020

Carey Logan, July 20, 2019

Carleton Gholz, February 25, 2020

Charles Moore, October 7, 2019

Chris "C-Minus" Rivas, December 12, 2020

Chris "DJ Fingers" Price, July 31, 2019; June 19, 2021

Chris "Peanut Butter Wolf" Manak, February 20, 2019*; June 26, 2020

Christopher Ramos, April 7, 2020; July 1, 2021

Clarice Hayes, June 2, 2021

Copez Wright, October 13, 2019

Common, March 20, 2020

Cornelius Harris, March 15, 2017*

Craig Seymour, March 21, 2020

D'Angelo, July 2, 2021

Dan Zieja, August 13, 2019

Darrell Dawsey, October 28, 2019

Darrick Grimmett, August 13, 2021

Dave Cooley, June 23, 2020; June 2, 2021

David Grandison Jr., February 6, 2019*

Dawn Elissa-Fischer, January 7, 2021

Demian Hoings, January 21, 2020

Denaun Porter, February 24, 2020

Dennis Coffey, March 16, 2017*; August 5, 2019

Derek Barbosa, January 1, 2020

Derek Dudley, March 28, 2020; June 24, 2021

Derreck "Dee Phunk" Johnson, February 28, 2020

Derrick Harvey, August 21, 2019

Dion Liverpool, August 20, 2019

DJ Dummy, June 7, 2021

DJ Henhouse, July 29, 2019

DJ Lefto, December 16, 2019

DJ Premier, June 7, 2021

DJ Rhettmatic, April 19, 2017*; February 27, 2019*; April 24, 2021

DJ Spinna, February 7, 2020; June 3, 2021

DJ Tony Tone, December 15, 2019

Drew Dixon, June 6, 2020

Eli Wolf, December 20, 2019; December 21, 2019; January 7, 2020

Eothen "Egon" Alapatt, January 4, 2021; January 8, 2021; April 21, 2021; June 29, 2021

Eric Coleman, June 22, 2020

Eugene "Hex" Howell, July 11, 2019

Frank Bush, September 5, 2019; May 29, 2021; June 6, 2021

Frank Sens, December 6, 2019

Frank Stratmann, January 16, 2020

Gilles Peterson, June 3, 2021

G. C. Cameron, April 19, 2021

Graham Finch, July 15, 2019

Guilty Simpson, October 10, 2019; June 19, 2021

Herman Hayes, July 21, 2019

Hi-Tek, April 18, 2021

Jack Splash, December 23, 2019; June 9, 2021

James "Jimmy Jam" Harris, September 14, 2022

James Poyser, September 12, 2019; June 4, 2021

Jamon Jordan, March 15, 2017*; March 16, 2017*

Janell Hunter, May 6, 2021

Jason "J-Rocc" Jackson, June 21, 2019; October 10, 2020

Jason Moran, June 28, 2018

Jay Boberg, February 10, 2020

Jeff Bubeck, April 20, 2021

Jeff Harleston, February 28, 2020

Jeff Jank, June 26, 2020; March 14, 2021

Jeff Peretz, September 25, 2019

Jeff "DJ Jazzy Jeff" Townes, April 21, 2021

Jeff Weiss, August 8, 2020; August 9, 2020

Jefferson Mao, January 21, 2020

Dr. Jeffrey Zonder, June 28, 2021

Jerry Barrow, October 28, 2019

jessica Care moore, February 4, 2020; June 3, 2021

Jocelyn Cooper, February 7, 2020

Jocelyne Ninneman, July 10, 2021

Joel Stone, August 16, 2019

John Salley, February 21, 2020

John Yancey, September 6, 2019; April 14, 2021

Jon Bellion, March 6, 2019*

Jonathan Dworkin, November 11, 2019; April 14, 2021

Jonathon Taylor, August 10, 2020; July 1, 2021

Joseph Patel, March 12, 2020

Joylette Hunter, April 22, 2020; October 14, 2020; April 24, 2021; July 1, 2021; July 6, 2021

JPEG Mafia, December 4, 2019

Junior Regisford, January 30, 2020

Kaiya Matthews, September 20, 2019

Kamaal "Q-Tip" Fareed, May 4, 2021

Karriem Riggins, October 4, 2020; January 13, 2021; January 14, 2021

Karyn Rachtman, March 3, 2020

Kelly "K-Fresh" Frazier, December 13, 2019

Kenny Dope, December 18, 2019

Kevin "DJ Head" Bell, March 6, 2020; June 7, 2021

Khary Kimani Turner, March 16, 2017*

Kieran Hebden, July 31, 2020

Kim Osorio, June 14, 2020

Kim Weston, August 11, 2019

Kindra Parker, April 10, 2020; December 26, 2020; May 28, 2021

Lara Gamble, June 10, 2019

Larick "Cricket" Mathews, December 30, 2020

LaRoy Glover, January 16, 2020

Lorenzo "Zo!" Ferguson, November 23, 2020

Malik Alston, July 23, 2019

Martha Yancey, August 21, 2019; July 5, 2021; July 6, 2021; July 10, 2021; July 11, 2021

Mark Hicks, July 5, 2020

Marsha Ambrosius, November 6, 2019

Mary Wright, October 13, 2019

Maureen Yancey, October 19, 2018; February 22, 2019*; September 26, 2019; December 5, 2019; August 1, 2019; April 17, 2021; April 24, 2021; June 30, 2021; July 9, 2021

Maurice "Bobo" Lamb, July 30, 2019; July 26, 2020; July 7, 2021

Michael "Serch" Berrin, January 15, 2020

Michael Buchanan, December 7, 2019; December 9, 2019; December 21, 2019

Michael McCoy, October 3, 2022

Michael Ross, March 28, 2017*

Micheline Levine, November 12, 2019; December 5, 2019; February 7, 2020; February 14, 2020; June 29, 2020

Mickey Stephenson, July 20, 2021

Miguel Atwood-Ferguson, February 10, 2018

Mike Chavarria, March 12, 2020

Mike Chavez, April 24, 2021

Monica Whitlow, April 2, 2021; April 4, 2021; June 25, 2021

Mr. Choc, June 4, 2021

Naim Ali McNair, April 27, 2021

Naomi Saalfield, July 22, 2020; January 11, 2021

Nate Smith, February 13, 2019*

Nicolay Rook, December 12, 2019

Nicole Hegeman, January 24, 2020

Nilusha Dassenaike, July 24, 2020

Olivia Fischa, January 5, 2021; June 26, 2021

Orlando Vesey, April 26, 2021

Paul Bender, July 20, 2020; January 14, 2021

Paul Riser, June 28, 2021

Paul Rosenberg, February 3, 2020

Paul Sewick, August 25, 2019

Perrin Moss, April 26, 2017*; January 9, 2021

Pete Rock, February 7, 2019*

Peter Adarkwah, August 27, 2019; June 16, 2021

Pharoahe Monch, February 28, 2020

Ron "Phat Kat" Watts, March 16, 2017*; November 4, 2019; June 10, 2021

Phonte Coleman, December 15, 2019; April 9, 2021

Pino Palladino, January 14, 2020

Piper Carter, July 29, 2019

Que.D, July 15, 2019; April 6, 2021; April 7, 2021

R. J. Rice, March 16, 2017*; January 10, 2020; March 9, 2020; June 28, 2021

R. L. "T3" Altman III, July 28, 2019; October 30, 2019; March 1, 2021; June 25, 2021

Raydar Ellis, September 5, 2019

Reta Hayes, July 21, 2019; October 17, 2019

Rich Medina, January 24, 2020

Robert Glasper, December 13, 2019

Rob Tewlow, January 6, 2020

Roger Erickson, March 21, 2020

Roger Linn, October 25, 2019

Roger Robinson, March 16, 2017*

Ronnie "Killa Ghanz" Kelly, February 23, 2020; June 3, 2021
Ross Allen, June 20, 2021
Royce da 5'9", July 22, 2019; January 16, 2020
Sacha Waldman, June 17, 2020
Saunte Lowe, January 5, 2021
Shannon Cason, January 23, 2021
Sheila Bowers, January 18, 2021; June 24, 2021
Simon Mavin, June 19, 2020; January 12, 2021
Skillz, December 5, 2019
Dr. Spero Cataland, October 31, 2019
Stephen Henderson, March 17, 2017*
Steve Mandel, April 28, 2020; May 28, 2021
Suave, September 9, 2019
Suemyra Shah, July 9, 2020; June 3, 2021
Tara Duvivier, February 20, 2020; June 7, 2021
Taz Arnold, August 5, 2020

Terrace Martin, June 1, 2021
Terrance Wright, June 26, 2021
Thad Baron, April 7, 2020
Tim Maynor, March 22, 2020; March 26, 2021; March 30, 2021; April 3, 2021
Tim Reid II, April 26, 2021
Timothy Anne Burnside, February 28, 2019
Tom Bacon, April 2, 2021
Tom Misch, June 20, 2020
Tre Hardson, March 29, 2017*; June 13, 2018; February 7, 2019
Dr. Valerie Israel, April 21, 2021
Vincent "Mase" Mason, October 15, 2019
Waajeed, April 26, 2021
Ward White, January 19, 2020
Wendy Goldstein, July 9, 2020; July 10, 2020
Young RJ, March 16, 2017*; June 29, 2021

BIBLIOGRAPHY

Selected Interviews with J Dilla

These are the important conversations with J Dilla conducted by journalists over the years, ordered by date.

Mao, Jefferson "Chairman." "Jay Dee: Electric Relaxation." *Vibe*, June/July 1996.

Patel, Joseph. Transcript of interview with Slum Village, conducted at A&M Records, Los Angeles. Unpublished. December 2, 1998.

Westwood, Tim. "Jay Dee aka J Dilla Interview." BBC Radio 1, February 2001. https://www.youtube.com/watch?v=woT27L1ra78.

Allen, Ross. "J Dilla in Conversation w/ Ross Allen." NTS, February 9, 2001. https://www.nts.live/shows/ross-allen/episodes/ross-allen-j-dilla-9th-february-2017.

Peterson, Gilles. "J Dilla Interview on Gilles Peterson Worldwide BBC Radio 2001." BBC, February 15, 2001. https://www.youtube.com/watch?v=l_1M0vM8d5c.

"McNasty Boy." *NME*, February 22, 2001. https://www.nme.com/news/music/jay-dee-1392144.

Haleem, Aadel. Interview of J Dilla at Roxy Blu in Toronto. RhymeRevolution.com, September 27, 2002. https://www.youtube.com/watch?v=1VLyTeEnD7U.

Alapatt, Eothen "Egon." Transcript of interview with J Dilla. Unpublished. July 2001.

Nileskär, Mats. "J Dilla Interview." *40 Years with P3 Soul*. Sveriges Radio, January 2003. https://sverigesradio.se/avsnitt/101147?programid=2680.

Sens, Frank "Y'skid." "Whatsup with Dilla (2003)" [Interview with J Dilla]. January 17, 2003. https://soundcloud.com/user4758833/whatsup-with-dilla-2003.

Hogan, Don. "Do the Math." *Rime*, May 1, 2003. https://www.stonesthrow.com/news/do-the-math/.

Turenne, Martin. "High Fidelity." *Urb*, March 2004. https://www.stonesthrow.com/news/high-fidelity/.

Samuel, Anslem. "Mighty Healthy." *XXL*, June 2005. https://www.stonesthrow.com/news/mighty-healthy/.

Peterson, Gilles. "Tribute to J Dilla." BBC Radio 1, February 2006. http://hiphophypedog.blogspot.com/2010/02/gilles-peterson-dilla-tribute-2006.html.

Blanco, Alvin. "J Dilla: Still Lives Through." *Scratch*, May/June 2006.

Samuel, Anslem. "J Dilla, The Lost Interview [circa 2004]." *XXL*, February 10, 2010. https://www.xxlmag.com/j-dilla-the-lost-interview-circa-2004/.

Court Documents

These documents were filed in the Superior Court of California, Los Angeles County, with regard to the estate of James Dewitt Yancey, deceased. Case #BP100879, ordered by date.

Yancey, James D. "California Statutory Will of James Dewitt Yancey." Signed and witnessed September 8, 2005, in Los Angeles, California. Filed October 2, 2006.

Erk, Arty, et al. "Petition for Will and Letters Testamentary and Authorization to Administer Under the Independent Administration of Estates Act." Filed October 2, 2006.

Erk, Arty, et al. "Affidavit Regarding Execution of California Statutory Will." Filed October 10, 2006.

Erk, Arty, et al. "Petition for Letters of Special Administration." Filed October 10, 2006.

Erk, Arty, et al. "Duties and Liabilities of Personal Representative and Acknowledgment of Receipt." Filed November 30, 2006.

Erk, Arty, et al. "Letters Testamentary." Filed November 30, 2006.

Alapatt, Eothen, et al. "Eothen Alapatt's Opposition to Ex Parte Application for Order Shortening Time." Filed March 27, 2008.

Erk, Arty, et al. "Declaration of Arty Erk in Support of Ex Parte Application for Expedited Hearing Date and Order Shortening Time for Notice of Petition to Discover Estate Assets and Compel Accounting Therefor." Filed March 27, 2008.

Erk, Arty, et al. "Ex Parte Application and Order for Expedited Hearing Date and Order Shortening Time for Notice of Petition to Discover Estate Assets and Compel Accounting Therefor." Filed March 27, 2008.

Erk, Arty, et al. "Petition to Discover Estate Assets and Compel Accounting Therefor." Filed March 27, 2008.

Bobb, Hon. Aviva K. Affidavit and Order re Citation. Filed April 3, 2008.

Bobb, Hon. Aviva K. Citation re Order to Show Cause. Filed April 3, 2008.

Erk, Arty, et al. "Amended Petition to Discover Estate Assets and Compel Accounting Therefor." Filed April 16, 2008.

Erk, Arty, et al. "Status of Administration Report." Filed April 16, 2008.

Erk, Arty, et al. "Inventory and Appraisal; Partial No. One." Filed April 18, 2008.

Hunter, Joylette, et al. "Petition for Family Allowance Before Inventory." Filed April 30, 2008.

Yancey, Maureen, et al. "Notice of Ruling on Status of Administration Report and Order to Show Cause re: Citation." Filed May 29, 2008.

Hunter, Joylette, et al. "Declaration of Martin N. Segal re Petition for Family Allowance." Filed June 5, 2008.

Erk, Arty, et al. "Response to Petition for Family Allowance Before Inventory." Filed June 6, 2008.

Yancey, Maureen, et al. "Objections to Status of Administration Report." Filed June 24, 2008.

Erk, Arty, et al. "Response to Objections to Status of Administration Report." Filed July 21, 2008.

Bobb, Hon. Aviva K. Order Extending Arty Erk Administration Until May 27, 2009. September 11, 2008.

Bobb, Hon. Aviva K. Order Regarding Lawsuit Against Eothen Alapatt. September 11, 2008.

Erk, Arty, et al. "Objections to Appraisal by Probate Referee." Filed December 4, 2008.

Erk, Arty, et al. "Petition to Collect Debt Due Decedent's Estate and Enforce Claim for the Benefit of Decedent's Estate; Request for Temporary Restraining Order; Memorandum of Points and Authorities and Declarations of Arty Erk and Micheline Levine in Support Thereof." Filed January 7, 2009.

Yancey, Maureen, et al. "First Supplement to Petition for Orders: 1) Vacating Order Approving Report of Status of Administration, and 2) Appointing Special Administrator." Filed January 12, 2009.

Bobb, Hon. Aviva K. Order on First Supplement to Petition for Orders: 1) Vacating Order Approving Report of Status of Administration, and 2) Appointing Special Administrator. February 3, 2009.

Bobb, Hon. Aviva K. Order on Objections to Appraisal by Probate Referee. February 3, 2009.

Bobb, Hon. Aviva K. Order on Petition to Discover Estate Assets and Compel Accounting Therefor. February 3, 2009.

Bobb, Hon. Aviva K. Order on First Supplement to Petition for Orders: 1) Vacating Order Approving Report of Status of Administration, and 2) Appointing Special Administrator. February 6, 2009.

Erk, Arty, et al. "Supplement to Response and Objections to Petition to Vacate Orders and Appoint Special Administrator." Filed February 6, 2009.

Bobb, Hon. Aviva K. Order on First Supplement to Petition for Orders: 1) Vacating Order Approving Report of Status of Administration, and 2) Appointing Special Administrator. February 9, 2009.

Yancey, Maureen, et al. "Order Prohibiting Payment of Attorneys Fees from Estate or from Any Corporation Owned by the Estate Without Further Order of the Court." Filed February 24, 2009.

Erk, Arty, et al. "Declaration of Micheline Levine." Filed July 7, 2009.

Borden, Alex R. "Declaration of Alex R. Borden in Support of Petitioner's Ex Parte Application for Order to Show Cause re: Preliminary Injunction and for Temporary Restraining Order." Filed December 15, 2009.

Borden, Alex R. "Declaration of Maureen Yancey in Support of Petitioner's Ex Parte Application for Order to Show Cause re: Preliminary Injunction and for Temporary Restraining Order." Filed December 15, 2009.

Borden, Alex R. "Declaration of Micheline Levine in Support of Petitioner's Ex Parte Application for Order to Show Cause re: Preliminary Injunction and for Temporary Restraining Order." Filed December 15, 2009.

Borden, Alex R. "Petition to Determine (In)validity of Purported Contract, for Declaratory and Injunctive Relief and for Restitution." Filed December 15, 2009.

Erk, Arty, et al. "Notice of Ruling and Regarding Continuance of Hearing." Filed February 26, 2010.

Erk, Arty, et al. "Second Supplement to First and Final Account and Report of Executor and Petition for Its Settlement; Objections to Petition for Allowance of Attorneys' Compensation for Services to PayJay Productions and for Extraordinary Services." Filed March 19, 2010.

Borden, Alex R. "Objections to First and Final Account and Report of Executor and Petition for Its Settlement; Objections to Petition for Allowance of Attorneys' Compensation for Services to PayJay Productions and for Extraordinary Services." Filed April 1, 2010.

Hunter, Joylette, et al. "Objection to Account of Executor and Request for Court Order." Filed April 9, 2010.

Erk, Arty, et al. "Amended First and Final Account and Report of Executor and Petition for Its Settlement; Objections to Petition for Allowance of Attorneys' Compensation for Services to PayJay Productions and for Extraordinary Services." Filed June 25, 2010.

Erk, Arty, et al. "Declaration of Arthur Erk." Filed October 13, 2010.

Hunter, Joylette, et al. "Request of Joylette Hunter re Petition for Court Approval of Settlement Agreement Terms." Filed November 18, 2016.

Borden, Alex R. "Allowance or Rejection of Creditor's Claim." Filed January 17, 2017.

Borden, Alex R. "First Account Current and Report of Administrator, Petition for Payment of Statutory Commissions and Extraordinary Commissions and for Additional Time Within Which to Close Estate." Filed March 21, 2018.

Borden, Alex R. "Second and Final Account and Report of Administrator; Petition for Order Determining That No Further Payments Are Required Under Family Allowance Order Dated July 25, 2008; Petition for Payment of Statutory Commissions and Extraordinary Commissions and for Final Distribution." Filed December 6, 2019.

Other Sources

These are books, periodicals, web pages, films, videos, liner notes, and other matter, ordered alphabetically.

Aciman, Alexander. "Meet the Unassuming Drum Machine That Changed Music Forever." *Vox*, April 16, 2018. https://www.vox.com/culture/2018/4/16/16615352/akai-mpc-music-history-impact.

Alapatt, Eothen "Egon," Eric Ducker, and Eddie "Stats" Houghton. "J Dilla: Shine On." *The Fader*, December 2006. https://www.thefader.com/2012/02/07/j-dilla-shine-on.

Alapatt, Eothen "Egon." "Erykah Badu." Interview transcript. Red Bull Music Academy, 2011. https://www.redbullmusicacademy.com/lectures/erykah-badu-frother-of-the-month.

Alapatt, Eothen. "Introduction," from liner notes for *The Diary*. Pay Jay Productions, Mass Appeal Records MSAP0032, 2016, CD.

Albin, T. Charter Township of Clinton Police Department. *General Incident Report #02-11915*. April 5, 2002.

"Allée Jay Dee." Montpellier.fr. Accessed July 13, 2021. https://www.montpellier.fr/structure/1509/240-allee-jay-dee-structure.htm.

Amano. "DILLA TRIBUTES/LINKS/COMMENTS." Okayplayer forums, February 13, 2006. https://board.okayplayer.com/okp.php?az=show_topic&forum=17&topic_id=57391&mesg_id=57391&listing_type=search.

"Announcing Reorganized J Dilla Estate and Plans for J Dilla Foundation." J-Dilla.com, January 24, 2010. http://web.archive.org/web/20110123200803/http://j-dilla.com/2010/01/24/announcing-reorganized-j-dilla-estate/.

Arango, Tim. "MCA Is History: Long-Lived Record Label to Be Merged into Geffen." *New York Post*, May 22, 2003.

Atkins, Brian "B. Kyle," dir. *Still Shining*. 2006. https://www.youtube.com/watch?v=2jhxIY3WNw0.

B., Marke. "Ken Collier: The Pivotal Figure of Detroit DJ Culture." Red Bull Music Academy, May 24, 2018. https://daily.redbullmusicacademy.com/2018/05/ken-collier.

Balfour, Jay. "J Dilla—Music from *The Lost Scrolls Vol. 1*." *HipHopDX*, February 12, 2013. https://hiphopdx.com/reviews/id.2039/title.j-dilla-music-from-the-lost-scrolls-vol-1.

Bassil, Ryan. "The Narrative Guide to Kendrick Lamar's 'To Pimp a Butterfly.'" *Vice*, March 24, 2015. https://www.vice.com/en/article/rzvbwe/the-narrative-guide-to-kendrick-lamars-to-pimp-a-butterfly-2015.

Batcheller, Pat. "CuriosiD: We Answered All Your Questions About the Mile Road System." WDET.org, August 8, 2019. https://wdet.org/posts/2019/08/08/88488-curiosid-we-answered-all-your-questions-about-the-mile-road-system/.

Battan, Carrie. "Detroit-Area Record Store Owner Gives Hundreds of Found J Dilla Items to Dilla's Mother." *Pitchfork*, April 30, 2012. https://pitchfork.com/news/46344-detroit-area-record-store-owner-gives-hundreds-of-found-j-dilla-items-to-dillas-mother/.

Bellion, Jon. "Jon Bellion *Definition* Album Is a Mix Between Dilla and Pixar." Video interview. MTV News, September 26, 2014. https://www.mtv.com/video-clips/1zvede/jon-bellion-definition-album-is-a-mix-between-dilla-and-pixar.

Benji B. J Dilla tribute show. BBC Radio 1Xtra, February 17, 2006.

Benji B. "Russell Elevado." Interview transcript. Red Bull Music Academy, 2007. https://www.redbullmusicacademy.com/lectures/russell-elevado-elevate-your-mind.

Bennett, Jessica. "Common Opens Up About Break-Up with Erykah Badu." *Ebony*, May 16, 2019. https://www.ebony.com/entertainment/common-opens-up-about-break-up-with-erykah-badu/.

Berry, Peter A. "10 Untold Stories from People Who Helped Make Kendrick Lamar's To Pimp a Butterfly Album." *XXL*, March 15, 2020. https://www.xxlmag.com/kendrick-lamar-to-pimp-a-butterfly-album-stories/.

Blair, Michael. "14 Years Ago Today, Slum Village Released Their Defining, Fantastic, Volume 2. AFH Took a Trip Down Memory Lane with the Remaining Founding Member, T3 (Food for Thought Interview)." *Ambrosia for Heads* (blog), June 13, 2014. https://ambrosiaforheads .com/2014/06/slumvillagefantasticvol2/.

Bowman, Patrick. "Sounwave Details the Making of Kendrick Lamar's Landmark 'To Pimp a Butterfly.'" *Spin*, April 24, 2015. https://www.spin.com/2015/04/sounwave-interview -kendrick-lamar-to-pimp-a-butterfly/.

Boyd, Herb. *Black Detroit: A People's History of Self-Determination.* New York: Amistad, 2017.

Brackett, David. "James Brown's 'Superbad' and the Double-Voiced Utterance." In *Interpreting Popular Music.* Cambridge: Cambridge University Press, 1995.

Brett, Thomas. "Roger Linn on Drum Machine Groove and J Dilla's Off-Beat Sound." *Brettworks* (blog), July 23, 2013. https://brettworks.com/2013/07/23/roger-linn-on-drum-machine -groove-and-j-dillas-off-beat-sound/.

Brewster, Bill. "I Feel Love: Donna Summer and Giorgio Moroder Created the Template for Dance Music as We Know It." *Mixmag*, June 22, 2017. https://mixmag.net/feature/i-feel -love-donna-summer-and-giorgio-moroder-created-the-template-for-dance-music-as -we-know-it.

Bromwich, Jonah. Review of *Rebirth of Detroit*, by J Dilla. *Pitchfork*, July 5, 2012. https:// pitchfork.com/reviews/albums/16731-rebirth-of-detroit/.

Brown, Harley. "Stacey 'Hotwaxx' Hale: The Godmother of House Music." Red Bull Music Academy, May 23, 2018. https://daily.redbullmusicacademy.com/2018/05/stacey-hale-interview.

Bry, David. "Soulquarians." *Vibe*, September 2000.

Burgess, Omar. "Dilla's Estate Threatened by Bootlegging." *HipHopDX*, June 25, 2008. https:// hiphopdx.com/news/id.7191/title.dillas-estate-threatened-by-bootlegging.

Burns, Todd L. "Put Your Hands Up: An Oral History of Detroit's Electronic Music Festival." *Resident Advisor*, May 10, 2010. https://ra.co/features/1186.

Callahan-Bever, Noah. Review of *Fantastic, Vol. 2*, by Slum Village. *Vibe*, August 2000.

Callwood, Brett. "Village of the Slummed." *Detroit Metro Times*, January 23, 2013. https://www .metrotimes.com/detroit/village-of-the-slummed/Content?oid=2146221.

Calyx: The Canterbury Music Website. "Alan Gowen: A Short Bio." Accessed June 12, 2021. http://www.calyx-canterbury.fr/mus/gowen_alan.html.

Cannon, Sean. "The Day J Dilla Met DJ Jazzy Jeff—And Blew His Mind." *Discogs Blog*, February 10, 2019. https://blog.discogs.com/en/j-dilla-dj-jazzy-jeff/.

Carlozo, Lou. "Prince's Drum Machine: How His Use of the Linn LM-1 Heralded a New Age of Pop Rhythm Creation." Reverb.com, June 24, 2019. https://reverb.com/news/prince-and -the-linn-lm-1.

Carlozo, Lou. "Roger Linn on Drum Samples, Prince, and Unlocking Virtuosity in Electronic Music." Reverb.com, August 15, 2017. https://reverb.com/news/roger-linn-on-drum -samples-prince-and-unlocking-virtuosity-in-electronic-music.

Carter, Kelley L. "Dollars to Donuts." *Vibe*, January 2009.

Carter, Kelley L. "Interview: Ma Dukes Speaks on Dilla's Legacy—And What Really Happened with His Estate." *Complex*, February 9, 2012. https://www.complex.com/music/2012/02 /interview-ma-dukes-speaks-on-dillas-legacy-and-what-really-happened-with-his-estate.

Carter, Kelley L. "Jay Dee's Last Days." *Detroit Free Press*, February 23, 2006. https://www.freep .com/story/entertainment/music/2006/11/27/jay-dee-s-last-days-the-untold-story-of -the/77378086/

Carter, Kelley L. "Service Praises Hip-Hop Maestro." *Detroit Free Press*, February 24, 2006.

Carvajal, Doreen. "Creative Turmoil at Arista; Founder and Chief Resists a Successor." *The New York Times*, November 27, 1999. https://www.nytimes.com/1999/11/27/business/creative -turmoil-at-arista-founder-and-chief-resists-a-successor.html.

Chafets, Ze'ev. *Devil's Night: And Other True Tales of Detroit.* New York: Random House, 1990.

"The 'Chamberlin,' Harry Chamberlin, USA, 1951." *120 Years of Electronic Music,* December 18, 2013. http://120years.net/the-chamberlin-harry-chamberlin-usa-1951/.

Chang, Jeff. "The Pure Movement and the Crooked Line: An Interview with Rennie Harris." In *Total Chaos: The Art and Aesthetics of Hip-Hop,* edited by Jeff Chang. New York: BasicCivitas Books, 2006.

Charnas, Dan. *The Big Payback: The History of the Business of Hip-Hop.* New York: New American Library, 2010.

Chaudhuri, Raj. "Donuts Dissected: 10 Years On." *Boiler Room.* Accessed February 7, 2016. https://boilerroom.tv/recording/donuts-dissected-10-years-on.

Chennault, Sam. "TDE: An Origin Story in Three Parts." *The Dowsers* (blog), December 12, 2017. https://the-dowsers.com/playlist/tde-origin-story-three-parts/.

Chidester, Bruce. "Ragtime—'Swing or Straight'?" *The Trumpet Blog,* October 5, 2013. http://www.thetrumpetblog.com/ragtime-swing-or-straight/.

Chinen, Nate. "Robert Glasper Experiment: So Is It Jazz?" *ArtsBeat* (blog). *The New York Times,* February 24, 2012. https://artsbeat.blogs.nytimes.com/2012/02/24/robert-glasper -experiment-so-is-it-jazz/.

Chinen, Nate. "The Corner of Jazz and Hip-Hop." *The New York Times,* February 24, 2012. https://www.nytimes.com/2012/02/26/arts/music/robert-glasper-experiment-to-release -black-radio.html.

Clarke, Kayla, and Victor Williams. "Community Steps Up to Help Dilla's Delights Donut Shop Owner After Cancer Battle." WDIV, January 3, 2020. https://www.clickondetroit.com/news /local/2020/01/03/community-steps-up-to-help-dillas-delights-donut-shop-owner-after -cancer-battle/.

"The 'Clavivox' Raymond Scott, USA, 1952." *120 Years of Electronic Music,* September 22, 2013. https://120years.net/the-clavivoxraymond-scottusa1952-2/.

Coleman, Brian. "A Discussion with the Roots' Secret Weapon: The Late, Great Richard Nichols." *Medium,* January 4, 2015. https://medium.com/@briancoleman/when-youve -reached-the-end-of-the-frontier-and-youve-afbf79ba1aa1.

Conniff, Tamara. "On the Fence." *The Hollywood Reporter,* January 23, 2001.

Connor, Jackson. "Doughnut Shop Honoring Late Producer J Dilla Finally Opens for Business." *First We Feast,* May 3, 2016. https://firstwefeast.com/eat/2016/05/dillas-delights-open-business.

Conot, Robert E. *American Odyssey: A History of a Great City.* Detroit: Wayne State University Press, 1986.

Cunningham, Jonathan. "Dilla Day Celebration Confirmed at the Fillmore Detroit." *Detroit Metro Times,* December 28, 2011. https://www.metrotimes.com/city-slang/archives/2011/12/28 /dilla-day-celebration-confirmed-at-the-fillmore-detroit.

Cunningham, Jonathan. "It's Gotta Be the Shoes." *Detroit Metro Times,* June 20, 2012. https:// www.metrotimes.com/detroit/its-gotta-be-the-shoes/Content?oid=2149049.

Danielsen, Anne, Carl Haakon Waadeland, Henrik G. Sundt, and Maria A. G. Witek. "Effects of Instructed Timing and Tempo on Snare Drum Sound in Drum Kit Performance." *The Journal of the Acoustical Society of America* 138, no. 4 (October 1, 2015): 2301–16. https:// doi.org/10.1121/1.4930950.

Danielsen, Anne, ed. *Musical Rhythm in the Age of Digital Reproduction.* Ashgate Popular and Folk Music Series. Farnham, England: Ashgate, 2010.

Danielsen, Anne. *Presence and Pleasure: The Funk Grooves of James Brown and Parliament.* Middletown, CT: Wesleyan University Press, 2006.

Datseris, George, Annika Ziereis, Thorsten Albrecht, York Hagmayer, Viola Priesemann, and Theo Geisel. "Microtiming Deviations and Swing Feel in Jazz." *Scientific Reports* 9, no. 1 (December 27, 2019). https://doi.org/10.1038/s41598-019-55981-3.

DeadlyMike. *Dilla Schroeder.* Digital illustration. Deviant Art, February 9, 2010. https://www .deviantart.com/deadlymike/art/Dilla-Schroeder-153547982.

Dean, Aria. "Worry the Image." *ARTnews*, May 26, 2017. https://www.artnews.com/art-in-america/features/worry-the-image-63266/.

Detroit Historical Society. "Conant Gardens Historic District." *Encyclopedia of Detroit*. Accessed June 1, 2021. https://detroithistorical.org/learn/encyclopedia-of-detroit/conant-gardens-historic-district.

Detroit Historical Society. "Eight Mile Road." *Encyclopedia of Detroit*. Accessed June 1, 2021. https://detroithistorical.org/learn/encyclopedia-of-detroit/eight-mile-road.

Detroit Historical Society. "Grand Bargain." *Encyclopedia of Detroit*. Accessed June 12, 2021. https://detroithistorical.org/learn/encyclopedia-of-detroit/grand-bargain.

Detroit Institute of Arts. Collection information for Diego M. Rivera, *Detroit Industry Murals*. Accessed June 12, 2021. https://www.dia.org/art/collection/object/detroit-industry-murals-58537.

"Detroit Maps." Accessed May 31, 2021. http://historydetroit.com/places/maps.php.

DeVito, Lee. "Detroit Doughnut Shop Dilla's Delights Surpasses Fundraising Goal to Move to Bigger Location." *Detroit Metro Times*, February 4, 2020. https://www.metrotimes.com/table-and-bar/archives/2020/02/04/detroit-doughnut-shop-dillas-delights-surpasses-fundraising-goal-to-move-to-bigger-location.

DeVito, Lee. "Dilla's Delights Is Closed for December While Owner Recovers from Cancer." *Detroit Metro Times*, December 18, 2019. https://www.metrotimes.com/table-and-bar/archives/2019/12/18/dillas-delights-is-closed-for-december-while-owner-recovers-from-cancer.

Dick, Kirby, and Amy Ziering, dir. *On the Record*. HBO Max, 2020.

Dirt Tech Reck. "You Should Know: Yamandu Roos." February 17, 2016. https://dirttechreck.com/you-should-know-yamandu-roos/.

DJ Dummy. *In Memory of J Dilla*. February 2006. CD.

Dolan, Matthew. "In Detroit Bankruptcy, Art Was Key to the Deal." *The Wall Street Journal*, November 8, 2014. https://online.wsj.com/articles/in-detroit-bankruptcy-art-was-key-to-the-deal-1415384308.

Dorris, Susan. "Detroit's 'Mile' Roads." Historydetroit.com. Accessed June 17, 2021. http://historydetroit.com/places/mile_roads.php.

Duelund, Theis. "The Rundown: L.A.'s Experimental Hip Hop Scene." *Los Angeles Magazine*, October 9, 2014. https://www.lamag.com/culturefiles/rundown-l-s-experimental-hip hop-scene/.

Eagle, Mike. Review of Rock the Bells Festival, Anaheim, CA, November 13, 2004. *Inside Pulse*, November 24, 2004. https://insidepulse.com/2004/11/24/29361/.

"Early DAWs: The Software That Changed Music Production Forever." *MusicRadar*, February 20, 2020. https://www.musicradar.com/news/early-daws-the-software-that-changed-music-production-forever.

Echlin, Hobey. "Dial 313 for the 411 on Hip-Hop." *Detroit Metro Times*, October 2–8, 1996.

Erk, Arty, Jonathan Dworkin, and Micheline Levine. Full-page advertisement with the headline "J Dilla a/k/a Jay Dee." *Billboard*, March 22, 2008.

Eustice, Kyle. "Common Reveals What His Break Up with Erykah Badu Taught Him." *HipHopDX*, March 3, 2018. https://hiphopdx.com/news/id.46112/title.common-reveals-what-his-break-up-with-erykah-badu-taught-him.

"Exclusive: Q-Tip Interview." Moovmnt, March 10, 2009. https://www.moovmnt.com/2009/04/19/exclusive-q-tip-interview/.

Fairfax, Jesse. "House Shoes Discusses 'Let It Go,' Continual Controversy Surrounding the Legacy of J. Dilla." *HipHopDX*, June 30, 2012. https://hiphopdx.com/news/id.20270/title.house-shoes-discusses-let-it-go-continual-controversy-surrounding-the-legacy-of-j-dilla.

Ferguson, Jordan. *Donuts*. 33 1/3 series. New York: Bloomsbury, 2014.

Ferreira, Adriana. "Cultura hip hop vai às telas de cinema." *Folha de S.Paulo*, July 21, 2005. https://www1.folha.uol.com.br/fsp/ilustrad/fq2107200517.htm.

Fintoni, Laurent. "Aron's Record Store and the Development of the LA Beat Scene." Red Bull

Music Academy, October 1, 2019. https://daily.redbullmusicacademy.com/2019/10/arons-record-store-la-beat-scene.

Fintoni, Laurent. "The 10-Year Mission to Release J Dilla's Legendary Lost Solo Album." The Vinyl Factory, April 3, 2016. https://thevinylfactory.com/features/the-10-year-mission-to-release-j-dillas-legendary-lost-solo-album/.

Fintoni, Laurent. "Give Them What They Want: The 10-Year Mission to Release J Dilla's Legendary Lost Solo Album." Fact, March 29, 2016. https://www.factmag.com/2016/03/29/j-dilla-the-diary-feature/.

Fintoni, Laurent. "Low End Ballers: Five Parties Taking Beats into the Future." Red Bull Music Academy, October 30, 2012. https://daily.redbullmusicacademy.com/2012/10/low-end-ballers.

Fintoni, Laurent. "'Prince Came to My Club': The Birth of the L.A. Beat Scene, as Told by Kutmah." Fact, April 3, 2013. https://www.factmag.com/2013/04/03/prince-came-to-my-club-the-birth-of-l-a-beat-scene-as-told-by-kutmah.

"Fire Damages Home of Rap Artist Q-Tip." The New York Times, February 9, 1998. https://www.nytimes.com/1998/02/09/nyregion/metro-news-briefs-new-jersey-fire-damages-home-of-rap-artist-q-tip.html.

Fitzgerald, Trent. "Get Well J Dilla!" Beats and Rants (blog), January 18, 2005. https://www.beatsandrants.com/2005/01/get_well_j_dill.html.

Fitzgerald, Trent. "J Dilla: Healthy and Productive." Beats and Rants (blog), May 12, 2005. https://www.beatsandrants.com/2005/05/j_dilla_healthy.html.

Fitzpatrick, Rob. "J Dilla: The Mozart of Hip-Hop." The Guardian, January 27, 2011. http://www.theguardian.com/music/2011/jan/27/j-dilla-suite-ma-dukes.

Foley, Aaron. "Baatin of Detroit's Slum Village Dead at 35." MLive, August 1, 2009. https://www.mlive.com/entertainment/detroit/2009/08/reports_baatin_of_detroits_slu.html.

Forster, Tim. "Dilla's Delights Is Crowd-Funding to Stay in Business." Eater Detroit, January 2, 2020. https://detroit.eater.com/2020/1/2/21047123/dillas-delights-closure-crowd-funding-reopening.

Frank, Aaron. "House Shoes: Seminal Producer Talks New Album, J Dilla Beef." LA Weekly, June 15, 2012. https://www.laweekly.com/house-shoes-seminal-producer-talks-new-album-j-dilla-beef/.

Frazier, Kelly "K-Fresh," with Tate McBroom. "Spiritualized: Jay Dee." Real Detroit Weekly, February 22–28, 2006.

Furman, Phyllis. "Label It the Day the Music Died." Daily News (New York), December 11, 1998.

Furman, Phyllis. "Seagram-Owned Universal Music Expected to Lay Off Thousands." Daily News (New York), January 19, 1999.

Gallo, Phil. "Vijay Iyer on Ferguson, Teaching at Harvard & Jazz's Relationship with Hip-Hop." Billboard, January 20, 2015. https://www.billboard.com/articles/news/6443754/vijay-iyer-interview-harvard-ferguson.

Gamble, Lara. "'I'll Forego All That Shit If J Dilla Was Still with Us': An Interview with B+." Passion of the Weiss, February 20, 2018. https://www.passionweiss.com/2018/02/20/ill-forego-all-that-shit-if-the-muthafucka-was-still-with-us-an-interview-with-b/.

Gardner, Adrianna. "'Rock the Bells' Evokes Spectacular Showcase." The Campus Times (University of La Verne), November 19, 2004. https://lvcampustimes.org/2004/11/rock-the-bells-evokes-spectacular-showcase/.

Garrison, Lucas. "All 71 People on Kendrick Lamar's 'To Pimp a Butterfly' Album." DJBooth, March 18, 2015. https://djbooth.net/features/2015-03-18-kendrick-lamar-to-pimp-a-butterfly-album-credits.

Ghansah, Rachel Kaadzi. "A River Runs Through It." The Believer, January 1, 2015. https://believermag.com/a-river-runs-through-it/.

Gierlowski, Anne G. State of Michigan Department of State Police. Laboratory Report #25117-02. Sterling Heights: Michigan Dept. of State Police, August 26, 2002.

Glass, Daniel. "Birth of Rock Backbeats and Straight Eighths." *Drum!*, July 16, 2013. https://drummagazine.com/birth-of-rock-backbeats-straight-eighths/.

Grady, Denise. "Is Your Cocktail Making You Sick?" *The New York Times*, January 5, 2017. https://www.nytimes.com/2017/01/05/well/live/is-your-cocktail-making-you-sick.html.

Graham, Adam. "Hometown Finally Honors Rapper." *The Detroit News*, February 9, 2012, sec. M.

Graham, Adam. "Sales of J Dilla's Records Halted, for Now." *The Detroit News*, April 28, 2012, sec. C.

Grier, Chaka V. "For R&B Singer Anna Wise, Music Is a Lifelong Journey." *Bandcamp Daily*, October 29, 2019. https://daily.bandcamp.com/features/anna-wise-as-if-it-were-forever-interview.

Hale, Andreas. "The Oral History of Kendrick Lamar's 'To Pimp a Butterfly.'" *Cuepoint*, February 9, 2016. https://medium.com/cuepoint/the-oral-history-of-kendrick-lamar-s-to-pimp-a-butterfly-622f725c3fde.

Hall, Rashaun. "Capitol Goes Slum-Ing." *Billboard*, April 20, 2002.

Hall, Rashaun. "Going for 'Common' Denominator: Artist Makes MCA Debut with *Like Water for Chocolate*." *Billboard*, February 19, 2000.

Hall, Rashaun. "MCA Shifts Its Urban Division in New Direction." *Billboard*, April 13, 2002.

Handley, Joel. "The Low-End Legacy of D'Angelo's *Voodoo*." Reverb.com, January 27, 2020. https://reverb.com/news/the-low-end-legacy-of-dangelos-voodoo.

Harris, Ross. *Ruff Draft Interviews*. Stones Throw Records, 2007. https://www.youtube.com/watch?v=xAlmingNBFg.

Hein, Ethan. "The Natural History of the Funky Drummer Break." *The Ethan Hein Blog*, May 25, 2009. http://www.ethanhein.com/wp/2009/the-natural-history-of-the-funky-drummer-break/.

Hernandez, Victoria. "J Dilla Donut Shop 'Dilla's Delights' Sells Out Three Times on Opening Day." *HipHopDX*, May 3, 2016. https://hiphopdx.com/news/id.38643/title.j-dilla-donut-shop-dillas-delights-sells-out-three-times-on-opening-day.

Hertzberg, Hendrik. "Jason Moran, New Master." *The New Yorker*, June 25, 2012. https://www.newyorker.com/culture/culture-desk/jason-moran-new-master.

Hilburn, Robert, and Geoff Boucher. "Geffen, A&M Labels Folded in Consolidation." *Los Angeles Times*, January 23, 1999.

Hill, Kristian R., dir. *God Said Give 'Em Drum Machines*. 2021.

Hip Hop Shop. "About Us." Accessed June 12, 2021. https://thehiphopshop.com/pages/about-us.

Historic Detroit. "Milner Hotel." Accessed June 12, 2021. https://historicdetroit.org/buildings/milner-hotel.

Hodgson, Jay. "Lateral Dynamics Processing in Experimental Hip Hop: Flying Lotus, Madlib, Oh No, J-Dilla and Prefuse 73." *Journal on the Art of Record Production* 5 (July 2011). https://www.arpjournal.com/asarpwp/lateral-dynamics-processing-in-experimental-hip-hop-flying-lotus-madlib-oh-no-j-dilla-and-prefuse-73/.

Holslin, Peter. "After Losing His Gear and Beats to Thieves, Nosaj Thing Tries to Move On." *LA Weekly*, May 12, 2015. https://www.laweekly.com/after-losing-his-gear-and-beats-to-thieves-nosaj-thing-tries-to-move-on/.

Horowitz-Ghazi, Alexi. "'A Lot of Detective Work': Piecing Together J Dilla's 'The Diary.'" *All Things Considered*. NPR, July 30, 2016. https://www.npr.org/2016/07/30/485700850/j-dilla-s-diary-is-now-in-the-hands-of-fans.

Houck, Brenna. "8 Things to Know About Dilla's Delights, Opening Tuesday in Downtown Detroit." *Eater Detroit*, May 2, 2016. https://detroit.eater.com/2016/5/2/11568364/new-dillas-delights-doughnuts-opening-detroit.

Houck, Brenna. "Inside Dilla's Delights, a Hip Hop–Inspired Doughnut Emporium in Downtown Detroit." *Eater Detroit*, May 7, 2016. https://detroit.eater.com/2016/5/7/11604822/dillas-delights-j-dilla-new-detroit-doughnut-shop-photos.

House Shoes's Twitter exchange with Jonathon Taylor, screenshot. Imgur, June 19, 2012. https://imgur.com/Gsedg.

Houghton, Edwin "STATS." "Erykah Badu, Common and Hiatus Kaiyote Live in Detroit." Okayplayer, August 14, 2013. https://www.okayplayer.com/news/erykah-badu-common-hiatus-kaiyote-live-in-detroit-photos.html.

Houghton, Edwin "STATS." "It Takes a Village to Pimp a Butterfly: Terrace Martin, Bilal, Robert Glasper and More Give Us the DVD Extraz To 'TPAB.'" Okayplayer, June 17, 2015. https://www.okayplayer.com/news/making-of-to-pimp-a-butterfly-bilal-robert-glasper-tpab-interview.html.

Houghton, Edwin "STATS." "OKP News: Ma Dukes Steps In, Dilla Record Sale on Hold." Okayplayer, April 27, 2012. https://www.okayplayer.com/news/okp-news-ma-dukes-steps-in-dilla-record-sale-on-hold.html.

Hunte, Justin. "J Dilla's Mother 'Ma Dukes' Yancey Finally Details House Shoes Beef." *HipHopDX*, February 8, 2016. https://hiphopdx.com/interviews/id.2848/title.j-dillas-mother-ma-dukes-yancey-finally-details-house-shoes-beef.

Internal Revenue Service. "The J Dilla Foundation Inc," November 20, 2020. https://apps.irs.gov/app/eos/detailsPage?ein=271536220&name=THE%20J%20DILLA%20FOUNDATION%20INC&city=&state=&countryAbbr=US&dba=&type=DETERMINATIONLETTERS,%20REVOCATION&orgTags=DETERMINATION LETTERS&orgTags=REVOCATION.

Internal Revenue Service. Letter to James Dewitt Yancey Foundation. December 20, 2010. Accessible through the IRS Tax Exempt Organization Search, https://apps.irs.gov/app/eos/.

Internal Revenue Service. Letter to the J Dilla Foundation c/o Maureen Yancey. May 16, 2020. https://apps.irs.gov/pub/epostcard/dl/FinalLetter_27-1536220_THEJDILLAFOUNDATION INC_01022010_01.tif.

Isenberg, Daniel. "What Is the J Dilla Ensemble?" *Complex*, February 10, 2012. https://www.complex.com/music/2012/02/what-is-the-j-dilla-ensemble/.

Iyer, Vijay S. "Microstructures of Feel, Macrostructures of Sound: Embodied Cognition in West African and African-American Musics." PhD diss., University of California, Berkeley, 1998. http://cnmat.org/People/Vijay/%20THESIS.html.

Jackman, Michael. "Still Standing: Stanley Hong's Mannia Café." *Detroit Metro Times*, November 21, 2015. https://www.metrotimes.com/the-scene/archives/2015/11/21/still-standing-stanley-hongs-mannia-cafe.

Jafa, Arthur. "Black Visual Intonation." In *The Jazz Cadence of American Culture*, edited by Robert G. O'Meally. New York: Columbia University Press, 1998.

JAS. "Hi Tek or Jay Dee?!?!?" Okayplayer forum, October 24, 2000. https://board.okayplayer.com/okp.php?az=show_topic&forum=17&topic_id=22689&mesg_id=22689&listing_type=search.

"J Dilla." *Crate Diggers*. Fuse, March 20, 2013. https://www.youtube.com/watch?v=XL3ENrZwjmw.

J Dilla and Madlib (JayLib). *Live at Detroit's Electronic Music Festival 2004 DEMF*. Accessed June 12, 2021. https://soundcloud.com/besttonyever/j-dilla-madlib-jaylib-live-at.

J Dilla Foundation. "Joylette Hunter Bio," June 2, 2012. https://kindraparkeronline.files.wordpress.com/2012/06/2joylette-bio.pdf.

"J. Dilla's Lost Scrolls." *Snap Judgment*. NPR, August 29, 2014. https://www.npr.org/2014/08/29/344255548/j-dillas-lost-scrolls.

"The Johnnie Mae Matthews Story." Soulful Detroit. Accessed May 25, 2021. https://soulfuldetroit.com/web08-johnniemaematthews/.

Jones, Charlie. "Detroit Record Store Unearths (and Flogs) J Dilla's Record Collection." *Dummy*, April 26, 2012. https://www.dummymag.com/news/detroit-record-store-sell-j-dilla-s-lost-records-collection/.

Jones, James T., IV. "Detroit Develops Its Own Rap." *USA Today*, October 10, 1990.

Jones, James T., IV. "Detroit's Salley, from Hoops to Hip-Hop." *USA Today*, September 3, 1992.

Jones, LeRoi. *Blues People: Negro Music in White America*. Westport, CT: Greenwood Press, 1980.

Jones, Todd E. Interview with Baatin of Slum Village. *MVRemix*, September 2003. https://www.mvremix.com/urban/interviews/baatin.shtml.

Jones, Todd E. "Dwele Interview." *MVRemix*, August 2003. https://www.mvremix.com/urban/interviews/dwele.shtml.

Karp, Hannah. "L.A. Reid's Epic Records Exit Followed Allegations by Female Staffer." *Billboard*, May 14, 2017. https://www.billboard.com/articles/news/7793105/la-reid-epic-records-exit-allegations-female-staffer.

Keil, Charles. *Urban Blues*. Chicago: University of Chicago Press, 1991.

Kellman, Andy. "R.J.'s Latest Arrival." AllMusic. Accessed June 12, 2021. https://www.allmusic.com/artist/rjs-latest-arrival-mn0000386400/biography.

"Kendrick Lamar's 'To Pimp a Butterfly': A Track-by-Track Guide." *Rolling Stone*, March 16, 2015. https://www.rollingstone.com/music/music-news/kendrick-lamars-to-pimp-a-butterfly-a-track-by-track-guide-200991/.

Kennedy, Randy. "Fate of Detroit's Art Hangs in the Balance." *The New York Times*, December 3, 2013. https://www.nytimes.com/2013/12/04/us/fate-of-detroits-art-hangs-in-the-balance.html.

Kennedy, Randy. "'Grand Bargain' Saves the Detroit Institute of Arts." *The New York Times*, November 7, 2014. https://www.nytimes.com/2014/11/08/arts/design/grand-bargain-saves-the-detroit-institute-of-arts.html.

Kenner, Rob. "J Dilla: The Essentials." *Complex*, February 7, 2016. https://www.complex.com/music/2016/02/j-dilla-essentials-guide.

King, Jason. "The Time Is Out of Joint: Notes on D'Angelo's Voodoo." Liner notes for D'Angelo, *Voodoo*. Light in the Attic, Modern Classics Recordings MCR 902, 2012, vinyl. https://passthecurve.com/post/41942596825/the-time-is-out-of-joint-notes-on-dangelos.

Kurlyandchik, Mark. "Dilla's Delights Doughnut Shop Opens in Detroit." *Detroit Free Press*, May 2, 2016. https://www.freep.com/story/entertainment/dining/2016/05/02/dillas-delights-doughnut-shop-opens-tuesday-detroit/83837342/.

Lea, Tom. "Rebirth: Maureen Yancey, Mother of J Dilla, on Releasing His Posthumous Work and Starting Her New Label." *Fact*, June 14, 2012. https://www.factmag.com/2012/06/14/rebirth-mareen-yancey-mother-of-the-late-j-dilla-on-releasing-his-posthumous-work-and-starting-her-new-record-label/.

"Let's Take It Back. J Dilla Remembered." *The Wire*, March 2016. https://www.thewire.co.uk/in-writing/the-portal/j-dilla-remembered.

Lewis, Barbara. "The DIA's Grand Bargain." WDET, November 30, 2015. https://wdet.org/posts/2015/11/29/82007-the-dias-grand-bargain/.

Linn, Roger. "MPC3000 Midi Production Center Software Version 3.0 Operators Manual." Akai Electric Co., Ltd, May 1994.

Littlejohn, Edward J. "Slaves, Judge Woodward, and the Supreme Court of the Michigan Territory." *Michigan Bar Journal*, July 2015. http://www.michbar.org/file/barjournal/article/documents/pdf4article2649.pdf.

"The Making of J Dilla's *The Diary*." Mass Appeal, May 19, 2016. https://www.youtube.com/watch?v=5hG-yzX9eEM.

"The Making of 'Mcnasty Filth'—Frank N Dank, Jaylib." FND TV, 2003. https://www.youtube.com/watch?v=DgEuY_JpwBU.

Mao, Jefferson "Chairman." "10 Facts About J Dilla You Might Not Know." *Complex*, February 10, 2012. https://www.complex.com/music/2012/02/10-facts-about-j-dilla-you-might-not-know/.

Mao, Jefferson. "Georgia Anne Muldrow and Dudley Perkins." Interview transcript. Red Bull Music Academy, 2007. https://www.redbullmusicacademy.com/lectures/georgia-anne-muldrow-and-dudley-perkins-the-universe-according.

Mao, Jefferson. "Jam and Lewis." Interview transcript. Red Bull Music Academy, 2016. https://www.redbullmusicacademy.com/lectures/jam-lewis-lecture.

Mao, Jefferson. "Q-Tip on Tribe Cuts, J Dilla, and the Zulu Nation." Video interview. Red Bull Music Academy, 2015. https://www.youtube.com/watch?v=8RWctL6Pk6A.

Mao, Jefferson. "Questlove Talks Drums, Dilla, and D'Angelo." Video interview. Red Bull Music Academy, 2014. https://www.youtube.com/watch?v=yCxVzCe2N1Y.

Maraniss, David. *Once in a Great City: A Detroit Story*. New York: Simon and Schuster, 2015.

Markman, Rob. "Jon Bellion's *Definition* Is What You Get When You Mix Disney with Dilla." MTV News, September 26, 2014. http://www.mtv.com/news/1945303/jon-bellion-definition-disney-dilla/.

Markman, Rob. "Kendrick Lamar Reveals To Pimp a Butterfly's Original Title and Its Tupac Connection." MTV News, March 31, 2015. http://www.mtv.com/news/2120689/kendrick-lamar-tu-pimp-a-caterpillar-tupac/.

Maroulis, Peter. "The Revolution (Evolution?) of Lo-Fi Hip-Hop." *DJBooth*, June 13, 2018. https://djbooth.net/features/2018-06-13-lo-fi-hip-hop-evolution.

Martins, Chris. "Rattling the Underground with Nosaj Thing and Low End Theory." *LA Weekly*, May 13, 2009. https://www.laweekly.com/rattling-the-underground-with-nosaj-thing-and-low-end-theory/.

McNamee, David. "Hey, What's That Sound: Linn LM-1 Drum Computer and the Oberheim DMX." *The Guardian*, June 22, 2009. http://www.theguardian.com/music/2009/jun/22/linn-oberheim-drum-machines.

McNary, Dave. "Seagram Lays Off Hundreds; Cuts Reduce Area's A&M, Geffen Music Labels to Skeletal Staffs." *Los Angeles Daily News*, January 22, 1999.

"Microtones, Birdsongs, and J Dilla: David Fiuczynski's Guggenheim Fellowship Composition to Premiere at Berklee on Friday, Dec. 7." JazzCorner.com, November 26, 2012. http://www.jazzcorner.com/news/display.php?news=3272.

Misch, Tom. "Beyond the Groove." July 27, 2014. https://www.youtube.com/watch?v=NT0UrxuCtWk.

Misra, Ria. "The Curious Plan to Make Detroit's Roads Extend from a Single Point." *Gizmodo*, May 8, 2015. https://gizmodo.com/the-curious-plan-to-make-detroits-roads-extend-from-a-s-1703191567.

Mitchell, Gail. "Capitol Cuts Back After Merger: Sales Staff Hardest Hit by Integration with Priority." *Billboard*, October 20, 2001.

Mitchell, Kimberly P. "Prom Is More Than Dresses in Detroit, It's Family, Friends, and a Community Celebration." *Detroit Free Press*, June 9, 2019. https://www.freep.com/picture-gallery/news/local/michigan/detroit/2019/06/09/detroit-prom-send-off-school-event-summer/1401559001/.

Morris, Jessie. "Kendrick Lamar Breaks Down the Making of 'To Pimp a Butterfly.'" *Complex*, February 8, 2016. https://www.complex.com/music/2016/02/kendrick-lamar-breaks-down-the-making-of-to-pimp-a-butterfly.

Murphy, Tom. "Flying Lotus on How J Dilla Really Did Change His Life by Making Music That Was Deep and Heartfelt." *Westword*, October 18, 2012. https://www.westword.com/music/flying-lotus-on-how-j-dilla-really-did-change-his-life-by-making-music-that-was-deep-and-heartfelt-5687960.

Murphy, Tom. "Thundercat on X-Men and His Last Conversation with J-Dilla Before He Died." *Westword*, February 22, 2017. https://www.westword.com/music/thundercat-on-x-men-and-his-last-conversation-with-j-dilla-before-he-died-8810415.

"Musicology: A Brief History of the Digital Audio Workstation." *Mixdown*, March 8, 2018. https://mixdownmag.com.au/features/columns/musicology-a-brief-history-of-the-digital-audio-workstation/.

National Association of Music Merchants. "Roger Linn." Video interview. NAMM Oral History Program, January 20, 2005. https://www.namm.org/library/oral-history/roger-linn.

Nelson, Valerie J. "Baatin Dies at 35; Rapper Co-founded Progressive Hip-Hop Group Slum Village." *Los Angeles Times*, August 2, 2009. https://www.latimes.com/local/obituaries /la-me-baatin2-2009aug02-story.html.

Newman, Melinda. "MCA Braces for Merger with Geffen: Layoffs Rock Staff, with More Possible." *Billboard*, June 21, 2003.

Norton, Perry L. "Woodward's Vision for Detroit." *Michigan Quarterly Review* 25, no. 2 (Spring 1986). https://quod.lib.umich.edu/m/mqrarchive/act2080.0025.002/22:4?rgn=full +text;view=image.

O'Neill, Connor Towne. "J Dilla's Last Album Is Both a Debut and a Finale." *The Village Voice*, March 22, 2016. https://www.villagevoice.com/2016/03/22/j-dillas-last-album-is-both-a -debut-and-a-finale/.

OpenMPT.org. Accessed June 12, 2021.

Orcutt, K. C. "Common Talks His Early Days, J. Dilla and More During 'Questlove Supreme' Podcast." *Revolt*, January 26, 2018. https://www.revolt.tv/2018/1/26/20824147/common -talks-his-early-days-j-dilla-and-more-during-questlove-supreme-podcast.

Ordonez, Jennifer. "MCA Records Chief Leaves Post, As Label Endures Slump." *The Wall Street Journal*, January 17, 2003. https://www.wsj.com/articles/SB1042743654669654504.

Orr, Dane. "Berklee Student Dane Orr Discusses the J Dilla Ensemble." Accessed June 12, 2021. Video interview. https://www.youtube.com/watch?v=rWi2k97-L2E.

Oumano, Elena. "Common, Sauce Money Prepare Bows on MCA." *Billboard*, February 20, 1999.

Oumano, Elena. "Roots Are Strong on MCA." *Billboard*, March 27, 1999.

Oumano, Elena. "The Roots Are Very Together on *Things*." *Billboard*, January 23, 1999.

Parfit. "DJ Premier Tells the Story of This Photo with D'Angelo, Alchemist and J. Dilla, In His Words." *Ambrosia for Heads* (blog), January 20, 2016. https://ambrosiaforheads .com/2016/01/dj-premier-tells-the-story-of-this-photo-with-dangelo-alchemist-j-dilla-in -his-words/.

Paysour, La Fleur. "J Dilla Hip-Hop Collection Donated to National Museum of African American History and Culture." News release. Smithsonian Institution, July 18, 2014. https://www.si.edu/newsdesk/releases/j-dilla-hip-hop-collection-donated-national -museum-african-american-history-and-culture.

Perkins, Tom. "Inside the Detroit Doughnut Shop Founded in Honor of a Hip-Hop Legend." *Vice*, August 3, 2016. https://www.vice.com/en/article/mgkpq3/inside-the-detroit-dough nut-shop-founded-in-honor-of-a-hip-hop-legend.

Peterson, Sean. "Something Real: Rap, Resistance, and the Music of the Soulquarians." PhD diss., University of Oregon, 2018. https://scholarsbank.uoregon.edu/xmlui/handle /1794/23759.

Philips, Chuck. "Company Town; Teller Enters the Online Fray with Record Label Atomic Pop." *Los Angeles Times*, February 12, 1999.

Phillips, Yoh. "The Night Jay-Z Stabbed Lance 'Un' Rivera and Almost Ended His Career." *DJBooth*, June 8, 2016. https://djbooth.net/features/2016-06-08-jay-z-stabbing-un-rivera -career-over.

Philp, Ray. "Ghettotech: An Oral History." Red Bull Music Academy, May 24, 2017. https:// daily.redbullmusicacademy.com/2017/05/ghettotech-oral-history.

Pizzo, Mike "DJ." "When J Dilla Said 'Fuck the Police.'" *Cuepoint*, August 25, 2015. https:// medium.com/cuepoint/when-j-dilla-said-f-the-police-8a33255db9e5.

Price, Joe. "Common Says It Was 'Hard to Eat' After Erykah Badu Breakup." *Complex*, May 16, 2019. https://www.complex.com/music/2019/05/common-erykah-badu-breakup.

Questlove. "Questcorner Reviews." Okayplayer, circa 2000–2001. http://web.archive.org /web/20080416043218/http://www.okayplayer.com/theroots/view.jsp.

Questlove. "Questlove Shares Candid Footage of J Dilla Playing Drums in Session w/ Common and the Soulquarians." Okayplayer, February 10, 2015. https://www.okayplayer.com/news /questlove-studio-footage-j-dilla-on-drums-common-soulquarians.html.

Rambeau, David, ed. *Conant Gardens: A Black Urban Community, 1925–1950*. Detroit: The Conant Gardeners, 2001.

Rapaport, Michael, dir. *Beats, Rhymes, and Life: The Travels of A Tribe Called Quest*. Rival Pictures, Om Films, 2011.

Rappcats. "J Dilla—THE MIDDLE FINGER—White Label 12-Inch." Rappcats, September 15, 2016. https://www.rappcats.com/middlefinger/.

Rasul, Haleem, dir. *The Jitterbugs: Pioneers of the Jit*, 2014.

"Rebirth of Detroit 'is a disgrace to Dilla.'" Reddit R/Hiphopheads forums, June 19, 2012. www .reddit.com/r/hiphopheads/comments/v9rgf/rebirth_of_detroit_is_a_disgrace_to _dilla/.

Reese, Ronnie. "Biography." J-Dilla.com, 2001. http://web.archive.org/web/20110704222231 /http://www.j-dilla.com/biography/.

Reese, Ronnie. "Son of Detroit: Jay Dee Remembered." *Wax Poetics* 17, June/July 2006.

Reese, Ronnie. "The Diary," from liner notes for *The Diary*. Pay Jay Productions, Mass Appeal Records MSAP0032, 2016, CD.

Reynolds, Simon. "The Cult of J Dilla." *The Guardian*, June 16, 2009. http://www.theguardian .com/music/musicblog/2009/jun/16/cult-j-dilla.

RITMO Centre for Interdisciplinary Studies in Rhythm, Time and Motion website. Accessed June 12, 2021. https://www.uio.no/ritmo/english/index.html.

Roberts, Randall. "The End of an Era: Low End Theory's Bittersweet Closing Caps a Year of Soul-Searching." *Los Angeles Times*, August 8, 2018. https://www.latimes.com/entertainment /music/la-et-ms-low-end-theory-20180807-story.html.

Rogers, Charles E. "R.J.'s 'Latest Arrival.'" *New York Amsterdam News*, January 31, 1987.

Roper, Tamara. "The Evolution of J Dilla." *Vice*, September 13, 2013. https://www.vice.com/en /article/6vmkwm/youneedtohearthis-dilla.

Rosenberg, Paul. "Proof and Dilla." *Paul Rosenblog* (blog), April 11, 2010. http:// bunyanchopshop.blogspot.com/2010/04/proof-dilla.html.

Rosenberg, Paul. "The Rhythm Kitchen Flyer." *Paul Rosenblog* (blog), January 25, 2008. http:// bunyanchopshop.blogspot.com/2008/01/rhythm-kitchen-flyer.html.

Rubin, Mike. "The 411 on the 313: A Brief History of Detroit Hip-Hop." *Complex*, October 10, 2013. https://www.complex.com/music/2013/10/history-of-detroit-rap/.

Russell, James. "Music Tech Legend Roger Linn: 'I Rarely Listen to Anything with Drum Machines in It.'" *MusicRadar*, July 3, 2019. https://www.musicradar.com/news/music-tech -legend-roger-linn-i-rarely-listen-to-anything-with-drum-machines-in-it.

Russonello, Giovanni. "Why J Dilla May Be Jazz's Latest Great Innovator." *A Blog Supreme*. NPR, February 7, 2013. https://www.npr.org/sections/ablogsupreme/2013/02/07/171349007/why -j-dilla-may-be-jazzs-latest-great-innovator.

Samuels, Anita M. "Geffen Shifts Its Hip-Hop Acts to MCA." *Billboard*, April 18, 1998.

Sanneh, Kelefah. "James Yancey, 32, Producer Known for Soulful Hip-Hop." *The New York Times*, February 14, 2006.

Scarth, Greg, and Oliver Curry. "DAW and Drum Machine Swing." *Attack*, July 1, 2013. https:// www.attackmagazine.com/technique/passing-notes/daw-drum-machine-swing/.

Scarth, Greg, and Roger Linn. "Roger Linn on Swing, Groove, and the Magic of the MPC's Timing." *Attack*, July 2, 2013. https://www.attackmagazine.com/features/interview/roger -linn-swing-groove-magic-mpc-timing/.

Schloss, Joseph G. *Making Beats: The Art of Sample-Based Hip-Hop*. Middletown, CT: Wesleyan University Press, 2004.

Schmidt, Torsten. "Brian Cross aka B+." Interview transcript. Red Bull Music Academy, 2005. https://www.redbullmusicacademy.com/lectures/brian-cross-brazilian-love-affair.

Scott, Damien, and Benjamin Chesna. "The Oral History of Okayplayer." *Complex*, March 8, 2013. https://www.complex.com/pop-culture/2013/03/the-oral-history-of-okayplayer.

Senske and Halloway. Charter Township of Clinton Police Department. *Domestic Violence*

Investigation Incident #02-8743. Clinton Township: Charter Township of Clinton Police Dept., March 11, 2002.

Serwer, Jesse. "Karriem Riggins and J Dilla Shine." *XLR8R*, August 14, 2006. https://xlr8r.com /features/karriem-riggins-and-j-dilla-shine/.

Setaro, Shawn. "Jon Bellion: From Pop Songs to Pixar." *Forbes*, June 22, 2016. https://www .forbes.com/sites/shawnsetaro/2016/06/22/jon-bellion-from-pop-songs-to-pixar/.

Sewick, Paul. "10,000 Acre Tract." *Detroit Urbanism* (blog), January 31, 2017. http:// detroiturbanism.blogspot.com/2017/01/10000-acre-tract.html.

Sewick, Paul. "Indian Villages, Reservations, and Removal." *Detroit Urbanism* (blog), March 7, 2016. http://detroiturbanism.blogspot.com/2016/03/indian-villages-reservations-and -removal.html.

Sewick, Paul. "Radial Avenues Part II: Woodward." *Detroit Urbanism* (blog), August 1, 2016. http://detroiturbanism.blogspot.com/2016/08/radial-avenues-part-ii-woodward.html.

Sewick, Paul. "Retracing Detroit's Native American Trails." *Detroit Urbanism* (blog), January 19, 2016. http://detroiturbanism.blogspot.com/2016/01/retracing-detroits-native-american.html.

Sewick, Paul. "The Grid Part I: The Survey of Michigan." *Detroit Urbanism* (blog), March 13, 2017. http://detroiturbanism.blogspot.com/2017/03/the-grid-part-i-survey-of-michigan.html.

Sewick, Paul. "The Grid Part II: The Survey of Metro Detroit." *Detroit Urbanism* (blog), March 30, 2017. http://detroiturbanism.blogspot.com/2017/03/the-grid-part-ii-survey-of-metro -detroit.html.

Sewick, Paul. "The Park Lots." *Detroit Urbanism* (blog), January 3, 2017. http://detroiturbanism .blogspot.com/2017/01/the-park-lots.html.

Sewick, Paul. "The Woodward Plan Part I: Origins." *Detroit Urbanism* (blog), April 4, 2016. http://detroiturbanism.blogspot.com/2016/04/the-woodward-plan-part-i-origins.html.

Sewick, Paul. "Woodward Plan Part II: Dawn of the Radial City." *Detroit Urbanism* (blog), April 25, 2016. http://detroiturbanism.blogspot.com/2016/04/woodward-plan-part-ii-dawn-of -radial.html.

Sewick, Paul. "Woodward Plan Part III: Interruptions." *Detroit Urbanism* (blog), June 6, 2016. http://detroiturbanism.blogspot.com/2016/06/woodward-plan-part-iii-interruptions.html.

Sicko, Dan. *Techno Rebels: The Renegades of Electronic Funk.* 2nd ed., rev. and updated. Detroit: Wayne State University Press, 2010.

Slopfunkdust. "88 Keys . . . GEEK DOWN!!! © J.Dilla." *FWMJ's Rappers I Know* (blog), December 22, 2010. https://www.rappersiknow.com/2010/12/22/88-keys-geek-down -%c2%a9-j-dilla/.

Smooth, Jay. "Jay Dee Sick But Recovering? ~~In a Coma, According to ?uestlove~~." HipHopMusic .com (blog), January 17, 2005. https://web.archive.org/web/20050207083505/http://hiphop music.com/archives/000748.html.

"Special Feature; R.J.'s Latest Arrival Is Holding On." *The Washington Informer*, March 25, 1987.

Spinologist. "Ambassador's on Soul Track Records Sound in Motion." Soul Source forum, April 15, 2008. https://www.soul-source.co.uk/forums/topic/70561-ambassadors-on-soul-track -records-sound-in-motion/.

Sryon. "Yancey Media Group to Release Previously Unheard J Dilla Records This 2013." *Hip-HopDX*, November 22, 2012. https://hiphopdx.com/news/id.21975/title.yancey-media -group-to-release-previously-unheard-j-dilla-records-this-2013.

Stadnicki, D. A. "Play Like Jay: Pedagogies of Drum Kit Performance After J Dilla." *Journal of Popular Music Education* 1, no. 3 (2017): 253–80.

Staskel, Ryan. "Album Review: J Dilla—*The Rebirth of Detroit*." *Consequence*, July 5, 2012. https://consequence.net/2012/07/album-review-j-dilla-the-rebirth-of-detroit/.

Stones Throw Records. "Jaylib Live 2004." February 6, 2009. https://www.stonesthrow.com /news/jaylib-live-2004/.

Stones Throw Records. "J Dilla and Madlib Live: Jaylib at Rock the Bells." July 25, 2004. https:// www.stonesthrow.com/news/j-dilla-and-madlib-live-jaylib-at-rock-the-bells/.

Stones Throw Records. "Paris Apeshit for Dilla." February 5, 2009. https://www.stonesthrow
.com/news/paris-apeshit-for-dilla.

Stones Throw Records. "RIP: J Dilla's Father Beverly Dewitt Yancey." September 25, 2012.
https://www.stonesthrow.com/news/beverly-dewitt-yancey/.

Strauss, Matthew. "Listen to Flying Lotus' Mix from the Day J Dilla Passed Away." *Pitchfork*,
February 10, 2016. https://pitchfork.com/news/63466-listen-to-flying-lotus-mix-from-the
-day-j-dilla-passed-away/.

Strauss, Neil. "A Major Merger Shakes Up the Rock World." *The New York Times*, December
21, 1998.

Strauss, Neil. "A Salute to Clive Davis, Ousted at Arista Records." *The New York Times*, April 12,
2000.   https://www.nytimes.com/2000/04/12/arts/a-salute-to-clive-davis-ousted-at-arista
-records.html.

Sugrue, Thomas J. *The Origins of the Urban Crisis: Race and Inequality in Postwar Detroit*.
Princeton, NJ: Princeton University Press, 2005.

Sullivan, Mary Ann. Images of the *Detroit Industry Murals* by Diego Rivera at the Detroit
Institute of Arts, 2010. https://homepages.bluffton.edu/~sullivanm/michigan/detroit
/riveramurals/intro.html.

Suosalo, Heikki. Review of *While the City Sleeps*, by the Spinners. *Soul Express Online*, October
2, 2018. https://www.soulexpress.net/spinners_whilethecitysleeps.htm.

Sylvester. Charter Township of Clinton Police Department. *General Incident Report #02-28099*.
Clinton Township: Charter Township of Clinton Police Dept., August 6, 2002.

Thomas, Datwon. "J Dilla: Soul Under Control." Platform.net, February 2001. Republished at
https://www.stonesthrow.com/news/soul-under-control/.

Thomas, Datwon. "Kendrick Lamar and Anthony 'Top Dawg' Tiffith on How They Built
Hip-Hop's Greatest Indie Label." *Billboard*, September 14, 2017. https://www.billboard
.com/articles/news/magazine-feature/7964649/kendrick-lamar-anthony-tiffith-interview
-billboard-cover-story-2017.

Timmhotep. "Fantastic Voyage: J Dilla, Your Favorite Producer's Favorite Producer, May
Have Passed On, But His Musical Legacy Will Never Fade Away." *The Source*, April 2006.
Republished at https://www.stonesthrow.com/news/fantastic-voyage/.

Tingen, Paul. "Inside Track: Kendrick Lamar's To Pimp a Butterfly." *Sound on Sound*, June 2015.
https://www.soundonsound.com/people/inside-track-kendrick-lamars-pimp-butterfly.

TonySwish. "J Dilla & Madlib (JayLib) - Live at Detroit's Electronic Music Festival 2004 DEMF."
https://soundcloud.com/besttonyever/j-dilla-madlib-jaylib-live-at.

"Tribe's Q-Tip Loses Unreleased Songs in Fire." MTV News, February 9, 1998. http://www.mtv
.com/news/1433421/tribes-q-tip-loses-unreleased-songs-in-fire/.

"TTP Overview." Answering TTP Foundation. Accessed June 12, 2021. https://www
.answeringttp.org/ttp-overview.

Turner, Khary Kimani, and Jonathan Cunningham. "Dilla: The Real Deal." *Detroit Metro
Times*, March 1, 2006. https://www.metrotimes.com/detroit/dilla-the-real-deal/Content?
oid=2184071.

Understanding TTP. "About TTP." Accessed June 12, 2021. https://www.understandingttp.com
/patient/about-ttp/.

Unikone. "Da' Enna C.—You Can't Use My Pen—1994." *HipHop-TheGoldenEra* (blog), July
16, 2018. http://hiphop-thegoldenera.blogspot.com/2018/07/da-enna-c-you-cant-use-my
-pen-1994.html.

"Universal Music Says Boberg Resigns as MCA President." Reuters, January 16, 2003.

Vanderpuije, John. "The Oral History of Jay Dee aka J Dilla's Classic Debut Album." Liner
notes for J Dilla, *Welcome 2 Detroit* 20th Anniversary Edition, BBE BBEBG001SLP, 2021,
vinyl.

Van Nguyen, Dean. "Kindred Soul." *Wax Poetics* 55 (Summer 2013).

Viega, Alex. "MCA Records Cuts Staff in Move to Restructure." Associated Press, June 10, 2003.

Vieira, Ricardo Miguel. "Still Dilla: Resurrecting a Lost Album by One of Hip Hop's Greatest." *Huck*, April 25, 2016. https://www.huckmag.com/art-and-culture/still-dilla-resurrecting -lost-album-one-hip-hops-greatest/.

Vouloumanos, Victoria. "An Exploration of Lo-Fi Hip-Hop, Part III: From Nujabes and J Dilla to YouTube Livestreams." Medium, December 8, 2019. https://medium.com/@ victoriavouloumanos/an-exploration-of-lo-fi-hip-hop-part-iii-from-nujabes-and-j-dilla -to-youtube-livestreams-f0a5cc719e50.

Walton, Scott. "Going in Style: Miami-Bound Salley Always Stands Out in a Crowd." *Detroit Free Press*, September 14, 1992.

Wang, Oliver. "The L.A. Roots of Kendrick Lamar's 'To Pimp a Butterfly.'" KCET, March 25, 2015. https://www.kcet.org/shows/artbound/the-l-a-roots-of-kendrick-lamars-to-pimp-a-butterfly.

Wang, Oliver, and Eothen Alapatt. "On the Rhodes Again: The Electric Piano of Harold B. Rhodes." Medium, November 23, 2017. https://medium.com/@oliverwang/on-the-rhodes -again-the-electric-piano-of-harold-b-rhodes-e3458f96e63e.

Watson, Elijah C. "J Dilla's Influence and Legacy Lives On in the World of Lo-Fi Hip-Hop." Okayplayer, October 7, 2020. https://www.okayplayer.com/music/j-dilla-lofi-hip-hop -influence.html.

Watson, Elijah C. "Thundercat and Kamasi Washington Discuss J Dilla, Kendrick Lamar in New Interview." Okayplayer, August 4, 2016. https://www.okayplayer.com/news/thundercat -kamasi-washington-discuss-j-dilla-kendrick-lamar-in-new-interview.html.

Weiner, Natalie. "'Love at First Sight, Creatively': Sonnymoon's Anna Wise on Working with Kendrick Lamar on 'Good Kid' and 'Butterfly.'" *Billboard*, March 24, 2015. https:// www.billboard.com/articles/columns/the-juice/6509570/anna-wise-kendrick-lamar -sonnymoon-good-kid-maad-city-to-pimp-a-butterfly.

Weiner, Natalie. "How Kendrick Lamar Transformed into 'The John Coltrane of Hip-Hop' on 'To Pimp a Butterfly.'" *Billboard*, March 26, 2015. https://www.billboard.com/articles /columns/the-juice/6509665/kendrick-lamar-to-pimp-a-butterfly-jazz-robert-glasper.

Weiner, Natalie, and Alex Gale. "Kendrick Lamar's 'To Pimp a Butterfly': 10 Key Collaborators." *Billboard*, March 16, 2015. https://www.billboard.com/articles/columns/the-juice/6502315 /kendrick-lamar-to-pimp-a-butterfly-10-key-collaborators.

Weingarten, Christopher R. "Hear the Lead Track from J Dilla's Lost Vocal Album." *Rolling Stone*, February 18, 2016. https://www.rollingstone.com/music/music-features/hear-the -lead-track-from-j-dillas-lost-vocal-album-the-diary-49800/.

Weiss, Jeff. "An Interview with J Dilla's Mother, Ms. Maureen Yancey." *LA Weekly*, July 24, 2008. https://www.laweekly.com/an-interview-with-j-dillas-mother-ms-maureen-yancey/.

Weiss, Jeff. "Frank Nitt Speaks on His New Delicious Vinyl EP and His Collaborations with J Dilla, and Premieres Exclusive MP3." *Pop & Hiss* (blog). *Los Angeles Times*, June 24, 2010. https://latimesblogs.latimes.com/music_blog/2010/06/dropping-jewels-frank-nitt-speaks -on-his-new-delicious-vinyl-ep-his-collaborations-with-j-dilla-and.html.

Weiss, Jeff. "It Was the Last Night at Low End Theory, and Tyler, the Creator, Tokimonsta and More Made Sure This Wasn't a Night of Mourning." *Los Angeles Times*, August 9, 2018. https://www.latimes.com/entertainment/music/la-et-ms-low-end-theory-final-20180809 -story.html.

Weiss, Jeff. "Jamie Strong Is the Most Influential Figure You've Never Heard of in the L.A. Music Scene." *LA Weekly*, September 30, 2015. https://www.laweekly.com/jamie-strong-is-the -most-influential-figure-youve-never-heard-of-in-the-l-a-music-scene/.

Weiss, Jeff. "Live: Thom Yorke and Flying Lotus Perform Surprise DJ Set at Low End Theory." *Pop & Hiss* (blog). *Los Angeles Times*, May 5, 2011. https://latimesblogs.latimes.com/music _blog/2011/05/live-thom-yorke-flying-lotus-perform-surprise-dj-set-at-low-end-theory .html.

Weiss, Jeff. "Who's Biting J Dilla's Beats?" *LA Weekly*, June 18, 2008. https://www.laweekly.com /whos-biting-j-dillas-beats/.

"What Causes Thrombotic Thrombocytopenic Purpura?" Hematology-Oncology Associates of CNY. Accessed June 12, 2021. https://www.hoacny.com/patient-resources/blood-disorders/what-thrombotic-thrombocytopenic-purpura/what-causes-thrombotic.

Whitall, Susan, and Chuck Bennett. "J Dilla Foundation Helps Pershing Music Program." *The Detroit News*, April 16, 2015. https://www.detroitnews.com/story/entertainment/people/2015/04/16/society-confidential-dilla-foundation-pershing-music-program/25898855/.

White, Michael. "Seagram Absorbs PolyGram, Creates World's Largest Music Company." Associated Press, December 11, 1998.

White, Paul. "The Return of Roger Linn." *Sound on Sound*, June 2002. https://www.soundonsound.com/people/return-roger-linn.

Wilkinson, Alec. "Jazz Hands." *The New Yorker*, March 3, 2013. https://www.newyorker.com/magazine/2013/03/11/jazz-hands.

Williams, Chris. "The Soulquarians at Electric Lady: An Oral History." Red Bull Music Academy, June 1, 2015. https://daily.redbullmusicacademy.com/2015/06/the-soulquarians-at-electric-lady.

Williams, Felicia A. "Slum Village, Fantastic, Vol. 2." *The Source*, May 1999.

Wilson, Jeff. "Seagram Fires 500 in Music Merger." Associated Press, January 21, 1999.

Wimbley, Randy, and David Komer. "J Dilla Music Tech Grant Awarded to Detroit Central HS in Memory of Late, Homegrown Music Star." Fox 2 Detroit, October 27, 2020. https://www.fox2detroit.com/news/j-dilla-music-tech-grant-awarded-to-detroit-central-hs-in-memory-of-late-great-homegrown-music-star.

Winistorfer, Andrew. "Oneness of Juju Were the Collision of Jazz, Funk, African Music and the Avant-Garde." *Vinyl Me, Please*, April 25, 2019. http://magazine.vinylmeplease.com/magazine/oneness-of-juju-interview/.

Young, Coleman, and Lonnie Wheeler. *Hard Stuff: The Autobiography of Mayor Coleman Young*. New York: Viking, 1994.

Zeman, David. "Former Piston Salley Is Sued for $375,000." *Detroit Free Press*, June 8, 1993.

Zlatopolsky, Ashley. "The Roots of Techno: Detroit's Club Scene 1973–1985." Red Bull Music Academy, July 31, 2014. https://daily.redbullmusicacademy.com/2014/07/roots-of-techno-feature.

Zo. "Throwback Thursday: That Time Thundercat Played Dilla's Flip of Herbie Hancock on Slum Village's 'Get Dis Money'—For Herbie Hancock." Okayplayer, February 5, 2015. https://www.okayplayer.com/news/throwback-thursday-j-dilla-slum-village-get-dis-money-thundercat-plays-sample-for-herbie-hancock-video.html.

Selected Discography

James Dewitt Yancey composed a countless number of beats in his lifetime, distributed occasionally in semi-formal "batches" sent to artists and executives, but often in informal dubs made for friends. The tracks and compilations were rarely named by James himself; they often acquired monikers as they made their way to artists, friends, and fans. Some beats were selected by artists and then finished by James himself in the studio; others, especially after his death, were simply lifted right from his beat cassettes or CDs as a bed for vocals. It's why many of his beats show up in more than one place under different song titles by different artists.

Thus the most complete and revelatory discography of J Dilla would be an inventory of every beat he ever made—and beside each one, a list of all the forms in which that beat made its way out into the world, whether on official releases, mixtapes, batches, or bootlegs; whether during his lifetime or posthumously. A project like this would need to live online, and is truly beyond the scope of the more selective discography that follows.

Following are the releases by J Dilla as a recording artist, followed by a list of the most notable tracks he produced over the years, and a list of his appearances as a vocalist or musician. Lastly, I have created a section called "Batches," in which I reference a select group of J Dilla's more intentional collections of raw beats. It is not comprehensive, but comprises the most widely known and circulated compilations.

As a Recording Artist

All tracks on these releases produced by James Dewitt Yancey, except where noted.

YEAR	ARTIST	TITLE	LABEL
1996	Jay Dee	*Jay Dee Unreleased EP*	House Shoes
1997	Slum Village	*Fan-Tas-Tic*	El-Azim Waajeed/ Donut Boy
2000	Slum Village	*Fantastic, Vol. 2*	Barak/Good Vibe
	J-88	*Best Kept Secret*	Superrappin/Groove Attack
2001	Jay Dee aka J Dilla	*Welcome 2 Detroit**	BBE
	Jay Dee	"Fuck the Police" b/w "Move"	Up Above
2002	Jay Dee	*The Official Jay Dee Instrumental Series: Unreleased Volume 1*	Bling47
2003	Jay Dee	*Vintage: Unreleased Instrumentals from Jay Dee of the Ummah (Volume 2)*	Bling47
	Jay Dee	*Ruff Draft / EP*	Mummy/Groove Attack
	Jaylib	*Champion Sound†*	Stones Throw
2006	J Dilla	*Donuts*	Stones Throw
	J Dilla	*The Shining*	BBE
2007	J Dilla	*Ruff Draft (Reissue)*	Stones Throw
	J Dilla	*Jay Love Japan*	Operation Unknown
	Jay Dee	*Jay Deelicious: The Delicious Vinyl Years*	Delicious Vinyl
2009	J Dilla	*Jay Stay Paid*	Nature Sounds
2012	J Dilla	*Dillatroit*	Mahogani/Yancey Media Group
	J Dilla	*Rebirth of Detroit*	Ruff Draft/Yancey Media Group
2013	J Dilla	*The Lost Scrolls Vol. 1 (EP)*	Ruff Draft/Yancey Media Group
	J Dilla	*Lost Tapes Reels + More*	Mahogani/Yancey Media Group
2014	J Dilla	*The King of Beats (Box Set)*	Yancey Media Group

* All tracks produced by J Dilla except "The Clapper," produced by Karriem Riggins; coproduced by J Dilla.

† Tracks produced by J Dilla: "L.A. to Detroit," "Nowadays," "The Red," "Raw Shit," "The Heist," "React," "Strip Club," "The Exclusive," "Starz."

YEAR	ARTIST	TITLE	LABEL
2015	J Dilla	*Dillatronic*	Yancey Media Group
2016	J Dilla	*The Diary*[*]	Pay Jay/Mass Appeal
2016	J Dilla	*The King of Beats*	Yancey Media Group
	Jay Dee	*Jay Dee a.k.a. King Dilla*	Yancey Media Group/Ne'Astra
	J Dilla	*Jay Dee's Ma Dukes Collection*	Yancey Media Group
2017	Slum Village	*Fantastic Vol. 0*	Barak/Ne'Astra
	J Dilla	*Motor City Collection*	Official Ma Dukes/Nature Sounds
	J Dilla	*J Dilla's Delights, Vol. 1*	Yancey Media Group
	J Dilla	*J Dilla's Delights, Vol. 2*	Yancey Media Group

As a Producer

These releases produced solely by James Dewitt Yancey, except where noted.

YEAR	ARTIST	TITLE	CREDIT	LABEL
1993	T.H.I.Q.U.E.	"Sweet One"	as James Yancy [*sic*], produced with Adé	Super Sonic
1994	Da' Enna C	"Now"	as J.D.	Up Top
1995	1st Down	"A Day wit the Homiez," "Front Street"	as Jon Doe	Payday/FFRR
	Little Indian	"One Little Indian (Jaydee's *hit Remix)"	as Jaydee	Premeditated
	Poe	"Fingertips"—on *Hello*	as JD (drum programming)	Modern/Atlantic
	The Pharcyde	"Runnin'," "Bullshit," "Splatittorium," "Somethin' That Means Somethin'," "Drop," "Y?"—on *Labcabincalifornia*. "Runnin' (Jay Dee Remix)," "Y? (Be Like That) (Jay Dee Remix)," "Runnin' (Jay Dee Extended Mix)," "Runnin' (Smooth Mix)"	as Jay Dee; co-producer, "Y?"	Delicious Vinyl

* J Dilla is the vocalist and featured artist; all tracks composed by other producers.

YEAR	ARTIST	TITLE	CREDIT	LABEL
1996	A Tribe Called Quest	"1nce Again," "Get a Hold," "Keeping It Moving," "Stressed Out," "Word Play"—on *Beats, Rhymes and Life*	as The Ummah	Jive
	Busta Rhymes	"Keep It Movin'," "Still Shining"—on *The Coming.* "Woo-Hah!! (The Jay-Dee Bounce Remix)," "Woo-Hah!! (The Jay-Dee Other Shit Remix)," "It's a Party (The Ummah Remix)," "Ill Vibe (The Ummah Remix)	as The Ummah	Elektra
	De La Soul	"Stakes Is High"—on *Stakes Is High.* "Stakes Is High (Remix)"	as Jay Dee; "Stakes Is High" co-produced by De La Soul	Tommy Boy
	Keith Murray	"Dangerous Ground"—on *Enigma.* "The Rhyme (Slum Village Street Mix)"	as The Ummah	Jive
	Mad Skillz	"It's Goin' Down," "The Jam"—on *From Where???*	as Jay Dee	Big Beat/ Atlantic
	The Pharcyde	"She Said (Remix)"	as Jay Dee	Delicious Vinyl
1997	Busta Rhymes	"So Hardcore"—on *When Disaster Strikes . . .*	as The Ummah	Elektra
	Crustation	"Purple (A Tribe Called Quest Edit)"	as The Ummah	Jive
	Janet Jackson	"Got 'Til It's Gone (Ummah Jay Dee's Revenge Mix)"	as The Ummah	Virgin
	Somethin' for the People	"All I Do (Jay Dee's *hit Mix)"	as The Ummah	Warner Bros.
	The Brand New Heavies	"Sometimes (The Ummah Remix)"	as The Ummah	Delicious Vinyl

YEAR	ARTIST	TITLE	CREDIT	LABEL
1998	5-Elementz	"Whutchawant," "Feed Back," "Rockshows," "Party Groove," "Janet Jacme," "E.G.O.," "Don't Stop," "Searchin,'" "Crazze"—on *The Album Time Forgot*	as Jay Dee	That Was Entertainment
	A Tribe Called Quest	"4 Moms," "Against the World," "Busta's Lament," "Da Booty," "Find a Way," "His Name Is Mutty Ranks," "Start It Up," "Steppin' It Up"—on *The Love Movement*	as The Ummah; contributions noted as JD	Jive
	A Tribe Called Quest and JD of Slum Village	"That Shit"—on *Funkmaster Flex • The Mix Tape, Vol. III*	as The Ummah	Loud
	Bizarre	"Butterfly"	as Jaydee for The Ummah	Federation
	Mood	"Secrets of the Sand (Remix)"	as J.D. of The Ummah	Blunt
1999	Heavy D	"Listen"—on *Heavy*	as Jay Dee	Universal
	Macy Gray	"I Try (Jaydee Remix)"	as Jaydee	Epic
	Nine Yards	"Always Find a Way (Jay Dee Remix)"	as Jay Dee	Virgin
	Phat Kat	"Dedication to the Suckers," "Don't Nobody Care About Us," "Microphone Master"—on *Dedication to the Suckers*	as Jay Dee	House Shoes
	Phife Dawg	"Bend Ova" (later "Ben Dova"), "Thought U Wuz Nice"	as Jay Dee for The Ummah	Superrappin/ Groove Attack

YEAR	ARTIST	TITLE	CREDIT	LABEL
1999	Q-Tip	"Wait Up," "Higher," "Moving with U," "Breathe & Stop," "Let's Ride," "Things U Do," "All In," "Go Hard," "End of Time," "Do It, Be It, See It," "Vivrant Thing"—on *Amplified*	as Jay Dee, produced with Q-Tip	Arista
	Que.D	"Underestimated," "Supa Shit," "Kilo," "Cash Flow," "Michelle," "Rock Box," "Don't Stop"—on *Quiet Delicious* (reissued as *Quite Delicious*)	as J.Dahmer	Waajid [*sic*] (reissued by Royal Flyness)
	The Roots	"Dynamite!"—on *Things Fall Apart*	as Jay Dee of The Ummah	MCA
2000	Bahamadia	"One-4-Teen (Jay Dee Remix)"	as Jay Dee	Good Vibe
	Black Star	"Little Brother"—on *The Hurricane (Music from and Inspired by the Motion Picture)*	as Jay Dee for The Ummah	MCA
	Busta Rhymes	"Enjoy Da Ride," "Live It Up," "Show Me What You Got"—on *Anarchy*	as Jay Dee	Elektra
	Common	"Time Travelin' (A Tribute to Fela)," "Heat," "Dooinit," "The Light," "Funky for You," "The Questions," "Time Travelin' Reprise," "A Film Called (Pimp)," "Nag Champa (Afrodisiac for the World),"	as The Soulquarians' Jay Dee for The Ummah; "Time Travelin'" produced with The Soulquarians; "Funky for You," "The Questions" produced with James Poyser	MCA

YEAR	ARTIST	TITLE	CREDIT	LABEL
2000	Common	"Thelonius," "Payback Is a Grandmother"—on *Like Water for Chocolate*		
	De La Soul	"Thru Ya City"—on *AOI: Mosaic Thump*	as Jay Dee for The Ummah	Tommy Boy
	Erykah Badu	"Didn't Cha Know?," "My Life," "Kiss Me on My Neck"—on *Mama's Gun*	as Jay Dee the Soulquarian; producer: "Didn't Cha Know"; co-producer: "Kiss Me on My Neck," "My Life"	Universal Motown
	Frank-n-Dank (as Jaydee presents . . .)	"Me and My Man," "Love (A Thing of the Past)," "Everybody Get Up!" "Give It Up II"	as Jay Dee	Fat Beats
	Guru	"Certified (featuring Bilal)"—on *Guru's Jazzmatazz: Streetsoul*	as Jay Dee	Virgin
	Innerzone Orchestra	"People Make the World Go Round (J-88 Mix)"	as J-88	Talkin Loud
	Mos Def	"Can U C the Pride in the Panther (Remix)"	as Jay Dee	Interscope
	Phife Dawg	"4 Horsemen"—on *Ventilation: Da LP*	as Jay Dee for The Ummah	Superrappin/ Groove Attack
	Royce da 5'9"	"Let's Grow"—on *Lyricist Lounge Volume 2*	as Jay Dee	Rawkus
	Spacek	"Eve (JayDee Mix)"	as Jay Dee	Blue/Island
	The Brand New Heavies	"Saturday Night (Jay Dee Remix)"	as Jay Dee	Delicious Vinyl

YEAR	ARTIST	TITLE	CREDIT	LABEL
2001	Bilal	"Reminisce"—on *1st Born Second*	as Jay Dee	Interscope
	Busta Rhymes	"Genesis," "Make It Hurt"—on *Genesis*	as J Dilla	J
	Chino XL	"Don't Say a Word," "How It Goes"—on *I Told You So*	as Jay Dee	Metro
	De La Soul	"Peer Pressure"—on *AOI: Bionix*	as Jay Dee	Tommy Boy
	Lucy Pearl	"Without You (Jay Dee Remix)"	as Jay Dee	Virgin
	Que.D	"In Yo Face"	as Jay Dee	Up Above
	Toshi Kubota	"Nothing But Your Love (Jay Dee Remix)"	as Jay Dee	Epic
2002	Busta Rhymes	"It Ain't Safe No More," "What Up," "Turn Me Up Some"—on *It Ain't Safe No More*	as J Dilla	J
	Common	"Soul Power," "Aquarius," "Electric Wire Hustler Flower," "New Wave," "Star *69 (PS with Love)," "Between Me," "You & Liberation," "I Am Music," "Jimi Was a Rock Star"—on *Electric Circus*	as Dilla, co-producer	MCA
	DJ Cam	"Love Junkee (Dilla Vocal Remix)"	as Jay Dee aka Dilla	Inflamable
	DJ Jazzy Jeff featuring Slum Village	"Are U Ready?"—on *The Magnificent EP*	as Jay Dee	Rapster
	Frank-n-Dank	"Push," "Where the Parties At?," "I'll Bet U Will"	as Jay Dee	Mummy/ Groove Attack
	Frank-n-Dank (as Jay Dee featuring . . .)	"Off Ya Chest," "Take Dem Clothes Off"	as Jay Dee	ABB

YEAR	ARTIST	TITLE	CREDIT	LABEL
2002	Slum Village	"Hoes," "Let's," "One"—on *Trinity (Past, Present and Future)*	as Jay Dilla	Barak/Capitol
	Talib Kweli	"Where Do We Go?," "Stand to the Side"—on *Quality*	as J Dilla	Rawkus
2003	ASD	"Komm Schon"—on *Wer Hätte Das Gedacht?* "Wenn Ihr Fühlt . . . "—on *Hey Du*	as J Dilla	Eimsbush
	Common	"Come Close Remix (Closer)"	as J Dilla	MCA
	Eric Roberson	"When Love Calls"—on *The Vault, Vol. 1*	as Jay Dee, produced with James Poyser	Blue Erro Soul
	Four Tet	"As Serious as Your Life (Jay Dee Remix)"	as Jay Dee	Domino
	T Love	"When You're Older (Ode to the Pickaninny)," "Who Smoked Sunshine?," "Long Way Back," "Chiquita"—on *Long Way Back*	as Jay Dee	Astralwerks
	Vivian Green	"Fanatic (Dilla's Remix)"	as J Dilla	Columbia
2004	Amp Fiddler	"Intro," "You Play Me," "Waltz of a Ghetto Fly"—on *Waltz of a Ghetto Fly.* "I Believe in You (Jaylib Mix)"*	as J Dilla	Genuine
	Brother Jack McDuff	"Oblighetto (J Dilla Remix)"—on *Blue Note Revisited*	as J Dilla	Blue Note
	De La Soul	"Verbal Clap," "Much More," "Shoomp"—on *The Grind Date*	as J Dilla	Sanctuary

* "Intro" and "Waltz of a Ghetto Fly" are the same beat as "Things U Do" by Q-Tip; "I Believe in You" is the same beat as "Raw Shit" by Jaylib.

YEAR	ARTIST	TITLE	CREDIT	LABEL
2004	Frank-n-Dank	"Okay," "Let's Go," "M.C.A. (Music Cemetery of America)"—on *Xtended Play Version 3.13*	as J Dilla	Needillworks
	Oh No	"Move"—on *The Disrupt*	as J Dilla	Stones Throw
	Slum Village	"Do You"—on *Detroit Deli (A Taste of Detroit)*	as J Dilla	Barak/Capitol
2005	Common	"Love Is . . . ," "It's Your World"—on *Be*	as Dilla	G.O.O.D./ Geffen
	Common	"The Movement"—on *26K*	as Dilla	Decon
	Dwele	"Keep On (featuring Slum Village)"—on *Some Kinda . . .*	as J Dilla	Virgin
	Dwight Trible and The Life Force Trio	"Antiquity"—on *Love Is the Answer*	as J Dilla	Ninja Tune
	Lawless Element	"The Shining"—on *Soundvision: In Stereo*	as J Dilla, produced with Young RJ	Babygrande
	M.E.D.	"Push," "So Real"—on *Push Comes to Shove*	as J Dilla	Stones Throw
	Slum Village	"It'z Your World," "Who Are We?"—on *Prequel to a Classic*	as J Dilla; "It'z Your World" produced with Young RJ	Barak
	Steve Spacek	"Dollar"—on *Space Shift*	as J Dilla	Sound in Color
2006	Busta Rhymes	"You Can't Hold the Torch"—on *The Big Bang*	as J Dilla	Aftermath
	Ghostface Killah	"Beauty Jackson," "Whip You with a Strap"—on *Fishcale**	as J Dilla	Def Jam

* "Beauty Jackson" is the same beat as "Hi" by J Dilla; "Whip You with a Strap" is the same beat as "One for Ghost" by J Dilla.

YEAR	ARTIST	TITLE	CREDIT	LABEL
2006	The Roots	"Can't Stop This"—on *Game Theory*[*]	as J Dilla; co-produced by The Roots and The Randy Watson Experience	Def Jam
2007	Common	"So Far to Go (with D'Angelo)"—on *Finding Forever*	as Dilla	G.O.O.D./ Geffen
	Phat Kat	"Nasty Ain't It," "My Old Label," "Cold Steel (with Elzhi)," "Game Time"—on *Carte Blanche*	as J Dilla	Look
2008	Guilty Simpson	"I Must Love You"—on *Ode to the Ghetto*	as J Dilla	Stones Throw
	Q-Tip	"Move," "Feva"—on *The Renaissance*	as J Dilla	Universal Motown
2009	Illa J	"Timeless," "We Here," "R U Listenin'?," "Alien Family (Interlude)," "Strugglin," "Showtime," "Swagger," "Mr Shakes (Skit)," "DFTF," "All Good," "Sounds Like Love," "Everytime," "Illasoul," "Air Signs"—on *Yancey Boys*	as Jay Dee; co-produced by Illa J and Mike Floss	Delicious Vinyl
	MF Doom	"Gazillion Ear," "Lightworks"—on *Born Like This*[†]	as J Dilla	Lex
	Mos Def	"History"—on *The Ecstatic*	as J Dilla	Downtown
	Raekwon	"House of Flying Daggers," "Ason Jones," "10 Bricks"—on *Only Built 4 Cuban Linx . . . Pt. II*[‡]	as J Dilla	Ice H2O

[*] "Can't Stop This" is the same beat as "Time: The Donut of the Heart" by J Dilla.

[†] "Lightworks" is the same beat as "Lightworks" by J Dilla.

[‡] "10 Bricks" is the same beat as "The Red" by Jaylib.

YEAR	ARTIST	TITLE	CREDIT	LABEL
2010	Erykah Badu	"Love"—on *New Amerykah Part Two (Return of the Ankh)*	as Jay Dilla	Universal Motown
	Slum Village	"Lock It Down," "We'll Show You"— on *Villa Manifesto*	as J Dilla; "We'll Show You" produced with Young RJ	Ne'Astra
2013	Frank-n-Dank	"Intro," "Get Cha Bitch," "Marijuana," "Rite Bites," "Street Life," "Pimp Strut," "Where the Parties At?," "Y'all Don't Want It," "Sex on the Beach," "All Seasons," "Alright," "Afterparty," "Ma Dukes," "Keep It Coming"—on *48 Hours*	as J Dilla	Delicious Vinyl
	Yancey Boys (Illa J and Frank Nitt)	"Dilltro," "Fisherman," "Lovin' U," "Go and Ask the DJ," "Jeep Volume," "Flowers," "Honk Ya Horn," "Slippin'," "Without Wings," "Beautiful," "Quicksand," "Rock My World," "The Throwaway," "This Evening"—on *Sunset Blvd.*	as J Dilla	Delicious Vinyl/ Yancey Media Group
2015	Slum Village	"Intro," "Love Is," "Tear It Down," "Expressive," "Windows," "Yes Yes (Remix)," "Right Back," "Too Much," "What We Have"— on *Yes!*	as J Dilla aka Jay Dee, produced with Young RJ	Ne'Astra/Yancey Music Group
2016	Phife Dawg	"Nutshell"	as J Dilla	Smoking Needles

As a Musician/Vocalist

YEAR	ARTIST	TITLE	ROLE	LABEL
1995	The Pharcyde	"All Live"—on *Labcabincalifornia*	Drums	Delicious Vinyl
1998	A Tribe Called Quest	"That Shit"—on *Funkmaster Flex • The Mix Tape, Vol. III*	Vocals	Loud
1999	Que.D	"Supa Shit"—on *Quite Delicious*	Vocals	Waajid [*sic*] (reissued by Royal Flyness)
2000	Common	"Heat," "Nag Champa (Afrodisiac for the World)," "Thelonius"—on *Like Water for Chocolate*	Vocals	MCA
	Erykah Badu	"Booty"—on *Mama's Gun*	Bass, Drum Programming	Universal Motown
2001	De La Soul	"Peer Pressure"—on *AOI: Bionix*	Vocals	Tommy Boy
2002	Common	"Jimi Was a Rock Star"—on *Electric Circus*	Moog Synthesizer, Drums, Electric Guitar, Bass, Drum Programming	MCA
	Frank-n-Dank	"Take Dem Clothes Off"—on *Off Ya Chest*	Vocals	ABB
2004	B.R. Gunna	"Do Your Thang, Stupid"—on *Dirty District: Vol. 2*	Vocals	Barak
	Dabrye feat. Jay Dee and Phat Kat	"Game Over"	Vocals	Ghostly International
	Slum Village	"Reunion"—on *Detroit Deli (A Taste of Detroit)*	Vocals	Barak/Capitol

YEAR	ARTIST	TITLE	ROLE	LABEL
2005	Diamond D	"We Gangstas"—on *The Diamond Mine*	Vocals	Diamond Mine
	Lawless Element	"Love," "Words from Dilla"—on *Soundvision: In Stereo*	Vocals	Babygrande
2005	Platinum Pied Pipers	"Shotgun," "Act Like You Know"—on *Triple P*; "Shotgun (Remix)"	Vocals	Ubiquity
	Sa-Ra	"Thrilla"—on *The Second Time Around*	Vocals	Sound in Color

Batches

TITLE	TRACKS
1995/1996 Batch ("Whatupdoe Sessions")	Includes the beats for "Still Shining," "Wordplay," "Stakes Is High"
1998 Batch ("Another Batch")	Includes the beats for "Don't Say a Word," "E=MC2," "Microphone Master"
1999 Batch ("The New Slave")	Includes the beats for "Breathe and Stop," "Payback Is a Grandmother"
2000 Batch ("Another Batch 2000")	Includes the beats for "Let's Grow," "Love" (Erykah Badu), "Enjoy Da Ride"
2001 Batch ("New Installment," "Da 1st Installment")	Includes the beats for "Ma Dukes"
2002 Batches, Vols. 1–5 ("Da 2nd Installment")	Includes the beats for *Champion Sound*, "You Can't Hold the Torch," "Push"
2003 Batches, Vols. 1–2	Includes the beats for *Jay Stay Paid*
2004 Batch ("Dill Withers," "The Motown Tape")	Includes the beat for "Move" (Q-Tip) and "Love" (J Dilla)

For the official *Dilla Time* listening guide, please visit www.DillaTimeBook.com.

Thanks

My gratitude, first and foremost, goes to everyone who sat for an interview for this book. I am honored by your trust and your candor, and my paramount wish is that I have done right by you and your story. Your names are inscribed in the Reporter's Notes and Sources section of this book.

Some additional needed recognition:

To James Dewitt Yancey, thanks for allowing me and Chino XL into your space, for humoring our two-man comedy show, and for two of the best beats you ever made. I doubt you would have imagined a future in which people would be writing voluminously about you; nor would I have imagined that I might be one of those people—which is why my dumb ass left my camera at the Atheneum and why I talked too much. Now, like you, I have learned the value of listening. I hope I've heard you.

I made my first trip to Detroit to work with Jay Dee; years later, I made my second to meet the family of the woman who became my wife. Wendy S. Walters imbued in me her love of the city. Her broad knowledge and incisive perspective enabled me to see how it connected to James Dewitt Yancey and so many other things; her mastery of language gave me the proper coaching to write about it; and her compassion got me through the process. Wendy's people have made a home for us in Detroit: I treasure Dr. Toni S. Walters, Jamie Kaye Walters, and Vincent M. Keenan, and am indebted to them for the support, guidance, and connections they provided that allowed me to bring my J Dilla students there in 2017, and to embark on the reporting and research that made this book possible.

I sing the praises of another Detroit family. When I told Maureen Yancey-Smith that I wanted to write a book about the gift her son gave to the world, she granted me abundant time and access, and her generosity and candor made it possible to tell a much deeper story about how a family created and sustained James. To know Maureen is itself a gift, and for that I am grateful. Before I ever thought of writing this book, I felt blessed by Herman Hayes's friendship, and Herm in return has a friend for life. I am endeared and indebted to Martha Yancey and John Yancey; to Reta, Clarice, Rashonda, and Al Hayes; to Faith Lamb; and to Maurice Lamb. To Joylette and Janell Hunter, and to Monica Whitlow: you are important, your stories matter, and thank you for sharing them with me. This work is dedicated to Ty-Monae Whitlow and Ja'Mya Yancey.

James was nurtured by a neighborhood brotherhood, and their love for him is manifest and enduring. They are Frank Bush, Derrick Harvey, R. L. Altman III, Qudduws Ware, Robert Waajeed O'Bryant, Titus Glover (RIP), and Terrance, Tobias, and Copez Wright. It's a fraternity that extended throughout Detroit, whose members include Charles Moore, Joseph Anthony Fiddler, Ron Watts, Andrés Hernández, Kevin Bell, Michael Buchanan, Karriem Riggins, Byron Simpson, Ralph James Rice Sr., Ralph James Rice Jr., Timothy Maynor, and DeShaun Holton (RIP). Later, James was adopted by a community in Los Angeles, among them Otis Jackson; Jason Jackson and Nazareth Nirza; Carlos Thurston and Christopher Rivas; Brian Cross and Eric Coleman; Eothen Alapatt, Chris Manak, and Jeffrey Carlson; and David Tobman (RIP). Thank you all for entrusting me with the preservation of those friendships.

Jeff Peretz, my greatest ally and friend in the creation of both the J Dilla course and book, gave an enormous amount of time and thought to this endeavor. For your flexibility and your friendship, eternal thanks.

I am overwhelmed by the patience, dedication, and professionalism of the team at MCD / Farrar, Straus and Giroux. For Sean McDonald, Rodrigo Corral, Olivia Kan-Sperling, Jackson Howard, Danny Vazquez, Janine Barlow, Debra Helfand, Logan Hill, Gretchen Achilles, Stephen

Weil, Claire Tobin, Sarita Varma, Daniel del Valle, Devon Mazzone, Flora Esterly, Zach Greenwald, and Rima Weinberg, I am so grateful.

And to the best agent and best friend a writer could hope for, David Dunton, it's true love.

Ahmir "Questlove" Thompson functions in this book as he does in life—a polymath in a category of his own. Not only did he study Jay Dee as a fan and then become James's friend and collaborator, Ahmir was the first writer to argue for his significance as a producer, on the pages of Okayplayer. He's never, ever stopped testifying. This book is simply the latest in a chain of events that Ahmir started. In that sense, this book would not be possible without him, and also because he was always so bountiful in his assistance and encouragement. Ahmir talks a lot about following his "North Stars." In this endeavor, Ahmir is mine.

My path to the study of James Dewitt Yancey began with the people who first schooled me back in the mid-1990s: Mike Ross, Rick Ross, Craig Bullock, and Joe Willis. It continued when Derek Barbosa (also known as Chino XL) and I made our pilgrimage to Detroit in 1999. More than a decade later, I began teaching at NYU, where I was mentored by Jason King, who in my estimation wrote the very first serious explication of J Dilla's musical impact on traditional musicians in his liner notes for a 2012 vinyl reissue of D'Angelo's *Voodoo*. It was Jason who encouraged me to not only lead a class on Dilla but take them to Detroit. I am grateful to my students for the honor of studying with them, and to the following people at NYU for their help in making the course a reality: Brianne Hayes, Alan Watson, Chelsea Falato, Allyson Green, Carrie Meconis, Annie Stanton, Bob Cameron, Michael Dinwiddie, Jeff Peretz, Bob Power, Nicholas Sansano, Michael McCoy, and Noah Simon. This book was supported by several Tisch Dean's Grants, and to my school I am most grateful. Thanks as well to my colleagues Sheril Antonio, Karen Shimakawa, Fred Carl, Jim Anderson, Marc Plotkin, J. D. Samson, Sofia Rei, Lauren Davis, Errol Kolosine, and Matthew D. Morrison; and to Harry Weingar, Piotr Orlov, Ashley Kahn, Kendra Foster, Vivien Goldman, Ned Sublette, Bob Christgau, Mike Errico, Ayanna Wilson, Kyle Alfred, and the rest of the adjunct faculty, staff, and students of the Clive

Davis Institute. My efforts on the ground in Detroit were assisted by
Stephen Henderson, Dr. Melba Joyce Boyd of Wayne State University,
Charles Ferrell of the Charles H. Wright Museum of African American
History, Sheila Cockrel, Bill Harris, Jeanette Pierce, Deidra Rice, Roger
Robinson, Khary Kimani Turner, Cornelius Harris, and Jamon Jordan,
whose knowledge of Detroit history approaches omniscience.

During my reporting and research for the book in Detroit, I had a
guardian angel, Mark Hicks, whom I've known since our days promoting records in the 1990s; and a guardian devil, Gene "Hex" Howell, a
pirate villain who sits on a throne of chrome, whose powers to summon
the right people at the right time border on supernatural, and who, for
whatever reason, decided to part the waters for me. Other Detroiters
who provided logistical and emotional support include the sublime Kof-
fey Brown; Joel Stone, senior curator at the Detroit Historical Society;
Brian D. James of the Motown Museum; Chrystal Wilson at the Detroit
Public Schools; Mary Wright and Vernon Chapel AME Church; Piper
Carter, Carleton Gholz, Malik Alston, Yuri Ramirez, Mike Vanover, David Grandison Jr., Boog Brown, Emery Petchauer, Michelle Mancinelli,
and the most important *d* in the D, dream hampton.

The following people provided vital assistance-in-a-pinch, connec-
tions, and advice that made this project immeasurably more compre-
hensive. My deepest thanks to Aaron Halfacre, Adam Mansbach, Adrian
Miller, Alex Atwell, Andre Barnes, Bill Johnson, Brian Cross, Brian D.
James, Brogues Cozens-McNeelance, Carla Reczek, Christine Kloostra,
Dalmar James, Dawn Elissa-Fischer, Dexter Story, Diana Boardley, DJ
Tony Tone, Drew Dixon, Dug Infinite, Duncan Murray, Elizabeth Clem-
ens, Eothen "Egon" Alapatt, Evan Krauss, Forest Erwin, Frank Bush, Gail
Mitchell, Gary Cohen, Grayson Kohs, Guttorm Andreasen, Guy Routte,
Harrison Remler, Heidi Robinson-Fitzgerald, Ian Schwartzman, Jabari
Canada, Jae Barber, James Lopez, Jerry Barrow, Joe Schloss, Johannes
Schultz, Karen Drew, Karen Rait, Kino Childrey, Lanre Gaba, Luxie
Aquino, Matthew Winne, Michael Arcilesi, Michael Berrin, Michael
Buchanan, Michael Castelaz, Micheline Levine, Mike Ross, Milo Bergé,
Nick Cianci, Nicole Hegeman, Paul Riser Jr., Paul Riser Sr., Paul Rosen-
berg, Phonte Coleman, Rachel Fryer, Renee Stromberg, Ross Hockrow,

Rudy Lauerman, Salaam Remi, Scott Barkham, Sharif Walters, Shawn Gee, Shawn Setaro, Shawn Wise, Sheila Bowers, Sophia Chang, Victor Anselmi, Vincent Bennett, and Zarah Zohlman. An extra special thanks to Sofia D'Angelo, who, before she graduated and became a rock star, was a resourceful, tireless research assistant for this project.

Dilla Time rests on a bedrock of foundational journalism, study, and response. I have deep respect for the following distinguished Dillologists: Aadel Haleem, Aaron Halfacre, Ahmir "Questlove" Thompson, Alvin Blanco, Anslem Samuel, Brian "B. Kyle" Atkins, Bowls, Connor Towne O'Neill, Datwon Thomas, Dean Van Nguyen, Dennis de Groot, DJ Dummy, Don Hogan, Dove Clark, Edwin "STATS" Houghton, Elijah C. Watson, Eothen "Egon" Alapatt, Frank "Y'skid" Sens, Gilles Peterson, Gino Sorcinelli, Giovanni Russonello, Jason King, Jeff Weiss, Jefferson "Chairman" Mao, Jerry Barrow, Jesse Fairfax, Jesse Moritz, John Vanderpuije, Jonathan Cunningham, Jordan Ferguson, Joseph Patel, J-Rocc, Kelefah Sanneh, Kelly "K-Fresh" Frazier, Kelley Louise Carter, Khary Kimani Turner, Kim Osorio, Lara Gamble, Laurent Fintoni, Martin Turenne, Mats Nileskär, Mike Rubin, Nate Chinen, Nate Patrin, Owen Smith-Clark, Pablo Ángel Zárate Pérez, Paul Rosenberg, Raj Chaudhuri, Raydar Ellis, Reggie Williams, Rob Kenner, Ronnie Reese, Ross Allen, Simon Reynolds, Timmhotep, Timothy Anne Burnside, and Tina Zafreen Alam.

A shout to my brilliant comrades in media, music, academia, and the arts, among them:

Aliya S. King, Andrew Barber, Angela Yee, Anthony Morris, Antoine Hardy, Antoine Harris, Bassey Ipki, Bevy Smith, Binta Brown, Britt Pham, Charles Hughes, Cheo Hodari Coker, Chris Morrow, Craig Seymour, D Nice, Daniel Schwartz, Danielle Young, Dante Ross, Danyel Smith, Dart Adams, Davey D, DJ Premier, Dimas Sanfiorenzo, Donnell Alexander, Donwill, Dyana Williams, Eb the Celeb, Ed Young, Elizabeth Mendez Berry, Elliott Wilson, Eric and Jeff and Dan Rosenthal, Fire, Frank DiGiacomo, Frank William Miller Jr., Frannie Kelley, Greg Tate, Harry Siegel, Havelock Nelson, Insanul Ahmed, Invincible, J Period, Jake Paine, Jamilah Lemieux, Jason Greene, Jay Smooth, Jayson Rodriguez, Jeff Chang, Jesse Serwer, Joan Morgan, Jody Rosen, Joe Levy, Joel Anderson,

John Bass, Jon Caramanica, Jon Pareles, Joy Reid, Kahlil Joseph, Kamilah Rouse, Kathy Iandoli, Keith Murphy, Kevin Beacham, Kevin Clark, Khris Davenport, Kierna Mayo, Kiese Laymon, Kirsten West Savali, Kris Ex, Kyle Eustice, Laiya St. Clair, Lisa Lucas, Mack Wilds, Marcel Williams, Marcus J. Moore, Maggie Rogers, Mark Anthony Neal, MeLa Machinko, Mendi and Keith Obadike, Michael Arceneaux, Michael Gonzales, Michael Skolnik, Michaelangelo Matos, Miles Marshall Lewis, Mimi Valdes, MiRi Park, Morgan Rhodes, Naima Cochrane, Naomi Zeichner, Nate Wilcox, Nelson George, Nina Gregory, Noah Callahan-Bever, Noah Yoo, Onye Anyanwu, the QLS crew, Rashaun Hall, Rebecca Carroll, Rick Rubin, Sarah Honda, Scott Poulson-Bryant, Sha Money XL, Shecky, Simone Jordan, Sowmya Krishnamurthy, Sway, Tamara Palmer, Tatiana Litvin, Terrell Jermaine Starr, Thembisa Mshaka, Thomas St. John, Tom Cole, Tray Chaney, Tressie McMillan Cottom, Wayne Marshall, Wendy Day, Wes Jackson, William E. Ketchum III, and Zenobia Simmons.

To my teachers, who taught me how to do the work: Adelaide Cromwell, Eileen Southern, Floyd Barbour, Howard Zinn, Hubert Walters, Joe Boskin, June Cross, Kim Nauer, Ophelia Barnes, and Samuel G. Freedman.

To friends who are family and family who are friends: Alex Horowitz and Ammon Shea; Amy Benson and Douglas Repetto; Andrew Carlson and Heather Waldon; Antonio and Brigitte Neves; Bill Adler and Sara Moulton; Bill Stephney and Tanya Cepeda; Craig Taborn; Derek Bermel and Andreia Pinto; Ellie Hisama and Anton Vishio; James, Andrea, Tori, and Hannah Lopez; John, Andrea, Juliana, Madeleine, Sophia, and Leah Mietus; Jumaane Saunders and Monica Amaro; Laila Al-Arian and Jonathan Brown; Maggie Malina and David Tischman; Margo Jefferson and Elizabeth Kendall; Mark, Amy, Jackson, and Rylan Brodie; Marti Rojas and Peter Asen; Patti Ybarra and Milind Shah; Paul Stache and Molly Johnson; Seith and Elyce Mann; Shelly John; and Stacey and Ed LeMelle. Love to my parents and bonus parents: Jane Charnas, Robert Charnas, Joan Charnas, and Lee Sartoph; to my siblings and bonus siblings, Hillary, Cortney, Perry, Ronnie, Jeff, and Avram; and to the Charnas, Cole, Walters, Keenan, Jay, and Sartoph families.

And then there is Isaac, who is worth more to me than all the words in all the books in all the world.

Index

Page numbers in *italics* refer to illustrations.

Illustration Credits